The
DOCTRINE *and*
RITUAL *of*
HIGH MAGIC

The
DOCTRINE *and*
RITUAL *of*
HIGH MAGIC

❧

ELIPHAS LÉVI

Translated
by MARK ANTHONY MIKITUK

Introduction and Notes
by JOHN MICHAEL GREER

A TarcherPerigee Book

An imprint of Penguin Random House LLC
375 Hudson Street
New York, New York 10014

Copyright ©2017 John Michael Greer and Mark Anthony Mikituk
Penguin supports copyright. Copyright fuels creativity, encourages diverse voices,
promotes free speech, and creates a vibrant culture. Thank you for buying an authorized edition of
this book and for complying with copyright laws by not reproducing, scanning, or distributing
any part of it in any form without permission. You are supporting writers and
allowing Penguin to continue to publish books for every reader.

Tarcher and Perigee are registered trademarks, and the colophon is a trademark of
Penguin Random House LLC.

Most TarcherPerigee books are available at special quantity discounts for bulk purchase for sales
promotions, premiums, fund-raising, and educational needs. Special books or book excerpts also can
be created to fit specific needs. For details, write: SpecialMarkets@penguinrandomhouse.com.

Library of Congress Cataloging-in-Publication Data
Names: Lévi, Eliphas, 1810–1875, author.
Title: The doctrine and ritual of high magic / Eliphas Lévi; translated by
Mark Anthony Mikituk; introduction and notes by John Michael Greer.
Other titles: Dogme et rituel de la haute magie. English
Description: New York: TarcherPerigee, 2017. | Includes index.
Identifiers: LCCN 2016040845 (print) | LCCN 2017002427 (ebook) |
ISBN 9780143111030 | ISBN 9781101992746
Subjects: LCSH: Magic.
Classification: LCC BF1612 .C713 2017 (print) | LCC BF1612 (ebook) |
DDC 133.4/3—dc23
LC record available at https://lccn.loc.gov/2016040845

Printed in the United States of America
5   7   9   10   8   6   4

Book design by Elke Sigal

CONTENTS

PART ONE
THE DOCTRINE OF HIGH MAGIC

CONTENTS

PART TWO
THE RITUAL OF HIGH MAGIC

CONTENTS

SUPPLEMENT TO THE RITUAL

GENERAL INTRODUCTION

John Michael Greer

All things considered, France in the year 1854 hardly seemed a propitious setting for a revival of the ancient traditions of magic. The Industrial Revolution launched in Britain a century before had leapt across the English Channel in the wake of the Napoleonic Wars and transformed France into one of the world's major economic powers. French scientists were on the cutting edge of scores of rapidly advancing fields of knowledge; railroads and telegraph lines spread across the French landscape; in the cafés of bustling Paris, members of the comfortable middle class could sit back, sip café au lait, and read up-to-date news reports from the front lines of the Crimean War and the Taiping Rebellion.

To many French people, the world seemed in that year to be marching steadily forwards into a new era of progress and modernity, with western Europe in the vanguard and France, by many measures, out in front of the other European nations. Yet this was the year that a previously obscure French writer published, under the pen name Eliphas Lévi, a book titled *Doctrine of High Magic* (*Dogme de la haute magie*). A sequel, *Ritual of High Magic* (*Rituel de la haute magie*), appeared the next year, and a single-volume edition that included both books found its way into print one year later. Nor did these publications languish in obscurity—quite the contrary. *The Doctrine and Ritual of High Magic* brought Lévi immediate fame and played a key role in kick-starting a revival of magic that remains a significant cultural presence today. Though modern occultism has many sources and streams, a surprisingly large number of them can be traced back to these works of Lévi's busy pen.

CƷ

Eliphas Lévi's real name was Alphonse Louis Constant. A shoemaker's son, he was born in Paris in 1810, when the Napoleonic Wars were at their height. He was a frail and studious child with strong religious feelings, and his parents encouraged him to study for the Catholic priesthood. His piety and intellectual gifts impressed his teachers to such an extent that once he became a deacon, he was appointed to a teaching position at the Petit Séminaire de Paris, a prestigious Catholic school.

This apparent stroke of luck proved fatal to his career in the church, however. Assigned to teach the catechism to a class of young women, he promptly fell in love with one of his pupils. While he did not act on the attraction, the experience convinced him that he was not suited for a celibate life, and he left the seminary before being ordained. Thereafter, he supported himself by a variety of odd jobs while making his first efforts towards a career as a writer.

France in the first half of the nineteenth century was wracked by political turmoil, with royalist supporters of the house of Bourbon, imperialist supporters of the heirs of Napoleon, republican proponents of the ideals of the Revolution, and the first wave of proponents of modern socialism among the many forces at work in the political smorgasbord of those years. Lévi was inevitably drawn into political journalism and proceeded to write his first major work, *The Bible of Liberty* (*La bible de la liberté*), which saw print in 1841. The French governing powers found plenty of objectionable material in this manifesto of Christian socialism; it was confiscated by the Paris police an hour after it went on sale, and Constant was arrested. His trial and eleven-month prison sentence, on a charge of inciting insurrection, afforded him his first real public exposure.

The years that followed saw Constant leading the ordinary life of an aspiring writer of the era: taking on an assortment of literary jobs to pay the bills while pursuing his own studies and a diverse range of interests during his off hours. Socialist journalism took up much of his time, but he also put his considerable knowledge of theology and Catholic tradition to good use, penning a substantial *Dictionary of Christian Literature* that remained in print for many years. In 1846 he married Noémie Cadiot, a talented young sculptor and author, but the marriage proved unsuccessful and they separated in 1853.

By that time Constant's studies had begun to move in unexpected directions. By 1839 he was a friend of Alphonse Esquiros, a romantic novelist interested in occultism, and it may have been contact with Esquiros and his circle that led Constant to begin reading forgotten tomes on magic and alchemy. He continued writing socialist tracts for a time, but his unsuccessful campaign for a seat in the newly constituted National Assembly, after the revolution of 1848, proved to be the last hurrah of his activist phase. From that point on, he was on the track of something different—and more profound.

In 1853 he met the most important of his occult teachers. Jósef Maria Hoëné-Wroński was at once one of the most brilliant and most eccentric figures in nineteenth-century French intellectual life: the inventor of Wronskian determinants—still much used in the study of differential equations—and of the caterpillar tread used to this day for tanks, bulldozers, and the like. Born in Poland in 1776, Wroński distinguished himself in the Polish cause when that country was conquered by the Russians and Germans. By 1800 he was, along with many other Polish exiles, in France, where he devoted himself to a variety of abstruse studies for the rest of his life. Occultism was only one of his many interests, but most of his later books focus on it increasingly, expounding an intricate system of thought derived from the Cabala, the ancient Jewish tradition of esoteric philosophy. Constant met Wroński just before the latter's death, but their brief acquaintance had a profound impact on the younger man.

It was apparently Wroński who showed Constant that the magical and alchemical writings he had encountered first by way of Alphonse Esquiros and his circle were not merely romantic curiosities but embodied a philosophy of life and a way of understanding the world that had not lost any of its relevance with the coming of the modern, up-to-date culture of the 1850s. That realization transformed Constant's life. Before long, he was devoting all his spare time to occult study and practice—a detail that may have had more than a little to do with the failure of his marriage—and assembling the first drafts of the book that would be his masterpiece. To distance this new work from his earlier writing, he adopted a pen name that was simply his own name loosely translated into Hebrew: Eliphas Lévi Zahed, or, for short, Eliphas Lévi.

The Doctrine and Ritual of High Magic was an immediate success, and in more than a financial sense. Irish poet William Butler Yeats, who was born in 1865 and grew up in a milieu powerfully shaped by Lévi's influence, reminisced in a 1917 book that in his youth, "one met everywhere young men of letters who talked of magic."[1] He was not exaggerating; from 1856 until the outbreak of the First World War, occultism was a massive presence not only in French culture but throughout Europe and America, and the revival of magic in those years sowed plenty of seeds that sprouted anew in the occult boom that got under way in the wake of the 1960s. Many others contributed to the rebirth of occultism, but Lévi was the most important of the first generation of occult authors, the one who proved that it was possible to restate the old teachings of magic in modern language and introduce them to a mass market.

Constant's life after the publication of *Dogme et rituel de la haute magie* was as placid as the years before it had been tempestuous. He lived quietly in rented apartments in Paris, writing and corresponding with an extensive circle of admirers and students. Further books on magic appeared at regular intervals— *History of Magic* (*Histoire de la magie*) in 1860, *The Key to the Great Mysteries* (*La clef des grands mystères*) in 1861, *Fables and Symbols* (*Fables et symboles*) in 1862, and *The Science of Spirits* (*La science des esprits*) in 1865—all of them developing and restating the insights introduced in *The Doctrine and Ritual of High Magic*. He died in 1875 after a short illness.

 C8

Even today, more than a century and a half after Constant's alter ego Eliphas Lévi burst on the scene, those who speak of magic as anything but a collection of discarded superstitions can expect reactions that range from blank incomprehension to reflexive contempt. Thus the first question that has to be asked and answered about Lévi's work, and especially his first and most influential book—the one you

---

1   In the epilogue to *Per Amica Silentia Lunae*; see W. B. Yeats, *A Vision and Related Writings* (London: Arena Books, 1990), 63.

now hold in your hands—is this: what exactly does magic have to offer to a world that, at least in theory, has left the Middle Ages behind?

We can begin to answer that question by sketching out four core themes of Lévi's approach to magic.

First, living amid the smoking ruins left behind by the eighteenth century's cult of reason, Lévi rejected the Enlightenment's blind faith in the omnipotence of the human intellect. The *philosophes* of the age of Voltaire and Rousseau had assumed as a matter of course that the replacement of traditional faith with rational understanding would lead to a glorious future of constant improvement, but their efforts instead opened the way to the chaos of the Revolution, the mass bloodshed of the Terror and the Napoleonic Wars, decades of political turmoil, and finally a despotism under Napoleon III that was, at best, no improvement on the corrupt autocracy of the overthrown Bourbon kings. The blowback of the Enlightenment project led a great many French intellectuals of Lévi's time to reject rationality out of hand and look for salvation in an assortment of deliberately irrational options.

Lévi himself was not among these. His position was far more nuanced. He argued that human understanding was certainly capable of knowing some things about the cosmos, and insisted that where accurate knowledge was possible facts should take precedence over faith. He had no time for the sort of fundamentalism that clings to the literal truth of traditional beliefs in the teeth of compelling evidence. He pointed out, though, that a great many things cannot be known by human reason and that some of these are enormously important in terms of their impact on human existence.

Faith, for Lévi, begins where reason can go no further. This rule applies just as much to the die-hard rationalist skeptic as it does to the devout Christian; neither one, after all, can carry out a complete, objective inventory of the things that exist in order to determine whether God is among them, and so the statements "there is a God" and "there is no God" are equally matters of faith. For that matter, the rationalist claim that human beings ought to make choices on the basis of reason, rather than any other criterion, isn't a statement of fact but, rather, a value judgment that rests on a galaxy of (usually) unexamined preconceptions every bit as resistant to objective proof as the theological claims of the believer.

Since every claim that can be made about things human beings cannot know is as faith based as any other, Lévi argued, the sensible course is to choose a faith that does not contradict anything that is known to be true about the world and yet appeals to those other human capacities—particularly the aesthetic sense and the needs of the heart—with which reason is not well equipped to deal. As a Roman Catholic by birth and training, Lévi found that faith in the Roman Catholic Church, and even the most cursory reading of the book that follows will show how often he turns to the Bible, and especially to the words of Jesus, as a source of guidance and inspiration. His approach to the Catholic Church and its teachings, however, had little in common with the sort of rigid literalism that has become standard issue in so much of the modern religious scene.

This brings us to the second of Lévi's four themes. The *philosophes* of the Enlightenment had argued that Christianity must be nonsense because Christian beliefs, taken in a purely literal sense, contradict known facts about the world. Voltaire's scornful dismissal of the Catholic Church—"Écrasez l'infâme!" (Smash the wretched thing!)—drew heavily on the assumption that all religious language must be taken in its most pigheadedly literal sense. Two other writers who influenced Lévi profoundly, Charles-François Dupuis and Constantin-François de Chasseboeuf, comte de Volney, carried out their own attempted demolition of Christianity on a similar basis; they argued that the narratives central to Christian faith had to be false because they paralleled mythological narratives in other faiths, particularly those of classical Greek and Roman religion—and these they assumed, as a matter of course, must be fatuous nonsense since their literal meanings did not fit the world as known to nineteenth-century science.

Not so fast, said Lévi. Literal meanings are not the only game in town. There are also symbolic meanings, and religions in particular have an extraordinarily long and rich history of using symbols, parables, and other indirect means of expression to communicate their teachings. What is more, religions have an equally long and rich history of using similar means to *conceal* their teachings from those who are considered not yet ready for them. Jesus of Nazareth, he noted, taught the crowds who gathered around him in parables, reserving more straightforward ways of discussing those teachings for his inner circle of apostles. As for Dupuis and Volney, he argued, they had found the most marvelous proofs of

Christianity's relevance and mistaken them for proofs of Christianity's falsehood—for what does the presence of common symbolic themes in different faiths indicate if not the presence of common truths shared by those faiths?

To Lévi, in other words, the teachings of Christianity were absurd only if they were taken in a literal sense that, he believed, the founders of the faith had never intended them to have. The same argument, in his view, applied to every other religion. The literal meaning was the proper spiritual food for children and the ignorant, who stood to benefit from a simple faith that taught basic lessons of morality. The inner meanings were reserved for those adults who had the intellectual and moral capacity to go beyond that simple faith without losing its benefits. In ancient times, the mysteries had unveiled the hidden truths behind the symbols and fables; Christianity, he argued, had done the same in its early days but had lost the keys to its own teachings in the last centuries of the Roman world, and thereafter those who preserved the heritage of the mysteries did so in secret, under the constant threat of exposure and extermination at the hands of the Inquisition and the mob.

The heirs of the mysteries, though, were said to have something more than a symbolic interpretation of religious teachings to pass on to their initiates. Whispered rumors and frantic accusations alike claimed that they also taught and practiced magic. Lévi rejected the notion that magic involved devil worship or supernatural powers; he argued, in fact, that there is nothing supernatural in the literal sense of that word—that is, above or outside of nature. He also rejected out of hand the idea that magic could overturn natural laws. If magic is not supernatural, then, what is it? and what can it accomplish?

His answer, the third theme of this book, was as simple as it was revolutionary: magic is a psychological process. The powers and potencies that mages invoke exist within their own minds, and the arduous training through which the apprentice becomes an adept is simply a process of learning how to use vivid symbols and symbolic acts energized by the will to draw on capacities of consciousness that most human beings never discover in themselves. The apparent absurdity of many magical rituals is thus beside the point, because any set of actions that has been given a symbolic meaning can be used to accomplish the redirection of the mind that makes magic work.

Consider the reasons why people down through the centuries have turned to magic. Some have used magic because they are poor and want to be rich; some have used it because they are unloved and want to find a willing partner; some have used it because they are weak and want to defend themselves against an enemy, or avenge a wrong done to them, or call down justice against an oppressor; some, more fortunate than the others, have used it because they feel powerless in the face of destiny but suspect that this is much less true than it seems. All these things can be changed, starting from the individual mind. There are many reasons why people are poor, but quite often the habits of the poor play a large role in keeping them mired in poverty; there are many reasons why people are unloved, and nearly always the most important factor is some detail of their personality that renders them unappealing to potential partners; weakness, in the same way, is tolerably often as much a matter of attitude as it is of external circumstances. Change the habits of thought and action that keep an undesired condition in place, and very often the condition will go away; embrace the habits of thought and action that will establish a desired condition, and that condition is likely to appear in short order—"like magic," as the saying goes.

⧼

Behind the three themes just surveyed lie two writers who had a profound influence on nineteenth-century thought. Lévi mentions neither of them, but his rehabilitation of magic would have been impossible without their paired impacts on his age, and his writings make a good deal more sense if these figures are recognized as part of the unstated background of his work.

The first of these writers was an Italian jurist and historian who worked in almost total obscurity during his lifetime but whose work burst on the European scene with immense force for most of a century after his own death. Giambattista Vico (1668–1744) spent his career laboring in a minor teaching post at the University of Naples and devoted his off hours to the project of a "philosophical philology"—that is, an approach to the humanities that was as profound and as challenging as the new philosophy of nature that was just then giving birth to modern science. His studies crystallized in a sprawling, difficult book, *Principles of the New Science Concerning the Common Nature of Nations* (for obvious reasons, this is normally shortened to *The New Science*). It was published in three editions of increasing complexity, in 1725, 1730, and 1744, but it attracted very little attention from anyone until 1824.

In that year Jules Michelet, a young professor of history in Paris, ran across a brief note on Vico in a book he was reading. He was so intrigued by the reference that he immediately set out to learn Italian so he could read Vico's work. "From 1824 on," Michelet later wrote, "I was seized by a frenzy caught from Vico, an incredible intoxication with his great historical principle."[2] That frenzy would go on to have a major impact on nineteenth-century culture, because Michelet became one of the most celebrated and widely read historians of the age, and his enthusiasm for Vico guaranteed a hearing for the Italian scholar's work.

Nineteenth-century writers and thinkers drew a great many things from the astonishingly rich treasury of *The New Science*. The current of thought that led to Eliphas Lévi started from one of them: Vico's redefinition of myth. Vico argued that it was a mistake to think of human consciousness as a constant untroubled by historical change. In particular, what Vico calls "the conceit of scholars"—the conviction on the part of intellectuals that their kind of knowledge must be as old as the world—tends to hide the reality that the earliest legacies of any human society reflect ways of thinking that differ radically from those of later ages. Where societies in their maturity and decadence rely on abstract concepts, societies in their infancy make use of concrete sensory images; where the thinkers of an old society construct theories, those of a young society tell stories, and the stories that embody the patterns most important to them are religious myths.

This differs sharply from the Enlightenment notion that mythology, and religion as well, are simply lumber rooms of ignorant folly long overdue for disposal. To Vico—and, as already noted, to Lévi as well—mythology is simply another method of communicating truths, but one that has become unfamiliar to modern people. Those who take the time to learn the language of myth, both men proposed, will discover that behind the seeming absurdity lies a forgotten world of meaning that reflects important realities about humanity and the universe.

---

2   Quoted in Edmund Wilson, *To the Finland Station* (New York: Farrar, Straus and Giroux, 1972), 4.

To borrow an example Lévi himself used repeatedly, the Thebaid—the sequence of ancient Greek myths surrounding the city of Thebes, in which the career of Oedipus, the self-sacrifice of Antigone, and the war of the *Seven Against Thebes* are the high points—cannot be understood if it is taken as nonsense or garbled history, despite the profusion of prophecies, monsters, miracles, and other apparent improbabilities with which it abounds. The vivid verbal images and riotous events of the myths communicate, to those who have ears to hear, some part of the knowledge of the ancient world. To Vico, that knowledge dealt with the same subjects as modern abstract thought; Lévi, on the other hand, drew from Renaissance sources the idea that the knowledge communicated by myth dealt with something beyond the ordinary.

It is at this point that the second of Lévi's unnamed sources enters the picture. Arthur Schopenhauer (1788–1860), like Giambattista Vico, had to face the experience of seeing his life's work comprehensively ignored at the time of its publication; unlike Vico, though, he lived long enough to see it rise out of obscurity to dominate the thinking of an age. Born in what is now the Polish city of Gdańsk and was then the German city of Danzig, Schopenhauer came of age during the golden age of German philosophy. Freed from the need for a professional career by a modest inheritance, he devoted his life first to philosophical studies in an assortment of German universities and then to the explication of his own distinctive philosophical vision. His doctoral dissertation, published in 1813 as *On the Fourfold Root of the Principle of Sufficient Reason* (*Über die vierfache Wurzel des Satzes vom zureichenden Grunde*), provided the foundation for his project; his greatest work, *The World as Will and Representation* (*Die Welt als Wille und Vorstellung*), followed in 1819, and an assortment of other writings filling in various details followed at intervals thereafter. These publications attracted next to no notice, and he labored in obscurity until 1851, when his ideas finally began to attract belated interest from intellectuals and avant-garde cultural figures across Europe.

Lévi's debt to Schopenhauer is profound and pervasive. The title of Schopenhauer's most important book, for example, can also be translated as *The World as Will and Imagination*—the German word *Vorstellung* includes both meanings— and it is thus no accident that will and imagination are the two primary forces in

Lévi's magic. Other such echoes can be found throughout Lévi's work. Schopenhauer's impact on Lévi, though, also reaches down into the realm of specifics, for the entire conception of magic Lévi presents can be found in embryo in one of Schopenhauer's less famous books.

This is *On the Will in Nature* (*Über den Willen in der Natur*), published in 1835. An omnivorous reader, Schopenhauer followed contemporary discussions about occultism, which had retained more of a foothold in the German-speaking lands of central Europe than elsewhere in the Western world. In the book just mentioned, which collects evidence from various sciences to support the central argument of *The World as Will and Representation*, Schopenhauer devoted a chapter to magic and occultism, and pointed out that both the traditional lore of magic and recent reports of apparently magical phenomena were dependent on the concentrated will of the magician.

Magic as the manifestation of the trained and focused will: this is the seed from which Lévi's conception of magic unfolded. The many echoes of Schopenhauer in Lévi's work likely also played an important role in making *The Doctrine and Ritual of High Magic* as popular as it was, for European avant-garde culture from the 1850s to the First World War was saturated with ideas drawn from Schopenhauer, and readers steeped in that milieu must have found themselves on familiar ground as they considered Lévi's interpretation of magic.

More generally, it was because Lévi wrote as a man of his time, interested in the same intellectual currents that were stirring the minds of many thoughtful people in the middle of the nineteenth century, that his work had such an impact. Other authors, in France and elsewhere, had written about occult topics in the decades immediately before *The Doctrine and Ritual of High Magic* saw print, but their approach to magic was by and large motivated by a rejection of the modern thought of their time, and so had little impact. Lévi's genius was that he made magic relevant to his world—and to ours.

છ

It was on the basis of that solid foundation in contemporary thought that Lévi proceeded to the most daring aspect of his study of magic. Like the insights offered by Vico and Schopenhauer, the three of Lévi's themes already covered, while not uncontroversial, fit without too much difficulty in the worldview common to Lévi's age and to ours. The same cannot be said of the fourth and most important theme of Lévi's work: the astral light.

This is Lévi's name for a concept familiar to nearly all students of spirituality in one form or another: a subtle medium that bridges the gap between one mind and another, has deep if obscure connections to the sun and the phenomenon of biological life, and can be concentrated, dispersed, and charged with intention by those who know its secrets. The astral light is the prana of the Hindu scriptures, the qi of Chinese tradition, the *ruach* of Jewish lore, the pneuma of the ancient gnostics, and the *anima mundi* of medieval and Renaissance Christianity; the Japanese call it *ki*, the Arabs *rūḥ*, the Yoruba *emi*, the Iroquois *orenda*, and the !Kung hunter-gatherers of the Kalahari Desert, *n/um*.[3] This list could be extended almost indefinitely; in fact, around the world and across the centuries, very nearly the only human cultures that have no common name for this medium are the societies of the modern industrial West.

Lévi was not the first figure to attempt to reintroduce this concept to the collective conversation of Western society. The most famous of his predecessors, Franz Anton Mesmer (1734–1815), called that subtle medium "animal magnetism" and developed an entire system of medical therapeutics that made use of it. (A few scraps of that system, wrenched out of their original context and carefully cleansed of their original connection to occultism, make up the current practice of hypnotism.) Mesmer was inevitably dismissed as a quack, a fate he has shared with many more recent discoverers of the same principle.

In speaking of the astral light and describing it as the great magical agent, the connecting link that enables magic to reach beyond the boundaries of any one mind, Lévi thus places himself squarely in the mainstream of the world's magical traditions. In the nineteenth century, furthermore, he was not quite as far from current scientific thought as he has since become. The physicists of his time theorized that all forms of energy were vibrations in a subtle substance called the ether, which filled the entire universe. Lévi was familiar with the theory and sug-

---

3   The ! and / represent two different clicking sounds made with the mouth in the !Kung language.

gested that the astral light might well be an ancient name for the ether, but he did not place any great importance on the identification. His goal was simply to explain the astral light in terms that his readers would find it easy to understand.

The importance of the astral light to Lévi's teachings is that it allows a psychological interpretation of magic to explain some of the things that magic is traditionally held to be able to do. According to the traditions of folklore and the manuals of magic alike, a magical blessing or curse can affect a person who does not know that the powers of magic have been invoked for his help or damnation. A purely psychological account that accepts modern notions about the absolute dependence of mind on matter, and conceives of thought as a mere side effect of certain lumps of meat called human brains, cannot explain this sort of action at a distance.

The existence of a medium that allows influences to pass from one mind to another takes care of this difficulty. It also solves several other crucial questions raised by any attempt to take traditional magical lore seriously in the modern world. The predictive power of astrology, for example, can readily be explained by a subtle medium that is influenced in complex ways by the angles the sun, moon, and planets make with one another in relation to an observer, while other forms of divination can be understood as different modes of sensing the flow of influences through the astral light.

Lévi argues that every thought, word, and action shapes the astral light to some extent. Under most conditions, though, these effects are short lived and have little impact, because they are poorly formulated and sent out into the astral light with very little momentum. The more clearly we formulate an intention and the more forcefully we back it up with concentration and will, on the other hand, the more influence it will have on the astral light, and the more effectively it will shape the thoughts and actions of other beings. One core aspect of the training of the magician, therefore, centers on learning how to use the imagination and will to define an intention clearly and project it out into the astral light with as much force as possible. Another consists of learning how not to be influenced by the intentions and imaginations of other beings, in order to have the freedom to act independently.

There is, however, a further dimension of magical training. Under certain conditions, after appropriate training and study, the aspiring magician can enter into a deeper and more fully conscious relation with the astral light, which allows that medium and its influences to be directed at will. The process that leads to this attainment, according to Lévi, is called the Great Work; it is the supreme secret of magic, and Lévi describes it in a galaxy of ways without ever stating in so many words the secret that underlies it.

This reticence is not mere obscurantism. The secret of the Great Work, as Lévi points out repeatedly, is incommunicable; like falling in love or facing death, it involves a shift in consciousness that cannot be translated meaningfully into words. Thus it cannot be taught to anyone who is not already capable of learning it independently, and each individual who sets out to master the secret has to tread the long road to adeptship alone. The secret can be expressed in symbols, though, for the benefit of those who are almost able to grasp it, and this Lévi does repeatedly, in a galaxy of different ways.

The Garden of Eden and the ancient Greek myths of the Thebaid are among the symbolic narratives he puts to work for this purpose; the tetragrammaton, the unspeakable four-lettered name of God in Jewish lore, is another; but among the simplest and most profound is a sequence of simple geometrical figures—a circle containing a cross, a six-pointed star formed of two triangles pointed in opposite directions, and a triangle—or, even more simply, the numbers four, two, and three. The circle and the number four relate to the four magical elements, fire, air, water, and earth; the star and the number two relate to the two contending-and-cooperating forces that Chinese philosophy calls yang and yin; the triangle and the number three relates to the resolution of those two forces. Unfold the hidden logic uniting these symbols, and you have grasped the supreme secret of Lévi's magic.

CB

The mysteries of the Great Work, and more generally the magical traditions Lévi sought to reintroduce to a civilization that had forgotten them, thus involve practice as well as theory: in Lévi's own formulation, doctrine is accompanied by ritual. It is entirely possible to approach the book that follows as a guide to an unfamiliar way of understanding the world, with no intention of putting that way into practice, and Lévi clearly had that possibility in mind. No small number of writers who came after him followed him along that line of approach. It is anything but an accident that H. P. Blavatsky's *Isis Unveiled* and Albert Pike's *Morals and Dogma of the Ancient and Accepted Scottish Rite of Freemasonry*, two of the most influential works of the late nineteenth-century occult revival, not only cite Lévi's writings but take his ideas about the nature of faith, the meaning of symbolism, and the psychological nature of ritual as basic presuppositions.

It is equally clear from the contents of Lévi's book, though, that he also meant it to be used by that minority of readers who were interested in exploring magic, not merely as a theoretical possibility, but also as a practical reality in their own lives. That intention was fulfilled abundantly in the decades that followed the publication of *The Doctrine and Ritual of High Magic*. The "young men of letters who talked of magic" about whom Yeats reminisced were matched, in intensity and cultural impact if not in number, by men and women who not only talked of magic but practiced it as well. For a century after Lévi's death, the great majority of practicing mages in the Western world drew extensively on his ideas; read the writings of Dion Fortune, Franz Bardon, Mouni Sadhu, Julius Evola's UR Group, and the Hermetic Order of the Golden Dawn, just to cite some or the more widely known names, and references to Lévi and his ideas stand out on every page.

The Doctrine and Ritual of High Magic is thus also a magical handbook, one that lays out a specific and entirely workable course of training that can be followed by the aspiring mage. A word of caution is in order, however, for those who choose to take up the challenge Lévi offers. Until quite recently, it was standard for authors of magical treatises to go out of their way not to make things too easy for their readers, and Lévi stands squarely in that tradition. His goal throughout *The Doctrine and Ritual of High Magic* is to force his readers to think for themselves, to look past the obvious surface meanings of his words to grasp a message that is not meant for the clueless. The tools he put to work in this traditional pastime of mages, though, were those of his own time and culture: above all, the dry wit and calculated absurdity for which nineteenth-century French literature is deservedly famous.

It is thus crucial to keep in mind that Lévi very often uses the same symbolic and allegorical way of speaking he traces out in the Bible, the Thebaid, and so many other sources. It is precisely when he seems to be saying something very straightforward, in the most simplistic of literal senses, that his real meaning is most likely to be concealed. Nor is there only one valid meaning to every phrase or passage. As Lévi himself points out, many magical teachings are meant to be taken in three different senses—physical, intellectual, and spiritual—and commonly the student discovers those meanings one at a time, as work pursued on the basis of one meaning develops the inner capacities needed to understand another meaning.

Those who are interested in practicing Lévi's magic, and in following the way of initiation this book outlines, are thus advised to read the book carefully, a sentence at a time; to think about ambiguities and potential double meanings; and to reread it frequently. A piece of advice found in the literature of medieval alchemy is worth following: "Lege, lege, lege, relege, ora, labora et invenies" (Read, read, read, read again, pray, labor, that you may discover).

The Doctrine and Ritual of High Magic, in other words, was not written for the clueless, or for those who expect the wisdom of the ages to be handed to them without effort. It reserves its gifts for those readers who are willing to grapple with its obscurities, delve below its surface meanings, and turn a wary eye on apparent absurdities, ambiguities, and obfuscations. It is what the alchemists of the Renaissance called a *lusus serius*, a "serious game" in which the author's playfulness frames themes of profound importance.

☙

The idea of helping to midwife a new English translation of Lévi's *Dogme et rituel de la haute magie* had been on my mind for most of a decade before this project came together. The commonly available English rendering by Arthur Edward Waite is profoundly unsatisfactory—pompous and turgid in style, full of errors and significant omissions, and burdened by notes that are far too busy denouncing, dismissing, and misstating Lévi's ideas to spare any time to help readers understand them. A more readable, accessible, and helpfully annotated translation was needed. Other commitments put out of reach the prospect of drafting a translation myself, though, and there the matter rested for some years.

I am grateful to Mark Mikituk for approaching me about the possibility of working together on this translation and even more for tackling the project promptly and capably, producing a clear, readable English version in a remarkably short time. I also owe thanks to Robert Mathiesen for his gracious assistance with the Greek passages in Lévi's text, to James Clark, Oliver C. Smith Callis, and Jean-Marc Viellevigne for their generous help with Lévi's illustrations, and to Mitch Horowitz of TarcherPerigee for his enthusiasm for the project. My thanks go to all.

TRANSLATOR'S NOTE

Mark Anthony Mikituk

Eliphas Lévi's *Doctrine and Ritual of High Magic* is an unusual work, and therefore, although it is unusual to do so, I would like to take a few moments of the reader's time to expound upon my qualifications for, and my method of, translating it.

John Michael Greer and I met through the magic of the Internet: in one of his blogs he mentioned his dissatisfaction with A. E. Waite's translation, and I had the temerity to offer my services as a professional translator, in the production of a new, annotated version.

I believe that in John Michael Greer's mind my main qualifications for the job, aside from the fact that I am a professional translator, was that I lacked virtually any other basis upon which to recommend myself: I belonged to no occult organization; I had very little experience with the occult beyond an expressed interest in it; I had not, and never did throughout this translation, read A. E. Waite's version of the work; and, as I said to Greer myself, I had "no skin in the game."

Thus I embarked upon this translation, as the fool would, naively, with just a bit of courage at hand.

But no fool is entirely naive, even at birth, and from the start I chose a particular method with regard to my translation, which was then confirmed by experience: I believed that any great work of the occult—as *The Doctrine and Ritual of High Magic* most certainly is—might have some ulterior, initially indefinable, motive, and that I should stick as closely as I possibly could to the original form of the work, in order not to make the mistake of failing to transmit some un-known quantity.

That intuition was quickly, and positively confirmed, by the effect the trans-lation of Levi's work had upon me. This was not some vulgar book, on magic or otherwise; it was written with the intention to act upon the reader's mind exactly like an initiatory experience, if that reader is of the right frame of mind. That is to say, although written as prose, this book is in fact poetry for the mind and acts as a key that can be used to open it.

In practice, as is the case when one translates poetry, this meant keeping as close as possible, not only to the sense, but also to the sound, the form and the rhythm, of the work. And so I have endeavored to keep the structure and rhythm of Lévi's work intact. As much as possible, I have stayed close to Lévi's words and tone, even if, perhaps, in English they at times seem a bit highfalutin. This is orig-inally a French work, after all.

Thus to the best of my ability I have attempted to intuit and reproduce *The Doctrine and Ritual of High Magic,* as Éliphas Lévi might have written it, had he done so in English.

Any errors are of course mine, but I would like to thank John Michael Greer for numerous pieces of advice and wisdom, and my wife, Géraldine, for her pa-tience.

PART ONE

❧

THE DOCTRINE OF HIGH MAGIC

INTRODUCTION TO
THE DOCTRINE OF HIGH MAGIC

Beyond the veil of all the hieratic and mystical allegories of the ancient doctrines, beyond the shadows and strange trials of all initiations, under the seal of all sacred writings, in the ruins of Nineveh or of Thebes,[4] on the eroded stones of the ancient temples and upon the darkened sides of the sphinxes of Assyria or of Egypt, in the marvelous or monstrous paintings which express the sacred pages of the Vedas for Indian believers, in the strange symbols in our books on alchemy, in the initiatory ceremonies practiced by all mystery cults, we find the traces of a doctrine which is the same everywhere and everywhere is carefully hidden. Occult philosophy seems to have been the wet nurse or the godmother for all religions, the secret lever of all intellectual powers, the key to all divine enigmas, and the absolute queen of society in the eras in which it was reserved exclusively for the education of priests and kings.

She reigned in Persia among the mages, who one day perished, as do perish the masters of the world, for having abused their power; she endowed India with the most amazing traditions and an incredible poetic treasure, with grace and terror in its symbols; she civilized Greece with the sounds of Orpheus's lyre;[5] she hid the principles of all the sciences and of all the progress of the human spirit in the audacious calculations of Pythagoras;[6] myths were full of her miracles, and

---

4   Important cities of the ancient kingdoms of Assyria and Egypt respectively.

5   Legendary musician and founder of the Greek mysteries.

6   Greek mathematician and mystic (c. 570 BCE–c. 500 BCE).

history, when it attempted to consider this unknown power, fused with mythology; she shook or strengthened empires through her oracles, made tyrants
turn pale upon their thrones, and dominated minds through curiosity or fear. For
this science, said the masses, nothing is impossible: she commands the elements,
knows the language of the celestial bodies, and directs the progress of the stars;
the dead rise in their tombs and articulate with fatal words the wind of the night
that whistles in their skulls. Mistress of love or hate, the occult science can, according to its desires, produce paradise or hell in the human heart; she disposes
at her leisure of all forms and allots as she so desires either beauty or ugliness; she
changes in turns, with the magical wand of Circe,[7] men into brutes and animals
into men; she even has at her command both life and death, and can confer riches
upon her adepts through the transmutation of metals, and immortality through
her quintessence and through her elixir, which is composed of gold and of light!
That is what magic was from Zoroaster[8] to Manes,[9] from Orpheus to Apollonius
of Tyana,[10] until positivist Christianity, triumphing at last with the pleasant reveries and the elephantine aspirations of the school of Alexandria, dared to publicly strike down that philosophy to which it was anathema and thus reduced it
to being even more occult and mysterious than ever.

Thus it was that strange and alarming rumors were heard at the expense of
initiates and adepts; these men were surrounded everywhere by a fatal influence:
they killed or made insane those who allowed themselves to be carried away by
their sickly sweet eloquence or the prestige of their knowledge. The women
whom they loved became stryges,[11] their children disappeared into their nocturnal conventicles, and people spoke in low and trembling voices of bloody
orgies and abominable feasts. They found bones in the basements of the ancient
temples, they heard screams during the night; the harvests began to wither and

---

7   Enchantress of ancient Greek legend who turned Odysseus's crew into swine.

8   Founder of the Zoroastrian religion, dates uncertain. From ancient Greek times
    on, he had a reputation in the Western world as a teacher of magic.

9   Also known as Mani, a Persian prophet of the third century CE. He taught that
    there were two gods, one good and one evil.

10 A famous Greek philosopher and magician of the first century CE.

11 Vampiric witches of ancient Greek legend.

flocks began to languish where the magician had passed by. Sicknesses which defied the medical arts now sometimes made their appearance in the world, as it has always been, they told us, due to the venomous gaze of the adepts. At last, a universal cry of condemnation rose up against magic, whose name alone became a crime, and the hatred of the vulgar was formulated in this command: "Magicians to the flames!" as was said several centuries previously: "Christians to the lions!"

Yet the multitudes never conspire against the real powers; they do not have the science of what is true, but only the instinct for what is strong.

The particularity of the eighteenth century was to make fun of both the Christians and of magic, while at the same time becoming infatuated with the homilies of Jean-Jacques Rousseau[12] and the magical illusions of Cagliostro.[13]

Nonetheless, at the heart of magic there is science, just as at the heart of Christianity there is love; and in the evangelical symbols, we see the Verb[14] incarnate adored in his infancy by the three mages guided by a star (the ternary and the sign of the microcosm), and receiving gold, incense, and myrrh from them: another mysterious ternary under whose symbol is allegorically contained the highest secrets of the Cabala.

Thus Christianity did not owe any hatred to magic; but human ignorance has always been afraid of the unknown. Occult science was obliged to hide in order to avoid the passionate aggressions of a blind love; she covered herself within new hieroglyphs, concealed her efforts, disguised her hopes. Thus was created the jargon of alchemy, a continual deception for the vulgar transmutation of gold and a living language only for the true disciples of Hermes.

What a remarkable thing! There exist among the sacred books of the Christians two works which the infallible Church makes no pretension to under-

---

12 French philosopher (1712–78).

13 Assumed name of the Sicilian occultist and adventurer Giuseppe Balsamo (1743–95).

14 In French, *verbe* means both "verb" and "word," and Lévi makes use of this ambiguity constantly. While it is customary to use the English term "Word" in this and similar contexts, we have used "Verb" instead to preserve the additional level of meaning Lévi had in mind.

standing and does not even try to explain: the prophecy of Ezekiel and the Book of Revelation; two Cabalistic keys doubtless reserved in heaven for the commentary of the three wise men; books that are closed to faithful believers with seven seals and perfectly clear to the unfaithful initiate of the occult sciences.

Another book also exists; but that one, even though it is in a way popular and can be found everywhere, is the most occult and the most unknown of all, because it contains the key to all the others; it is amongst the public without being known by the public; we do not think of finding it where it is, and we would lose our time multiplied by a thousand looking for it where it is not if we suspected its existence. This book, perhaps more ancient than Enoch's, was never translated, and it is still written in primitive characters on detached pages like the tablets of the ancients.[15] A distinguished scholar revealed it,[16] without anyone remarking it; he did not quite reveal the secret itself, but its antiquity and the singular way in which it was conserved; another scholar, but of a more fantastical than judicious spirit, spent thirty years studying this book and only suspected the whole of its importance. It is, in fact, a monumental and singular work, simple and powerful as the architecture of the pyramids, and in consequence as durable as them; a book which synthesizes all the sciences, and thus all the infinite combinations that can resolve all scientific problems; a book which speaks by making us think; inspiration and regulator of all possible ideas; perhaps the masterpiece of the human spirit, and certainly the most beautiful of things left to us by antiquity; universal key, whose name was only understood and explained by the enlightened scholar Guillaume Postel;[17] a unique text, whose first characters alone sent the religious mind of Saint-Martin[18] into an ecstasy and legitimized the unfortunate Swedenborg.[19] This book, which we shall discuss later, and its rigorous and mathematical explanation, shall be the complement and the crown to our conscientious work.

---

15   This book is, of course, the tarot deck.

16   Lévi refers here to French scholar Antoine Court de Gébelin (c. 1728–84), who first proposed that the tarot was a relic of ancient Egyptian teaching.

17   French diplomat and Cabalist (1510–81).

18   French occultist and mystic Louis-Claude de Saint-Martin (1743–1803).

19   Swedish scientist and mystic Emanuel Swedenborg (1688–1772), who wrote extensively about his encounters with angels and spirits.

The original alliance between Christianity and the science of the mages, if it is properly demonstrated for once, would not be a discovery of mediocre importance, and we doubt not that the result of a serious study of magic and the Cabala would bring serious minds to a reconciliation, until now regarded as impossible, between science and doctrine, and between reason and faith.

We have said that the Church, whose special characteristic is that of repository of the keys, does not pretend to have those to the Book of Revelation or the visions of Ezekiel. For Christians, and in their opinion, the scientific and magical keys of Solomon are lost. Nonetheless, it is certain that, in the domain of intelligence governed by the Verb, nothing which is written is lost. Things of which men cease to have knowledge of only stop existing for them, at least as verbs; they enter then into the domain of enigmas and mysteries.

Indeed, the antipathy and even the open war of the official Church against all that deals with the domain of magic, which is like a personal and emancipated priesthood, is due to causes which are necessary and even inherent to the social and hierarchical constitution of the Christian priesthood. The Church ignores magic, because it must ignore it or perish, as we we shall prove later on; it also does not recognize that its mysterious founder was greeted in his crib by the three mages, that is to say by the hieratic ambassadors from the three parts of the known world and from the three analogical worlds of occult philosophy.

In the school of Alexandria, magic and Christianity almost held hands under the auspices of Ammonius Saccas and of Plato. The doctrine of Hermes is found almost in its entirety in the writings attributed to Dionysius the Areopagite.[20] Synesius[21] draws the map from a treatise on dreams, which would be commented on later by Cardano,[22] and composed into hymns which could be used in the liturgy of Swedenborg's church, if that church's visionaries could have a liturgy. It is that time of ardent abstractions and passionate semantic dis-

---

20   Written in the fifth century CE, these rephrased the magical Platonism of Iamblichus and Proclus in Christian terminology and had an immense influence both on Christian theology and on European magic.

21   Synesius of Cyrene (370–413), an important Christian Neoplatonist philosopher.

22   Italian astrologer and mathematician Girolamo Cardano (1501–76), the inventor of the combination lock, was an influential writer on astrology.

putes to which one has to connect the philosophical reign of Julian,[23] called the Apostate, because, in his youth, he had grudgingly professed to the Christian faith. Everyone knows that Julian had made the mistake of being Plutarch's hero out of season and was, if we may say so, the Don Quixote of Roman knighthood; but what everyone does not know is that Julian was a visionary and initiate of the first order; that he believed in the unity of God and in the universal dogma of the Trinity; that in a word, the only thing he sought from the old world was its magnificent symbols and its highly graceful images. Julian was not a pagan, he was a gnostic enchanted by the allegories of Greek polytheism, who made the mistake of finding the name of Jesus Christ less sonorous than that of Orpheus. The emperor in him paid for his taste for the schools of philosophy and rhetoric; and after he had provided himself the spectacle of expiring like Epaminondas[24] with phrases from Cato,[25] he received from the public, already completely Christian, curses for a funeral sermon and a scathing epithet as his final fame.

But let us pass over the little things and the little men of the late Empire and get to the Middle Ages. Here, take this book: read the seventh page, then sit down upon this coat which I shall lay down, and we will roll back the coverings before our eyes. . . . Your head is turning, is it not, and you feel as if the earth is fleeing from beneath your feet. Hold firm and do not look. . . . The vertigo stops; we are there. Stand up and open your eyes, but do not allow yourself to make any Christian sign or pronounce any Christian word. We are in a landscape by Salvator Rosa.[26] It is a troubled desert, which seems to be coming to rest after a storm. The Moon no longer appears in the sky; but do you not see little stars dancing in the heath? Do you not hear flying about you gigantic birds who seem in passing to be murmuring strange words? Let us approach in silence that crossroad among the rocks. A husky and funereal trumpet is heard; black torches

---

23 Flavius Claudius Julianus (332–363), the last pagan emperor of Rome.

24 An ancient Greek general who died of his wounds after the battle of Mantinea in 362 BCE.

25 Roman politician and writer Marcus Porcius Cato (234 BCE–149 BCE).

26 Italian painter (1615–73), known for the extravagant romanticism of his scenes.

are lit from all sides. A tumultuous assembly presses about an empty chair; they look and they wait. All of a sudden everyone prostrates themselves, and they murmur: "There he is! There he is! It is him!" A prince with the head of a goat arrives in leaping strides; he sits upon the throne; he turns and presents a human figurine to the assembly, while bending down, to which, then, everyone heads, with black votive candles in hand, to give it a greeting and a kiss, then the prince rises with a strident laugh and distributes gold, secret instructions, occult medicines, and poisons to his acolytes. All the while fires are being lit, alder wood and ferns are being burnt pell-mell along with human bones and the fat from torture victims. Druidesses with golden sickles, wearing crowns of smallage and vervain, sacrifice children stolen before their baptism and prepare a horrific banquet. The tables are set: masked men sit beside half-nude women, and we begin the bacchanalian feast; nothing is missing except salt, which is the symbol of wisdom and of immortality. The wine flows like water and leaves stains resembling blood; the speech is obscene, and the wild caresses begin; now the entire assembly is drunk with wine, with crimes, with lust, and with song; we rise in disorder, and we run to form infernal round dances. . . . Then come all the monsters of legend, all the ghosts of nightmares; enormous toads put flutes to their lips the wrong way and blow while pressing their sides with their legs; limping beetles join the dance, crayfish play the castanets, and crocodiles play upon their scaly skins like harps; elephants and mammoths arrive dressed as Cupids and raise their legs as they dance. Then the frenzied round dances break up and disperse. . . . Each male dancer carries off a screaming, wild-haired female. The lamps and candles made of human tallow go out and are left smoking in the shadows. . . . We hear cries here and there, outbreaks of laughter, blasphemies and rough breathing. . . . Come, wake up and do not make the sign of the cross: I have brought you back home and you are in your bed. You are a bit tired, a bit broken even, from your voyage and your night; but you have seen a thing of which everyone speaks without knowing of it; you are initiated into the terrible secrets like those in the cave of Trophonius:[27] you have witnessed the witches' Sabbath! Now you must

---

27   One of the oracles of ancient Greece, associated with a deep cavern in which fearsome visions were seen.

simply avoid going insane, keep up a healthy fear for the law, and stay a respectful distance from the Church and its burning stakes!

Would you like to see something less fantastic, more real, and even more truly terrible? I will have you witness the torment of Jacques de Molay and his accomplices, or his brothers, in martyrdom. . . .[28] But do not be fooled, and do not confuse the guilty with the innocent. Did the Templars really adore Baphomet?[29] Did they give a humiliating embrace to the backside of the Goat of Mendes?[30] What, then, was this secret and powerful association that put the Church and State in peril? Judge nothing lightly, they are guilty of a great crime: they allowed the profane a glimpse into the sanctuary of the ancient initiation; they gathered once again and shared amongst themselves, in order to become the masters of the world, the fruits of the science of good and evil. The judgment which condemns them comes from a higher power than even the Pope's or King Philip's tribunal. "On the day that you eat this fruit, you shall surely die," God himself said, as we read in the Book of Genesis.

What is happening in the world, and why do priests and kings tremble? What secret power menaces the tiaras and the crowns? Here are a few madmen who run from country to country, and who hide, they say, the philosopher's stone beneath the tatters of their poverty. They can change earth into gold, yet they lack shelter and bread! Their foreheads are encircled with a halo of glory and with a reflection of disgrace! One of them had found the universal science, and knew not how to die in order to escape the tortures of his triumph: that is Raymond Lully the Majorcan.[31] Another cures imaginary maladies with fantastical remedies and formally denies the proverb which notes the inefficiency of cauterizing a wooden leg: that

---

28   The Knights Templar, many of whom were burnt at the stake as heretics between 1307 and 1314.

29   According to the inquisitors who tried the Knights Templar, an idol the Templars worshipped.

30   Originally a sacred goat in the Egyptian city of Mendes, one of many sacred animals in Egypt, the Goat of Mendes was conflated by later occult writers with the Christian devil, Baphomet, and a great many other goatish figures of myth and legend.

31   Catalan mystic Ramon Llull (1235–1315), inventor of a system of mental training, the Llullian art, much studied by Renaissance occultists. Lévi's interpretation of the tarot draws some of its core ideas from Llull's teachings.

is the marvelous Paracelsus,[32] always as drunk and as lucid as one of Rabelais's heroes. Here is Guillaume Postel, who naively writes to the fathers of the council of Trent because he has found the absolute doctrine, hidden since the beginning of the world, and which he hesitates to share more widely. The council doesn't even fret about this madman, doesn't bother to condemn him, and moves on to examine more serious questions about efficient grace and sufficient grace. The one whom we see die poor and abandoned, that is Cornelius Agrippa,[33] the least magician of all, and the one whom the vulgar continue to take for the most sorcerous, because he was occasionally satirical and a hoaxer. What secret, then, have all these men carried to their tomb? Why do we admire them without knowing them? Why do we condemn them without a hearing? Do you ask why? And why did they become initiates of these terrible occult sciences of which the Church and society are afraid? Why do they know what other men ignore? Why do they hide what everyone is burning to know? Why are they invested with a terrible and unknown power? The occult sciences! Magic! Here are words which say it all and could make you think still harder! *De omni re scribili et quibusdam aliis.*[34]

What is this magic, then? What was the power of these overly persecuted and proud men? Why, if they were so strong, were they not victorious over their enemies? Why, if they were foolish and weak, did we give them the honor of fearing them so much? Is there a magic, is there an occult science which is a veritable power and which works wonders capable of competing with the miracles of the authorized religions?

To these two important questions we answer with a word and with a book. The book will be the justification of the word, and here is that word: *yes*, there existed and there still exists a powerful and real magic; *yes*, what all the legends said

---

32   Pseudonym of the Swiss physician, alchemist, and occultist Philippus Aureolus Theophrastus Bombast von Hohenheim (1493–1541).

33   German occultist Heinrich Cornelius Agrippa (1486–1535), author of the most famous magical text of the late Renaissance, *Three Books of Occult Philosophy*.

34   Latin: "About everything that can be written, and certain other things too." A typical Lévi joke; the actual phrase, a Latin proverb, uses the word *scibili*, "that can be known," rather than *scribili*, "that can be written," or, alternatively, "scribbled."

about it were true; in this case only, and contrary to what ordinarily happens, popular exaggerations were not simply off track but less than the reality.

Yes, there exists a formidable secret whose revelation has already overturned the world, as the religious traditions of Egypt attest, symbolically summarized by Moses, at the start of Genesis. This secret forms the fatal science of good and evil, and its result, when it is divulged, is death. Moses symbolizes it as a tree which is *at the center* of the terrestrial Paradise, and which is near, which even embraces with its roots, the tree of life; the four mysterious rivers have their source at the foot of this tree, which is guarded by the sword of fire and by the four forms of the biblical sphinx, Ezekiel's Cherubim. . . . Here I must stop, I am afraid I have already said too much.

Yes, there exists a unique doctrine, universal, imperishable, strong as supreme reason, simple as all that is great, intelligible as all that is universally and absolutely true, and this doctrine was the father of all others.

Yes, there exists a science that confers upon man apparently superhuman prerogatives; here they are as I find them listed in a Hebrew manuscript from the sixteenth century:

"Here now are the privileges and powers of he who holds the key of Schlomoh[35] in his right hand, and in his left the blossoming almond tree branch:

א Aleph.—He sees God face-to-face, without dying, and speaks casually with the seven spirits who command the entire celestial army.

ב Beth.—He is above all afflictions and all fears.

ג Gimel.—He reigns with all of heaven and is served by all of hell.

ד Daleth.—He has his health and his life at his command, as well as the life of others.

---

35   The Hebrew form of the name Solomon.

ה Heh.—He can neither be surprised by misfortune nor struck down by disasters, nor vanquished by his enemies.

ו Vav.—He knows the reason for the past, the present, and the future.

ז Zayin.—He has the secret of the resurrection of the dead and the key to immortality.

"Those are the seven great privileges. Here are those which come afterwards:

ח Cheth.—To find the philosopher's stone.

ט Teth.—To have the universal medicine.

י Yod.—To know the laws of perpetual movement and to be able to demonstrate them with the squaring of the circle.

כ Kaph.—To change not only all metals into gold but also the earth itself, and even the refuse of the earth.

ל Lamed.—To tame the most ferocious animals and know the words to say which numb and charm serpents.

מ Mem.—To master the well-known art which produces universal science.

נ Nun.—To speak knowledgeably about all things, without preparation or study.

"Here at last are the seven minor powers of the mage:

ס Samekh.—To know at first sight the depths of men's souls and the mysteries of women's hearts.

ע Ayin.—To force nature to surrender to him when he desires.

פ Peh.—To predict all future events which do not rely on a superior free will or an imperceptible cause.

צ Tzaddi.—To be able to immediately provide the most effective consolations and all the most advantageous pieces of advice.

ק Qoph.—To triumph over adversities.

ר Resh.—To tame love and hate.

ש Shin.—To have the secret to riches, to always be the master over them and never the slave. To know how to take pleasure even from poverty and to never fall into abjection nor misery.

ת Tav.—Let us add to these three septenaries that the wise man governs the elements, that he calms storms, that he heals the sick by touching them, and that he raises the dead!

"But there are things which Solomon sealed up with his triple seal. The initiates know, and that suffices. As to others, whether they laugh, or believe, or doubt, or threaten, or be fearful, what matter is it to science and to us?"

Such are, in fact, the results of occult philosophy, and we are in the position of not having to fear any accusation of folly or suspicion of charlatanism in affirming that all these privileges are real.

To demonstrate that this is so is the goal of all our work on occult philosophy.

The philosopher's stone, the universal medicine, the transmutation of metals, the squaring of the circle, and the secret of perpetual movement are neither scientific hoaxes nor wild dreams; they are terms that must be understood in their true sense and express all the different uses of the same secret, the different characters of the same operation, that we define in a more general manner by simply calling it the Great Work.[36]

There also exists in nature a force much more powerful than steam. With its use, a single man who could seize it and direct it, could disrupt and change the face of the world. This force was known to the ancients: it consists of a universal agent whose supreme law is balance and whose control is directly related to the great arcanum of transcendental magic. Through the control of this agent, we can even change the order of the seasons, produce daytime phenomena at night, communicate instantly from one end of the world to another, see like Apollonius what is happening on the other side of the world, heal or strike at a distance, give speech a real impact and a universal effect. This agent, which just barely revealed itself with the fumbling of Mesmer's disciples,[37] is precisely what the adepts of the Middle Ages called the raw material of the Great Work. The Gnostics made of it the flaming body of the Holy Spirit, and it was that which they adored in the secret rites of the sabbath or of the temple, under the hieroglyphic figure of Baphomet or of the androgynous goat of Mendes. All this shall be demonstrated.

Such are the secrets of occult philosophy, such is how magic appears in history; let us now observe it in books and in works, in the initiations and in the rites.

The key to all the magical allegories is found in the folios which we have indicated, which we believe to be the work of Hermes.[38] Around this book, which we can call the keystone of the entire edifice of the occult sciences, have gathered all number of legends, which are either the result of a partial translation or commentaries which are ceaselessly renewed under a thousand different forms. Sometimes these ingenious myths group together harmoniously and form a grand saga which characterizes an era without the masses being able to explain why or how. It is thus

---

36   This paragraph should be read and reread by anyone who hopes to understand what Lévi is saying.

37   The Austrian physician Franz Anton Mesmer (1734–1815) believed he had discovered a previously unknown life force he called "animal magnetism"—in Lévi's view, another name for the magical agent discussed in this paragraph. Mesmer's students and disciples abandoned this concept and ended up inventing hypnotism.

38   Once again, the tarot is meant here.

ℓe fabulous story of the Golden Fleece summarizes, while veiling them, the nermetic and magical doctrines of Orpheus, and if we only go back to the mysterious poems of Greece, it is because the sanctuaries of Egypt and India in some way dismay us with their wealth and leave us embarrassed for choice in the middle of so many riches; and then we are not very far from the Thebaid, that frightening synthesis of all doctrine present, past, and future, that, so to speak, infinite myth that touches, like the divine Orpheus, the two extremes of the human life cycle.[39] What a strange thing! The seven doors of Thebes, defended and attacked by the seven leaders who have sworn upon the blood of their victims, have the same meaning as the seven seals of the sacred book accounted for by seven spirits, and attacked by a seven-headed monster after having been opened by a living and immolated lamb in the allegorical book of Saint John! The mysterious origin of Oedipus,[40] whom we find suspended like a bloody fruit from a tree on Mount Cithaeron, recalls the symbols of Moses and the tales of Genesis. He fights against his father and kills him without knowing him: dreadful prophecy of the blind emancipation of reason without science; and then he arrives before the sphinx! The sphinx, symbol of symbols, eternal enigma for the vulgar, the granite pedestal of the science of the Sages, the devouring and silent monster who expresses by its invariable form the unique doctrine of the great universal mystery. How does the quaternary become the duality, and how is it explained by the ternary? In other more illustrative and vulgar terms, what animal is on four feet in the morning, two at noon, and three in the evening? Philosophically speaking, how does the doctrine of the elemental forces produce the duality of Zoroaster, and how is it summarized by the triad of Pythagoras and Plato? What is the final reason for the allegories and the numbers, the last word of all symbolism? Oedipus answers with a simple and terrible word which kills the sphinx and which will have him become the perspicacious king of Thebes: the word for the enigma, is man!

---

39   Lévi uses the Thebaid as a generic title for the cycle of Greek legends surrounding the city of Thebes. The following paragraphs refer to many details of the story, which can be read in any good account of Greek myth and legend.

40   One of the central figures of the Thebaid, Oedipus, son of the king of Thebes, was abandoned at birth, raised by shepherds, and unwittingly killed his father and married his mother.

The poor man, he saw too much and not clearly enough, and soon he would expiate his deadly and incomplete clairvoyance through a voluntary blinding, and then he would disappear into the middle of a storm, like all civilizations which one day will have guessed, without having understood, the full implications and the whole mystery, the word for the enigma of the sphinx. All is symbolic and transcendental in this epic saga of human destinies. The two feuding brothers express the second part of this great mystery, which is divinely completed by the sacrifice of Antigone;[41] and then war, the last war, the feuding brothers killed one by the other, Capaneus killed by the thunderbolt he had defied, Amphiaraus devoured by the earth, are all allegories which by their truth and their grandeur fill with wonder those who penetrate the triple hieratical meaning. Aeschylus[42] commented on by Ballanche[43] provides only a very weak notion of its meaning, whatever the majesty of Aeschylus's primal poetry and the beauty of Ballanche's book.

The secret book of ancient initiation was not ignored by Homer, who draws its plan and its main figures on Achilles's shield, with exacting precision.[44] But Homer's graceful fictions soon seem to make us forget the simple and abstract truths of the primal revelation. Man takes to the form and forgets the idea; the signs, in multiplying, lose their power; magic as well, at that time, becomes corrupt and then descends with the witches of Thessaly into the most profane enchantments. Oedipus's crime bore its fruits of death, and the science of good and evil elevates evil as a sacrilegious divinity. Men, tired of the light, take refuge in the shadow of corporeal substance: the dream of the void which God fills soon seems to them greater than God himself, and hell is created.

When, in the course of this work, we will make use of these sacred words:

---

41   Oedipus's granddaughter, who performed funeral rites for her brother at the cost of her own life.

42   Ancient Greek playwright whose *Oedipus the King* and *Antigone* recount parts of the Thebaid.

43   French philosopher Pierre-Simon Ballanche (1776–1847), whose philosophy of history drew on the story of Antigone and her brothers.

44   The shield of Achilles, carved with the images of all things in the heavens and the earth, is described in detail in book 18 of Homer's *Iliad*. It was a favorite subject for occult speculation.

God, Heaven, Hell, let it be known, once and for all, that we distance ourselves as far from the meaning given these words by the profane as far as initiation is separate from vulgar thought.[45] God, for us, is the Azoth of the sages, the efficient and final principle of the Great Work. We shall explain later what is obscure in these terms.

Let us go back to the myth of Oedipus. The crime of the king of Thebes is not to have understood the sphinx, it is to have destroyed the bane of Thebes without having been pure enough to complete the expiation in the name of his people; soon after, a plague takes revenge for the death of the sphinx, and the king of Thebes, forced to abdicate, sacrifices himself to the terrible spirit of the monster, which is more alive and more devouring than ever, now that it has passed from the domain of form into that of idea. Oedipus had seen what man is, and he puts out his eyes so as not to see what God is. He had divulged half of the great magical arcanum and, to save his people, he must carry, with himself, into exile and into the grave the other half of this terrible secret.

After the colossal myth of Oedipus, we find the graceful poem of Psyche, of which Apuleius is certainly not the inventor.[46] The great magical arcanum reappears here in the symbol of mystical union between a god and a feeble mortal abandoned alone and naked on a rock. Psyche must be unaware of the secret of her ideal kingship, and if she looks at her husband, she loses him. Apuleius here comments on and interprets the allegories of Moses; but did not the Elohim of Israel and the gods of Apuleius also come from the sanctuaries of Memphis and Thebes? Psyche is the sister of Eve, or rather she is Eve spiritualized. Both of them wish to know, and lose their innocence in order to gain the honor of a trial. Both of them are worthy of descending into the hells, one to bring back Pandora's ancient box, the other to search for and crush the head of the ancient serpent, which is the symbol of time and of evil. Both of them commit a crime which must be ex-

---

45   Once again, anyone who hopes to understand what Lévi is trying to say should pay close attention to this sentence.

46   Another classic story from Greek mythology, the tale of Cupid and Psyche. Lucius Apuleius, a Roman writer and philosopher who lived in the second century CE, included a famous version of the story in his work *The Golden Ass*, mentioned a little further on.

piated by the Prometheus of ancient times and the Lucifer of Christian legend, one is liberated, the other is subdued by Hercules and by the Savior.

The great magical secret is thus Psyche's lamp and dagger, it is Eve's apple, it is the sacred fire revealed by Prometheus, it is Lucifer's burning scepter, but it is also the holy cross of the Redeemer. To know this well enough in order to abuse it or divulge it, is to merit every type of torture; to know it as one should know it, to use it and to hide it, is to be master of the absolute.

All is enclosed in one word, and in one word of four letters: it is the Tetragrammaton of the Hebrews, the Azoth of the alchemists, the Thoth of the Bohemians, and the Taro of the Cabalists. This word, expressed in so many ways, means God to the profane, signifies man for the philosophers, and gives adepts the last word of the human sciences and the key to divine power; but only he alone who understands the necessity of never revealing it knows how to use it. If Oedipus, instead of killing the sphinx, had tamed it and harnessed it to his chariot in order to enter Thebes, he would have been a king free of incest, free of calamity, and free of exile. If Psyche, by dint of submissions and caresses, had gotten Love to reveal himself, she would never have lost him. Love is one of the mythological images of the great secret and the great agent, because he expresses both an action and a passion, a void and a plenitude, an arrow and a wound. Initiates should understand me, and, due to the profane, one cannot speak too much about it.

After Apuleius's marvelous *Golden Ass*,[47] we find no more magical sagas. Science, vanquished in Alexandria by the fanaticism of Hypatia's murderers,[48] is Christianized, or rather hides under Christian veils with Ammonius, Synesius, and Dionysius the Areopagite, an author's pseudonym. One had, in those times, to make up for miracles by having them appear to be superstition, and make up for occult science by having it written in an unintelligible language. They resuscitated hieroglyphic writing, and they invented pentacles and characters which summarized an entire doctrine in a sign, a whole series of tendencies and revela-

---

47 The famous tale by Lucius Apuleius, a lively story of love and magical transformation in which the hero is turned into an ass and freed from that form, after many adventures, by the goddess Isis.

48 Hypatia, a pagan philosopher in Alexandria in the fifth century CE, was dragged from her chariot and murdered by Christian monks.

tions in a word. What was the goal of aspirants to the science? They were searching for the secret of the Great Work, or the philosopher's stone, or perpetual movement, or the universal medicine, expressions which often saved them from persecution and hatred by having themselves labeled as madmen and which all express one of the aspects of the great magical secret, as we shall demonstrate later. This absence of sagas lasted until the *Roman de la rose*,[49] but the symbol of the rose, which also expresses the sense of mystery and magic in the poem by Dante, is borrowed from the high Cabala, and it is time for us to tackle this immense and hidden source of the universal philosophy.

The Bible, with all the allegories which enclose it, expresses only in an incomplete manner the veiled religious science of the Hebrews. The book of which we spoke of, and for which we will explain its hieratic characters, the book which Guillaume Postel called the Genesis of Enoch, which certainly existed before Moses and the prophets, and whose doctrine is identical in substance with that of the ancient Egyptians, also had its exotericism and its veils. When Moses spoke to the people, says the sacred book allegorically, he wore a veil over his face, and he removed that veil to speak to God: that is the cause of those so-called absurdities in the Bible, which allowed Voltaire to exercise his satirical wit so often. The books were only written to recall tradition, and they were written in symbols which are unintelligible to the profane. The Pentateuch and the poems of the prophets for that matter were just elementary books, of doctrine or of morals or of liturgy: the true secret and traditional philosophy was only written later, under even less transparent veils. And it was thus that was born a second unknown bible, or rather, misunderstood by Christians, a collection, they say, of monstrous absurdities (and here believers, confused by the same ignorance, speak like skeptics); a monument, we say, which assembles all of which the philosophical genius and the religious genius have ever been able to do or to make which is sublime, a treasure surrounded by thorns, a hidden diamond in a rough and obscure stone: our readers will have already guessed that we wish to speak of the Talmud.

What a strange destiny the Jews have! The scapegoats, the martyrs, and the

---

49   A famous medieval romance, written by Guillaume de Lorris and Jean de Meun in the thirteenth century.

saviors of the world! A long-lasting family, a courageous and hardy race, whose persecutions always left them intact, because they had not yet accomplished their mission! Do not our apostolic traditions say that after the decline in faith of the Gentiles, salvation must come again from the house of Jacob, and that then the crucified Jew who was adored by the Christians will hand back the empire of the world into the hands of God his Father?

We are seized with admiration when we penetrate the sanctuary of the Cabala, by the sight of a doctrine so logical, so simple, and at the same time so absolute. The necessary union of ideas and of signs; the consecration of the most fundamental realities with primitive characters, the trinity of words, of letters and of numbers; a philosophy as simple as the alphabet, profound and infinite as the Verb; theorems more complete and illuminating than those of Pythagoras; a theology which we summarize by counting on our fingers; an infinity that could be held in the hollow of a child's hand; ten numbers and twenty-two letters, a triangle, a square, and a circle: those are the whole of the elements of the Cabala. They are the elementary principles of the written Verb, the reflection of that spoken Verb which created the world!

All the truly dogmatic religions came out of the Cabala and return there; all that is scientific and grand in the religious dreams of all the enlightened, Jacob Boehme,[50] Swedenborg, Saint-Martin, etc., are borrowed from the Cabala; all the Masonic brotherhoods owe to it their secrets and their symbols. The Cabala alone devotes itself to the alliance of universal reason and the divine Verb; it establishes, through the counterweight of two apparently opposing forces, the eternal balance of being; it alone reconciles reason with faith, power with liberty, science with mystery: it has the keys to the present, the past and the future!

To become initiated into the Cabala, it does not suffice to read and meditate on the writings of Reuchlin, Galatinus, Kircher, or Pico della Mirandola;[51] one must also study and understand the Hebrew writers in Pistorius's collection, the Sepher Yetzirah most of all, then the philosophy of love by Leo the Hebrew. One

---

50   German mystic Jakob Böhme (1575–1624), whose writings played a major role in inspiring the Rosicrucians and other Christian occultists.

51   Four Christian scholars of the Renaissance who wrote essays surveying the Cabala.

must also approach the great book Zohar, read carefully, in the 1684 collection entitled *Cabala Denudata*,[52] the treatise on the pneumatic Cabala and the treaty on the revolution of souls; then boldly and courageously enter into the enlightening darkness of the entire dogmatic and allegorical main body of the Talmud. And then we could understand Guillaume Postel and admit in a low voice that apart from his premature dreams and overly generous emancipation of woman, the famous and knowledgeable visionary might not be as crazy as he is called by people who have not read him.

We have just rapidly sketched out the history of occult philosophy, we have pointed out the sources and analyzed in but a few words the principal books. This work does not deal only with science; magic, or rather magical power, is composed of two things: a science and a force. Without force, science is nothing, or rather is in danger. To take science only by force; such is the supreme law of the initiations. And the great revealer has said: "The kingdom of heaven suffereth violence, and the violent take it by force." The door of truth is closed like the sanctuary of a virgin; one must be a man to enter. All the miracles are promised to faith; but what is faith if not the audacity of a will which does not hesitate in the darkness, and which walks towards the light through all trials and by overcoming all obstacles!

We do not have to repeat here the story of the ancient initiations; the more dangerous and terrible they were, the more effective they were: and the world, then, had men to govern and instruct it. The priestly art and the royal art consisted mostly of trials of courage, trials of discretion, and trials of will. It was a novitiate which was similar to those unpopular priests of today known under the name of Jesuits, who would still be governing the world if they had been truly wise and intelligent.

After having spent our life in search of the absolute in religion, in science, and in justice; after having turned around the circle of Faust,[53] we have arrived at the

---

52   Translated into English by S. L. Mathers as *The Kabbalah Unveiled*.

53   A legendary German wizard. In the two greatest versions of the Faust story, those by the English playwright Christopher Marlowe and the German poet and polymath Johann Wolfgang von Goethe, Faust decides to take up the study of magic because he has explored all other branches of scholarship without finding satisfaction; this is the "circle of Faust" Lévi mentions.

first doctrine and the first book of humanity. Here we stop, here we have found the secret of human omnipotence and indefinite progress, the key to all symbolism, the first and last of all the doctrines. And we have understood what this term so often repeated in the Gospels means: the kingdom of God.

To give a fixed point in support of human activity is to resolve Archimedes's problem by understanding the use of his famous lever.[54] That is what the great initiators who shook the world did, and they could not have done so except by means of the great and incommunicable secret. As a guarantee, incidentally, of its new youth, the symbolic phoenix never appears to the world without having solemnly consumed the remains and the proof of its previous life. That is why Moses kills all those in the desert who could have had knowledge of Egypt and its mysteries; that is why Saint Paul, in Ephesus, burns all the books which deal with the occult sciences; that is why, finally, the French Revolution, daughter of the Johannite Grand Orient[55] and of the ashes of the Templars, despoils the churches and curses the allegories of the divine cult. But all the doctrines and all the renaissances outlaw magic and throw the mysteries into the fire or into oblivion. This is because any cult or any philosophy which comes into the world is the offspring of humanity, which cannot live without killing its mother; this is because the symbolic serpent always turns around and devours its tail; this is because there must be as raison d'être for any plenitude a void, for any magnitude a space, for any affirmation a negation; it is the eternal realization of the allegory of the phoenix.

Two illustrious scholars have already preceded me along the road I walk, but they passed by, in a manner of speaking, during the night and without light. I

---

54   The Greek mathematician and inventor Archimedes is said to have claimed that he could move the world if only he had a lever long enough and a fixed point on which to balance it.

55   One of several grand lodges of French Freemasonry before the Revolution, the Grand Orient de France was deeply involved in alternative political and religious thought. The term "Johannite" refers to the belief in an alternative Christianity passed on by the heirs of the apostle St. John, as distinct from the Catholic Church as the heir of St. Peter.

speak of Volney[56] and of Dupuis,[57] of Dupuis most of all, whose immense erudition only managed to produce one negative work. He saw only astronomy as the origin of all cults, thus taking the symbolic Cycle for the dogma, and the calendar for legend. He only lacked one single body of knowledge, that of true magic, which encloses the secrets of the Cabala. Dupuis passed through the ancient sanctuaries like the prophet Ezekiel in the valley full of bones,[58] and he understood only death, for lack of knowing the word which gathers together the virtue of the four winds of heaven, and which could turn that immense ossuary into a living people by crying out to the ancient symbols: "Rise up! Take on a new form and walk!"

What no one has been able to or has dared to do before us, the time has come when we will have the audacity to try. We wish, like Julian, to rebuild the temple, and we do not believe that in doing so we deny a wisdom which we love, and that Julian himself would have found it worthy of adoration if the hateful and fanatical quacks of his time had permitted him to include it in his empire. The temple for us has two columns, upon one of which Christianity wrote its name. We thus do not wish to attack Christianity; far from it, we wish to explain and complete it. Intelligence and will have alternatively exercised their power in the world; religion and philosophy still battle in our times and must finally end up in agreement. Christianity's initial goal was to establish, through obedience and faith, a supernatural or religious equality between men and to immobilize intelligence with faith so as to provide a point of support for virtue, which had just destroyed the aristocracy of science, or rather replaced that aristocracy, which had already been destroyed. Philosophy, on the contrary, worked to bring men back through liberty and reason to natural inequality, and to substitute, by founding the reign of industry, virtue with practical knowledge. Neither of these two actions was complete and sufficient, neither of them brought men to perfection and happiness. What we dream of today, almost without daring to hope for it, is an

---

56   French philosopher Constantin-François de Chasseboeuf, comte de Volney (1757–1820).

57   French scholar Charles-François Dupuis (1742–1809). Dupuis and Volney both argued that Jesus Christ was not a historical person but an astrological myth.

58   Ezekiel 37:1.

alliance between these two forces regarded for so long as opposites, and this alliance we have reason to desire: for the two great powers of the human soul are no more opposed to one another than the male sex is opposed to the female sex; without a doubt they are different, but their apparently contrary dispositions only come from their natural tendency to meet and to unite.

Is this then nothing less than a universal solution to all problems?

Without a doubt, since we are trying to explain the philosopher's stone, perpetual movement, the secret of the Great Work and the universal medicine, we will be accused of madness, like the divine Paracelsus, or of charlatanism, like the great and unfortunate Agrippa. Even though Urbain Grandier's burning stake is extinguished,[59] there remain the nameless proscriptions of silence or of slander. We do not seek them, but we are resigned to them. We did not look to have this work published on our own, and we believe that, if the time has come to speak, the words will come of their own, from us or from others. Thus we shall remain calm, and we shall wait.

Our work is divided into two parts: in one we establish the Cabalistic and magical doctrine in its entirety, the other is dedicated to the cult, that is to say, ceremonial magic. One is what the ancients called a clavicule; the other is what country people still call a grimoire.[60] The number and the subject of the chapters, which correspond between the two parts, are anything but arbitrary and are all found indicated in the great universal key for which we give for the first time a complete and satisfying explication.[61] May this work now go where it wishes and become what Providence desires of it: it is done, and we believe it to be durable, because it is as strong as all that is reasonable and conscientious.

—*Eliphas Lévi*

---

59   The victim of a famous French witchcraft trial, burned at the stake in 1634.

60   Many medieval books on magic include one or the other of these words in the title. The Latin word *clavicule* means "key"; "grimoire" is originally an old French variant of the word meaning "grammar," and indicates that the book is what we would now call an ABC of magic.

61   The "great universal key" is of course the tarot deck.

1 א A

THE INITIATE

The Magus

DISCIPLINA.

AIN SOPH.

KETHER.[62]

When a certain philosopher[63] took as the basis for a new revelation of human knowledge the following reasoning: "I think, therefore I am," he changed in a way, and without his realizing it, the ancient concept of the Supreme Being according to Christian revelation. Moses has the Being of beings say, "I am he who is." Descartes has man say, "I am he who thinks," and, because thinking is to speak internally, Descartes's man can say just as the God of St. John the Evangelist said: "I am he within whom and by whom is expressed the Verb." *In principio erat verbum.*[64]

---

62   The words placed at the beginning of each chapter have been much used as seed thoughts for meditation in occult schools and may well have been intended for that purpose by Lévi. *Disciplina* is the Latin word for "training"; *Ain Soph*, from the Hebrew for "without limit," is a name for that which exists before the Cabalistic Tree of Life; while *Kether* is from the Hebrew word for "crown" and is the name of the first of the ten spheres (sephiroth) of the Tree of Life.

63   René Descartes (1596–1650), French rationalist philosopher.

64   Latin, "In the beginning is the Verb/Word."

What is a principle? It is a basis for speech, it is the raison d'être of the verb. The essence of the verb is in the principle: the principle is that which is; intelligence is a principle which speaks.

What is the intellectual light? It is the word. What is revelation? It is the word; being is the principle, the word is the means, and plenitude, or development and the perfection of being, is the end; to speak is to create.

But to say "I think, therefore I exist" is to assume the consequent of the principle, and recent objections raised by a great writer[65] have sufficiently proven the philosophical imperfection of this method. "I am, therefore something exists," seems to us a more primal and simple basis for experimental philosophy.

I am, therefore being exists.

---

65   Lamennais. (Lévi's note.) French Catholic priest and philosopher Hugues-Félicité Robert de Lamennais (1782–1854) wrote an extensive critique of rationalist philosophy.

Ego sum qui sum:[66] that is God's first revelation in man and of man in the world, and it is also the first axiom of occult philosophy.

אהיה אשר אהיה[67]
Being is being.

Thus the principle behind this philosophy is what is, and there is nothing hypothetical or uncertain about it.

Mercurius Trismegistus began his admirable symbol known by the name of the Emerald Tablet with this triple affirmation: "True, without error, certain, and most true."[68] Thus the truth is confirmed by experience in physics, certitude is freed from any alloy of falsehood through philosophy, absolute truth is arrived at by analogy in the domain of religion or the infinite, those are the primary requirements of the true science, and it is that which magic alone can provide to its adepts.

But, before anything else, who are you, you who hold this book between your hands and are beginning to read it?

On the pediment of the temple which antiquity had dedicated to the god of light, we read the following two-word inscription: Know Thyself.

I have the same recommendation to give to anyone who wishes to come closer to science.

Magic, which the ancients called *sanctum regnum*, the holy kingdom, or the kingdom of God, *regnum Dei*, is only appropriate for kings and for priests: are you priests, are you kings? The calling of magic is not a vulgar calling, and its royalty has nothing to do with the princes of this world. The kings of science are the priests of truth, and their reign is hidden from the multitude, as are their sacrifices and their prayers. The kings of science are those who know the truth, and

---

66   Latin, usually translated "I am that I am." According to Exodus 3:14, this is the divine name given to Moses on Mount Sinai.

67   *Ehyeh asher ehyeh*, "I am that I am," the same name given in Hebrew.

68   The Emerald Tablet, one of the oldest and most succinct writings of western alchemy, begins with the words cited by Lévi.

the truth has set them free according to the formal promise of the most powerful of initiators.[69]

One who is a slave to his passions or to the prejudices of this world will not know how to become an initiate, he will never be able to do so, as long as he does not reform himself; and so he will not know how to become an adept, because the word adept means he who succeeded by his will and through his works.

One who loves his ideas and is afraid to lose them, who is suspicious of new truths and is not disposed to doubt everything rather than accept something at random: he can close this book, which is useless and dangerous to him: he will understand it poorly and will be troubled by it, but he would be even more troubled if by chance he were to understand it better.

If you hold something dearer in this world than reason, the truth, and justice; if your will is uncertain and faltering, either for good, or for evil; if logic frightens you, if the naked truth makes you blush; if your feelings are hurt when your errors are touched upon, throw this book away at once, and then act, in not reading it, as if it did not exist for you, but do not denounce it as dangerous: the secrets it reveals will only be understood by a small number, and those who understand will not reveal them. Showing the light to birds of the night is like hiding it from them, because it blinds them and becomes for them more obscure than darkness. I will thus speak clearly, I will tell all, and I have the firm belief that only initiates, or those worthy of being initiates, will read everything and understand something.

There is a true and a false science, a divine magic and a magic that is infernal, that is to say misleading and obscure: we will reveal one and unveil the other; we will distinguish the magician from the sorcerer and the adept from the charlatan.

The magician disposes of a force which he knows, the sorcerer struggles to abuse that of which he is ignorant.

The devil, if it can be permitted to use this reviled and vulgar word in a book of science, surrenders himself to the magician, and the sorcerer surrenders himself to the devil.

The magician is the sovereign pontiff of nature, the sorcerer is but its desecrator.

---

69   A reference to John 8:32.

The sorcerer is to the magician what the superstitious and the fanatic is to the truly religious man.

Before going further, let us clearly define magic.

Magic is the traditional science of the secrets of nature, which comes to us from the mages.

By using this science, the adept is invested with a sort of relative omnipotence and can act in a superhuman manner, that is to say in a manner which is not within the common reach of men.

It is in this manner that several famous adepts such as Hermes Trismegistus, Osiris, Orpheus, Apollonius of Tyana, and others which it could be dangerous or inconvenient to name, were adored, or invoked after their death, as gods. It is in this manner that others, following the flux and reflux of opinion, which makes for the vagaries of success, became the henchmen of hell or dubious adventurers, like the emperor Julian, Apuleius, Merlin the enchanter, and the arch-sorcerer, as the illustrious and miserable Cornelius Agrippa was called in his time.

To reach the *sanctum regnum*, that is to say the science and the power of the mages, there are four things which are required: an intelligence enlightened by study, an audacity which nothing can stop, a will which nothing can break and a discretion that nothing can corrupt or intoxicate.

TO KNOW, TO DARE, TO WILL, TO BE SILENT, those are the four verbs of the mage which are written in the four symbolic forms of the sphinx. These four verbs can be combined together in four ways and can be explained four times through the others.[70]

On the first page of the book of Hermes; the adept is depicted wearing a large hat, which, if he lowers it, could hide his entire head.[71] He holds one hand up towards the sky, which he seems to be commanding with his wand, and the other hand is on his chest; he has before him the principal symbols or instruments of science, and he hides others in an illusionist's satchel. His body and his arms form the letter Aleph, the first of the alphabet, which the Hebrews borrowed from the Egyptians; but we will be coming back to this symbol again later.

---

70   See the game of Taro. (Lévi's note.)

71   This paragraph is a description of trump I of the tarot, the Magician.

The mage is actually what the Hebrew Cabalists called the microprosopus,[72] that is to say the creator of the little world. The first magical science, and also the first of all the works of science, was knowledge of oneself, it is that which contains all the others and which is the principle of the Great Work, it is the *creation* of oneself: this word needs to be explained. *the basis for the essence speech, of the verb*

The supreme reason being the only invariable principle, and in consequence imperishable, since change is what we call death, intelligence, which adheres strongly to and in a certain way relates to this principle, is thus also invariable and therefore immortal. We understand that to adhere invariably to reason one must have become independent from all the forces which produce, through their fatal and necessary movement, the alternatives of life and death. To know how to suffer, abstain, and die, these are the first secrets that raise us above pain, sensual desires, and the fear of the void. The man who looks for and finds a glorious death has faith in immortality, and all of humanity believes in it with him and for him, because humanity raises altars or statues of him as a sign of immortal life.

Man only becomes king of the animals by subjugating or taming them, otherwise he will be their victim or their slave. Animals represent our passions, they are the instinctive forces of nature.

The world is a battlefield where liberty battles with the force of inertia by using the active force. The physical laws are the millstone and you will be the grain, if you do not know how to be the miller.

You are called to be the king of the air, of water, of the earth, and of fire; but to reign over these four symbolic animals, you must conquer them and place them in chains.

He who aspires to become a sage and to know the great mystery of nature must be the heir and the despoiler of the sphinx; he must have a human head to possess speech, the wings of an eagle to conquer the heights, the body of a bull to plow the depths, and the claws of a lion to make space for himself to the left and the right, in front and behind.

You who wish to be an initiate, are you as wise as Faust? Are you as imper-

---

72   Latin, "lesser face."

turbable as Job? That is not so, is it? But you can become so if you wish. Have you conquered the whirlwinds of vague thoughts? Are you decisive and not capricious? Do you only accept pleasure when you want it, and do you want it only when you should? That is not so, is it? It has never been so, has it? But it could be so if you wish.

The sphinx does not only have the head of a man, he also has the breasts of a woman; can you resist the attractions of women? That is not so, is it? And here you laugh while answering, and you brag about your moral weakness to glorify the vital and material force within you. So be it, I allow you to pay homage to the donkey of Sterne or Apuleius;[73] the donkey has its merits, I will not deny that, for it was dedicated to Priapus as the goat was to the god of Mendes. But let us leave that for what it is, and know only if he is your master or you are his. Only the person who is his own master can truly possess the pleasure of love, for he has vanquished the love of pleasure. To be able to do and to abstain from doing, is to be twice able. Woman shackles you through your desires: be the master of your desires, and you will shackle woman.

The greatest insult to a man is to call him a coward. But what exactly is a coward?

A coward is he who neglects to take care of his moral dignity in order to blindly obey his natural instincts.

In the presence of danger, in fact, it is natural to be fearful and attempt to flee: why then is this shameful? Because honor requires us to prefer our duty to our attractions and our fears. What, from this point of view, is honor? It is the universal presentiment of immortality and esteem for the ways to achieve it. The last victory that man can have over death is to triumph over the desire for life, not out of despair, but from the greatest hope that is contained in the faith, in all that is beautiful and honest, by the consent of the entire world.

---

73   Laurence Sterne (1713–68), author of *The Life and Opinions of Tristram Shandy, Gentleman*, and again Lucius Apuleius, author of *The Golden Ass*. Both works feature a donkey as a major plot engine.

To learn to overcome yourself is thus to learn to live, and the austerities of Stoicism were not just a vain display of freedom!

To give in to the forces of nature is to follow ordinary communal life, it is to be the slave to second causes.

To resist nature and overcome it is to create a personal and imperishable life, it is to gain freedom from the vicissitudes of life and of death.

Any man who is prepared to die rather than deny truth and justice is truly alive, because in his soul he is immortal.

The goal of all ancient initiations was to find or to shape such men.

Pythagoras trained his disciples through silence and all kinds of abstinence; in Egypt, initiates were trained in the four elements; in India, we know what prodigious austerities the fakirs and brahmins were condemned to do, to reach the kingdom of free will and divine independence.

All of this ascetic scourging is borrowed from the initiation rites of the ancient mysteries, and they stopped because potential initiates could no longer find initiators; the directors of consciences have with time become as ignorant as the common man, the blind tired of following the blind, and nobody wanted to submit to trials which lead only to doubt and despair: the path of the light had been lost.

To do something, one must know what one wants to do, or at least have faith in someone who knows. But how can I risk my life on some adventure and follow someone who does not know himself where he is going?

One should not head recklessly onto the road of the high sciences, but once en route, one must succeed or perish. To doubt is to become insane; to stop is to fall; to retreat is to plunge into an abyss.

You who have begun reading this book, if you understand it and if you wish to read it to the end, it will make of you a monarch or a madman. Make of this volume what you will, you will not be able to scorn it nor forget it. If you are pure, this book will be a light for you; if you are strong, it will be your weapon; if you are holy, it will be your religion; if you are wise, it will balance your wisdom.

But if you are wicked, this book will be like an infernal torch for you, it will dig into your breast, tearing into it like a dagger; it will remain in your memory like a great regret; it will fill your imagination with chimeras, and it will drive you through folly to despair. You will want to laugh at it, and all you will be able to do is gnash your teeth, because this book is to you like the steel file in the fable was to the serpent who tried to bite it, and who ended up wearing down all its teeth.[74]

Let us now start the series of initiations.

I said that revelation is the verb. The verb, in fact, or the word, is the cloak of existence and the characteristic sign of life. Every form is the cloak of a verb, because the founding idea of the verb is the only raison d'être of the forms. Every figure is a character, and all characters belong and return to a verb. That is why the ancient sages, for whom Trismegistus was their voice, had formulated their sole doctrine in these terms:

What is above is like what is below, and what is below is like what is above.

In other words, the form is proportional to the idea, the shadow is the measure of the body calculated by its relation to the luminous rays. The scabbard is as deep as the sword is long, the denial is proportional to the contrary affirmation, production is equal to destruction in the movement which preserves life, and there is no point in infinite space which is not the center of a circle whose circumference extends and retracts perpetually in space.

Each individuality is thus perpetually perfectible, since morality is analogous to the physical order, and since we cannot conceive of a point that could not dilate, extend, and send out rays within a philosophically infinite circle.

What we can say about the soul in its entirety we can say about each faculty of the soul.

Intelligence and man's will are instruments whose reach and power are incalculable.

But intelligence and will are assisted by a little known faculty and whose great power belongs exclusively to the domain of magic: I speak of imagination, which the Cabalists called the diaphane or the translucent.

The imagination, in fact, is like the eye of the soul, and it is within it that the forms materialize and are conserved, it is through imagination that we can see the reflections of the invisible world, it is the mirror of visions and the apparatus

---

74   A reference to "The Serpent and the File," a fable by Jean de La Fontaine.

of a magical life: it is through imagination that we cure diseases, that we influence the seasons, that we prevent death, that we bring the dead back to life, because it is imagination which excites the will and which gives it power over the universal agent.

Imagination determines the form of the child in the center of the mother and determines the destiny of men; it gives wings to contagion and commands weapons in wartime. Are you in danger during a battle? Do you think you are invulnerable like Achilles, are you the so-called Paracelsus? Fear attracts bullets, and courage turns back cannonballs. We know that amputees often complain about the limbs they no longer have. Paracelsus worked on living blood by treating the results of a phlebotomy[75] with medicines; he cured headaches at a distance by working on cut hairs; through the science of the unity of imagination and the solidarity of all parts, he was well in advance of all the theories and experiments done by our most famous magnetists. So miraculous were his cures, that another name was added to his original name Philippus Theophrastus Bombast, that of Aureolus Paracelsus, and then even adding the epithet of divine!

The imagination is the instrument of the *adaptation of the Verb*.

Imagination applied to reason is genius.

Reason and genius both account in part for the diversity of its works.

There is a principle, there is a truth, there is a reason, there is an absolute and universal philosophy.

What is within the unity is considered the principle, and what returns to the unity is considered the end.

One is within one, that is to say all is within all.

The unity is the principle of numbers, it is also the principle of movement, and in consequence of life.

All of the human body comes down to a single organ, which is the brain.

All the religions come down to the unity of a single doctrine, which is the affirmation of being and its equality with itself, which constitutes its mathematical value.

---

75   Physicians in Paracelsus's time treated many diseases by extracting blood from the patient; Paracelsus is said to have poured medicine into the extracted blood, and the patient got well.

There is only one doctrine in magic, and it is this: the visible is a manifestation of the invisible, or, in other terms, the perfect Verb is in the things which are noticeable and visible, in exact proportion to the things which are not noticeable by our senses and are invisible to our eyes.

The mage raises a hand towards the sky and lowers another towards the earth, and he says: On high, the immensity! Down here, the immensity as well; immensity equals immensity. This is true of visible things as it is for invisible things.

The first letter of the holy alphabet, Aleph א, represents a man who is raising a hand towards the sky and who is lowering the other towards the earth.[76]

It is the expression of the active principle of all things, it is the creation in the heavens, which corresponds to the all-powerful Verb here below. This letter, all on its own, is a pentacle, that is to say a character expressing universal science.

The letter א can replace the sacred symbols of the macrocosm and the microcosm, it explains the masonic double triangle and the shining five-pointed star: because the Verb is the triangle and revelation is the star. God, in giving man reason, gave him the word, and revelation, multiple in its forms, but singular in its principle, is entirely within the universal Verb, the interpreter of absolute reason.

That is what the so poorly understood word Catholicism means, which, in modern priestly language signifies infallibility.

The universal in reason is the absolute, and the absolute is infallible.

If absolute reason brought all of society to irresistibly believe in the word of a child, that child would be infallible, for God and for all of humanity.

Faith is nothing but reasonable confidence in the unity of reason and in the universality of the Verb.

To believe is to acquiesce to what we do not yet know but which reason renders us certain that we shall know, or at least recognize, one day.

Thus the so-called philosophers are absurd who say: I will not believe what I do not know.

Pathetic wretches! If you knew, would you have need to believe?

---

76   This is again the posture of the figure in trump I of the tarot, the Magician.

But can I believe anything, and without reason? Certainly not! Blind and bold belief is superstition and folly. One must believe in causes which reason forces us to admit the existence of after witnessing effects known and appreciated by science.

Science! A great word and a great problem!

What is science?

We will answer that question in the second chapter of this book.

I ask myself honestly to
let go of all struggles
and if I feel uncertain + fearful
about what will happen
Remind myself that my struggling
seeks to hide what I know

2 ב B.

THE COLUMNS OF THE TEMPLE

The Priestess

CHOKMAH.

DOMUS.

GNOSIS.[77]

Science is the complete and absolute possession of the truth.

Thus the sages from all the centuries trembled before this absolute and terrible word; they feared to usurp the first privilege of the divinity, by making use of the word "science,"[78] and they contented themselves with the word gnosis, which only expresses the idea of knowledge through intuition, rather than the word science and the verb to know, which express awareness.

What does man actually know? Nothing, but he is not permitted to ignore anything.

He knows nothing, and he is called to become acquainted with everything.

---

77 Chokmah, meaning "wisdom" in Hebrew, is the name of the second sphere of the Cabalistic Tree of Life; *domus* is "house" in Latin; and *gnosis* is the Greek word for personal, experiential, or intuitive knowledge, as distinct from abstract book learning.

78 Note that the French word *science* means knowledge in general, and is not restricted to "science" in the usual modern English sense of the word.

Yet knowledge supposes duality. The knowing subject must have a knowable object.

Duality is the generator of society and laws; it is also the number of gnosis. Duality is the unity multiplying itself to create; and it is for that reason that the sacred symbols have Eve arising out of Adam's chest.

Adam is the human tetragram, who is summed up in the mysterious yod, image of the Cabalistic phallus. Add the threefold word Eve to yod and you form the name Jehovah, the divine tetragram, which is the Cabalistic and magical word par excellence—

יהוה

—that the high priest in the temple pronounced as Jodheva.[79]

It is thus that complete unity within the fecundity of the threefold form, and with it, the quaternary, is the key to all the numbers, to all movement and to all forms.

The square, by spinning around itself, produces a circle equal to itself, and that is the quadrature of the circle, where the circular movement of the four equal angles rotate around a single point.[80]

What is above, said Hermes, is equal to what is below: that is the duality which serves to measure the unity; and the relation of equality between above

---

79   According to Jewish tradition, the high priest of the Temple of Solomon in Jerusalem, once each year on the Day of Atonement, pronounced the sacred Name of God aloud in the Holy of Holies of the temple. "Jodheva" is a pronunciation of that Name in some traditions of Cabalistic mysticism; the Hebrew letters הוה, HVH, spell the name of Havah or Eve, the first woman; add to this the name of the first letter of the Name, yod, and you have "Yodhavah" or "Yodheva."

80   A very elusive paragraph. "The quadrature of the circle" normally refers to one of two things: the first is the division of a circle into four parts, a simple geometrical operation; the second is the construction of a square and a circle with exactly equal areas or perimeters, which has been proven to be impossible by ordinary geometrical means. What Lévi is suggesting is something quite different, which may be understood by meditating on the image he describes and those that follow in the next few paragraphs.

and below is the creative principle, it is the ideal phallus; and the principle having been created, is the formal cteïs.

The insertion of the vertical phallus into the horizontal cteis[81] forms the Gnostic stauros,[82] or the philosophical cross of the masons. Thus the crossing of the two produces four, which when moving determines the circle with all its degrees.

א is man; ב is woman;[83] 1 is the principle; 2 is the Verb; A is the active; B is the passive; the unity is Boaz; the duality is Jachin.[84]

In Fu Hsi's trigrams, the unity is the yang; the duality is the yin.[85]

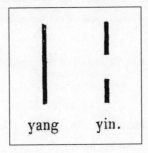

yang   yin.

Boaz and Jachin are the names of the two symbolic columns which were in front of the main doorway of the Cabalistic temple of Solomon.

In the Cabala, these two columns explain all the mysteries of antagonism, whether natural, political, or religious, and it explains the generative conflict between man and woman: because, according to the law of nature, woman must resist man, and man must seduce her or subdue her.

---

81   Cteis is a Greek word for "vagina." The sexual symbolism is quite deliberate, and appears throughout this book and Lévi's other work.

82   *Stauros* is Greek for "cross." The gnostics traditionally saw the cross as T-shaped.

83   These are, respectively, the first two Hebrew letters, aleph and beth.

84   Boaz and Jachin are the names of the two great bronze pillars of the Temple of Solomon. In Masonic symbolism, they relate to the numbers one and two.

85   Lévi is quite correct here; in Chinese lore, Fu Hsi is the traditional creator of the eight *kua,* or trigrams, that are the foundation of the *I Ching,* or *Book of Changes,* made of solid (yang) and broken (yin) lines.

The active principle searches for the passive principle, the full loves the empty. The mouth of the serpent attracts its tail, and, in turning on itself, it both runs away from itself and chases itself.

Man created woman, and universal creation is the spouse of the first principle.

When the principal being became the creator, he raised a yod or a phallus, and to give it a place in the full uncreated light he had to dig a cteïs, or a pit of shadow, equal to the dimension determined by his creative desire and attributed to him by the ideal yod of the radiant light.

That is the mysterious language of the Cabalists in the Talmud, and because of ignorance and vulgar maliciousness, it is impossible for us to explain or simplify it more.

What then is creation? It is the house of the creator Verb. What is the cteïs? It is the house of the phallus.

What is the nature of the active principle? It is to spread outwards. What is the nature of the passive principle? It is to gather and fertilize.

What is man? He is the initiator, he who fractures, who plows and who sows.

What is woman? She is the teacher, she who consolidates, who waters and who harvests.

Man makes war, and woman brings peace; man destroys to create, woman builds to preserve; man is the revolution, woman is the conciliation; man is the father of Cain, woman is the mother of Abel.

What is wisdom? It is the conciliation and the union of the two principles, it is the gentleness of Abel directing the energy of Cain, it is man following the gentle inspirations of woman, it is debauchery conquered by legitimate marriage, it is revolutionary energy softened and tamed by the gentleness of order and peace, it is pride subdued by love, it is science recognizing the inspirations of faith.

And so human science becomes wise, because it is modest, and submits to the infallibility of universal reason, taught by love or by universal charity. It can then be called gnosis, because it at least knows what it cannot yet brag about mastering perfectly.

The unity can only be manifested in the duality; the unity itself and the idea of unity already make two.

The unity of the macrocosm is revealed by the two opposing points of the two triangles:

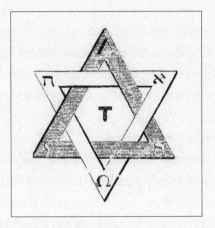

The human unity is completed by the left and the right. Primitive man is androgynous. All the organs of the human body come in twos, except for the nose, the tongue, the umbilicus, and the Cabalistic yod.

The divinity, one in his essence, has two essential conditions as the fundamental basis for his being: necessity and liberty.

The laws of supreme reason require God and regulate liberty, which is necessarily reasonable and wise.

To render light visible, God has only to imagine shadow.

To make truth manifest, he made doubt possible.

Shadow is a foil for light, and the possibility of error is necessary for the temporal manifestation of the truth.

If the shield of Satan did not stop Michael's lance, the angel's power would be lost in the abyss, and this would have resulted in infinite destruction, from the highest to the lowest.

Satan is thus as necessary to Michael as the pedestal is to a statue, and Michael is as necessary to Satan as a brake to a locomotive.

In the analogical and universal dynamic, we can only lean on that which resists.

The universe is balanced by two forces which maintain its equilibrium: the force which attracts and the force which repels. These two forces exist in physics, in philosophy, and in religion. They produce equilibrium in physics, criticism in philosophy, and gradual revelation in religion. The ancients represented this mystery in the battle between Eros and Anteros,[86] in the combat between Jacob and the angel,[87] by the mountain of gold held in equilibrium, using the symbolic serpent of India, by the gods on one side and the demons on the other.[88]

It is symbolized by the caduceus of Hermanubis, by the cherubim of the Ark, by the two sphinxes on Osiris's chariot, and by the two Seraphim, the black and the white.

Its scientific reality is demonstrated by the phenomenon of polarity and by the universal law of sympathies and antipathies.

The unintelligent disciples of Zoroaster divided the duality without bringing it to the unity, thus separating the columns of the temple and wishing to tear God apart. The duality in God only exists through the ternary. If you conceive of the absolute as two, you must immediately think of them as three in order to find the unitary principle again.

This is why the material elements which are analogous to the divine elements are thought of as four, are explained by two, and only exist in the end as three.

Revelation is the duality; all verbs are twofold and suppose two.[89]

The morals which result from this revelation are founded upon antagonism, which is the consequence of the duality. The spirit and the forms are attracted and repelled by one another like the idea and the sign, like truth and fiction. Supreme reason requires doctrine in communicating to finite intelligences, and the doctrine, in passing through the domain of ideas and forms, participates in two worlds and necessarily has two meanings, which speak successively or at once, either to the spirit or to the flesh.

There are also two forces in the domain of morality: one which attacks, and

---

86   In Greek myth, Love and Hatred, or more precisely Love and "Unlove."

87   Genesis 32:24–32.

88   This is the churning of the Ocean of Milk, the creation myth recounted in the Hindu Puranas.

89   That is, every verb has a subject and, at least by implication, an object.

the other which represses or expiates. These two forces are represented in the Genesis myths by the distinctive characters of Cain and Abel.[90]

Abel oppresses Cain with his moral superiority; Cain, to free himself, immortalizes his brother by killing him, and becomes the victim of his infamy. Cain could not allow Abel to live, and Abel's blood no longer allows Cain to sleep.

In the Gospel, the character of Cain is replaced by that of the prodigal son, whose father forgives him of everything because he returns after having greatly suffered.[91]

Within God, there is mercy and justice: he does justice to the just and gives mercy to the sinners.

In the soul of the world, which is the universal agent, there is a current of love and a current of wrath.

This ambient fluid which penetrates all things; this detached ray of the Sun's glory which is fixed by the weight of the atmosphere and by the central attractive force, this body of the Holy Spirit that we call the universal agent and which the ancients represented with the symbol of the snake biting its tail, this electromagnetic ether, this vital and luminous calorific is symbolized in the ancient monuments by Isis's belt, which turns and returns in a knot of love around the two poles, and by the serpent biting its tail, emblem of prudence and of Saturn.

Movement and life consist of the extreme tension between two forces.

It would please God, said the Master, if you were entirely cold or entirely hot![92]

Indeed, a great wrongdoer is more alive than a cowardly and apathetic man, and his return to virtue will be due to the energy of his wanderings.

The woman who must crush the head of the serpent[93] is intelligence, which is always surmounting the current of blind forces. She is, say the Cabalists, the virgin of the sea, whose humid feet the infernal dragon comes to lick with his tongues of fire, and then falls asleep from delight.

---

90   According to Genesis 4:1–15, the first murderer and his victim.

91   The reference is to Luke 15:11–32.

92   A paraphrase of Revelation 3:15.

93   A reference to Genesis 3:15.

These are the hieratic mysteries of duality. But there is one, the last of them all, that should not be revealed: the reason for this, according to Hermes Trismegistus, is due to the stupidity of the vulgar, who would add to the necessities of science the entire immoral range of a blind destiny. One must contain the vulgar, he also says, by the fear of the unknown; and the Christ said it as well: Do not cast your pearls before swine, lest they trample them under their feet, and turn and devour you.[94] The tree of the knowledge of good and evil, whose fruits cause death, is the symbol of this hieratic secret of the duality. This secret, in fact, if it is revealed, can only be misunderstood, and would ordinarily result in the impious negation of free will, which is the moral principle of life. It is thus natural that the revelation of this secret causes death, and it is not even the greatest mystery of magic; but the secret of duality leads to that of the quaternary, or, more precisely, it proceeds from and is resolved by the ternary, which contains the word of the enigma of the sphinx as it must have been found in order to save life, to expiate the involuntary crime, and secure the kingship of Oedipus.

In the hieroglyphic book of Hermes,[95] which is also called the book of Thoth, the duality is represented either by a high priestess with the horns of Isis, her head veiled, with an open book which she partially hides under her cloak, or by the sovereign woman, the Greek goddess Juno, holding one hand raised towards the sky and the other lowered towards the earth, as if with her gesture she were formulating the unique and dualistic doctrine which is the basis for all magic and which is the first marvelous symbol in Hermes's Emerald Tablet.

In the Revelation of Saint John, there are the two witnesses, or martyrs, to which prophetic tradition ascribes the names of Elijah and Enoch:[96] Elijah, the man of faith, of zeal and miracles; Enoch, the same whom the Egyptians called Hermes and the Phoenicians honored under the name of Cadmus, author of the sacred alphabet and the universal key to the initiations of the Verb, father of the Cabala, he, say the saintly allegories, who did not die like other men but was raised to the heavens to return in the end times. Much the same thing was said

---

94   A paraphrase of Matthew 7:6.

95   See the game of Taro. (Lévi's note.)

96   Revelation 11:3–11.

about Saint John himself, who rediscovered and explained in his Apocalypse the symbols of the Verb of Enoch. This resurrection of Saint John and Enoch, awaited for at the end of the centuries of ignorance, shall be the renewal of their doctrine through the intelligence of the Cabalistic keys which open the temple of the unity and the universal philosophy, which have too long remained occult and the exclusive reserve of the elect whom this world has made to die.

But we have said that the reproduction of the unity by the duality inevitably leads to the notion and doctrine of the ternary, and we arrive finally to that great number, which is the fulfillment and the perfect Verb of unity.

THE TRIANGLE OF SOLOMON

The Empress

PLENITUDO VOCIS.

BINAH.

PHYSIS.[97]

T he perfect Verb is the ternary, because it supposes an intelligent principle, an expressive principle, and a spoken principle.

The absolute, which is revealed by the word, gives this word a meaning which is true to itself, and creates a third "itself" in the understanding of this word.

It is thus that the Sun is made manifest by the light and demonstrates this manifestation, or renders it effective, through its heat.

The ternary is outlined in space from the sky's zenith, infinite in height, which is attached by two straight and diverging lines to the orient and the occident.

But reason compares this visible triangle to another invisible triangle, which it affirms to be equal to the first: it is the one which has as its summit the depths

---

97   *Plenitudo vocis* is Latin for "fullness of voice"; Binah, "understanding," is the third of the ten sephiroth of the Cabalistic Tree of Life; *physis* is Greek for "nature."

and whose base is inverted and parallel to the horizontal line which goes from the orient to the occident.

These two triangles reunited in a single figure, which is that of the six-pointed star, forms the sacred seal of Solomon, the shining star of the macro-cosm.[98]

This symbol, which is the great pentacle, expresses the idea of the infinite and the absolute, which is to say that it is the simplest and most complete synopsis of all things.

On its own, grammar attributes three persons to the verb. The first person is he who speaks, the second is he to whom we speak, the third is he about whom we speak.

The infinite prince, in creating, speaks of himself to himself.

That is the explanation of the ternary and the origin of the dogma of the Trinity.

The magical doctrine is also of one in three and three in one.

That which is above resembles or is equal to that which is below.

Thus, two things which resemble each other and the verb which expresses their resemblance makes three.

The ternary is the universal doctrine.

In magic it is principle, fulfillment, and adaptation; in alchemy it is azoth, in-corporation, and transmutation; in theology it is God, incarnation, and re-demption; in the human soul it is thought, love, and action; in the family it is father, mother, and child. The ternary is the goal and ultimate expression of love: we search for another to become two in order to become three.

There are three intelligible worlds which correspond to each other through a hierarchical analogy: the natural or physical world, the spiritual or metaphysical world, and the divine or religious world.

From this principle results the hierarchy of states of mind divided in three orders, which are again subdivided, as always, by the ternary.

All these revelations are logical deductions from the first mathematical no-tions of being and number.

---

98   See figure on page 43. (Lévi's note.)

The unity, to become active, must multiply. An indivisible principle, which is immobile and infertile, would be a dead and incomprehensible unity.

If God was only one, he would never be creator and father. If he was two, there would be infinite antagonism or division, and the result would be the division or death of all things: thus he is three in order to create from himself, and in his image, the infinite multitude of beings and numbers.

Thus he is truly unique, of himself, and threefold in our conception of him, which also makes us see him through our intellect and in our love as both threefold and unique.

This is a mystery for the believer and a logical necessity for the initiate of the true and absolute sciences.

The Verb made manifest by life is realization or incarnation.

The life of the Verb, in completing its cyclical movement, is adaptation or redemption. This threefold doctrine was known to all the sanctuaries enlightened by the tradition of the sages. Do you wish to know which is the true religion? Look for the one which understands the most about the divine order, the one which humanizes God and deifies man, the one which keeps the ternary doctrine intact, the one which incarnates the Verb by having the most ignorant among us see and touch God, and finally the one whose doctrine is suitable for all and can be adapted by everyone; the religion which is hierarchical and cyclical, which has for its children allegories and symbols, which contains for completed men a high philosophy, and has sublime hopes and sweet consolations for old men.

The first sages who searched for the cause of causes saw good and evil in the world; they observed shadow and light; they compared winter to spring, old age to youth, life to death, and they said, "The first cause is beneficial and harsh, it vivifies and it destroys."

Are there, then, two contrary principles, one good and one evil? So proclaimed the disciples of Manes.

No, the two principles of the universal equilibrium are not contrary, even if they are opposites in appearance: because it is a single, unique wisdom which opposes one against the other.

The good is to the right, evil is to the left, but supreme grace is above the two, and it puts evil in service to the triumph of good, and the good in reparation for evil.

The principle of harmony is in the unity, and it is why magic finds so much power in odd numbers.

But the most perfect of odd numbers is three, because it is the trilogy of the unity.

In Fu Hsi's trigrams, the superior ternary is composed of three yangs, or masculine figures, because in the idea of God, which is considered the principle of fertility in the three worlds, one cannot accept anything of the passive.

It is for this reason also that the Christian trinity does not accept the personification of the mother, which is implied in the son. It is also for this reason that it is contrary to the laws of orthodox hieratic symbolism to personify the Holy Spirit as a woman.[99]

Woman comes from man just as nature comes from God: also the Christ raises himself to heaven and *assumes* the Virgin mother; we speak of the ascension of the Savior and the assumption of the mother of God.

God, considered as the father, has nature for a daughter.

God, as the son, has the Virgin for a mother and the Church as a spouse.

As the Holy Spirit, he regenerates and fertilizes humanity.

It is thus, in Fu Hsi's trigrams, that the three superior yangs correspond to the three inferior yins, because Fu Hsi's trigrams comprise a pentacle similar to the two triangles of Solomon but with a ternary explanation of the six brilliant points of the star.

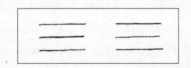

Dogma is not divine unless it is truly human, that is to say it summarizes the highest reason of humanity: also, the Master whom we call the Man-God called himself the Son of Man.

Revelation is the expression of the belief in the human Verb as accepted and formulated by universal reason.

---

99   A point of Catholic doctrine with which many Christians, ancient and modern, have disagreed.

That is why we say that within the Man-God, divinity is human and humanity is divine.

We write all this philosophically speaking, and not theologically, and this has nothing to do with the Church's teachings, which condemn and must always condemn magic.

Paracelsus and Agrippa did not raise altar against altar but submitted themselves to the dominant religion of their times. To the elect of science, the things of science; to the faithful, the things of faith!

The Emperor Julian, in his hymn to the royal Sun,[100] provides a theory of the ternary which is almost exactly the same as that of the visionary Swedenborg.

The Sun of the divine world is the uncreated infinite spiritual light; it is the light which verbalizes, if we can so phrase it, in the philosophical world and becomes the home of souls and of the truth, then it becomes corporeal and becomes the visible light of the sun of the third world, the central sun of our suns, of which the fixed stars are ever-living sparks.

The Cabalists compare the spirit to a substance which remains fluid in the divine milieu and under the influence of the essential light but whose exterior hardens like wax exposed to the air of the coldest regions of reasoning or of the visible forms. These husks or petrified envelopes (we would express it better by saying "carnified," if the word existed in French) are the cause of errors or of evil, which are due to the weight and the hardness of these envelopes of the soul. In the book of Zohar and in the book of the revolutions of souls, perverted minds, or wicked demons, are called nothing other than husks or cortices.[101]

The husks of the world of the spirits are transparent, those of the material world are opaque; bodies are only temporary crusts from which souls must be delivered; but those who obey the body in this life produce an interior body or a fluidic crust which becomes their prison and their torment after death, until they manage to melt it in the heat of the divine light, to which their weight stops them from rising; they only manage this after infinite efforts and with the help of the

---

100   The most famous of Julian's writings, a Greek hymn in praise of the sun god Helios.

101   The literal translation of the Hebrew word qlippoth, the term for demons in Cabalistic writings.

just, who assist them, and during all this time they are devoured by the internal activity of the captive spirit as if they were in a raging furnace. Those who arrive at the pyre of expiation burn themselves like Hercules atop Mount Oeta and thus deliver themselves from their suffering;[102] but most lack the courage to face this final test, which appears like a second and more horrible death to them than the first, and thus remain in hell, which is eternal by law and fact, but into which souls are never thrown or held against their will.

The three worlds correspond to each other through the thirty-two paths of light which are the rungs of the divine ladder; every true thought corresponds to a divine grace in heaven and to a helpful deed on earth. Every grace of God arouses a truth and produces one or more acts, and reciprocally every act stirs a truth or a lie in the heavens, a grace or a punishment. When a man pronounces the Tetragrammaton, write the Cabalists, the nine heavens are shaken, and all the spirits cry out to each other: "Who thus disturbs the kingdom of heaven?" And then the earth reveals to the first heaven the sins of the foolhardy person who took the eternal one's name in vain, and the accusing Verb is transmitted from circle to circle, from star to star, and from hierarchy to hierarchy.

All words have three meanings, all actions a threefold result, all forms a threefold idea because the absolute corresponds from world to world with its forms. Every resolution of human will modifies nature, interests philosophy, and is written in heaven. There are then two inevitabilities, one resulting from the will of the Uncreated in accord with his wisdom, the other resulting from the wills of the created in accord with the necessity of second causes and their relationships with the first cause.

Thus nothing is indifferent in life, and our most apparently simple resolutions are often what decide an incalculable series of good or evils, especially with regard to connections between our diaphane and the great magical agent, as we shall explain elsewhere.

The ternary, being the fundamental principle of the entire Cabala, or sacred

---

102   The legendary Greek hero Hercules, when he had been tricked into putting on a
       garment soaked in the poisonous blood of Nessus, achieved immortality by burn-
       ing himself alive on Mount Oeta. This scene had much the same significance for
       ancient Greeks as the crucifixion of Jesus has for Christians.

tradition of our fathers, had to be the fundamental dogma of Christianity, where it explains the apparent dualism by the intervention of a harmonious and all-powerful unity. The Christ did not write down his dogma; he only revealed it in secret to his favorite disciple, the only Cabalist, and a great Cabalist among the apostles. Thus the Book of Revelation is the book of gnosis, or the secret doctrine of the first Christians, a doctrine whose key is indicated by a secret verse of the Paternoster, which the Vulgate does not translate, and that in the Greek rite (the custodian of the traditions of Saint John) only the priests are allowed to pronounce. This entirely Cabalistic verse is found in the Greek text of the Gospel according to Saint Matthew and in several Hebrew copies. Here it is in those two sacred languages.[103]

כִּי לְךָ הַמַּמְלָכָה וְהַגְּבוּרָה וְהַתִּפְאֶרֶת לְעוֹלְמֵי עוֹלָמִים אָמֵן:

Ὅτι σοῦ ἐστιν ἡ βασιλεία καὶ ἡ δύναμις καὶ ἡ δόξα εἰς τοὺς αἰῶνας, Ἀμήν.

The sacred word Malkuth, placed in Kether, which is its Cabalistic correspondence, and the balance between Geburah and Chesed repeated in the circles or the heavens which the gnostics call Aeons, gives with this occult verse the keystone for the entire Christian temple. The Protestants translated it and kept it in their New Testament, without discovering its lofty and marvelous meaning, which would have revealed to them all the mysteries of the Book of Revelation; but it is a tradition in the Church that the revelation of these mysteries is reserved for the end times.

Malkuth, supported by Geburah and by Chesed, is the temple of Solomon, which has Jachin and Boaz for columns. It is the Adamic doctrine, supported on one side by the resignation of Abel and on the other by the work and remorse of Cain; it is the universal balance of reality based on necessity and on liberty, on stillness and movement; it is the demonstration of the universal lever vainly sought after by Archimedes. A scholar who used his talent to obscure, and who

---

103 This is the familiar ending verse of the Lord's Prayer as recited in Protestant churches: "For Thine is the kingdom and the power and the glory, forever and ever, amen." It is found in some early copies of the Gospel of Matthew but not in others.

died without wanting to be understood, solved this supreme equation, which he found in the Cabala, and who feared above all we would not understand, if he explained the origin of his discoveries more clearly. We heard one of his disciples and admirers angrily protest, perhaps in good faith, upon hearing him called a Cabalist, and still we must say, to the glory of this scholar, that his studies considerably reduced our work with regard to the occult sciences, and more importantly that the key to the high Cabala, indicated in the occult verse we just cited, was learnedly applied to an absolute reform of all the sciences in the books of Hoene Wronski.[104]

The secret virtue of the Gospels is thus contained in three words, and those three words founded the three doctrines and three hierarchies. All of science rests on three principles, just like a syllogism with three terms. There are also three distinct classes, or three original and natural ranks, among men, who are all called to climb from the lowest to the highest rank. The Hebrews call these series or degrees of progress of the spirit, Assiah, Yetzirah, and Briah.[105] The Gnostics, who were the Christian Cabalists, called them Hyle, Psyche and Gnosis;[106] the supreme circle was called Atziluth by the Hebrews and Pleroma[107] by the gnostics.

In the Tetragrammaton, the ternary, taken at the start of the word, expresses divine copulation, taken at the end, it expresses the feminine and maternity. Eve's name has three letters, but primitive Adam is expressed by the single letter Yod, such that Jehovah should be pronounced as Ieva. This brings us to the great and supreme mystery of magic, expressed by the quaternary.

---

104   Polish mathematician and occultist Jósef Maria Hoëné-Wroński, Lévi's most important teacher.

105   The four Cabalistic worlds are Atziluth, the world of origination; Briah, the world of creation; Yetzirah, the world of formation; and Assiah, the world of action, which is the material world.

106   Greek for "matter," "spirit," and "wisdom."

107   Greek for "fullness." According to gnostic teachings, the pleroma was the eternal source of all realities.

4 ד D.

THE TETRAGRAMMATON

The EmperoR

HESED.

PORTA LIBRORUM.

ELEMENTA.[108]

In nature there are two forces which produce an equilibrium, and the three are but one law. That is the ternary summarized in the unity, and, in adding the idea of the unity to that of the ternary, we arrive at the quaternary, the first square and perfect number, source of all numerical combinations and the principle behind all the forms.

Affirmation, negation, discussion, solution, these are the four philosophical operations of the human spirit. Discussion reconciles negation with affirmation and renders them necessary to each other. It is thus that the philosophical ternary, produced by the antagonistic duality, is completed by the quaternary, the square base for all truth. In God, following the established dogma, there are three persons, and these three persons are but one God. Three in one produces the idea

---

108 Chesed, "mercy," is the fourth sephira of the Cabalistic Tree of Life; *porta librorum* is Latin for "gate of books," and *elementa* is Latin for "elements." The second is likely a misprint for *porta librarum*, "gate of balance."

of four, because the unity is necessary to account for the three. In almost all languages, the name of God is made of four letters,[109] and in Hebrew these four letters are only three, because there is one that is repeated twice: the one which expresses the Verb and the creation of the Verb.

Two affirmations render possible or necessary two corresponding negations. Being is signified, the void is not. The affirmation, like the Verb, produces another affirmation, like the realization or incarnation of the Verb, and each of these affirmations correspond to the negation of its opposite.

It is thus, as the Cabalists say, that the name of the demon, or of evil, is composed of the letters of the name of God, or of good, in reverse.

This evil is the lost reflection or the imperfect mirage of the light in the shadow.

But all that exists, either for the good or for evil, either in the light or in the shadow, exists and is revealed by the quaternary.

The affirmation of the unity supposes the number four, if this unity is not to return back into unity itself like a vicious circle. Also the ternary, as we have already observed, is explained by the duality, it resolves itself by the quaternary, which is the squared unit of number pairs and the quadrangular base of the cube, the unity of construction, of solidity, and of measurement.

The Cabalistic Tetragrammaton, Jodheva, expresses God in humanity and humanity in God.

The four astronomical cardinal points are, relative to us, the yes and the no of light: the orient and the occident, and the yes and the no of heat: the south and the north.

What is in visible nature, as we already know from the unique doctrine of the Cabala, reveals what is in the domain of invisible nature, or the domain of second causes, which are all proportional and analogous to manifestations of the first cause.

This first cause is the one which is always revealed by the cross: the cross,

---

109   This is not quite true, but many European names of God do have this peculiarity; consider French *Dieu*, Spanish *Dios*, German *Gott*, Latin *Deus*, Greek Θεος (*Theos*), etc.

that unity composed of two, which divide each other to form four; the cross, that key to the mysteries of India and of Egypt, the Tau of the patriarchs, the symbol of the divine Osiris, the Stauros of the Gnostics, the keystone of the temple, the symbol of occult masonry; the cross, that central point at the junction of the right angles of two infinite triangles; the cross, which, in the French language, seems to be the first root and fundamental substantive of the verb "croire" (to believe) and the verb "croître" (to grow), thus reuniting the ideas of science, of religion, and of progress.[110]

The great magical agent reveals itself through four types of phenomenon and was subjected to the groping of the profane sciences under four names: heat, light, electricity, magnetism. It has also been given the names of Tetragrammaton; I.N.R.I.,[111] Azoth, ether,[112] od,[113] magnetic fluid,[114] the soul of the Earth,[115] serpent, Lucifer, etc.

The great magical agent is the fourth emanation of the life principle, of which the Sun is the third form (see the initiates of the school of Alexandria and the doctrine of Hermes Trismegistus).

Thus the eye of the world (as the ancients called the Sun) is the mirage of the reflection of God, and the soul of the Earth is under the permanent gaze of the Sun which the Earth perceives and keeps through impregnation.

The Moon takes part in this impregnation of the Earth by sending the Earth

---

110 A bit of wordplay that does not translate well into English: in French, "cross" is *croix*, which does in fact look like it should be a noun related to the verbs *croire* and/or *croître*.

111 The initials of *Iesus Nazarethus Rex Iudaeorum*, "Jesus of Nazareth, King of the Jews," the placard traditionally posted on the cross. These four letters saw much use in Christian Cabalistic symbolism and magic.

112 In the physics of Lévi's time, a subtle substance through which light waves were believed to propagate. Many mages adopted this label for the great magical agent, and some traditions still use the term.

113 The term used by Baron Karl von Reichenbach for the life force.

114 Franz Anton Mesmer's term for the same force.

115 Renaissance magical philosophy's term for the same force. It is interesting how often this supposedly nonexistent phenomenon has been discovered and how remarkably consistent are the descriptions its finders give of it.

a solar image during the night, so that Hermes was correct in saying, when speaking of the great agent: "The Sun is its father, the Moon is its mother." He then adds: "The wind carried the great agent in its belly,"[116] because the atmosphere is the recipient of, and like a crucible for, the Sun's rays, and through the great agent, with its continual outflows and currents, which are analogous to those of the Sun itself, is formed that living image of the Sun which entirely penetrates the Earth, enlivens it, fertilizes it, and determines all that is produced on its surface.

This solar agent lives through two contrary forces: a force of attraction and a force of projection, which is why Hermes says that it always goes back up and comes back down.

The force of attraction is always fixed in the center of objects, the force of projection is fixed on their contours or their surface.

It is through this dual force that all is created and all subsists.

Its movement is successive and indefinite, or rather simultaneous and perpetual, rolling and unrolling through spirals of contrary movements which never meet.

To understand the movement of this terrestrial Sun, so as to be able to benefit from its currents and direct them, is to have accomplished the Great Work, and it is to be master of the world.

Armed with such a power, you can make yourself adored, the vulgar will believe you to be God.

The absolute secret for directing the currents was possessed by a few men and can be found again. It is the great magical arcanum: it depends on an incommunicable axiom and on an instrument which is the great and unique athanor of the Hermetics of the highest grade.

The incommunicable axiom is enclosed Cabalistically within the four letters of the tetragrammaton in this manner:

---

116   These are both passages from the Emerald Tablet.

in the letters of the words AZOTH and INRI, written Cabalistically, and in the monogram of Christ as it was appended to the labarum,[117] and which the Cabalist Postel interprets with the word ROTA, with which the adepts formed their taro or tarot, by repeating the first letter twice, to indicate the circle and have it understood that the word is inversed.

All of magical science consists in the understanding of this secret. To have this knowledge and to dare to use it is omnipotence in human affairs; to reveal it to the profane is to lose it; to reveal it even to a disciple is to abdicate in favor of that disciple, who from that moment, would have the power of life and death over his initiator (I speak here from the magical point of view) and will certainly kill him, out of fear of dying himself. (This has nothing to do with acts treated as murder in criminal law, which serve as a basis and starting point for our laws and ignore instances of murder through bewitchment and occult influences.) We enter here into strange revelations, and we expect every expression of disbelief and the shrugging shoulders of fanatic disbelievers, because the religion of Voltaire also has its fanatics—apologies to the great shades who must now be sulking in a pathetic manner within the vaults of the Pantheon,

---

117 The labarum was a Roman standard bearing the Chi-Rho, a symbol made of the Greek letters XP (chi and rho), the first two letters of Χριστος, or Christ, which was used after the Christianization of the empire. The Chi-Rho still has a role in some Catholic uses.

while Catholicism, always strong due to its practices and its prestige, praises them.

The perfect word, that which is adequate for the thought it expresses, always contains potentially or supposes a quaternary: the idea of those three necessary and correlative forms, and also the image of the thing expressed with the three terms of judgment which qualify it. When I say: Being exists, I implicitly affirm that nothingness does not exist.

A height, a width which the the height divides geometrically in two, and a depth separated from the height by the intersection of the width, such is the natural quaternary composed of two lines which cross each other. There are also in nature four movements produced by two forces which support each other by their orientation in opposite directions. Yet the law which rules objects is analogous and proportional to the law which governs intellects, and the law which governs intellects is the very manifestation of the secret of God, which is to say the mystery of creation.

Suppose a watch with two parallel springs, with a gear which makes them move in opposing directions, so that one, in extending, contracts the other: such a watch would wind itself, and you would have discovered perpetual motion.[118] This gear must work in both directions and be of great precision. Is it nowhere to be found? We do not believe so. But when someone will have discovered it, he will be able to understand by analogy all the secrets of nature: *progress as a direct result of resistance.*

The absolute movement of life is the perpetual result of two contrary tendencies which never oppose one another. When one of them appears to yield, it is a spring which stretches, and you can expect a reaction whose timing and character is quite possible to predict; it is thus that during the era of the greatest Christian fervor, the reign of the Antichrist was known and predicted.

But the Antichrist will prepare and determine the new occasion and the definitive triumph of the Man-God. This is also a rigorous and Cabalistic conclusion which is contained in the premises of the Gospels.

---

118   Not literally true—the watch would run down due to friction—but the image
       Lévi offers will yield much to meditation.

Thus Christian prophecy contains a quadruple revelation: first, the fall of the ancient world and the triumph of the Gospel under the first coming; second, the great apostasy and the arrival of the Antichrist; third, the fall of the Antichrist and the return of Christian ideas; fourth, the definitive triumph of the Gospel, or the Second Coming, designated by the name "the last judgment." This quadruple prophecy contains, as we can see, two affirmations and two negations, the idea of two ruins or universal deaths and two rebirths; because for every idea which appears on the social horizon we can assign without fear an orient and an occident, a zenith and a nadir. It is in that way that the philosophical cross is the key to the prophecy, and we can open all the doors of science with Ezekiel's pentacle, whose center is a star formed by the crossing of two crosses.

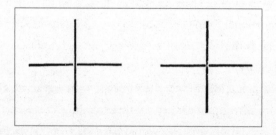

Is not human life also formed by those three phases or successive transformations: birth, life, death, immortality? And notice here that the immortality of the soul, required as the complement of the quaternary, is proven Cabalistically by analogy, which is the unique doctrine of the truly universal religion, just as it is the key to science and the inviolable law of nature.

Death, in fact, can no more be an absolute end than birth a real beginning. Birth proves the preexistence of the human being, since nothing is produced from nothing, and death proves immortality, since being cannot stop being any more than nothingness cannot stop not being. Being and nothingness are two absolutely irreconcilable ideas, with the difference that the idea of nothingness (a totally negative idea) comes from the idea of being itself, thus nothingness cannot even be understood as an absolute negation, while the idea of being can never even be compared to that of nothingness, and it is even less the case that it can come out of nothingness. To say the world came out of nothingness is to utter a monstrous absurdity. All that is proceeds from what was; in consequence, nothing that is could ever not be. The succession of forms is produced by alternate movements: they are the phenomena of life that replace one another without destroying themselves. Everything changes, but nothing perishes. The Sun does not die when it disappears at the horizon, the forms, even the most mobile ones, are immortal and subsist always in the permanence of their raison d'être, which is the combination of the light with the powerful aggregates of molecules of the first substance. They are also conserved in the astral fluid and can be evoked and reproduced according to the will of the sage, as we shall see when we examine second sight and the evocation of memories in necromancy and other magical operations.

We will come back to the great magical agent in the fourth chapter of the Ritual, where we will finish describing the characters of the great arcanum and the means of seizing this formidable power.

Let us say a few words here about the four elements of magic and about the elementary spirits.

The magical elements are: in alchemy, salt, mercury, sulfur, and azoth;[119] in the Cabala, the macroprosopus, the microprosopus, and the two mothers;[120] in hieroglyphics, the man, the eagle, the lion, and the bull;[121] in ancient physics, using the vulgar ideas and terms, air, water, earth, and fire.

In magical science, we know that water is not ordinary water; that fire is not simply fire, etc. These expressions hide a higher meaning. Modern science has broken down the four elements of the ancients and has found many so-called simple bodies. What is simple is the primitive substance properly so called; thus there is only one material element, and this element is always manifested by the quaternary in its forms. We will thus keep the learned distinction of the ele-

---

119 The first three are not the material substances usually so called. Alchemically, salt is the principle of solidity, mercury of fluidity, sulfur of volatility, and azoth is the universal solvent that permits their separation and recombination.

120 These are, among other things in Cabalistic symbolism, the sephiroth Chokmah, Tiphareth, Binah, and Malkuth respectively.

121 The symbols of the four evangelists—Matthew is the man, John the eagle, Mark the lion, and Luke the bull—and also of the four signs of the zodiac—the man is Aquarius, the eagle is the highest of the three forms of Scorpio (the others being the scorpion and the serpent), the lion is Leo, and the bull is Taurus.

mentary aspects as accepted by the ancients, and we will recognize air, fire, earth, and water as the four positive and visible elements of magic.

The subtle and the thick, the rapid solvent and the slow solvent, or the instruments of hot and cold, form in occult physics the two positive principles and the two negative principles of the quaternary and must be drawn so:

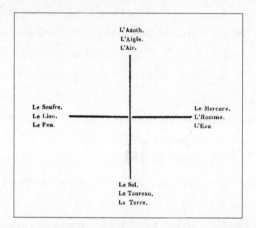

Air and earth thus represent the male principle, fire and water belong to the female principle, since the philosophical cross of the pentacles is, as we have already said, a primitive hieroglyph and elementary lingam of the gymnosophists.[122]

These four elementary forms correspond to the following four elementary ideas:

Spirit,

Matter,

Movement,

Rest.

---

122   From Greek for "naked philosophers," an old term for the ascetic sages of India.

All of science, in fact, is in the understanding of these four things, which alchemy reduces to three,

The Absolute,

The Fixed,

The Volatile;

and which the Cabala relates to the actual idea of God, which is absolute reason, necessity and liberty, the threefold notion expressed in the occult books of the Hebrews.

Under the names of Kether, Chokmah, and Binah for the divine world, Tiphereth, Chesed, and Geburah in the moral world; and finally Yesod, Hod, and Netzach in the physical world, which, along with the moral world, is contained in the idea of kingdom or Malkuth: we will explain in the tenth chapter of this book this theogony, which is as rational as it is sublime.

The created intelligences, having been called forth during emancipation by trial, were placed from their birth between these four forces, the two positive and two negative ones, and immediately began to affirm or deny the good, to choose life or death. To find the fixed point, that is to say the moral center of the cross, is the first problem given to them to solve; their first conquest must be that of their own freedom.

Thus certain of them begin by being pulled to the north, others to the south, certain to the right, others to the left, and as long as they are not free, they cannot make use of reason, nor be incarnated in anything other than animal forms. These unemancipated intelligences, slaves of the four elements, are what the Cabalists call the elementary demons, and they people the elements which correspond to their state of servitude. Thus, sylphs, undines, gnomes, and salamanders truly exist, certain of them wandering and seeking to become incarnate, others already incarnate and living on Earth. They are perverted and imperfect men.

We will come back to this subject in the fifteenth chapter, which deals with enchantments and demons.

It is also a tradition of occult physics, which led the ancients to admit the existence of the four ages of the world; only they did not tell the vulgar that these four ages had to succeed each other, like the four seasons of the year, and be renewed like them. Thus the golden age has passed, and it is still to come. But this has to do with the spirit of prophecy, and we will talk about it in the ninth chapter, which deals with the initiate and the seer.

Let us now add the unity to the quaternary, and we will have together and separately the ideas of divine synthesis and analysis, the god of the initiates and the god of the profane. Here the doctrine is popularized and becomes less abstract; the great hierophant intervenes.

THE PENTAGRAM

The Hierophant

GEBURAH.

ECCE.[123]

Up until now we have expounded upon the most arid and abstract aspects of magical doctrine; here begin the enchantments; here we can announce wonders and reveal the most hidden of things.

The pentagram expresses the domination of the mind over the elements, and it is by this symbol that we enchain the demons of air, the spirits of fire, the specters of water, and the ghosts of the earth.

---

123 Geburah, "severity," is the fifth sephira of the Cabalistic Tree of Life; *ecce* is Latin for "behold!"

Armed with this symbol and properly prepared, you can see the infinite by using that faculty which is like the eye of your soul, and you will have the legions of angels and columns of demons serve you.

And let us first state the principles:

There is no invisible world, there are only degrees of perfection in the different systems.

Objects and crude representations are like the temporary crust of the soul.

The soul can perceive objects on its own, without the intercession of the corporeal organs, through its own sensibility and its diaphane. It can see either spiritual or corporeal objects that exist in the universe.

Spiritual and corporeal are words which only express the degrees of subtlety or the density of the substance.

What we call our imagination is simply the inherent property of our soul to assimilate images and the reflections contained in the living light, which is the great magnetic agent.

These images and reflections are revelations when science intervenes to reveal the object or the light to us. The man of genius differs from the dreamer and the madman only in that his creations are analogous to the truth, whereas those of dreamers and madmen are lost reflections and misplaced images.

Thus, for the sage, to imagine is to see, just as for the magician, to speak is to create.

We can thus really and truly see demons, souls, etc., by means of the imagination; but the imagination of the adept is diaphanous, while the imagination of the vulgar is opaque; the light of truth crosses one as though through a splendid window and refracts in the other as though through a glazed mass full of dross and foreign objects.

That which contributes the most to the errors of the vulgar and to extravagances of folly are people's depraved reflections of the imagination.

But the seer knows with the certainty of science that the things he imagines are true, and experience always confirms his visions.

We will explain in the Ritual by what means we can acquire this lucidity.

It is by means of this light that static visionaries are able to communicate with all the worlds, as happened so often to Emanuel Swedenborg, despite his not being perfectly lucid, since he did not discern the reflection of the rays and often confused simple reveries with his most admirable dreams.

We say dreams because the dream is the result of a natural and periodic ecstasy called sleep. To be in ecstasy is to dream; magnetic somnambulism is a reproduction, and a way, of ecstasy.

Errors in somnambulism are caused by reflections from the diaphanes of people who are awake, and even more so by reflections due to hypnotism.

Dreams are visions produced by the refraction of rays of truth; reverie is hallucination caused by a reflection.

The temptation of Saint Anthony, with his nightmares and his monsters, represents confusion between reflections and direct rays. As long as the soul fights, it remains rational; when it succumbs to this kind of invasive intoxication, it is deranged.

Untangling the direct ray and separating it from reflection, this is the work of the initiate.

Now let us speak clearly and say that this work has always been accomplished by a few elite persons in the world; that revelation through intuition is thus permanent, and that there is no insurmountable barrier which separates souls, because in nature there is no sudden break, nor are there absolute barriers that separate one psyche from others. All is transition and nuance, and if we suppose perfectibility, if not infinite, at least indefinite, of the human faculties, we would see that any man can manage to see all, and in consequence to know all, at least in one circle which he can indefinitely expand.

There is no vacuum in nature, all is filled.

There is no real death in nature, all is alive.

"Do you see that star?" said Napoleon to Cardinal Fesch. "No, Sire." "Really! Well, *I* see it." And he certainly did see it.

It is for this reason that we accuse great men of having been superstitious: it is that they saw what the vulgar did not see.

Men of genius differ from ordinary seers by the faculty they have for making other men *sense* what they see themselves and to be *believed* out of enthusiasm and sympathy.

They are the *mediums* of the divine Verb.

Let us now speak about how this occurs.

All the forms correspond to ideas, and there is no idea which does not have its own particular form.

The primordial light, the vehicle for all ideas, is the mother of all the forms and transmits them from emanation to emanation, they are only weakened or altered because of the density of the environments.

The secondary forms are reflections which return back to the home of the emanated light.

The forms of objects, being a modification of light, stay in the light where reflections refer to them. Also, the astral light or terrestrial fluid, which we call the great magical agent, is saturated with images or reflections of all kinds, which soul can evoke and submit to its diaphane, as the Cabalists say. These images are always present in us and are only erased by the stronger imprint of the reality of the waking world or by preoccupation with our thoughts, which render our imagination inattentive to the mobile panorama of the astral light. When we sleep, this spectacle presents itself to us, and it is thus that we produce reveries: reveries which are incoherent and vague, unless some dominant will remains active during sleep and gives, unbeknownst to our intellect, a direction to the reverie, which then transforms it into a dream.

Animal magnetism is nothing but artificial sleep produced by the union, either voluntary or forced, of two souls, one of whom keeps vigil while the other sleeps, that is to say while one directs the other in its choice of reflections in order to transform reveries into dreams and know the truth through images.

Thus somnambulists do not really go to the places where the hypnotist sends them; they evoke images in the astral light and can see nothing that does not exist in that light.

The astral light has a direct effect upon the nerves, which are conductors in the animal economy and which carry it to the brain; also, in the state of somnambulism we can see with our nerves without even having need for the radiant light, since the astral fluid is a latent light, just as physics has recognized that there exists a latent calorific.

Hypnotism with two participants is without a doubt a marvelous discovery, but hypnotism with a single participant who renders himself lucid at will and who directs himself is the perfection of the magical art and the secret of this great work is not lost: it was known and practiced by a large number of initiates, most of all by the celebrated Apollonius of Tyana, who left behind a theory, as we shall see in our Ritual.

The secret to hypnotic lucidity and the way of magnetic phenomena is twofold: the harmony of intellects and the perfect union of wills in a direction made possible and determined by science; this is with regard to hypnotism as practiced with several participants. Solitary hypnotism requires preparations of which we spoke in our first chapter, when we listed and showed with all their difficulties the qualities required to be a veritable adept.

We will elucidate this important and fundamental point more and more in the chapters which follow.

This empire of will over the astral light, which is the physical soul of the four elements, is symbolized in magic by the pentagram, whose figure we placed at the head of this chapter.

The elementary spirits are also brought under the power of this sign when we use it with intelligence, and we can, by placing it in a circle or on a table of evocation, render them docile, or, as it is called in magic, bind them.

Let us explain this marvel in a few words. All the created spirits communicate between themselves by signs, and all adhere to a certain number of truths as expressed by certain determined forms.

The perfection of the forms increases with a detachment of the spirits, and those which are not weighed down by the chains of matter recognize with their first intuition if a sign is the expression of a real power or of an imprudent will.

The intelligence of the sage thus gives validity to his pentacle, just as his science gives weight to his will, and the spirits understand this power immediately.

And so, with the pentagram we can force the spirits to appear in dreams, when we are awake or asleep, *by bringing their reflection before our diaphane, a reflection which exists in the astral light, if their reflection ever existed, or a reflection which is analogous to their spiritual Verb, if they never existed on earth.* This explains all visions and more important demonstrates why the dead always appear to seers either the way they had been on earth or the way they still are in the tomb, never as they are in an existence which escapes the perceptions of our actual organism.

More than others, pregnant women are influenced by the astral light, which participates in the formation of their child and which incessantly presents them with reminiscences of the forms of which they are full. It is in this way that through vague similarities very virtuous women deceive malicious observers. They imprint, often when they consummate their marriage, an image that affected them in dream, and it is thus that the same physiognomies are perpetuated century after century.

The use of the Cabalistic pentagram can thus determine the image of the child to be born, and an initiated woman could give her son the traits of Nero or Achilles, or those of Louis XIV or of Napoleon. We will indicate how this is done in the Ritual.

The pentagram is what we call, in the Cabala, the sign of the microcosm, the sign whose strength Goëthe glorifies in a fine monologue by Faust:

Ah! how all my senses trembled at the sight! I feel the youth and holy joy of life overflowing in my nerves and in my veins. Was he a God, the being who traced that sign which calmed my giddy soul, filled my poor heart with joy, and, in a mysterious rush, revealed the forces of nature around me? Am I a God? All has become so clear to me; I see in these simple lines the energy of nature revealing itself in my soul. Now for the first time I recognize the truth in the words of the sage: The world of the spirits is not closed! Your meaning is obtuse, your heart is dead. Rise! Bathe, O adept of science, with your breast, still enveloped in a terrestrial veil, bathe in the splendors of the breaking day! (*Faust, Part One*, scene 1)

It was on the 24th of July of the year 1854 that the author of this book, Eliphas Lévi, conducted an experiment in evocation by pentagram in London, after having prepared himself using all the ceremonies indicated in the Ritual.[124] The success of that experiment, whose rationale and details we shall provide in chapter 13 of the Doctrine and the Ceremonies in chapter 13 of the Ritual, has established a new fact of pathology that true men of science will admit without hes-

---

124   See chapter 13 of "The Ritual." (Lévi's note.)

itation. The experiment, which has been repeated three times, gave truly extraordinary results; positive results without any hallucinatory influence. We invite unbelievers to make a conscientious and reasoned attempt before shrugging their shoulders and smiling.

The figure of the pentagram, enhanced by occult science, and which served the author in this trial, is the one found at the start of this chapter, and which we cannot find as complete in either the Keys of Solomon[125] or the magical calendars of Tycho Brahe and Duchenteau.[126]

We need but observe that the usage of the pentagram is very dangerous for those who do not have a complete and perfect knowledge. The direction of the points of the star are not arbitrary and can change the character of the entire intervention, as we will explain in Ritual.

Paracelsus, that innovator in magic who surpassed all the other initiates through the success of his achievements that only he was able to do, affirms that all the magical figures and all the Cabalistic signs of pentagrams which the spirits obey can be summarized by two of them, which are the synthesis of all the others: the sign of the macrocosm, or the seal of Solomon, which we have already shown, and which we reproduce here,

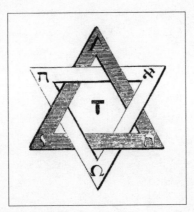

---

125   The two most influential medieval handbooks of magic, the *Key of Solomon* and the *Lemegeton*, or *Lesser Key of Solomon*, which contain many magical emblems.

126   The *Magical Calendar*, attributed to the great Danish astrologer and astronomer Tycho Brahe (1546–1601), published in 1620, and reprinted with additions by Duchenteau in 1755. It is not a calendar in the modern sense of the word but a very extensive table of Renaissance occult symbolism.

and that of the microcosm, even more powerful than the first, that is to say the pentagram, of which Paracelsus gives, in his occult philosophy, a meticulous description.

If one asks how a sign could have so much power over the spirits, we would then ask in return why the Christian world prostrated itself before the sign of the cross. A sign is nothing on its own and only has power through the doctrine by which it is summarized and the Verb. Yet a sign which summarizes and expresses all the occult powers of nature, a sign which has always communicated to the elementary spirits and others a power superior to their nature, naturally makes them respect and fear it and forces them to obey, through the empire of science and will over ignorance and weakness.

It is also through the pentagram that we measure the exact proportions of the great and only athanor necessary for the confection of the philosopher's stone and for the completion of the Great Work. The most perfect alembic which can produce the quintessence is based on this figure, and the quintessence itself is symbolized by the sign of the pentagram.

6] F.

MAGICAL EQUILIBRIUM

The Lovers

TIPHARETH.

UNCUS.[127]

The supreme intelligence is necessarily reasonable. God, in philosophy, can only be a hypothesis, but it is a hypothesis decreed by common sense and human reason. To personify absolute reason is to determine the divine ideal.

Necessity, liberty, and reason, that is the great and supreme triangle of the Cabalists, they name reason Kether, necessity Hokhmah, and liberty Binah, in their first divine ternary.

Destiny, will, and power, such is the magical ternary which, in human terms, corresponds to the divine triangle.

Destiny is the inevitable chain of effects and causes in a given order.

Will is the directive faculty of the intelligent forces which reconciles the liberty of individuals with the necessity of things. *fatality = predetermined*

Power is the wise use of the will, which puts even destiny in service to the fulfillment of the sage's desires.

When Moses hit the rock, he did not create the source of water, he revealed

---

127   Tiphareth, "beauty," is the sixth sephira of the Cabalistic Tree of Life; *uncus* is
      Latin for "hook."

it to the people, because an occult science had revealed it to him through the means of a divining rod.

It is thus with all the miracles of magic: a law exists, the vulgar are unaware of it, the initiate makes use of it.

The occult laws are often diametrically opposed to common conceptions. Thus, for example, the vulgar believe in the sympathy between similar objects and the war between opposites; it is the obverse law which is the true one.[128]

Formerly we said nature abhors the void; we should have said nature is in love with the void, if the void, in physics, was not the most absurd of fictions.

The vulgar habitually mistakes shadows for the reality in all things. He turns his back to the light and gazes into the obscurity which he himself projects.

The forces of nature are at the disposal of he who knows how to resist them. Have you mastered yourself to the point that you never become intoxicated? Then you dispose of the terrible and fatal power of intoxication. If you wish to intoxicate others, give them the desire to drink, but do not drink yourself.

Such a person disposes of the love of others and is master of his own. If you wish to possess, do not give of yourself.

The world is magnetized by the Sun's light, and we are magnetized by the astral light of the world. What operates in the body of the planet is repeated in us. There are in us three analogical and hierarchical worlds, as in the whole of nature.

Man is the microcosm, or the little world, and, following the doctrine of analogies, all that is in the big world is repeated in the little. There are thus in us three centers of attraction and fluidic projection: the brain, the heart or the epigastrium,[129] and the genitals. Each of these organs is unique and dual, that is to say that we find the idea of the ternary in them. Each of these organs attracts from one side and repulses from the other. It is through the means of these devices that we communicate with the universal fluid, transmitted in us through the nervous system. It is also these three centers which are the seat of a triple magnetic operation, as we shall explain elsewhere.

---

128   The obvious example is magnetism: similar poles repel each other, while opposite poles attract. The same law applies to a very broad range of phenomenon.

129   Also known as the solar plexus, an important nerve center below the level of the heart.

When a mage has achieved lucidity, either through the intermediary of a pythoness or through his own efforts, he communicates and directs at will the magnetic vibrations in the entire mass of the astral light, whose currents he divines with the aid of a magical wand, which is a perfected divinatory wand. By means of these vibrations, he influences the nervous system of people subject to his action, precipitates or suspends currents of life, calms or torments, heals or renders sick, kills or resuscitates. . . . But here we shall stop before the smiles of the incredulous. Let us leave to them the easy triumph of denying what they do not know.

We shall demonstrate later that death is always preceded by a lethargic sleep and only operates by degrees; that resurrection in certain cases is possible, that the lethargy is a real death, but uncompleted, and that many deaths are only completed after burial. But this is not the subject matter of this chapter. We were saying, then, that a lucid will can act upon the mass of astral light, and, with the participation of other wills which it absorbs and carries away, can incite large and irresistible currents. Let us also say that the astral light condenses or rarefies, depending on whether currents accumulate more or less in certain centers. When it lacks sufficient energy to fuel life, the sicknesses of sudden decomposition follow. Gastroenteritis, for example, has almost no other cause, and the bacterial columns observed or supposed by scholars could be the effect rather than the cause. Thus one must treat gastroenteritis by insufflation,[130] if, with such a treatment, the operator does not set out to perform an exchange with the patient which proves to be too great for the operator.

All intelligent efforts of the will are a projection of human fluid or light, and here it is important to distinguish human light from astral light and animal magnetism from universal magnetism.

In using the word fluid, we employ a common expression, and we are trying to be understood by that means; but we are far from accepting that latent light is a fluid. Everything leads us, on the contrary, to prefer describing this exceptional phenomenon as a system of vibrations. Whatever the case, this light, being the

---

130 Insufflation is the magical art of communicating a force to a person or thing by breathing on it.

instrument of life, is naturally fixed in all the living centers; it attaches itself to the cores of the planets as it also does in the heart of man (and by heart we mean, in magic, the great sympathetic[131]), but it identifies with the actual life of the being it animates, and it is through this property of sympathetic assimilation that it is divided without confusion. Thus it is terrestrial in its relation to the earth and exclusively human with regard to its relation to man.

It is for that reason that electricity, heat, light, and magnetism produced by ordinary physical means not only do not produce but tend, on the contrary, to neutralize the effects of animal magnetism. The astral light, subordinate to a blind mechanism and proceeding from given self-regulating centers, is a dead light and operates mathematically according to the impulses given to it or according to its predestined laws; the human light, on the contrary, is only fatalistic among the ignorant who attempt things at random; for the sighted, it is subordinate to intelligence, subject to imagination, and dependent on will. This light, which is incessantly projected by our will, forms what Swedenborg calls personal atmospheres. The body absorbs that which surrounds it and endlessly radiates by projecting miasmas and invisible molecules; it is the same with the spirit, so that this phenomenon, called by several mystics respiration, has in reality the influence that we attribute to it, either physical or moral. It is truly contagious to breathe the same air as the sick and to find oneself in the same circle of attraction and expansion as the wicked.

When the magnetic atmosphere of two people is so balanced that the attractive qualities of one absorbs the expansion of the other, an attraction is produced that we call sympathy; and thus imagination, in evoking all the rays or analogic reflections that it is experiencing, creates a poem of desires which carries off the will, and if the persons are of a different sex, there is produced in them, or more often in the weakest of the two, a total intoxication due to the astral light, which we call passion, in the precise sense of that word,[132] or love.

Love is one of the great instruments of magical power; but it is formally for-

---

131   That is, the sympathetic nervous system, of which the solar plexus is the most important center.

132   A neat etymological point, as the word "passion" has the same relation to "passive" that "action" has to "active."

bidden to the mage, at least in the form of intoxication or passion. It would be a great tragedy if Samson were to allow himself to be put to sleep by Delilah![133] The Hercules of science who exchanges his royal scepter for Omphale's spindle will soon feel Deianira's vengeance and all that will remain for him is the pyre on Mount Oeta as escape from the devouring restraints of Nessus's tunic.[134] Sexual love is always an illusion, since it is the result of an imaginary mirage. The astral light is the universal seducer symbolized by the serpent of Genesis. This subtle agent, always active, always luxuriant with life blood, always embellished with seductive dreams and sweet images; this blind force is subordinate to every will, either for good or for evil; this continually reemerging *circulus* of an uncontrolled life, which causes giddiness in the imprudent; this corporeal spirit, this fiery body, this impalpable and always present ether; this immense seduction of nature, how can it be completely defined and how can its action be qualified? Indifferent, in a way, on its own, it lends itself just as easily to good as to evil; it carries the light and propagates darkness; we can also call it Lucifer or Lucifuge:[135] it is a serpent, but it is also an aureole; it is a fire, but one that can as easily belong to the torments of hell as to the offerings of incense promised in heaven. To take possession of it, one must, like the predestined woman, place one's feet on its head.

That which corresponds to the Cabalistic woman, in the elementary world, is water, and that which corresponds to the serpent is fire. To tame the serpent, which means to dominate the circle of astral light, one must manage to get outside the currents, that is to say one must isolate oneself. That is why Apollonius of Tyana covered himself entirely in a coat of fine wool upon which he placed his feet, and which he brought up to his head; then he rounded his spinal column into a half circle, closed his eyes after having completed several rites which must have consisted of magnetic passes of the hand and sacramental words

---

133   Judges 16:18.

134   In Greek myth, Hercules at one point in his adventures dressed as a woman and worked as a spinster for Queen Omphale. Deianira was Hercules's wife, who gave him a garment soaked in Nessus's poisonous blood in the mistaken belief that this would ensure his fidelity; he burned himself alive on a pyre on Mount Oeta to escape its torments.

135   Lucifer means "light bringer," Lucifuge means "flees the light." Both are traditional names of the devil.

whose goal was to fixate the imagination and determine the action of the will. The coat of wool is often used in magic; it is the usual vehicle for witches going to a Sabbath, which proves that the witches were not really going to the Sabbath, but that the Sabbath had found the witches isolated in their coats and then brought to their *translucid* the images related to their magical preoccupations, mixed with the reflections of all the acts of the same type that had been completed before them in the world.

This torrent of universal life is also symbolized in religious doctrines by the expiatory fires of hell. It is the instrument of initiation, it is the monster to be tamed, it is the enemy to be vanquished; it is that which sends to our evocations and conjurations of the goetia so many larvae and ghosts; it is within it that are conserved all the forms whose fantastical and fortuitous assemblage people our nightmares with such abominable monsters. To allow oneself to be carried away, rudderless, by this whirling river is to fall into an abyss of madness even more terrifying than death; to chase the shadows of this chaos and make it give us the perfect forms of our thoughts is to be a man of genius, is to create, is to have triumphed over hell!

The astral light directs the animal instincts and battles against man's intelligence, which it tends to pervert through the lavishness of its reflections and the lies of its images, a fatal and necessary action which controls and renders even more deadly the elemental spirits and souls in pain, whose disturbed wills search for sympathies in our weaknesses and tempt us less in order to drag us to perdition than to become our friends.

This book of conscious beings, which, according to Christian dogma, must become manifest on the last day, is nothing other than the astral light in which the impressions of all the Verbs are conserved, that is to say of all the actions and of all the forms. Our acts modify our *magnetic respiration* in such a way that a seer can say, when approaching a person for the first time, if that person is innocent or guilty, and what are their virtues or their crimes. This faculty, which is a part of divination, was called the discernment of spirits by the Christian mystics of the primitive Church.

People who renounce the empire of reason and who love losing their will in the pursuit of reflections of the astral light are subject to alternative bouts of furor and sadness which remind us of all the wonders of demonic possession; it is true that through the use of these reflections, impure spirits can act upon such souls, make them docile instruments, and even accustom them to torturing their own organism, in which they come to reside through *obsession* or through *embryonization*. These Cabalistic words are explained in the Hebrew book of *The Revolution of Souls*,[136] whose succinct analysis can be found in our thirteenth chapter.

It is thus extremely dangerous to play at the mysteries of magic; most importantly it is totally reckless to practice rites out of simple curiosity, to try things out as though to tempt the superior powers. The curious who, without being adepts, get involved in evocations or occult magnetism resemble children who would play with fire beside a barrel of gunpowder: sooner or later they will be the victims of a terrible explosion.

To isolate oneself from the astral light, it does not suffice to wrap oneself in woolen material; one must also, and most importantly, have achieved an absolute tranquility of the mind and heart; have left the domain of the passions; and have made sure of one's ability to keep an inflexible will while acting sincerely. One must also repeat these acts of will often, because as we will see in the introduction to the Ritual, the will is only secured through acts, just like religions have no power or duration over time except through their ceremonies and their rites.

There are intoxicating substances which, by exciting the nervous system, augment the power of representations, and in consequence that of astral seduction; by the same means, but going in the opposite direction, we can terrify and trouble the spirit. These substances, having magnetic qualities of their own which are further magnetized by practitioners, are what we call potions or enchanted beverages. But we will not discuss this dangerous application of magic, which Cornelius Agrippa himself calls poisonous magic. There no longer exist, it is true, burning stakes for sorcerers, but there are still, and now more than ever, punishments meted out against wrongdoers. Let us limit ourselves then to observing, on this occasion, the reality of this power.

To command the astral light, one must also understand dual vibration and

---

136 A medieval Jewish treatise on the Cabala that sets forth the concept of reincarnation.

know the balance of forces that is called magical equilibrium, and is expressed, in the Cabala, by the senary.

This equilibrium, considered in its first cause, is the will of God; in man, it is liberty; in matter, it is mathematical equilibrium.

Equilibrium produces stability over time.

Liberty gives birth to the immortality of man, and the will of God puts the laws of eternal reason to work. Equilibrium in thought is wisdom, equilibrium of forces is power. Equilibrium is strict. If one observes the law, equilibrium is there; if we violate the law, even ever so lightly, it no longer is.

It is for this reason that nothing is useless or lost. All speech and all movement are either for or against equilibrium, for or against truth: because equilibrium represents truth, which is composed of the "for" and "against" reconciled, or at least balanced against each other.

We explain in the introduction to Ritual how magical equilibrium must be produced, and why it is necessary to the success of all operations.

Omnipotence is the most absolute liberty. Yet absolute liberty could not exist without perfect equilibrium. Magical equilibrium is thus one of the primary conditions for the success of operations in science, and we must search for the same equilibrium in occult chemistry by learning to combine opposites without having one neutralize the other.

It is through magical equilibrium that we can explain the great and ancient mystery of existence and the relative necessity of evil.

That relative necessity provides, in black magic, the measure of the power of demons or impure spirits, whose fury and even apparent force is increased by virtuous acts that are committed on earth.

In the eras when the saints and angels openly produced miracles, sorcerers and devils also did marvels and wonders.

It is rivalry which often makes for success: we always lean on that which resists.

7 I G.

THE FLAMING SWORD

The Chariot

NETZACH.

GLADIUS.[137]

The septenary is the sacred number in all theogonies and in all symbols, because it is composed of the ternary and the quaternary.

The number seven represents the power of magic in all its force; it is the spirit assisted by all the elemental powers; it is the soul served by nature, it is the *sanctum regnum* which is spoken of in the Keys of Solomon, and it is represented in the Tarot by the crowned warrior with a triangle on his armor, and standing on a cube, to which are harnessed two sphinxes, one white, the other black, who pull in contrary directions while turning their heads to look at each other.

This warrior is armed with a flaming sword, and in his other hand he holds a scepter upon which are mounted a triangle and a ball.

The cube is the philosopher's stone, the sphinxes are the two forces of the great agent, corresponding to Jachin and Boaz which are the two columns of the temple; the armor is the science of divine things which renders the sage invulnerable to human attacks; the burning sword is the symbol of victory over vice,

---

137   Netzach, "victory," is the seventh sephira of the Cabalistic Tree of Life; *gladius* is Latin for "sword."

of which there are seven, like the virtues; the ideas of these virtues and these vices were drawn by the ancients in the form of the symbols of the seven planets known at that time.

Thus faith, that aspiration to the infinite, that noble confidence in oneself, supported by the belief in all the virtues, faith, which in people of feeble nature can degenerate into pride, was represented by the Sun; hope, the enemy of avarice, is represented by the Moon; charity, opposed to lust, is represented by Venus, the brilliant star of the morning and dusk; strength, superior to wrath, is represented by Mars; prudence, opposed to sloth, is represented by Mercury; temperance, opposed to gluttony, is represented by Saturn, to whom we give a stone to eat in the place of his children; and finally, justice, opposed to envy, is represented by Jupiter, vanquisher of the Titans. Those are the symbols which astrology borrows from the Hellenic cult. In the Cabala of the Hebrews, the Sun represents the angel of light; the Moon, the angel of aspirations and dreams; Mars, the exterminating angel; Venus, the angel of loves; Mercury, the civilizing angel; Jupiter, the angel of power; Saturn, the angel of the solitudes. We also name them Michael, Gabriel, Samaël, Anaël, Raphaël, Zachariel and Orifiel.

These powers which dominate souls divide out human life into periods that astrologers measure by the revolution of the corresponding planets. But one must not confound Cabalistic astrology with judicial astrology.[138] We shall explain this distinction. Childhood is dedicated to the Sun, adolescence to the Moon, youth to Mars and Venus, virility to Mercury, maturity to Jupiter, and old age to Saturn. All of humanity lives under the laws of development which are analogous to those of the individual. It is on that basis that Trithemius established his prophetic key of the seven spirits,[139] which we shall discuss later, and it is the means through which we can, by following the analogical dimensions of successive events, predict with certainty great future events and establish in advance, from period to period, the destinies of the peoples of the world.

---

138 Judicial astrology is the branch of astrological practice that predicts future events from a horoscope.

139 The *De septem secundeis* (*On the Seven Secondary Causes*), which propounds a cyclic theory of history based on the rulerships of seven planetary angels over periods of time.

Saint John, the custodian of the Christ's secret doctrine, recorded this doctrine in the Cabalistic Book of Revelation, which he represented as closed by seven seals. We find in it the seven spirits of ancient mythology, with the cups and the swords of the Tarot. The hidden doctrine underneath these emblems is pure Cabala, already lost by the Pharisees in the time of the arrival of the Savior; the scenes which succeed each other in this marvelous prophetic saga are so many pentacles of which the ternary and the quaternary, the septenary and the duodenary are the keys. The hieroglyphic figures are analogous to those of the book of Hermes or of Enoch's Genesis, to use the uncertain title which only expresses the personal opinion of the scholar Guillaume Postel.

The cherub or symbolic bull which Moses placed at the door to the Edenic world, and which holds in its hand the flaming sword, is the sphinx with the body of a bull and the head of a human; it is the ancient Assyrian sphinx, against which Mithras's struggle and triumph was the hieroglyphic analysis. This armed sphinx represents the law of mystery which guards the door to initiations in order to ward off the profane. Voltaire, who knew nothing of all this, laughed greatly when he saw an ox holding a sword. What would he have said if he had visited the ruins of Memphis and Thebes, where he would have had as an answer to his little sarcasms, so appreciated in France, that echo of centuries past which sleeps in the sepulchers of Psammetichus and Ramses?[140]

Moses's cherub also represents the great magical arcanum, of which the septenary expresses all the elements, without, however, providing the last word. This *verbum inenarrabile*[141] of the sages of the school of Alexandria, this word which the Hebrew Cabalists write as יהוה and translate with אראריתא,[142] thus expressing the triplicity of the secondary principle, the dualism of the means and the unity as much of the first principle as of the end, and also the alliance of the ternary with the quaternary in a word composed of four letters, which form

---

140   Three pharaohs of ancient Egypt were named Psammetichus, and six more were named Ramses.

141   Latin for "unspeakable word."

142   יהוה is the tetragrammaton YHVH; אראריתא is ARARITA, the initials of a Hebrew sentence meaning "One is His beginning; one is His individuality; His permutations are One."

seven by the means of a triple and a double repetition; this word is pronounced Ararita.

The virtue of the septenary is absolute in magic, because this number is the determining factor in all things; also, all religions have consecrated it in their rites. The seventh year for the Jews was a jubilee;[143] the seventh day is consecrated to rest and prayer; there are seven sacraments, etc.

The seven colors of the prism, the seven notes of music, also correspond to the seven ancient planets, that is to say to the seven chords of the human lyre. The spiritual heaven has never changed, and astrology has remained more invariable than astronomy. The seven planets, in fact, are none other than hieroglyphic symbols of the keyboard of our emotions. To make talismans of the Sun, the Moon or of Saturn, is to magnetically attach one's will to signs which correspond to the principal powers of the soul; to consecrate something to Venus or to Mercury, is to magnetize that thing in a direct intention, for either pleasure, science, or profit. The metals, the animals, the analogous perfumes are in this matter our assistants. The seven magical animals are, among the birds, corresponding to the divine world, the swan, the owl, the vulture, the dove, the stork, the eagle and the hoopoe; among fish, corresponding to the spiritual or scientific world, are the seal, the catfish,[144] the pike, the grayling, the mullet, the dolphin, and the squid or cuttlefish; among the quadrupeds, corresponding to the natural world; are the lion, the cat, the wolf, the goat, the monkey, the stag, and the mole. Blood, fat, liver, and bile from animals are used for enchantments; brains are combined with the perfumes of the planets,[145] and it is accepted by the practices of the ancients that they possess magnetic virtues corresponding to the seven planetary influences.

---

143   Leviticus 25:3–22.

144   "Oelurus" in the original; Lévi has copied this from Cornelius Agrippa, in which it appears as *aelurus*, the Latin word for "cat."

145   Renaissance magic made extensive use of animal substances in this way, though most modern Western magical traditions have found less problematic ways to invoke the septenary powers.

TABLE OF PLANETARY SYMBOLS

PLANET	BIRD	FISH	ANIMAL	STONE	METAL	EMBLEM
Sun	Swan	Seal	Lion	Carbuncle	Gold	Lion-headed serpent
Moon	Owl	Catfish	Cat	Crystal	Silver	Sphere with two crescents
Mars	Vulture	Pike	Wolf	Diamond	Iron	Dragon biting sword
Venus	Dove	Grayling	Goat	Emerald	Copper	Lingam
Mercury	Stork	Mullet	Monkey	Agate	Fixed Mercury	Caduceus and cynocephalus
Jupiter	Eagle	Dolphin	Stag	Sapphire	Tin	Eagle clutching pentagram
Saturn	Hoopoe	Squid	Mole	Onyx	Lead	Old man or serpent & stone

The talismans of the seven spirits are made either from precious stones, such as carbuncle, crystal, diamond, emerald, agate, sapphire, and onyx; or from metals, such as gold, silver, iron, copper, fixed mercury, tin, and lead. The Cabalistic signs of the seven spirits are: for the Sun, a serpent with the head of a lion; for the Moon, a globe cut across with two crescents; for Mars, a dragon biting the guard of a sword; for Venus, a lingam;[146] for Mercury, the Hermetic caduceus and the cynocephalus;[147] for Jupiter, the flaming pentagram held in the talons or the beak of an eagle; for Saturn, a limping old man or a serpent wrapped around a solar stone. We find all these signs engraved in the stones of the ancients, and particularly on talismans from gnostic eras, known by the name Abraxas.[148] In Paracelsus's collection of talismans, Jupiter is represented by a priest in ecclesiastical vestments, and in the Tarot it is figured by a great hierophant crowned with a tiara made of three diadems who is holding a cross with three tiers, forming the magical triangle and representing both the scepter and the key to the three worlds.

By uniting all that we have said about the unity the ternary and the quaternary, we have all that there remains to be said about the septenary, that great and complete magical unity, composed of four and of three.[149]

---

146 That is, a penis.

147 The baboon, so called because of its doglike head, which was sacred to the Egyptian god Thoth.

148 "Abraxas gems," so called because the gnostic word of power "Abraxas" often appears on them, survive in large numbers from late Roman times.

149 See, for the planets and the colors of the septenary used for magnetic purposes, the learned work of M. Ragon regarding occult masonry. (Lévi's note.)

8 ח H.

REALIZATION

Adjustment

HOD.

VIVENS.[150]

Causes are revealed by effects, and effects are proportional to the causes. The divine Verb, the unique word, the tetragrammaton, affirmed itself with the quaternary creation. Human fecundity demonstrates the existence of divine fecundity; the yod of the divine name is the eternal virility of the first principle. Man understood that he was made in the image of God when he understood God by aggrandizing, unto infinity, the idea he had of himself.

In understanding God as an infinite man, man says of himself; I am the finite God.

Magic differs from mysticism in that it does not make a priori judgments until after having established the a posteriori basis for those judgments, that is to say after having understood the cause through the effects contained in the very energy of the cause, by means of the universal law of analogy; also in the occult sciences everything is real, and theories are only established on the basis of experience. Realities make up the proportions of the ideal, and the mage only

---

150 Hod, "splendor," is the eighth sephira of the Cabalistic Tree of Life; *vivens* is Latin for "living."

admits something as certain into the domain of ideas that has been demonstrated by realization. In other terms, what is true in the cause becomes realized in the effect. What does not become realized is not. The realization of the word, is the Verb properly speaking. A thought is realized in becoming speech; it is realized by the signs, by the sounds, and by the depictions of the signs: that is the first degree of realization. The thought is then imprinted upon the astral light by means of the signs of writing or of speech; it influences other minds by being reflected in them; it refracts when crossing the diaphane of other men, and takes on new forms and proportions, which are then translated into acts which modify society and the world: that is the last degree of realization. Men born into a world modified by an idea carry within them its imprint, and this is also how the Verb is made flesh. The imprint of Adam's disobedience, conserved within the astral light, could not be erased except by the stronger imprint of the obedience of the Savior, and it is thus that we can explain original sin and redemption in a natural and magical sense.

The astral light or the world soul was the instrument of Adam's omnipotence, which then became the instrument of his torment, after having been corrupted and confused by his sin, which was to confuse an impure reflection with the primitive images which composed, for his still virgin imagination, the book of universal science.

The astral light, depicted in the ancient symbols by a serpent biting its tail, represented in turns vice and prudence, time and eternity, the tempter and the Redemptor. This light, being the vehicle of life, can serve as much as the auxiliary to good as to evil, and can be taken for the fiery form of Satan as much as for the body of the Holy Spirit. It is the universal weapon in the battle between the angels, and it feeds the flames of hell as much as the lightning of St. Michael. We can compare it to a horse whose nature is analogous to that of the chameleon and who will always reflect the armor of its rider.

The astral light is the realization or the form of the intellectual light, just as the latter is the realization or the form of the divine light.

The great initiator of Christianity, understanding that the astral light was overburdened with the impure reflections of Roman depravity, wished to separate his disciples from the ambient sphere of reflections and have them pay attention only to the interior light, so that through a common faith they could communicate together via new magnetic cords which he called grace, and thus vanquish the overwhelmed currents of universal magnetism, to which he gave the names of devil and Satan, to express their putrefied state. To oppose one current against another current is to renew the power of fluidic life. For that matter, the prophets simply figured out, through the accuracy of their calculations, the propitious time for moral reactions.

The law of realization produces what we call magnetic respiration, with which objects and places are impregnated, and which gives them an influence in conformity with our dominant desires, especially those objects and places which are confirmed and realized by acts. In fact, the universal agent, or the latent astral light, always searches for equilibrium; it fills the void and sucks in the full, which renders vice contagious like certain physical maladies and powerfully serves proselytism and virtue. It is for this reason that the cohabitation of antipathetic beings is an ordeal; it is for this reason that the relics, either of the saints or of the great evildoers, can produce sudden supernatural conversions or perversions; it is for this reason that sexual love can often be produced by a breath or by touch, and not only by the touch of the person themselves but through objects that they have touched or magnetized without knowing it.

The soul inhales and exhales exactly like the body. It inhales what it believes to be happiness, and exhales the ideas which result from its intimate sensations. Sickly souls have bad breath and vitiate their moral atmosphere, that is to say they mix impure reflections with the astral light which penetrates them, thus creating harmful currents. We are often surprised when we are assailed, in public, by bad thoughts which we would not have thought possible of ourselves, and we do not realize that they are due to some unhealthy nearby person. This is a secret of great importance, because it leads to the manifestation of the conscience, one of the most incontestable and terrible powers of the art of magic.

Magnetic respiration produces a radiation around the soul of which it is the center, and it surrounds itself with the reflection of its works, which makes a heaven or a hell for itself. There are no solitary acts and there can be no hidden acts; all that we truly want, that is to say all of which we confirm by our acts, remains written in the astral light, where our reflections are kept; these reflections continually influence our thoughts through the mediation of the diaphane, and it is thus that we become and we remain the child of our own works.

The astral light, transformed into human light at the moment of conception, is the first mantle of the soul, and, by combining with the most subtle fluids, it forms the ethereal body, or the astral ghost, of which Paracelsus speaks of in his philosophy of intuition (*Philosophia sagax*). This astral body, when departing the body at death, attracts to itself, and keeps for a long time, through the sympathy between homogeneous matter, the reflections of its passed life; if a powerfully sympathetic will attracts it into a particular current, the astral body manifests itself naturally, because there is nothing more natural than miracles. It is thus that apparitions are produced. But we will develop this more completely in the chapter dedicated to Necromancy.

This fluidic body, which like the mass of astral light is subjected to two contrary movements, the attractive to the left and the repulsive to the right, or, reciprocally, in the two sexes, produces in us the struggles between different attractions and contributes to the anxiety of our conscience: often it is influenced by other spirits, and thus are produced either temptations or subtle and unexpected grace. This is also the explanation for the traditional dogma of the two angels who help us and test us. The two forces of the astral light can be depicted by a balance where our good intentions for the triumph of justice and the emancipation of our liberty are weighed.

The astral body is not always of the same sex as the terrestrial body, which is to say that the proportions of the two forces, varying from right to left, often seem to contradict the visible organism; this is what produces the apparent errors in human passion and can explain, without in any way justifying them morally, the amorous singularities of Anacreon or of Sappho.[151]

A skilled magnetizer must be able to appreciate all these nuances, and we provide in our Ritual the means of recognizing them.

There are two types of realizations, the true and the fantastic. The first is the exclusive secret of magicians; the other belongs to enchanters and sorcerers.

---

151   Ancient Greek poets whose love poetry celebrated gay and lesbian relationships, respectively.

Myths are fantastic realizations of religious dogma, superstitions are the spells of false piety, but myths and superstitions act more effectively upon the human will than a purely speculative philosophy which excludes all practice. It is for this reason that Saint Paul opposes the conquests of the folly of the Cross to the inertia of human wisdom. Religion *realizes* philosophy by *adapting it* to the weaknesses of the vulgar: according to the Cabalists this is the secret reason and occult explanation for the dogmas of incarnation and of redemption.

Thoughts which are not translated into speech are thoughts which are lost to humanity; words which are not confirmed by acts are idle words, and there is not far to go from idle speech to lies.

It is thought formulated into words and confirmed by acts which constitutes the good deed or the crime. Thus either by vice or by virtue, there is no speech for which we are not responsible; moreover, there are no indifferent acts. Maledictions and benedictions always have an effect, and all action, whatever it may be, whether it is inspired by love or by hate, produces effects analogous to its motive, its reach, and its direction. The emperor whose images had been mutilated, and who, as he brought his hand to his face, said: "I have not been hurt," made a false appraisal and by it diminished the merit of his clemency. What honorable man can look calmly upon the insults made to his portrait? And what if such insults, even done without our knowledge, fell upon us through their fatal influence; what if the art of enchantments was real, as the adept is not permitted to doubt, how much more would we find the words of the emperor imprudent and reckless!

There are people that one can never offend with impunity, and if one's offense to them is fatal, then one begins to die from that point on. There are those one cannot encounter without it having an effect and whose gaze can change the direction of one's life. The basilisk who kills with its gaze is not a fable; it is a magical allegory. In general, it is bad for your health to have enemies, and one cannot brave anyone's disapproval with impunity. Before opposing a force or a current, one must assure oneself that one has the strength or that one is supported by the contrary current; otherwise one will be crushed or struck down, and many sudden deaths have no other cause. The terrible deaths of Nadab and

Abihu, of Uzziah, of Ananias and Sapphira,[152] were caused by the electrical currents of the beliefs of those they had offended; the torments of the Ursuline nuns of Loudun,[153] of the nuns of Louviers,[154] and of the Jansenist convulsionaries,[155] were due to the same principle and are explained by the same natural occult laws. If Urbain Grandier[156] had not been executed, one of two things would have occurred, either the possessed nuns would have died in terrible convulsions or a phenomenon of diabolical frenzy would have overcome them, and in multiplying so many wills by so much power, Grandier, despite his science and reason, would himself have suffered from hallucinations to the point of accusing himself like the unfortunate Gaufridi[157] had done before him, or he would have died suddenly under all the terrible circumstances of a poisoning or divine vengeance.

In the eighteenth century, the unfortunate poet Gilbert fell victim to his own audacity in braving the current of popular opinion and even the philosophical fanaticism of his era.[158] Guilty of philosophical treason, he died raving mad, assailed by the most incredible terrors, as if God himself had punished him for having inappropriately defended His cause. In actual fact, he died a victim of a law of nature that he could not have known: he had opposed himself against an electrical current and was struck down.

---

152   Biblical characters struck down by divine wrath, as described in Leviticus 10:1–2, II Chronicles 26:16–23, and Acts 5:1–11.

153   The site of a famous witchcraft trial in 1634. Several nuns of the Ursuline convent at Loudun, who were thought to be possessed by the devil, accused their father confessor of witchcraft.

154   An almost identical case that occurred in Louviers in 1647.

155   The Jansenists were a seventeenth- and eighteenth-century offshoot of Catholicism in France, some of whom were famous for going into seemingly miraculous convulsions at the tomb of a Jansenist priest in Paris.

156   The father confessor of the nuns of Loudon. As noted previously, he was burned at the stake in 1634.

157   Father Louis Gaufridi, who was burned at the stake in 1611 after similar accusations by a possessed nun.

158   French satirist Nicolas Gilbert (1750–80), whose writings mocked the popular atheism of his time.

If Marat had not been assassinated by Charlotte Corday,[159] he would certainly have been killed by a reaction from public opinion. That which caused his leprosy was the hatred of decent, everyday people, and he had to fall victim to it.

The public disapproval which arose due to the Saint Bartholomew's Day massacre was the sole cause of the horrible sickness and subsequent death of Charles IX,[160] and Henry IV,[161] if he had not been supported by his immense popularity, which he owed to the power of projection or the sympathetic strength of his astral life, Henry IV, we say, would not have survived long after his conversion, and would have died due to the scorn of the Protestants, combined with the distrust and resentment of the Catholics.

Unpopularity can be a proof of integrity and of courage, but it is never a proof of prudence or good politics; injuries done to public opinion are deadly for men of the State. We can remind ourselves again of the premature and violent ends of several famous men, whom it is not convenient to mention here.

Stigmatization due to public opinion can be of great injustice, but it will in any case always be the reason for lack of success, and often for sudden death.

On the other hand, the injustices caused to a single man can and should, if we do not notice them, cause the downfall of an entire people or society: it is what we call the cry of the blood, because at the heart of all injustice there is the germ of a homicide.

It is because of these terrible laws of solidarity that Christianity so highly recommends forgiveness of insults and reconciliation. He who dies without for-

---

159   French journalist and revolutionary Jean-Paul Marat (1744–93), who played a central role in launching the Terror in revolutionary France and was stabbed to death, while in his bathtub, by Charlotte Corday. He did not have leprosy but rather a skin disease that was not well differentiated from leprosy by the medical authorities of Lévi's time.

160   King of France (1550–74). On his orders, over a three-day period beginning on Saint Bartholomew's Day, August 24, 1572, Protestant nobles who had come to Paris to celebrate a royal wedding were slaughtered by royal troops with the assistance of Catholic mobs.

161   King of France (1553–1601). The leader of the Protestant party, he converted to Catholicism in order to become king.

giving throws himself into eternity armed with a dagger and devotes himself to the horrors of eternal murder.

The effectiveness of paternal or maternal benedictions or maledictions is a traditional and overwhelming belief among the people. In fact, the more that the ties which unite two people are close, the more that the hatred between them has terrible effects. Althea's brand which burns up the blood of Meleager is, in mythology, the symbol of this formidable power.[162] Parents should always take heed, because one does not kindle hell in one's own blood and one does not curse one's own children without being burnt and cursed oneself. It is never a crime to forgive, and it is always dangerous and evil to cast a curse.

---

162   In Greek mythology, when the hero Meleager was a child the fates decreed that he would live only until a certain piece of firewood, then in the household fire, was consumed. His mother, Althea, promptly pulled the piece out of the fire, quenched it, and set it aside for safekeeping. Years later, Meleager killed his uncle and brother in a fight, and Althea put the piece of wood back in the fire, killing Meleager.

9 ט I.

INITIATION

The Hermit

YESOD.

BONUM.[163]

The initiate is he who possesses the lamp of Trismegistus, the mantle of Apollonius, and the staff of the patriarchs.

Trismegistus's lamp is reason enlightened by science; Apollonius's mantle is full and whole self-possession, which isolates the sage from the instinctive currents; and the staff of the patriarchs is the assistance of the occult and perpetual forces of nature.

Trismegistus's lamp illuminates the present, the past, and the future; lays bare the conscience of man; and illuminates the most hidden secrets of women. The lamp shines with a triple flame; the mantle is folded three times; the staff is divided into three parts.

The number nine is that of the divine reflections: it expresses the divine idea in all its abstract power, but it also expresses the extravagance in belief and, in consequence, superstition and idolatry.

---

163 Yesod, "foundation," is the ninth sephira of the Cabalistic Tree of Life; *bonum* is Latin for "good."

That is why Hermes made it the number of initiation, because the initiate reigns over superstition and through superstition. Only he can walk in the darkness, supported as he is by his staff, enveloped in his mantle and illuminated by his lamp.

Reason was given to all men, but not all men know how to make use of it; it is a science which must be learned. Liberty is offered to all, but not everyone can be free; it is a right which must be won. Strength is for all, but not everyone knows how to rely on it; it is a power which must be seized.

We arrive at nothing if it requires no effort. The destiny of man is that he enriches himself with what he gains, and that, then, like God, he basks in the glory and pleasure of giving.

The magical science was once called the priestly and royal art, because initiation gave the sage dominion over souls and the aptitude to govern wills.

Divination is also a privilege of the initiate; since divination is simply the knowledge of the effects contained in the causes, and science applied to the facts of the universal doctrine of analogy.

Human acts are not only written in the astral light, they also leave their traces on the face, they modify one's bearing and walk, they change the tone of one's voice.

Every man thus carries with him the story of his life, which may be read by an initiate. The future is always the consequence of the past, and unexpected circumstances barely change the rationally expected results.

We can thus predict each man's destiny. We can judge an entire existence based on a single movement; a single bit of awkwardness presages a series of misfortunes. Caesar was assassinated because he blushed in embarrassment due to being bald; Napoleon died on St. Helena because he liked the poems of Ossian;[164]

---

164   Written by James Macpherson but credited to an ancient Scots bard named Ossian, these poems were extraordinarily popular in the early nineteenth century, though they are almost forgotten today. Napoleon was among the many famous fans of the poems.

Louis Philippe had to leave the throne as he did because he carried an umbrella.[165] These are paradoxes for the vulgar, who do not understand the occult relations of things, but they are reasons for the initiate, who understands all and is surprised by nothing.

The initiation protects a person from the false lights of mysticism; it gives human reason its relative value and its proportional infallibility, by linking it to supreme reason through the chain of analogies.

Thus the initiate has neither doubtful hopes nor absurd fears, because he has no unreasonable beliefs; he knows what he is capable of, and it costs him nothing to dare to do it. So for him to dare something is to be able to do it.

Here then is a new interpretation of the attributes of the initiate: his lamp represents knowledge, the mantle which envelops him represents discretion, and his staff is the emblem of his strength and audacity. He knows, he dares, and he keeps silent.

He knows the secrets of the future, he dares in the present, and he stays silent about the past.

He knows the weaknesses of the human heart, he dares to make use of them to complete his work, and he does not speak about his projects.

He knows the reason for all the symbolisms and all the cults, he dares to practice them or to abstain from doing so without hypocrisy and without impiety, and he does not speak about the unique doctrine of high initiation.

He knows of the existence and the nature of the great magical agent, he dares to perform the acts and pronounce the words which subject it to human will, and he does not speak of the mysteries of the great arcanum.

You may also notice that he is often sad, never beaten nor desperate; often poor, never degraded nor miserable; often persecuted, never deterred nor vanquished. He remembers the bereavement and the murder of Orpheus, the exile

---

165   Louis Philippe I, the last king of France, was driven from the throne by a revolution in 1848. These statements are far less absurd than they appear at first glance: what Lévi is saying, of course, is that Caesar was assassinated because his actions were too heavily influenced by his vanity, Napoleon fell from power because he mistook himself for the hero of an overblown romantic poem, and Louis Philippe was driven from the throne because he was unable to rekindle the mystique of monarchy in an age typified by the middle-class image of an umbrella tucked under the arm.

and solitary death of Moses, the martyrdom of the prophets, the tortures of Apollonius, the cross of the Savior; he knows in what abandonment Agrippa died, whose memory is still denigrated; he knows to what weariness the great Paracelsus succumbed, and all that which Raymond Lully must have suffered to at last arrive at a bloody death. He remembers Swedenborg pretending to be mad, or even actually losing his reason, so as to have his science pardoned; he remembers Saint-Martin, who hid all his life;[166] Cagliostro, who died abandoned in the dungeons of the Inquisition; Cazotte,[167] who climbed the scaffold. As the successor to so many victims, the initiate does not dare less, but he understands even more the necessity to keep quiet.

Let us imitate his example, let us learn through perseverance; when we know, let us dare and let us stay silent.

---

166 Louis-Claude de Saint-Martin published all his esoteric works under the pen name the Unknown Philosopher.

167 French author Jacques Cazotte (1719–92), a follower of the occult teachings of Louis-Claude de Saint-Martin, was guillotined during the Terror.

10 ׳ K.

THE CABALA

Fortune

MALKUTH.

PRINCIPIUM.

PHALLUS.[168]

All religions have preserved the memory of a primordial book written in pictures by the sages of the world's first centuries, and whose symbols, which were later on simplified and vulgarized, provided writing with its letters, the Verb with its characters, and occult philosophy with its mysterious signs and pentacles.

This book, attributed by the Hebrews to Enoch, the seventh master of the world, attributed to Hermes Trismegistus by the Egyptians, and attributed to Cadmus, the mysterious founder of the Holy City,[169] by the Greeks, was the symbolic summary of the original tradition, which has since been named Kabbalah or Cabala, from a Hebrew word which is the equivalent of tradition.[170]

---

168 Malkuth, "kingdom," is the tenth sephira of the Cabalistic Tree of Life; *principium* is Latin for "beginning"; and *phallus* should need no translation. In Cabalistic tradition, Malkuth is related to the genitals.

169 Thebes, Greece.

170 The Hebrew word קבלה, Cabala, literally means "tradition."

This tradition rests entirely on the unique doctrine of magic: the visible is for us the proportional measure of the invisible. The ancients observed that equilibrium is, in physics, a universal law, which results in the apparent opposition of two forces, and they then derived metaphysical equilibrium from physical equilibrium, and declared that in God, that is to say the first living and active cause, we should be able to recognize two properties that are necessary to one another: stability and movement, necessity and liberty, rational order and willful autonomy, justice and love, and in consequence also severity and mercy; and it is these two attributes which the Jewish Cabalists in a way personified with the names Geburah and Chesed.

Above Geburah and Chesed resides the supreme crown, the balancing power, the principle of the balanced world or kingdom, that we find designated by the name Malkuth in the occult and Cabalistic verses of the Lord's Prayer, of which we have already spoken.

But Geburah and Chesed, maintained in equilibrium from above by the crown and from below by the kingdom, are two principles that we can consider, either in the abstract or in their realization. As abstraction or idealization, they take on their superior names of Chokmah, wisdom, and Binah, intelligence. When realized, they are called stability and progress, that is to say eternity and victory: Hod and Netzach.

According to the Cabala, this is the basis for all religions and for all sciences, the first and immutable idea of things: a triple triangle and a circle, the ternary idea explained by balance multiplied by itself in the domains of the ideal, and then the realization of that idea in forms. The ancients then tied the first notions of this simple and grand theology to the idea of numbers, qualifying all the numbers of the original decade as follows:

1. Kether.—The Crown, the balancing power.
2. Chokmah.—Wisdom, balanced in its immutable order by the initiative of intelligence.
3. Binah.—Active Intelligence, balanced by Wisdom.
4. Chesed.—Mercy, the second conception of Wisdom, always benevolent, because it is strong.

5. Geburah.—The Rigor necessitated by Wisdom itself and by benevolence. To suffer evil is to hold back good.

6. Tiphareth.—Beauty, luminous and balanced conception in the forms, the intermediary between the crown and the kingdom, the principle mediator between the creator and creation. (What a sublime and poetic idea do we not find here of His sovereign calling!)

7. Netzach.—Victory, that is to say the eternal triumph of intelligence and justice.

8. Hod.—The Eternity of victories of spirit over matter, of the active over the passive, of life over death.

9. Yesod.—The Foundation, that is to say the basis of all belief and all truth, it is what we call in philosophy the ABSOLUTE.

10. Malkuth.—The Kingdom, it is the universe, it is all of creation, the work and the mirror of God, the proof of supreme reason, the formal consequence which forces us to climb back up to the virtual premises, the enigma whose word is God, that is to say: supreme and absolute reason.

These ten first notions attached to the ten first characters of the original alphabet, signifying both the principles and the numbers, are what the masters of the Cabala call the ten Sephiroth.

The sacred tetragrammaton, drawn in this manner,

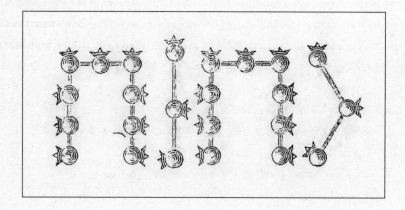

THE CABALA

indicates the number, the source, and the relationship of the divine names. It is in
the name of Iot-Chavah, written with these twenty-four signs crowned with a
triple crown of light, that one must find the twenty-four thrones of heaven and
the twenty-four crowned elders of the Book of Revelation. In the Cabala, the
occult principle is called the Ancient of Days, and this principle multiplied and as
if reflected in the second causes creates these images, that is to say there are as
many old men as there are diverse concepts of His unique essence. These images,
less perfect as they move away from their source, cast a final reflection or a final
glimmer in the darkness which represents a horrible and disfigured old man: it is
what is coarsely referred to as the devil. Thus an initiate dared to say: "The devil
is God as understood by the wicked"; and another, in stranger, but no less vigorous terms, added: "The devil is formed from the rifts within God." We could
summarize and explain these very original assertions by remarking that, within
the symbolism itself, the demon is an angel fallen from heaven for having wished
to usurp the divinity. This pertains to the allegorical language of the prophets
and of legends. Philosophically speaking, the devil is a human idea of divinity surpassed and dispossessed of heaven through the progress of science and of reason.
Moloch, Adramelech, and Baal,[171] were all, for the primordial Orientals, the per-
sonifications of the unique god, disgraced by barbaric attributes. The god of the
Jansenists, in creating hell for the majority of humans and basking in the eternal
tortures of those he had not wished to save, is an even more barbaric idea than
that of Moloch:[172] and thus the god of the Jansenists is already, for wise and enlightened Christians, a veritable Satan fallen from heaven.

The Cabalists, in multiplying the divine names, related them all either to the
unity of the Tetragrammaton, or to the ternary figure, or to the Sephirothic
ladder of the decad; they draw the ladder of the divine names and numbers
like this:

---

171   Gods of the nations neighboring Israel, who are repeatedly denounced and ridi-
      culed in the Old Testament.

172   The Jansenists were French followers of Jean Calvin (1509–64), the Protestant re-
      former who taught that God deliberately predestined most human souls to eter-
      nal damnation for his own greater glory.

י

יה

שדי

יהוה

אלהים

אלוהים

אראריתא

אלוה ודעת

אלהים גבור

אלהים צבאות[173]

a triangle that we can translate into Roman letters as follows:

J

JA

SDI

JEHU

ELOHIM

SABAOT

ARARITA

ELVEDAAT

ELIM GIBOR

ELIM SABAOT

The aggregation of all these divine names formed from the unique Tetragrammaton, but outside of the Tetragrammaton itself, is one of the bases of the

---

173   These names are Y, Yah, Shaddai, Yahweh, Elohim, Elohim (spelled another way), ARARITA, Eloah va-Daath, Elohim Gibor, and Elohim Sabaoth. The triangle of Latin letters below is a partial equivalent using common Latin spellings of Hebrew holy names; the number of letters is the crucial factor.

Hebrew ritual, and makes up the occult power the Cabalistic rabbis invoke under the name of Shemhamphorash.[174]

We have spoken here about the Tarot cards from the Cabalistic point of view. We have already indicated the occult source of their name. This hieroglyphic book is composed of a Cabalistic alphabet and a wheel or circle of four decades, specified by four symbolic and typical figures, each having as a spoke in the wheel a ladder of progressive figures representing Humanity: man, woman, young man, and child; master, mistress, warrior, and valet. The twenty-two characters of the alphabet represent first of all the thirteen doctrines, then the nine beliefs authorized by the Hebrew religion, a powerful religion founded upon the highest reason.

Here is the religious and Cabalistic key of the Tarot, expressed in verses in the manner of the ancient legislators:

1	א	All things proclaim an active, thinking cause.
2	ב	The living unity heeds number's laws.
3	ג	That which contains all is by nothing bound.
4	ד	Before all else, He everywhere is found.
5	ה	He, the sole Master—praise to Him alone!
6	ו	To pure hearts His true doctrine He makes known.
7	ז	Faith's works a single guide have, under heaven.
8	ח	So one sole altar and one law are given.
9	ט	What the Eternal founds, forever stays.
10	י	From high, down to our time, He rules each phase.
11	כ	Great is His mercy, and His wrath severe.
12	ל	He sends a king unto His people dear.
13	מ	The tomb but leads to new lands by and by,
		Life is immortal, death alone shall die.

Such are the pure doctrines, the sacred immutabilities; Let us now conclude with the revered numbers.

---

174   More correctly, ha-Shem ha-Mephoresh, "the divided Name," a set of seventy-two three-letter names of God used in Cabalistic mysticism.

14	נ	The angel of good brings temperance and peace.
15	ס	The other, pride and anger without cease.
16	ע	The lightning and the fire heed God's commands.
17	פ	The evening star's sweet dew is in His Hands.
18	צ	He sets the Moon to watch our ways forlorn.
19	ק	His Sun, the source wherein all is reborn.
20	ר	The dust of tombs is raised up by His breath.
0 or 21	ש	Where countless mortals stumble down to death.
21 or 22	ת	Above the Mercy Seat shines His bright crown,
		As from above the cherubs He looks down.

With the aid of this purely doctrinal commentary, we can already understand the figures of the Cabalistic alphabet of the Tarot. Thus figure No. 1, called the Mage, represents the active principle in the unity of the divine and human self-regulation; figure No. 2, crudely called the Priestess, describes the dogmatic unity founded upon the numbers, it is the Cabala or Gnosis personified; No. 3 represents divine Spirituality under the symbol of a winged female who holds in one hand the apocalyptic eagle, and, in the other, the world attached to the end of her scepter. The other figures are just as clear and as easily explainable as these first ones.

Let us now get to the fours signs, that is to say Wands, Cups, Swords, and Circles or Pentacles, crudely called Coins. These symbols are the hieroglyphs of the Tetragrammaton: thus, the Wand, is the phallus of the Egyptians or the Yodh of the Hebrews; the Cup is the cteis[175] or the primordial Heh; the Sword is the conjunction of the two, or the lingam, symbolized in precaptivity Hebrew by the Vav, and the Circle or Pentacle, the image of the world, is the final Heh of the divine name.

Now let us take the Tarot and gather together, four by four, all the pages which form Guillaume Postel's Wheel or ROTA; let us place together the four aces, the fours twos, etc., and we will have ten packs of cards which provide the hieroglyphic explanation of the triangle and the divine names on the decimal

---

175   As mentioned, the Greek word for "vagina." For some reason this has never entered into common use in English, while the equivalent Greek word for penis, *phallos*, has found wide used, via Late Latin, in the English word "phallus."

scale which we have provided above. We can then read them thus, by relating each number to the corresponding Sephirot:

יהוה

Four letters make the Name that rules all names.

1 Kether

The four Aces.

The crown of God has four uprising flames.

2 Chokmah

The four Twos.

Four streams lead Wisdom out to all four sides.

3 Binah

The four Threes.

Four proofs of Understanding He provides.

4 Chesed

The four Fours.

Four blessings unto us His Mercy moves.

5 Geburah

The four Fives.

Four times four crimes Severity reproves.

6 Tiphareth

The four Sixes.

His Beauty is revealed through four pure rays.

7 Netzach

The four Sevens.

Four times His mighty Victory we praise.

8 Hod

The four Eights.

Four times He triumphs in Eternity.

9 Yesod

The four Nines.

Beneath His throne, Foundations four we see.

10 Malkuth

The four Tens.

His unique Kingdom is four times the same,

Conforming ever to His crown of flame.

We see by this simple arrangement the Cabalistic meaning of each card. Thus, for example, the five of wands strictly symbolizes the Geburah of Yod, that is to say the justice of the Creator or the anger of man; the seven of cups signifies the victory of mercy or the triumph of woman; the eight of swords signifies conflict or eternal equilibrium; and so on. We can understand in this way how the ancient pontiffs proceeded in order to make this oracle speak: the cards cast randomly always provided a new Cabalistic meaning, but rigorously true in their combination, which was the only fortuitous aspect; and since the ancients' faith did not accept anything as accidental, they read the answers provided by Providence in the oracles of the Tarot, which the Hebrews called Teraph or Teraphim,[176] just as the first Cabalistic scholar, Gaffarel,[177] one of Cardinal Richelieu's official magicians, had sensed.

As to the four court cards, here is a final couplet to explain them:

King, Queen, Knight, Page.

Husband, young man, child, all humanity,

By these four rungs, climb back to unity.

---

176 Teraphim are mentioned in several places in the Old Testament; most modern scholars consider them to be statues of household guardian spirits.

177 French astrologer and linguist Jacques Gaffarel (1601–81), who was in fact employed by Cardinal Richelieu.

At the end of the Ritual we will provide more details and complete documents regarding the marvelous book of the Tarot, and we will demonstrate that it is the primordial book, the key to all the prophecies and all the dogmas, in one word the book which inspired all inspired books, which was neither intuited by Court de Gébelin through his science, nor Alliette or Etteilla[178] through his singular intuitions.

The ten Sephiroth and the twenty-two Tarot trumps form what the Cabalists call the thirty-two Paths of Wisdom. As to particular sciences, they divide them into fifty chapters, which they call the Fifty Gates (we know that "door" signifies government or authority for the Orientals).[179] The rabbis also divide the Cabala into Bereshith, or universal Genesis, and Merkabah, or Ezekiel's chariot;[180] then, from the two ways of interpreting the Cabalistic alphabet they form two sciences, called Gematria and Temurah,[181] and with them they form that well-known art, which is nothing other than the complete science of the symbols of the Tarot and their complex and varied use in the divination of all secrets, of philosophy, or of nature, or even of the future. We will speak again about this in chapter 20 of this book.

---

178   French cartomancer Jean-Baptiste Alliette (1738–91), who published his books under the pseudonym Etteilla, his last name spelled backwards.

179   A custom among the Turks, to be precise. In nineteenth-century Europe, the government of the Ottoman Empire was known as the Sublime Porte.

180   The first chapter of Genesis, and the vision of the chariot in the book of Ezekiel, are the two main sources of the mystical symbolism of the Cabala.

181   Two methods of Cabalistic analysis. Each Hebrew letter represents a number as well as a sound. Gematria consists of adding up the number values of the letters of a word and using the resulting number as a key to its inner meaning. Temurah substitutes one set of letters for another using special rules.

11 ʾ L.

THE MAGICAL CHAIN

MANUS.

STRENGTH.[182]

T he great magical agent, which we have called the astral light, which others call the world soul, which the ancient alchemists refer to under the names of Azoth and Magnesia, this unique and incontestable occult force is the key to all influences, the secret to all the powers; it is Medea's flying dragon, the mysterious serpent of Eden; it is the universal mirror of visions, the knot of sympathies, the source of love, of prophecy, and of glory. To take possession of this agent is to have the powers of God himself; all real, effective magic, all true occult power, comes from it, and all the true books of science have no other goal than to demonstrate this.

In order to take possession of the great magical agent, two operations are required: to concentrate and project; in other terms, to fixate and move.

The author of all things provided stability as a foundation and guarantee for movement; the mage must act in the same manner.

---

182 *Manus* is Latin for "hand," and Strength is the eleventh tarot trump in the original order of the cards, though some modern decks switch the eighth and eleventh trumps, Justice and Strength.

We say that enthusiasm is contagious. Why? It is because enthusiasm is not produced without fixed beliefs. Faith produces faith; to want with reason is to want with a, I will not say infinite, but with an indefinite power.

That which acts in the intellectual and moral sphere affects the physical world even more; and when Archimedes called for a fulcrum with which to raise the world, he was simply looking for the great magical arcanum. On one of the arms of the hermaphrodite drawn by Heinrich Khunrath[183] we read this word: COAGULA, and on the other arm: SOLVE.

To gather and to disperse are the two verbs of nature; but how does one gather, and how does one disperse the astral light or the world soul?

We gather in isolation, and we disperse through the magical chain.

The isolation of thought means absolute independence, the isolation of the heart is total liberty, the isolation of the senses is perfect abstinence.

Any man who has prejudices and fears, any individual who is a slave to his passions, is incapable of gathering or coagulating, to use Khunrath's expression, the astral light or world soul.

All true adepts were independent under torture, sober and chaste until death; and the reason for this anomaly is that, to command a force, you cannot be taken over by that force to such an extent that it commands you.

But then, those men will cry out who look to magic as a means of satisfying their natural desires, what use does this power serve if one cannot use it to satisfy oneself? If I told you, you poor people who ask such a question, how would you understand me? Are pearls then nothing, because they have no value for Epicurus's flock of piglets?[184] Did Curtius not find it more worthwhile to command those who had gold rather than to possess it himself?[185] Does one not need to be a little more than just an ordinary man if one hopes to become godlike? Incidentally, I am sorry to distress or discourage you, but I am not reinventing the high

---

183 German alchemist (1560–1605), whose works are full of many complex symbolic figures.

184 Epicurus was the founder of the Epicurean school of philosophy, which held that pleasure was the only purpose in life.

185 Curtius Rufus, a Roman politician of the first century CE.

sciences here; I teach them and I am attesting to their strict requirements by mentioning their primary and most inexorable conditions.

Pythagoras was a chaste and sober free man; Apollonius of Tyana and the emperor Julian were men of frightful austerity; people questioned Paracelsus's sex, so resistant was he to amorous temptations; Raymond Lully pushed the strictures of his life to the point of the most exalted asceticism; Girolamo Cardano so exaggerated his practice of fasting that he almost died of starvation, if we are to believe tradition; Agrippa, poor and running from town to town, almost died of penury rather than submit to the caprices of a princess who threatened the liberty of science. What, then, was happiness for these men? Knowledge of the great secrets and the understanding of power. That was enough for these great individuals. Must one be like them to know what they knew? Certainly not, and this book which I write is the proof; but, to do what they did, it is absolutely necessary to use the same means that they used.

But what did they actually do? They surprised and enthralled the world, they reigned more truly than kings. Magic is an instrument of divine grace or diabolical pride, but it is death to the joys of the world and the pleasures of a mortal life.

Then what is the use of studying it? the Epicureans would say.

—Simply to know, and perhaps also to learn to guard against stupid incredulity and puerile credulity. Men of pleasure (and for half of those men I count many a woman), is it not a very great pleasure to satisfy curiosity? Read on, then, without fear, for you shall never become magicians against your own will.

But these dispositions of absolute renouncement are only necessary for establishing the universal currents and changing the face of the world; there are magical operations, relative to and limited within a given circle, which do not require such heroic virtues. We can act upon the passions with passions, determine the sympathies and antipathies, even afflict and heal, without having the omnipotence of the mage; one must simply be forewarned of the risk that one runs of a reaction proportional to any action and to which one can easily fall victim. All this is explained in the Ritual.

To create a magical chain is to establish a magnetic current which becomes stronger depending on the length of the chain. We shall see in the Ritual how these currents can be produced, and the different manners of forming a chain. Mesmer's wooden tub was a rather imperfect magical chain; many great circles of the illumined, in various northern countries, have more powerful chains. Even a certain society of Catholic priests famous for their occult powers and their unpopularity[186] was established according to the plan and following the requirements of the most powerful magical chains, and that is the secret of their power, which they attribute solely to grace or the will of God, a vulgar and easy solution to all the questions regarding the effects of power upon influence or upon unconscious impulses. In our Ritual, we will assess the value of the series of truly magical ceremonies and evocations which make up the Great Work of that vocation under the name of the exercises of Saint Ignatius.

Every enthusiasm propagated in society due to a series of communications and predetermined practices produces a magnetic current that is also conserved or augmented by that current. The effect of the current is to enchant and often overly stimulate impressionable and weak persons, excitable constitutions, and temperaments disposed to hysteria or hallucinations. These persons soon become powerful vehicles for magical power and strongly project the astral light in the same direction as the current; thus to oppose oneself to manifestations of power is in a way to fight against destiny. When the young Pharisee called Saul or Schol had thrown himself, with all the fanaticism and stubbornness of a sectarian, in the way of the invading Christian religion, he unknowingly put himself at the mercy of the power he thought he was fighting; he was immediately struck by a formidable magnetic bolt, rendered even more immediate no doubt by the combined effects of cerebral congestion and sunburn.[187] The conversion of the young Israelite Alphonse Ratisbonne is a contemporary example of precisely the same nature.[188] We know of such a sect of enthusiasts, whom people mock from a distance but join despite themselves when they approach them, even if it is to fight against them. I would add that magical circles and magnetic currents are estab-

---

186   That is, the Jesuit order.

187   Acts 9:1–9.

188   A French Jew (1814–84) who converted to Catholicism after seeing a vision of the Virgin Mary in 1842.

lished on their own, and in accordance with their inexorable laws influence those who submit to their effects. Each one of us is attracted into a circle of relations which is their world and under which we are influenced. Jean-Jacques Rousseau, that legislator of the French Revolution, that man which the most spiritual nation in the world accepted as the incarnation of reason, was dragged into the saddest act of his life, the abandonment of his children, through the magnetic influence of a circle of libertines and due to the magnetic current from a dinner service. He naively and simply gives an account of this in his *Confessions*, and it is an event no one had noticed. Great circles make great men, and vice versa. There are no misunderstood geniuses; there are *eccentric* men, and that word seems to have been invented by an adept.[189] A man eccentric in his genius is one who looks to form a circle and fights against the central forces of attraction of magical chains and established currents. His destiny is to be broken by the fight or to succeed. What is the dual condition for such a success? A central fixed point and a persevering circular initiative. The man of genius is one who has discovered a real law, and in consequence possesses an invincible power of action and direction. He may die before completing his work, but what he wished for is accomplished despite his death, and often because of his death: because death is a veritable assumption for the genius. "And I, if I be lifted up from the earth," said one of the greatest initiators, "will draw all men unto me."[190]

The law of magnetic currents is that of the movement of the astral light itself. This movement is always dual and multiplies itself in the opposite direction. A great action always entails an equal reaction, and the secret of great success is all about predicting the reactions. It is in this manner that Chateaubriand, inspired by his disgust for the revolutionary saturnalia, predicted and prepared the immense success of his *Génie de christianisme*. To oppose oneself to a current which is beginning its circle, is to wish to be broken as the great and unfortunate emperor Julian was; to oppose a current which has run the entire circle of its action is to take the head of the opposing current. A great man is he who arrives in time and who knows how to innovate appropriately. Voltaire, if he had been born in

---

189   The word "eccentric" literally means "off center."

190   John 12:32.

the time of the apostles, would have been unable to find an echo for his words and would perhaps have been no more than an ingenious parasite at the banquets of Trimalchio.[191] In the era in which we live, everything is ready for a new explosion of evangelical enthusiasm and Christian selflessness, precisely because of the universal disenchantment with egotistical positivism and a cynical public with the crudest of appetites. The success of certain books and the mystical tendencies in people are unequivocal symptoms of this general disposition. We are restoring the churches and are building new ones; the more we feel empty of beliefs, the more we hope for them; the entire world again awaits for the Messiah, and it will not be long before he arrives. Thus there will be, for example, someone who is highly placed due to his rank or his wealth, a pope, a king, or even a Jewish millionaire, who will publicly and solemnly sacrifice all of his material interests in the name of the salvation of humanity; he will become the redemptor of the poor, the actual propagator and even the victim of the doctrines of devotion and charity, and he will cause a great upswelling of support around him and a complete moral upheaval in the world. But the high position of this person is what is most necessary because, in our time of misery and charlatanism, all Verbs coming from below bear the suspicion of having arisen out of ambition and self-interested deceit. You, then, who are nothing and have nothing, do not hope to be among either the apostles or the messiahs. Do you have faith and do you wish to act upon your faith? Then first achieve the means to act, which is the influence which comes with rank and the prestige of wealth. In the past we created gold with science, today we must remake science with gold. We fixed the volatile, now we must make volatile the fixed; in other terms, we materialized the spirit, we must now spiritualize matter. The most sublime word is not heard today if it does not have the guarantee of a name, that is to say of a success which represents material value. How much is a manuscript worth? What the author's signature is worth in the bookstore. The business firm Alexandre Dumas and Co., for example, represents one of the greatest literary guarantees in our time; but the Dumas brand

---

191   A character in *The Satyricon*, a famous novel by the Roman author Petronius Arbiter. Trimalchio is a nouveau-riche Roman who flaunts his wealth by throwing orgiastic parties.

is only valued for its habitual products: novels. Were Dumas to devise some magnificent utopia or an admirable solution for our religious problems, we would consider his discoveries as the amusing caprices of a novelist, and no one would take them seriously, despite the European fame of the Panurge[192] of modern literature. We are in a century of established positions: everyone is worth what he is worth socially and commercially. The unlimited liberty of speech produces so much argument that we no longer ask today: What does he say? But: Who said so? If it is Rothschild, or His Holiness Pius IX, or even Monsignor Dupanloup,[193] then that is something. If it is just so-and-so, even if so-and-so is (which is entirely possible, after all) a prodigy or even an ignored genius of science and good sense, then it is nothing.

To those who would then tell me: If you have the secret to great success and the power to change the world, why do you not use it? I would answer: This science came to me too late, and I lost a great deal, in order to acquire it, of the time and resources which might allow me to make use of it; but I offer it up to those who are in a position to use it. Famous men, the rich and great of this world, who are not satisfied with what you have, and who sense in your heart a more noble and vaster ambition, do you wish to become the fathers of a new world, the kings of a renewed civilization? A poor and obscure savant has found Archimedes's lever, and he offers it to you solely for the good of humanity, without asking you for anything in exchange.

The phenomena which recently agitated America and Europe with regard to talking tables and fluidic manifestations[194] are nothing other than magnetic currents which are beginning to form, and solicitations whose nature is to invite us, in the name of the salvation of humanity, to reconstitute the great sympathetic and religious chains. The stagnation of the astral light would be the death of the human species, and the current torpor of this secret agent has already manifested itself through terrifying symptoms of decomposition and death. Cholera morbus,

---

192 In *Gargantua and Pantagruel*, by François Rabelais (1483–1553), Panurge is a drinking, whoring, laughing boon companion of Pantagruel's.

193 Félix Dupanloup (1802–78), a charismatic Catholic bishop and theologian in Lévi's time.

194 The Spiritualist movement, which began in the United States in 1848.

for example, and the sicknesses found in potatoes and grapes, have no other cause, as was seen by the two shepherd children of La Salette in their obscure and symbolic daydreams.[195]

Their story was met with unexpected faith, and the immense confluence of pilgrims caused by the very singular and vague story of these two illiterate children with almost no morals is proof of the magnetic reality of the occurrence and of the fluidic tendency of the Earth itself to work towards healing its inhabitants.

Superstitions are instinctive, and all that is instinct has a reason for existing in the nature of things itself: that is what the skeptics from all the ages have not properly considered.

Thus we attribute all these strange occurrences of moving tables to the universal magnetic agent, which is looking for a chain of enthusiasm in order to form new currents. On its own, it is a blind force, but which can be directed by the will of men and which is influenced by contemporary opinion. This universal fluid, if we wish to call it a fluid, being the common environment of all nervous organisms and the vehicle for all sensitive vibrations, establishes between impressionable persons a veritable physical solidarity and transmits from individuals to other individuals impressions from the imagination and thought. The movement of an inert object, determined by the undulations of the universal agent, thus obeys the dominant impression and thereafter reproduces in its revelations all the lucidity of the most marvelous of daydreams or all the strangeness and all the lies of the most incoherent and vaguest of dreams. The knocking sounds arising from furniture, the noises of agitated cookware, musical instruments playing on their own,[196] all of these are illusions produced by the same cause. The convulsive miracles of Saint-Médard[197] were of the same order and often seemed to defy the laws

---

195   La Salette, in southeastern France, was in 1846 the site of a famous apparition of the Virgin Mary, seen by the children Mélanie Calvat and Maximin Giraud.

196   All of these were common features of Spiritualist exhibitions.

197   The tomb of François de Pâris, in the cemetery of Saint-Médard in Paris, was a place of pilgrimage for believers in the Jansenist heresy in eighteenth-century France. Many of the pilgrims went into convulsions and miraculous healings were claimed.

of nature. On one hand, exaggerations produced by fascination resulting from intoxication due to the congestion of the astral light; and, on the other hand, oscillations or actual movements imprinted on inert matter by the subtle and universal agent of the movement of life: this is what is at the foundation of all these marvelous occurrences, as we can easily convince ourselves of by reproducing the most impressive of these miracles at will, by means indicated in the Ritual, and by observing the evident absence of trickery, hallucination, or error.

It has happened several times to me, after experimenting with the magical chain with persons of good faith who were not sympathetic to my beliefs, that I was suddenly awakened during the night, by images and truly terrifying communications. One night, among others, I truly felt as if a hand was strangling me; I woke up, lit my lamp, and began to calmly work, making use of my insomnia to chase away the ghosts of sleep, when various books besides me began to move noisily, their pages trembling and rubbing against one another, the wood paneling crackled as though it were about to split, and dull knocking sounds came from the ceiling. I observed these effects, which were no less impressive even if they were caused solely by my imagination, with calm curiosity. Incidentally, besides not being afraid at all, I was not at all occupied with occult matters at the time they occurred.

It was in reaction to such occurrences that I was led to attempt experiments in evocation with the aid of the ceremonial magic of the ancients, and from which I obtained truly extraordinary results that I shall describe in chapter 13 of this work.

12　ל　M.

THE GREAT WORK

DISCITE.

The Hanged Man

CRUX.[198]

T he Great Work is, above all else, the creation of man by himself, that is to say the full and entire conquest of his faculties and his future; it is above all the perfect emancipation of his will, which assures him the universal empire of Azoth and the domain of Magnesia, which means full control over the universal magical agent.

This magical agent, which the ancient hermetic philosophers disguised under the name of the first matter, determines the forms of the modifiable substance, and through its use we can actually arrive at metallic transmutation and the universal medicine. This is not just hypothesis, it is previously tested and rigorously demonstrable scientific fact.

Nicolas Flamel[199] and Raymond Lully,[200] both poor men, evidently gave away

---

198　*Discite* is Latin for "learn!" *Crux* is Latin for "cross."

199　French alchemist (1330–1418), whose *Hieroglyphic Figures* were a major source for many later alchemists.

200　The Catalan polymath Ramon Llull, known as Raymond Lully, was credited with dozens of alchemical books he did not write. The mistaken attribution was not known in Lévi's time.

immense riches. Agrippa only got to the first part of the Great Work, and he died in the attempt, struggling for sole possession of himself and to fix his independence.

There are two hermetic operations: one which is spiritual, the other material, and these two depend upon each other.

All hermetic science is contained in the doctrine that Hermes originally engraved, or so it is said, on a tablet of emerald. We have already described the first articles; here are those which have to do with the Great Work:

You shall separate earth from fire, the subtle from the coarse, carefully, and with much labor.

It ascends from the earth to heaven, then descends again to earth, and receives the power of the superiors and the inferiors.

Thus you shall have the glory of the entire world, and all obscurity shall flee before you.

It is the strong fortitude of all fortitudes, vanquishing every subtle and penetrating every solid thing.

Thus the world was created.

To separate the subtle from the coarse, in the first operation, which is entirely done from within, is to liberate one's soul from all prejudice and vice: which is done with the use of the philosophical salt, that is to say wisdom; and with mercury, that is to say, with one's own skill and work; and finally with sulfur, which represents the vital energy and the heat of the will. By these means we are able to transform less precious things, even the filth of the earth, into spiritual gold. It is in this manner that one must understand the unwashed parables of the philosophers, of Bernard Trevisan,[201] of Basilius Valentinius,[202] of Mary the Egyptian,[203] and other prophets of alchemy, but in their works, as in the Great Work, one must carefully separate the subtle from the coarse, the mystic from the pos-

---

201   Italian alchemist (1406–90), author of *The Parable of the Fountain*.

202   Pseudonym of a German alchemist, probably Johann Thölde (1565–1624). Author of *The Twelve Keys* and many other important alchemical works.

203   Also known as Mary the Prophet, a pioneering Jewish-Egyptian alchemist who lived sometime during the first three centuries CE.

itive, the allegory from the theory. If we wish to read them with pleasure and in-telligence, one must first understand them entirely allegorically, and then descend from the allegories to reality by the path of correspondences, or analogies, indi-cated in the unique doctrine:

That which is above is like that which is below, and vice versa.

The word ART backwards, or read in the manner of the sacred and pri-mordial writings, that is to say from right to left, expresses, with three initials, the different degrees of the Great Work. T signifies ternary, theory, and travail; R, realization; A, adaptation. We shall provide, in chapter 12 of the Ritual, the recipes of the great masters for adaptation, and in particular the one contained in the hermetic fortress of Heinrich Khunrath.

We indicate here for our readers for the purposes of research the admirable treatise attributed to Hermes Trismegistus entitled *Minerva Mundi*.[204] This treatise is found in only a few publications of Hermes's, and contains, in the form of alle-gories, with much poetry and profundity, the doctrine of the creation of beings by and of themselves, or the law of creation which results from the accordance of two forces, the forces the alchemists call the fixed and the volatile, and which are, in the absolute, necessity and liberty. Therein is explained the diversity of forms spread throughout nature by the diversity of spirits, and the monstrosities of nature by the divergence of efforts. The reading of and meditation upon this work is indispensable to all adepts who wish to deepen their understanding of the mys-teries of nature and to begin to work more seriously towards the achievement of the Great Work.

When the masters of alchemy said that one needs little time or money to ac-complish the great works of science, when they affirm moreover that only a single vessel is required, when they speak of the great and unique athanor which anyone can put to use, and which is available to everyone and that men possess it without knowing, they are alluding to philosophical and moral alchemy. In fact, a strong and decided will can arrive at absolute independence rather quickly, and we posses the chemical instrument, the great and unique athanor, which serves to

---

204   Also known as *The Virgin of the World*, an ancient Greek treatise attributed to Her-mes Trismegistus.

separate the subtle from the coarse and the fixed from the volatile. This instrument, as complete as the world itself, and as precise as mathematics, and that is designated by the sages with the symbol of the pentagram or the five-pointed star, which is the absolute sign of human intelligence. I shall imitate the sages by not naming it: it is very easy to guess it.

The Tarot drawing which corresponds to this chapter was poorly understood by Court de Gébelin and Etteilla, who believed that all they saw was an error committed by a German card maker. This drawing represents a man, his hands tied behind his back, with two money bags attached to his armpits, hanging by one foot from a gallows made of two tree trunks which each have six cut branches and a crossbeam that completes the letter Tav in the Jewish alphabet ת; the legs of the figure are crossed and his elbows form a triangle with his head. Whereas the triangle with a cross mounted on it signifies, in alchemy, the end and the perfection of the Great Work, the letter ת, which is the last letter of the sacred alphabet, has an identical meaning.

This hanged man is thus the adept, tied by his spiritual commitments, spiritualized where his feet are turned towards heaven; he is also the Prometheus of antiquity, punished with immortal torture for his glorious theft. Crudely speaking, he is the traitor Judas, and his torment threatens the revealers of the great arcanum. Finally, for the Jewish Cabalists, this hanged man, which corresponds to their twelfth dogma, that of the promised Messiah, is a protest against the Savior recognized by the Christians, and which seems to still say to him: How will you save others, you who could not manage to save yourself?

In the *Sefer Toledot Yeshu*, an anti-Christian rabbinical compilation, we find a singular parable: Yeshu, says the rabbinic author of the legend, was traveling with Simon Bar-Jonah and Judas Iscariot. They arrived late and tired at an isolated house; they were very hungry and could find nothing to eat aside from a very small and thin young goose. It was too little for three people; to share it would have meant arousing their hunger even more, rather than satisfying it. They decided to draw straws; but, because they were falling down from lack of sleep, "Let us sleep first," said Yeshu, "while our meal cooks; when we wake we will tell each other our dreams, and he who had the most beautiful dream will eat the little goose all for himself." And thus was it done. They slept and then awoke. "I," said

Saint Peter, "I dreamed that I was the vicar of God." "I," said Yeshu, "that I was God himself." "And I," Judas responded hypocritically, "I dreamed that while sleepwalking I got up and went quietly downstairs, removed the goose from its spit, and ate it." After this they all went downstairs, but the goose had in fact disappeared: Judas had dreamed while completely awake.[205]

This legend is a Jewish positivist protest against Christian mysticism. In fact, while the believers were having nice dreams, the exiled Israelite, the Judas of Christian civilization, worked, sold, agitated, became rich, and made off with the realities of our present life and was thus able to help his cult, which had been proscribed for so long. The ancients worshiped the Ark, and those who stayed faithful to the cult of the strongbox, now have the Market for a temple, and it is from there that they govern the Christian world. Judas can, in fact, laugh and congratulate himself for not having slept like Saint Peter.

In the ancient precaptivity writings, the Hebrew Tav had the shape of a cross, which also confirms our interpretation of the twelfth card of the Cabalistic tarot. The cross, generator of the four triangles, is also the sacred symbol of the duodenary, and the Egyptians called it, for that reason, the key to heaven. Also Etteilla, troubled by his long search to conciliate the analogical necessities of the drawing with his own personal opinion (in this he had been influenced by the scholar Court de Gébelin), placed in the hand of his hanged man the hermetic caduceus formed by two serpents and a Greek Tav and then stood him upright and called him Prudence. Since he understood the necessity of the Tav or the cross on the twelfth page of the book of Thoth, he should have understood the multiple and magnificent symbol of the hermetic hanged man, the Prometheus of science, the living man who does not touch the ground except with his thought and whose foundation is in heaven, the free and sacrificed adept, the revealer threatened with death, Judaism's polemic against Christ, which seems to be an involuntary admission of the occult divinity of the crucified, the sign of the work accomplished, the termination of the cycle, the intermediary Tav, which summarizes, for a first time before the last denary, the signs of the sacred alphabet.

---

205   This anecdote is not found in the actual text of the *Sefer Toledot Yeshu* but in the rabbinical commentaries about this work. (Lévi's note.)

13 מ N.

NECROMANCY

EX IPSIS.

MORS.[206]

We have said that within the astral light are conserved the images of people and things. It is also in this light that we can evoke the forms of those who are no longer of this world, and it is by this means that are accomplished such mysteries, as disputed as they are real, like necromancy.

The Cabalists who spoke of the world of the spirits were simply recounting what they had seen in their evocations.

Eliphas Lévi Zahed,[207] who writes this book, has evoked, and he has seen.

Let us first say what the masters wrote of their visions or of their intuitions in what they called *the light of glory*.

We read in the Hebrew book of the *Revolution of Souls* that there are three types of souls: the daughters of Adam, the daughters of angels, and the daughters of sin. There are also, according to the same book, three types of spirits: captive spirits, errant spirits, and free spirits. Souls are sent off in couples. There are,

---

206   *Ex ipsis* is Latin for "out of itself," and *mors* Latin for "death."

207   These Hebrew names when translated into French are Alphonse Louis Constant. (Lévi's note.)

however, male souls born widowed, and whose wives are being held captive by Lilith and Na'amah, the queens of the stryges: they are souls who must expiate their rashness through a vow of celibacy. Thus when a man renounces from early childhood his love for women, he renders the wife who was destined for him a slave to the demons of debauchery. Souls meet and multiply in heaven as well as in bodies on earth. Immaculate souls are the daughters of the kisses of angels.

Nothing can enter heaven which does not come from heaven. After death, then, the divine spirit which animated a man returns alone to heaven, and leaves on earth and in the atmosphere two cadavers: one terrestrial and elementary, and another aerial and astral; one is already inert, the other is still animated by the universal movement of the world soul but is destined to slowly die, absorbed by the astral powers which produced it. The terrestrial corpse remains visible; the other is invisible to the eyes of terrestrial and living bodies and can only be seen through applications of the astral light upon the *translucent*, which communicates its impressions to the nervous system and thus affects the organ of sight to the point of being able to see the forms which are conserved and the words which are written in the book of the vital light.

After a time, a man's astral corpse evaporates like pure incense by rising towards the upper regions, but if that man lived in crime, his astral corpse, which holds him prisoner, continues to search for the objects of his passion and wishes to live again. He torments the dreams of young girls, bathes in the vapors of spilt blood, and loiters around places where the pleasures of life have flowed; he still watches over the treasures he had possessed and hoarded; he exhausts himself with painful efforts, in order to make himself material organs so as to live again. But the celestial bodies suck him up and drink him; they feel his intellect weaken, his memory slowly fading, his entire being dissolving. . . . His old vices appear to him as monstrous figures and chase him; they attack and devour him. . . . The poor devil thus gradually loses all the members of his body which had served him in his iniquity; and then he dies for a second time and forever, because he then loses his personality and his memory. Souls which must live but are not yet entirely purified stay captive in their astral corpse for more or less time, where they are burnt by the odic light which wishes to assimilate and dissolve him. It is in order to escape their astral corpse that souls sometimes enter into the living, and live within them in a state Cabalists call embryonate.

It is these aerial corpses which we evoke through necromancy. It is the larvae, of dead or dying substances, that we contact; ordinarily they cannot communicate except through the ringing in our ears produced by the nervous trembling which I have spoken of, and they are normally understood only by reflecting upon our thoughts or our dreams.

But to see these strange forms one must enter into an exceptional state, between sleep and death, which is to say that one must magnetize oneself and reach a sort of lucid and alert hypnotic state. Necromancy obtains real results, and magical evocations can produce actual visions. We have said that within the great magical agent, which is the astral light, are conserved the imprint of all things, all images which have been formed either by rays or by reflections; it is within this light that our dreams appear, it is this light which intoxicates madmen and pulls their sleepy judgment into chasing the most bizarre ghosts. To see without illusions in this light, one must push aside the reflections with a powerful will and only attract the rays to oneself. To dream awake, is to see within the astral light; the orgies of the Sabbath, as recounted by so many witches during their criminal trials, had appeared to them in the same manner. Often the preparations and the substances used to arrive at this result were horrific, as we shall see in Ritual; but the results were never in doubt. They saw, they heard, they touched the most abominable things, the most fantastic, the most impossible. We shall return to this subject in our fifteenth chapter; here we are solely concerned with the evocation of the dead.

In the spring of the year 1854, I went to London to escape my personal sorrows and dedicate myself, without distraction, to science. I had letters of introduction to eminent people who were curious about revelations from the supernatural world. I saw several of them, and I found in them, along with their very courteous behavior, a foundation based on indifference or frivolity. They asked of me before anything else for miracles as though they were addressing a charlatan. I was a bit discouraged because, to tell the truth, far from being disposed to initiating others into the mysteries of ceremonial magic, I was always afraid of, for myself, the illusions and the fatigue; incidentally, these ceremonies require expensive materials which are difficult to find. Thus I isolated myself in the study of the high Cabala, and I no longer thought of English adepts, when one day, upon returning to my hotel, I found an envelope addressed to me. This envelope contained half of a card which was cut crosswise, and upon which I first recognized the symbol of the seal of Solomon and also a very small piece of paper upon which had been written in pencil: "Tomorrow, at three o'clock, in front of Westminster Abbey, we shall present you with the other half of this card." I went to this very singular rendezvous. A carriage was parked there. I held, without affectation, my piece of the card in my hand; a servant approached me and waved to me while opening the door to the car. In the car was a woman dressed in black, whose hat was covered with a very thick veil; she indicated that I should climb in beside her, while showing me the other half of the card I had received. The door closed, the car began to move, and, the woman having lifted up her veil, I could now see that I was dealing with an older person who had gray eyebrows and black eyes which were extremely bright and strangely fixed. "Sir," she said to me, with a very heavy English accent, "I know that the law of secrecy is very strict among adepts; a friend of Sir B*** L***,[208] whom you met, knows that you were asked to perform certain experiments, and that you refused to satisfy their curiosity. Perhaps you do not have the necessary equipment: I wish to assemble a complete magical study for you; but I ask of you, before all else, complete secrecy. If you do not swear upon your honor, I will give the order for you to be driven back to your hotel." I made the promise asked of me, and I am still faithful to it by mentioning neither the name, nor station, nor the abode of this lady, who I soon accepted as an initiate, not precisely of the first order, but of a very high rank. We had several long conversations, during which she always insisted on practical experience in order to complete the initiation. She showed me a collection of clothes and magical instruments, she even lent me some interesting books which I did not have; in short, she convinced me to attempt the experiment of a complete evocation at her place, which I prepared for during twenty-one days by strictly observing the practices described in the thirteenth chapter of the Ritual.

---

208   This is clearly supposed to be Sir Edward Bulwer-Lytton, the author of several popular novels on occultism.

All was ready by the 24th of July, it concerned the evocation of the divine ghost of Apollonius, and I was to ask him about two secrets: one which concerned me, and one which the lady was interested in. She had at first planned on being present for the evocation with another person she trusted; but at the last moment that person took fright, and since the ternary or the unity is strictly required for these magical rites, I was left to conduct it alone. The study which had been prepared for the evocation was in a small tower: inside it we had placed four concave mirrors and a sort of altar whose base was made of white marble encircled by a magnetized iron chain. Upon the white marble was engraved in gold the sign of the pentagram, as it is shown on page 73 of this work; and the same sign was drawn, in various colors, on the new and white lambskin which had been laid under the altar. In the middle of the marble table there was a small copper brazier with alder and bay wood charcoal; another brazier was placed before me on a tripod. I was dressed in robes like that of our Catholic priests, but that they were more ample and longer, and on my head I wore a crown of vervain leaves intertwined with a golden chain. In one hand I held a new sword and in the other the Ritual. I lit the two braziers with the required and prepared substances, and I began reciting, in a low voice at first, then raising my voice by degrees, the invocations from the Ritual. The smoke expanded, the flames made all the objects which they illuminated shimmer, and then they went out. The white smoke slowly rose above the marble altar. I seemed to feel the earth tremble; my ears were ringing and my heart beat strongly. I put several branches and perfume in the braziers, and as the flames rose again, I distinctly saw, in front of the altar, the larger-than-life figure of a man, which then dissipated and faded away. I renewed my evocations, and I had just placed myself within the circle I had drawn beforehand between the altar and the tripod: it was then that I saw appear within the mirror in front of me, behind the altar, a white form, getting larger and appearing to draw nearer. I closed my eyes and called out to Apollonius three times; and when I opened them again, a man stood before me, entirely covered in some kind of shroud, who seemed to me to be more gray than white; his form was thin, sad, and beardless, which was not exactly the image I had of Apollonius beforehand. I felt an extraordinarily cold sensation, and when I opened my mouth to question the ghost, I was unable to utter a sound. I then put my hand upon the sign of the pentagram, and I directed the point of my sword towards him, commanding him mentally, by that sign, to stop trying to frighten me and to obey me. Then the form became more confused and suddenly disappeared. I commanded him to return: I then felt a kind of breath pass near me, and something touched my hand which held the sword, and I immediately felt my arm become numb right up to my shoulder. From this I hypothesized that the sword offended the spirit, and I drove the point of the sword into the circle surrounding me. The human figure reappeared right afterwards, but I felt such a great weakness in my limbs, and such a sudden failing which overtook me that I took two steps back to sit down. The moment I sat down, I fell into a deep lethargy accompanied by dreams, of which there only remained vague and confused memories once I re-awakened. For several days afterwards, my arm remained numb and painful. The figure never spoke to me, but it seemed to me that the questions I had had for him had been answered for me in my mind. To the lady's question, an interior voice answered within me: Dead! (The question was with regard to a man which the lady wished to have news of.) As for me, I wished to know if reunification and forgiveness was possible between two people I was thinking about, and the same interior echo replied mercilessly: Dead!

I relate here the events as they happened, I do not insist that anyone believe me. The effect of this experience on me was inexplicable. I was no longer the same man, something from another world had passed within me; I was no longer either cheerful, or sad, but I felt a singular attraction to death, without being, however, at all tempted to commit suicide. I carefully analyzed what I had gone through; and, despite a very strong feeling of nervous repugnance, I twice repeated, at a few days interval, the same experience. The story of what happened during my subsequent trials does not differ enough from the first experience for me to need to add to this already perhaps too long narrative. But the result of the two other evocations was the revelation of two Cabalistic secrets, which could, if they were known to the world, quickly transform the foundations and the laws of our entire society.

Should I conclude from all this that I actually evoked, saw, and touched the great Apollonius of Tyana? I am not enough of a crackpot to believe so, nor so irresponsible as to confirm it. The effect of the preparations, the perfumes, the mirrors, the pentacles was a veritable intoxication of the imagination, which must have acted strongly upon an already impressionable and nervous person. I cannot explain by what physiological laws I saw and touched; I only confirm that I saw and that I touched, that I saw clearly and distinctly, without dreaming, and that suffices in order to believe in the genuine efficacy of magical ceremonies. I also believe the practice to be dangerous and harmful; one's health, both moral and physical, would not withstand such exercises if they were to become habitual. The older lady of whom I spoke, and who has since caused me some trouble, is the proof of this: because, despite her denials, I have no doubt that she often makes use of goetia and necromancy. She at times completely lost her reason, at other times, she became senselessly angry without being able to explain why. I left London without seeing her again, and I will faithfully keep the promise I made to say nothing to anyone which might reveal her identity or even raise suspicions about her practices, which I am sure she conducts without the knowledge of her family, which is, or so I understand, relatively numerous and of a high social position.

There are evocations of intelligence, evocations of love, and evocations of hate; but nothing proves, once again, that the spirits actually leave the upper spheres to meet with us, and the contrary is more probable. We evoke the memories which they have left in the astral light, which is the common reservoir of universal magnetism. It is in this light that in the past the emperor Julian saw the Gods as old, sick, and decrepit: another proof of the influence of current and accepted opinion on the reflections of this same magical agent, which makes tables speak and gives answers by knocking on walls. After the evocation of which I just spoke about, I carefully reread the life of Apollonius, who historians have described as an ideal of old-world beauty and elegance. I remarked that Apollonius, towards the end of his life, was shaven and tortured for a long time in prison. Those circumstances, which I no doubt retained from a previous reading, without remembering it, may have contributed to the unattractive appearance of my vision, which I consider solely as a voluntary waking dream. I saw two other persons, whom there is no need to name, and both were different, by their costume and their aspect, from what I expected to see. I recommend, by the way, the greatest prudence to any who wish to attempt the same type of experiments:

there results from them great fatigue and often even distresses abnormal enough to cause sickness.

I shall not end this chapter without mentioning here the rather strange opinion of certain Cabalists who distinguish apparent death from true death, and who believe that they rarely coincide. According to them, most people who are buried are still alive, and many others who we believe to be alive are actually dead.

Incurable madness, for example, would be for them an incomplete death, but a real one, which leaves the terrestrial body under the purely instinctive control of the astral body. When the human soul suffers a violence which it cannot cope with, it then separates from its body, and leaves in its place the animal or astral soul, which makes of the human remains something which is less alive in a way than an animal. We recognize, they say, deaths of this type by the complete extinction of the affectionate and moral senses; they are not bad, they are not good: they are dead. These beings, who are the poisonous mushrooms of the human species, absorb as much life as they can from the living; that is why their approach numbs the soul and makes the heart cold.

These cadaverous beings, if they existed, would do all the things we once attributed to revenants and vampires.

Are there not beings beside whom we feel less intelligent, less good, sometimes even less honest?

Are there not beings whose approach extinguishes all belief and all enthusiasm, and who tie you to them through your weaknesses, dominate you through your bad tendencies, and who slowly kill your morals, in a torment similar to that of Mezentius?[209]

They are the dead, who we take to be living; they are vampires, whom we take to be friends!

---

209   A tyrant of classical legend, who punished his subjects by shackling them to corpses.

14 ⅃ O.

TRANSMUTATIONS

Art

SPHERA LUNAE.

SEMPITERNUM.

AUXILIUM.[210]

Saint Augustine seriously doubted that Apuleius could have been changed into an ass by a witch from Thessaly.[211] The theologians argued at length regarding the transmutation of Nebuchadnezzar into a wild animal.[212] This simply proves that the eloquent doctor of Hippo was unaware of the magical arcanum, and that the theologians in question were not very advanced in exegesis. We will examine, in this chapter, marvels which are even more incredible yet incontestable. I wish to speak of lycanthropy, or the nocturnal transformation of men into wolves, well known around campfires in our countryside, due to all the stories told about werewolves: stories so well documented, that, in order to explain them, incred-

---

210 *Sphera lunae* is Latin for "sphere of the moon," *sempiternum* Latin for "forever," and *auxilium* Latin for "help."

211 This transformation is the main plot engine of Apuleius's novel *The Golden Ass*. Augustine was from the African town of Hippo, thus Lévi's comment later in the paragraph.

212 Daniel 4:29–33.

ulous science has had to resort to claims of mass delusions and hoaxes. But such hypotheses are puerile and explain nothing. Let us look elsewhere for the secret to the observed phenomena regarding this subject and note to start with:

1. That no one has ever been killed by a werewolf, except through suffocation, with no blood being spilt and no wounds.
2. That werewolves who were hunted down, chased, even wounded, were never killed on the spot.
3. That persons suspected of these transformations were always found in their homes after the hunt for a werewolf, sometimes about to die but always in their natural form.

Now let us observe certain phenomena of another order.

Nothing is more attested to and incontestably proven than the visible and real presence of Father Alphonsus de Liguori besides the dying Pope, while at the same time he was observed at home, at a great distance from Rome, in prayer and ecstasy.

The simultaneous presence of the missionary Francis Xavier in several places at once has also been just as rigorously observed.[213]

One might say that they are miracles; I would answer that miracles, when they are real, are simply phenomena to be studied by science.

The apparition of persons who are dear to us coinciding with the moment of their death are phenomena of the same order and attributable to the same cause.

We have spoken about the astral body, which is the intermediary between the soul and the physical body. This body often remains aware while the physical body sleeps, and travels by thought within all the space open to it through universal magnetism. It thus stretches the sympathetic chain which keeps it attached to our hearts and brains without breaking it, and this is what makes awakening with a start so dangerous to people who are dreaming. In fact, an overly loud noise can abruptly break the chain, causing sudden death.

---

213   Both of these events were investigated extensively by the Catholic Church during the process by which Liguori and Xavier were declared saints.

The form which our astral body takes on conforms to the habitual state of our thoughts, and it modifies, over time, the traits of the material body. It is for this reason that Swedenborg, during his hypnotic visions, often saw spirits in the form of diverse animals.

We now dare to say that a werewolf is nothing but the astral body of a man, to whom the wolf represents wild and bloodthirsty instincts, and who, while his ghost wanders about in the countryside, is sleeping restlessly in his bed while dreaming that he is an actual wolf.

What renders the werewolf visible is the almost hypnotic overexcitement caused by the fright of the people who see him, or the disposition, more common among simple people in the countryside, to communicate directly with the astral light, which is the common milieu of visions and dreams. The attacks on the werewolf cause actual harm to the sleeping person through odic[214] and sympathetic congestion of the astral light, through the correspondence between the immaterial body and the material body. A great number of people might think they are dreaming when reading about such things and might ask us if we are in possession of our senses, but we ask that the men of science simply reflect upon the phenomena surrounding pregnancy and the influence of a woman's imagination upon the form of their offspring. A woman who has witnessed the suffering of a man who was severely beaten will give birth to a child whose limbs have all been broken.[215] Please explain how the impression made upon the soul of the mother by a horrible spectacle can harm and break the limbs of her infant, and we shall explain how attacks made and received in dreams can actually break and even seriously wound the body who receives them in the imagination, especially when their body is suffering and under nervous and magnetic influences.

It is these phenomena and the occult laws which produce them that are related to the effects of enchantments, which we shall speak of later. Diabolic obsessions, and most nervous sicknesses that affect the brain, are wounds caused to

---

214 As already noted, "Od" and "Odyle" were terms used by Baron Karl von Reichenbach for the phenomenon that Lévi calls the astral light.

215 This was considered a fact by medical authorities in Lévi's time.

the nervous system due to a perverted astral light, that is to say one that is absorbed or projected in abnormal proportions. All extraordinary and extranatural tensions of the will dispose one to obsessions and nervous sicknesses; forced celibacy, asceticism, hatred, ambition, unrequited love, are all the principal generators of infernal forms and influences. Paracelsus says that the menstrual blood of women engenders phantoms in the air; a convent, from this point of view, would be a seminary of nightmares, and we could compare it to those demons with heads like the Lernaean hydra,[216] which were reborn without end and multiplied through the blood from their wounds.

The phenomena related to the possession of the Ursulines of Loudun, so fatal to Urbain Grandier, were misunderstood. The nuns were actually possessed due to hysteria and a fanatical imitation of the secret thoughts of their exorcists, transmitted to their nervous system via the astral light. They received the impressions of all the hatred that this unfortunate priest had inspired, and this entirely internal communication appeared to them as diabolical and miraculous. Thus in this unfortunate affair everyone was of good faith, even Laubardement,[217] who, in blindly executing the biased sentences of Cardinal Richelieu, believed that he was fulfilling the duties of a true judge and did not at all suspect himself of being a servant to Pontius Pilate, such that it was impossible for him to see the priest of Saint-Pierre-du-Marché, who was a strong and free-thinking spirit, as a disciple of Christ and a martyr.

The possession of the nuns of Louviers is barely more than a copy of that of Loudun: demons are not very inventive and often plagiarize each other. The trial of Gaufridi and of Madeleine de la Palud are of a much stranger aspect. Here the victims accuse themselves. Gaufridi admits to being guilty of removing from several women, by a simple breath up their nostrils, their freedom to defend themselves against seduction. One young and beautiful girl, of noble family, breathed upon by him, recounts, in the greatest of details, scenes of the most monstrous and grotesque lechery. Such are the ordinary hallucinations of false

---

216 In Greek legend, a monster killed by Hercules; it had nine heads, and as soon as one was cut off, two more sprouted from the stump.

217 The prosecutor in the trial of Urbain Grandier.

mysticism and poorly preserved celibacy. Gaufridi and his mistress were obsessed by their reciprocal chimeras, and in the head of one were reflected the nightmares of the other. Did not the Marquis de Sade himself attract certain sick and retarded characters?

The scandalous trial of Father Girard is recent proof of the delirium of mysticism and the singular neuralgia which can follow in its wake. The convulsions of Cadière, her ecstasies, her stigmata—all of it was as real as the mad debauchery which was perhaps involuntary on the part of her director. She accused him once he wished to take leave of her, and the conversion of this girl was a form of vengeance, because nothing is more cruel than depraved love. The powerful person[218] who had intervened in Grandier's trial in order to defeat a possible sectarian, saved Father Girard in the name of the honor of the Jesuits. Grandier and Girard both arrived at the same results by very different paths, of which we will be especially concerned with in the sixteenth chapter.

We act through our imagination upon the imagination of others, through our astral body upon theirs, and through our organs upon their organs. In this way, through the sympathy either of attraction or of obsession, we possess one another, and we identify with those upon whom we wish to act. It is the reaction against this control that produces in the most ardent sympathies a subsequently even more pronounced antipathy. Love has a tendency to identify beings; yet, in identifying them, it often renders them rivals, and in consequence enemies, if the basic disposition of two characters is unsociable, as would be, for example, pride; to equally saturate two united souls with pride is to divide them by rendering them rivals. Antagonism is the necessary result of the plurality of the gods.

When we dream about a living person, it is their astral body which presents itself to ours in the astral light, or at least the reflection of that same body, and the manner in which we are affected by our encounter with it often reveals hidden dispositions that this person holds with regard to us. Love, for example, creates the astral body of one in the image and resemblance of the other, such that

---

218   Cardinal Richelieu.

woman's animus[219] is like a man and man's anima is like a woman. It is this exchange that the Cabalists wished to express in an occult manner when they said, in explaining an obscure term in Genesis: "God created love by placing one of Adam's ribs in the breast of Eve and some of Eve's flesh in the breast of Adam, such that at the bottom of the heart of woman is a man's bone and at the bottom of the heart of man is the flesh of woman," an allegory that is certainly not without profundity and beauty.

In the preceding chapter we mentioned a concept that the masters of the Cabala called the embryonate of souls. This embryonate, which is completed after the death of the person who has possessed someone else, is often started while that person is still living, either through obsession or through love. I knew a young woman whose parents inspired great fear in her, and who out of the blue perpetrated the acts upon an inoffensive person that she had feared her parents would do to her. I knew another who, after having taken part in the evocation of a guilty woman tormented in the other world for eccentric acts, began to imitate without reason the acts of the dead woman. It is to this occult power that one must attribute the redoubtable influence of the curse of one's parents, redoubtable to all the peoples of the Earth, and the real danger of magical operations when one has not managed to isolate oneself as the true adepts do.

This aspect of astral transmutation, which really exists in love, explains the allegorical miracles of the wand of Circe. Apuleius speaks of a Thessalonian who could transform into a bird; he got the servant of this woman to fall in love with him so he could learn the secrets of her mistress, and only managed to get transformed into an ass.[220] The allegory explains the most hidden secrets of love. The Cabalists still say that when we love an elementary woman, whether she be an undine or a sylph or a gnomide,[221] we immortalize her within us or we die with

---

219 Lévi writes "le medium animique de la femme," which is impossible to render exactly into English, as *âme* and *animique* share none of the same connotations of their closest English cognates, "soul" and (far worse) "soulful." As Lévi's argument is essentially the same as Jung's—and may well have inspired Jung—using the psychologist's coinage here seems reasonable.

220 Another reference to *The Golden Ass*.

221 A female gnome.

her. We have seen that elementary beings are imperfect and still mortal humans. The revelation of which we speak, and which we saw as a myth, is thus the doctrine of moral solidarity in love, which is the basis of love itself and is the only explanation for all holiness and all power.

Who, then, is this female magician who changes her adorers into swine and whose enchantments are destroyed the moment she falls in love? It is the courtesan of old, the girl of marble of all the eras. The loveless woman absorbs and debases all that approaches her; the woman who loves spreads enthusiasm, greatness, and life.

We have spoken a great deal of an adept of the last century who was accused of charlatanism, and who in his lifetime was named the divine Cagliostro. We know that he conducted evocations and that he was surpassed in his art only by the visionary Schröpfer.[222] We know that he boasted of binding sympathies, and that he said that he knew the secret of the Great Work; but what made him even more famous was a certain elixir of life which instantly gave vigor and the sap of youth to old men. This mixture had for its base Malvasian wine, and was obtained by the distillation of the sperm of certain animals with the juice of several plants. We have the recipe, and I am sure you understand why I must keep it a secret.

---

222 See, in "The *Ritual*," the secrets and forms of Schröpfer for the evocations. (Lévi's note.)

15 ס P.

BLACK MAGIC

SAMAEL.

AUXILIATOR.[223]

W e shall now enter into the subject of black magic. We shall face, within its veritable sanctuary, the black god of the Sabbath, the formidable goat of Mendes. Here, those who are fearful should close this book, and persons subject to nervous reactions would do well to distract themselves or abstain; but we have imposed a task upon ourselves, and we shall finish it.

Let us begin by dealing with the subject in a frank and bold manner:

Does the devil exist?

What is the devil?

Regarding the first question, science is silent; philosophy denies his existence indiscriminately, and only religion responds in the affirmative.

Regarding the second question, religion claims that the devil is a fallen angel; occult philosophy accepts this and explains this definition.

We shall not repeat what we have already said, but we shall add here a new revelation:

---

223   Samael is a Hebrew name of the devil; *auxiliator* is Latin for "helper."

THE DEVIL, IN BLACK MAGIC, IS THE GREAT MAGICAL AGENT
USED FOR PURPOSES OF EVIL BY A PERVERSE WILL.

The ancient serpent of legend is nothing other than the universal agent, it is
the eternal fire of terrestrial life; it is the soul of the Earth and the living hearth
of hell.

We have said that the astral light is the receptacle of forms. Evoked through
reason, these forms are produced in harmony; evoked through madness, they
turn up disordered and monstrous: such is the cradle of nightmares of Saint Anthony and the phantoms of the Sabbath.

Do the evocations of goetia and demonomania give results? Yes, most certainly, incontestable results which are more terrible than those recounted in
legends!

When we call upon the devil with the required ceremonies, the devil comes
and we see him.

In order not to die, struck down by this vision, in order not to become cata-
leptic or insane, one must already be crazy.

Grandier was a libertine through impiety, and perhaps also through skep-
ticism; Girard was corrupt and a corrupter through enthusiasm, due to his ascetic
turmoils and the blindness of his faith.

We shall provide, in the fifteenth chapter of our Ritual, all the diabolical evocations and practices of black magic, not so as to make use of them, but so that we
know them, judge them, and so that we can protect ourselves forevermore from
such aberrations.

M. Eudes de Mirville,[224] whose books on table turning recently created a
buzz, will be both happy and unhappy with the solution we provide here regarding the question of black magic. Indeed, we accept, as he does, the reality and
magnificence of the effects, we also assign to them the same cause as he does; the
ancient serpent, the prince of the occult of this world; but we are not in agreement
as to the nature of this blind agent, which is at the same time, but under different
managers, the instrument of all good and of all evil, the servant of the prophets

---

224   Jules Eudes de Mirville, a popular Catholic author of Lévi's time, who attacked
        Spiritualism in several books.

and the inspirer of the pythonesses.[225] In a word, the devil, for us, is the power used for a period of time in the service of error, just as mortal sin is, in our eyes, the persistence of the will in absurdity. M. de Mirville is thus right a thousand times, but he is wrong, very wrong, in a single instance.

What one must exclude from the kingdom of beings is the arbitrary. Nothing occurs either by accident or by the autocracy of a good or bad will. There are two chambers in heaven, and the deviations of Satan's tribunal are restrained by the senate of divine wisdom.

225　An old word for female oracles.

16 ‫ע‬ Q.

ENCHANTMENTS

FONS.

OCULUS.

FULGUR.[226]

A man who looks upon woman with impure desire profanes that woman, said the great Master.[227] What we wish for with dedication, we actually do. All true will is confirmed by acts; all will confirmed by an act is an action. All action is subject to judgment, and that judgment is eternal. These are the doctrines and principles.

According to these principles and these doctrines, the good or evil that you wish, either upon yourself or upon others, to the extent of your will and within the sphere of your action, will infallibly occur, either to others or to yourself, if you confirm your will and settle upon your determination through acts.

The acts must be analogous to the will. The will to harm or to be loved must be confirmed, to be efficacious, by acts of hate or love.

All that which carries the imprint of a human soul belongs to that soul; all

---

226 *Fons* is Latin for "fountain," *oculus* for "eye," and *fulgur* for "thunderbolt."
227 Matthew 5:28.

that which a man appropriates in any manner becomes his body, in the largest sense of the word, and that which is done to the body of a man is felt, either indirectly or directly, through his soul.

It is for this reason that every type of hostile action towards another is regarded by moral theology as the beginning of a homicide.

Enchantment[228] is homicide, and it is a homicide that is all the more cowardly since it eludes the right to defense of the victim and the vengeance of the law.

This principle being established, to the satisfaction of our conscience and in order to warn off the weak, we affirm fearlessly that enchantment is possible.

Let us go further and affirm that not only is it possible, but in a certain way necessary and inevitable. It occurs ceaselessly in the social world, unbeknownst to both those who perform it and those who suffer from it. Involuntary enchantment is one of the most terrible dangers of human life.

The sympathy of the passions necessarily submits the most ardent desire to the strongest will. Moral sicknesses are more contagious than physical ones, and there are fads and fashions whose success is comparable to leprosy or cholera.

We can die from a bad acquaintance as if it were a contagious contact, and the horrible malady that, during the last few centuries, in Europe, has punished the profanation of the mysteries of love,[229] is a revelation of the analogical laws of nature, and represents only a weakened image of the moral corruption which results every day from dubious sympathies.

Rumor speaks of a jealous and cowardly man who, to avenge himself upon a rival, voluntarily infected himself with an incurable illness, and makes of it a mutual bane and the anathema of a shared bed. This horrible story is that of every magician, or rather every sorcerer who practices enchantment. He poisons himself in order to poison; he damns himself in order to torture; he inhales hell to exhale it; he injures himself until death in order to kill; but if he has the unfortunate courage, it is definite and certain that he will poison and kill through the projection of his perverse will alone.

---

228 The word translated as "enchantment" here, *envoûtement*, has no exact English equivalent; it usually implies hostile magic, such as an attempt to kill by magic.

229 That is, syphilis, which was unknown in Europe until the beginning of the sixteenth century.

There exists loves which kill as easily as hate, and the enchantments of benevolence are a torture for the wicked. Prayers which we address to God in the hopes of converting a man bring misfortune upon him if he does not wish to be converted. It is, as we have already mentioned, tiring and dangerous to fight against the fluidic currents excited by chains of united wills.

There are thus two types of enchantments: involuntary enchantment and voluntary enchantment. We can also distinguish between physical enchantment and moral enchantment.

Strength attracts strength, life attracts life, good health attracts good health: it is a law of nature.

If two children live together, and especially if they sleep together, and if one is weak and one is strong, the strong one will absorb the weak one, and the weak one will waste away. That is why it is important that children always sleep separately.

In boarding schools, certain students absorb the intelligence of other students, and in any circle of men one always finds one individual who takes hold of the wills of the others.

Enchantment through currents is very common, as we have remarked previously: we are carried away by the masses, in both moral and physical senses. But what we wish to note in particular in this chapter is the almost absolute power of the human will in the determination of its acts and the influence of all exterior demonstrations of will even upon exterior things.

Voluntary enchantments are still common in the countryside, because the natural forces, among ignorant and solitary people, act without being weakened by any doubts or diversions. A frank hatred, absolute and without any mix of unrequited passions or personal cupidity, is the kiss of death for he who is their object in certain given conditions. I say without any mix of amorous passion or cupidity, because a desire, being an attraction, counterbalances and annuls the power of the projection. Thus, for example, someone who is jealous will never efficaciously enchant his rival, and an eager heir will not decrease by his will alone the number of days left to a miserly and hardy uncle. Enchantments which are attempted under these conditions fall back upon those who perform them and are more salutary than noxious to the person who is their object, because he is freed from their hateful action, which destroys itself by too much enthusiasm.

The French word *envoûtement*, so very energetic in its Gallic simplicity, admirably expresses the thing which it signifies: *envoultement*, which is the action of taking, in a manner of speaking, and enveloping someone in a vow, in a formulated wish.

The instrument of enchantments is none other than the great magical agent itself, which, under the influence of a malicious will, truly and positively becomes demonic.

Properly speaking, evil spells, that is to say a ceremonial performance with the object of enchantment, act only upon the performer, and serve to fix and confirm his will by formulating it with perseverance and effort, the two conditions which render the will efficacious.

The more that the performance is difficult or horrible, the more effective it is, because it acts more fully upon the imagination and attests to the effort required, which is in direct relationship to the sense of resistance to it.

This is what explains the strangeness and even atrocity of magical performances during antiquity and the Middle Ages: the satanic masses, the sacraments administered to reptiles, the spilling of blood, the human sacrifices, and other monstrosities which are the essence of the reality of goetia or necromancy. It is such practices which have attracted onto sorcerers the just repression of the law throughout the ages. Black magic is in fact simply a combination of sacrilege and progressive murder whose goal is to forever pervert the human will and to produce in a man the hideous phantom of the devil. It is thus, properly speaking, the religion of the devil, the cult of shadows, the hatred of the good brought to its climax; it is the incarnation of death and the permanent creation of hell.

The Cabalist Bodin, who was falsely suspected of being weak minded and superstitious, had no other motive in writing his *Demonomania* than the need to guard minds against an overly dangerous incredulity. Initiated through the study of the Cabala and the true secrets of magic, he trembled at the thought of the dangers to which society would be exposed by way of this power if it were left in the hands of the wickedness of men. He thus attempted that which M. Eudes de Mirville, who is still among us, has also just done: he gathered the facts without explaining them, and denounced to the sciences, inattentive or elsewhere preoccupied, the existence of occult influences in the criminal performance of bad magic. Bodin was ignored in his time and so will M. Eudes de Mirville be, because it is not enough to indicate phenomenon while presupposing the cause in order to impress serious people; that cause must be studied, explained, and proven to exist, and that is our task here. Will we be more successful?

One can die from being loved by certain beings just as much as from their hatred: there are absorbing passions under whose influence we feel weakened like the victims of vampires. It is not only the wicked who torment the good, but without knowing it the good torture the wicked. Abel's kindness was a long and painful enchantment for the ferocity of Cain.[230] The hatred of the good among wicked men derives from the instinct for survival itself; incidentally, they deny that what torments them is the good, and endeavor, for their peace of mind, to deify and justify evil. Abel, in the eyes of Cain, was a hypocrite and a coward who dishonored human dignity through his scandalous submissiveness to the divinity. How much must this first murderer have suffered before coming to that terrible assault upon his brother? If Abel had been able to understand him, he would have been terrified.

Antipathy is nothing other than the presentiment of a possible enchantment, an enchantment which could be of love or of hatred, because we often see love following after antipathy. The astral light warns us of influences to come by acting upon a more or less sensitive, and more or less aware, nervous system. The instantaneous sympathies of sudden love are explosions of astral light set in motion just as exactly, and no less mathematically explainable and demonstrable, as strong electrical discharges from batteries. We can see from this how many unforeseen dangers menace the profane who play unceasingly with fire near the gunpowder they do not see.

We are saturated with astral light, and we project it unceasingly to make room for more and to attract more. The nervous apparatus destined either for attraction or for projection are in particular the eyes and the hands. The polarity of the hands resides in the thumb, and it is for this reason, according to the magical

---

230   Genesis 4:3–8.

tradition still kept in our countryside, that one must, when one finds oneself in suspect company, hold one's thumb folded and hidden behind the hand, while refusing to stare at anyone but trying to be the first to look upon those from whom we have something to fear, so as to avoid fluidic projections and mesmerizing looks.

There also exist certain animals whose property is to break the currents of the astral light through an ability for absorption which is particular to them. These animals are violently antipathetic to us and have a look in their eyes which is mesmerizing, such as the toad, the basilisk, and the tard.[231] These animals, if tamed and carried or kept alive in the rooms where we live, guarantee hallucinations and the illusions of astral intoxication: ASTRAL INTOXICATION, a word which we write here for the first time, and which explains all the phenomena related to wild passions, mental elation, and madness.

Go and raise toads and tards, my dear sir, a disciple of Voltaire would tell me here; carry them around with you and write no more. To which I would respond that I would consider that most seriously when I felt disposed to laugh at that which I know nothing of, and to treat as mad those men whose science and wisdom I do not understand.

Paracelsus, the greatest of Christian mages, countered enchantments by performing contrary ones. He made up sympathetic remedies and applied them, not to the suffering limbs, but to the representations of those same limbs, formed and consecrated according to ceremonial magic. His success was phenomenal, and never has any doctor gotten close to achieving the same success as the marvelous cures of Paracelsus.

But Paracelsus had discovered magnetism well before Mesmer and had pushed to its limits this marvelous discovery, or rather this initiation into the magic of the ancients, who understood, more than us, the great magical agent, and who did not

---

231   The word *tard*, referring to an animal, appears in no French dictionary available to us, and the identity of this creature is therefore a pretty problem. It is perhaps most likely an obsolete word for "frog," as "tadpole," *têtard*, is probably a shortened form of *tête tard*, "frog head," or possibly *petit tard*, "little frog." Less likely but still possible is local dialect for the thrush or common blackbird, whose genus is *Turdus*.

think of the astral light, of azoth, of the universal magnesia of the sages, as a particular and animal fluid solely emanating from a few special beings.[232]

In his occult philosophy, Paracelsus opposes ceremonial magic, whose terrible power he was certainly aware of but whose practices he wished to disparage, so as to discredit black magic. He places the omnipotence of the mage in the internal and occult *Magnes*. The most skillful magnetizers of our day could say no better. However, Paracelsus wants us to use the magical symbols, and more importantly the talismans, in order to cure maladies. We will have cause to come back to the subject regarding Paracelsus's talismans in our eighteenth chapter, when touching upon, according to Gaffarel, the great question of occult iconography and numismatics.[233]

We can also cure an enchantment by substitution, when that is possible, and through the rupture or the diversion of the astral current. The customs in the countryside are most admirable and most certainly come from afar: they are the remains of the teachings of the Druids, who had been initiated into the mysteries of Egypt and India by wandering hierophants. We know then, in popular magic, that an enchantment, which is to say a determined and confirmed will to do evil, always obtains its desired effect, and that it cannot be recanted without risk of death. The sorcerer who delivers someone from a charm must have another object for his malice, or it is certain that he himself will be struck and then die, a victim to his own evil spells. The astral movement being circular, all azotic or magnetic emissions which do not encounter their *medium* return powerfully to their point of departure: which explains one of the strangest stories from any sacred book, the tale of demons sent into pigs, who then ran into the sea.[234] This work of high initiation was nothing other than the rupture of an infected magnetic current by evil willpowers. "I am legion," said the instinctive voice of the patient, "for we are many."[235]

---

232 This latter opinion was held by some of Mesmer's followers, though not by Mesmer himself.

233 Numismatics is the study of coins and coin-like objects, including—as Lévi means to suggest here—talismans.

234 Matthew 8: 28–34.

235 Mark 5:9.

Demonic possessions are nothing other than enchantments, and there exist in our time innumerable quantities of the possessed. A saintly religious man who devotes himself to the service of the insane, Brother Hilarion Tissot[236] has managed, through long experience and the constant practice of the Christian virtues, to cure many patients, and without knowing it he practices the magnetism of Paracelsus. He attributes most of these maladies to disorders of the will or the perverse influence of foreign wills; he sees all crime as acts of folly and would like us to treat the wicked as patients, rather than exciting them and rendering them even more incurable under the pretext of punishing them. How much time will pass before the poor Brother Hilarion is recognized as a man of genius! and how many serious men in reading this chapter, will still say that Hilarion Tissot and I should treat each other according to the ideas which are common to us, by not publishing our theories if we do not wish to be taken for doctors who should be sent to the asylum!

And yet it turns! So cried Galileo, while stamping his foot on the earth.[237] You shall recognize the truth, and the truth shall set you free, says the Savior of men. We might add: You will love justice, and justice will render you healthy. A vice is a poison, even for the body: true virtue is a guarantee of longevity.

The methods of *ceremonial enchantment* vary depending on the times and the people, and all men of artifice and domination find within themselves its secrets and practices, without even calculating precisely or reasoning their order. They follow the instinctive inspirations of the great agent, which assimilate marvelously, as we have already said, into our vices and virtues; but we can say that, in general, we are under the power of the wills of others through the analogy of our desires and most of all through our vices. To coddle the weaknesses of an individual is to seize hold of him and make of him an instrument corresponding in kind to the same errors or the same depravities. Yet when two analogical natures

---

236 French priest and physician Joseph-Xavier Tissot (1780–1864), whose name in religion was Brother Hilarion. He founded several treatment centers for mental illness in early nineteenth-century France.

237 According to a common legend, when Galileo was forced by the Catholic Church to renounce his belief in the Copernican system, he muttered under his breath, "Eppur si muove" (And yet it moves).

in error subordinate themselves to one another, there is created a sort of substitution of the weakest by the strongest, and a veritable obsession with one mind by the other. Often the weaker one struggles and wishes to rebel but then falls lower than ever into servitude. It was in this way that Louis XIII conspired against Richelieu and then obtained grace of a sort by abandoning his accomplices.[238]

We all have a ruling vice which is, for our soul, like the umbilical cord of its birth into sin, and it is through it that the enemy can always grab hold of us: it is vanity for some, laziness for others, egoism for a great many. If a cunning and wicked mind makes use of this resource, then you are lost. You then become, not mad, not idiotic, but positively alienated, using the full meaning of this expression, that is to say subject to a foreign impulse. In this state, you feel instinctive horror for anything that would bring you back to reason, and you do not even want to hear representations which are contrary to your lunacy. It is is one of the most dangerous sicknesses which can affect human morale.

The only remedy to this enchantment is to seize upon madness in order to cure madness, and to force the patient to find imaginary satisfactions in the contrary order to the ones to which he lost himself. Thus one can, for example, cure a power-hungry person by having him desire the glories of heaven; cure a depraved person through true love, a natural remedy; provide honorable success to a vain person; show selflessness to an avaricious person and provide them with a just profit through the participation in a generous endeavor, and so on.

By acting in this manner upon morals, we can cure a great number of physical maladies, because morals influence the physical by virtue of the magical axiom: "That which is above is like that which is below." It is for this reason that the Master said, in speaking of a paralytic woman: Satan has bound her.[239] Sickness often comes from a vice or an abuse, and you will always find at the source of a physical illness a moral disorder: it is an invariable law of nature.

---

238 Cardinal Richelieu was Louis XIII's chief minister; the king hated him but was unable to govern without him. On several occasions, conspiracies of courtiers against Richelieu that might have succeeded given royal support were defeated when the king abruptly turned his back on the conspirators.

239 Luke 13:16.

17 פ R.

ASTROLOGY

STELLA.

OS.

INFLEXUS.[240]

Of all the arts arising from ancient Zoroastrianism, astrology is now the most misunderstood. We no longer believe in the universal harmony of nature and the necessary links between all effects and all causes. True astrology, incidentally, the kind which is related to the universal doctrine and the Cabala, was profaned by the Greeks and the Romans in their decadence; the doctrine of the seven heavens and the three mobiles,[241] the primordial emanations of the ten spheres, the characters of the planets governed by the angels whose names were changed from the divinities of paganism, the influence of the spheres upon each other, the destinies attributed to the numbers, the proportional scale between the celestial hierarchies that correspond to human hierarchies, all this was materialized and

---

240   *Stella* is Latin for "star," *os* Latin for "mouth," and *inflexus* Latin for "bent."

241   These are basic elements of the old Earth-centered cosmologies. The seven heavens are the realms of the seven planets known to the ancients; the three mobiles, or sources of motion, are the three spheres thought to lie beyond the realm of the planets, which accounted for the motion of the stars as observed from Earth.

rendered into superstition by the decadent readers and interpreters of natal horo-scopes in the Middle Ages. To bring astrology back to its primitive purity, in a sense, requires the creation of an entirely new science; let us simply attempt to in-dicate the main principles, along with their most immediate and imminent con-sequences.

We have said that the astral light receives and conserves all the imprints of visible matter; the result of which is that the daily disposition of the stars is re-flected in this light. This, being the principal agent of life, affects conception, the embryo, and the birth of infants through a series of devices destined to that end by nature. What is more, if this light is sensitive enough to the images it receives to affect a pregnancy with the visible imprints of the fantasies or delights of the mother, there is even stronger reason to believe that it transmits to the mobile and still uncertain infant atmospheric impressions and the diverse influences of a particular moment, from the entire planetary system and from one or another more particular disposition of the stars.

Nothing is indifferent in nature; a stone more or less on the road could break or profoundly modify the destinies of the greatest men or the greatest empires; there is even stronger reason to believe the position of one star or another in the sky would not be indifferent to the destiny of the child who is being born, and who by his birth enters into the same universal harmony as the astral world. The stars are linked to one another by attractions which keep them in equilibrium and regularly cause them to move in space; these networks of light travel from all the spheres to all the spheres, and there is no single point on any planet which is not connected to these indestructible threads. The precise place and time of birth must therefore be calculated by a true adept in astrology; then, when he has made the exact calculation of the astral influences, he must count the prob-abilities of state, that is to say the facilities or obstacles that the child will find one day in his condition, in his parents, in the temperament he received from them, and, in consequence, in his natural tendencies, for the accomplishment of his destiny. Beyond this, the astrologer must take into account human liberty and initiative, if the child manages one day to become a true man and extract himself with courageous will from fatal influences and the chain of destinies. You can now see that we do not give *too* much weight to astrology but also that what we leave to it is incontestable: it is the scientific and magical calculation of the probabilities.

Astrology is as old as, or even older than, astronomy, and all the visionary sages of antiquity gave it their entire confidence; thus one must not carelessly condemn and reject that which comes to us surrounded and supported by such imposing authorities.

Many long and patient observations, conclusive comparisons, and often-repeated experiments must have brought the ancient sages to their conclusions, and one must, if one pretends to refute them, begin the same work all over again in the contrary direction. Paracelsus was perhaps the last of the great practical as-trologers; he cured the sick with talismans created under the influence of the stars and recognized in all bodies the mark of their dominant star, and it was this, ac-cording to him, which was true universal medicine; the absolute science of nature, lost due to the errors of man and rediscovered only by a small number of initiates. To recognize the sign of each star in men, in animals, and in plants is the true natural science of Solomon, that science which is said to be lost but whose principles are, however, kept, like all other secrets, in the symbolism of the Ca-bala.[242] We understand that to read the writing of the stars one must know the stars themselves, know what is obtained by the Cabalistic domification[243] of the sky, and by the intelligence of the Cabalistic planisphere, as rediscovered and ex-plained by Gaffarel.[244] In this planisphere, the constellations form Hebrew letters and the mythological figures can be replaced by the symbols of the Tarot. It is to this very planisphere that Gaffarel attributes the origin of the writings of the pa-triarchs, and they had found in the chains of attractions between the stars the first outlines of the primordial characters;[245] the book of the heavens thus served as a

---

242 This is also known as the doctrine of signatures, the belief that the magical and medicinal powers of every natural thing can be known from its outwards form.

243 "Domification" means to divide into houses or, as modern astrologers would say, signs and constellations.

244 In his book *Curiositez inouyes* (*Unheard-of Curiosities*), published in 1629, Jacques Gaffarel included a chart that identified the Hebrew letters with constellations. A planisphere is a map of the heavenly sphere laid out on a flat surface, such as a sheet of paper.

245 The Hebrew alphabet.

model for Enoch, and the Cabalistic alphabet was a summary of the entire sky. The above does not lack in either poetry or more important in probability, and the study of the Tarot, which is evidently the primordial and hieroglyphic book of Enoch, as had been understood by Guillaume Postel, suffices to convince us.

The signs imprinted in the astral light by the reflection and the attraction of the stars is reproduced, then, as was discovered by the sages, in all bodies which are formed with the participation of this light. Men carry the signs of their star on their foreheads and most of all on their hands; animals, in their entire form and in their particular signs; plants reveal them in their leaves and their seeds; minerals, in their veins and in their level of friability. The study of these characteristics was the work of an entire life for Paracelsus, and his figures and talismans are the results of his research; but he did not provide the key, and the Cabalistic astral alphabet, with its correspondences, is incomplete; the science of unconventional magical writing was arrested, within the public domain, at Gaffarel's planisphere.

The serious art of divination rests entirely upon the knowledge of these signs. Chiromancy[246] is the art of reading the writing of the stars in the lines of the hand, and metoposcopy[247] looks for the same characters or their analogues on the foreheads of those who consult it. In effect, the lines formed on the human face due to nervous contractions are determined by destiny, and the influence of the nervous tissue is absolutely analogous to the networks formed between worlds and the chains of attractions between the stars. The destinies of life are thus necessarily written in our lines, and we often recognize at first glance, on the forehead of a stranger, one or more mysterious letters from the Cabalistic planisphere. This letter represents a thought system, and those thoughts must dominate the existence of this man. If the mark is troubled and has difficulty outlining itself, there is a battle in him between his destiny and his will, and in his emotions and strongest tendencies his entire past is revealed to the mage; the future is then easy to estimate, and if at times events mislead the wisdom of the diviner, the pa-

---

246 Commonly known today as palmistry.

247 All but forgotten today, metoposcopy was the art of reading fortunes in faces, as chiromancy, or palmistry, is the art of reading hands.

tient nonetheless remains impressed and convinced by the superhuman science of the adept.

The head of man is based on the model of the celestial spheres; it attracts and emits, and it is the head which, when a child is conceived, is formed and manifests itself first. It is thus affected in an absolute manner by the astral influences, and its numerous protuberances are witness to the diverse attractions. Phrenology,[248] a science whose problems test the patience and faith of scholars, must thus find its final solution in a purified and scientific astrology.

According to Ptolemy, the Sun dries and the Moon humidifies; according to the Cabalists, the Sun represents strict Justice, and the Moon is sympathetic Mercy. It is the Sun which creates storms; it is the Moon which, through a sort of soft atmospheric pressure, like breathing, raises and lowers the sea. We read in the Zohar, one of the great sacred books of the Cabala, that "the magical Serpent, son of the Sun, will devour the world, when the Sea, daughter of the Moon, puts her foot down on its head and subjugates it." It is for this reason that, among the ancients, Venus was daughter of the Sea, just as Diana was identified with the Moon; it is for this reason that the name Mary signifies star of the sea or salt of the sea.[249] It was to consecrate this Cabalistic doctrine within the beliefs of the vulgar that it was said in prophetic language: It is woman who must crush the head of the serpent.[250]

Girolamo Cardano, one of the boldest of seekers and undeniably the most skilled astrologer of his time; Girolamo Cardano, who was, if we believe the legend surrounding his death, a martyr to his faith in astrology, left us a calculus with which each of us can predict the good or bad fortune for all the years of our life. His theory rests upon his own experiments, and he claims that his calculations have never been wrong. To know what one's fortune will be in a particular year, one summarizes the events of those that preceded it by four, eight, twelve,

---

248 Phrenology is a system of reading the mental characteristics of a person in the shape of his or her skull. In Lévi's time it was considered a valid science, even by the most skeptical scientists.

249 This is a traditional Catholic etymology for the name of Mary but does not seem to be correct. Current authorities argue about the original source of the name.

250 A reference to Genesis 3:15.

nineteen, and thirty years. The number four is fulfillment; the number eight, that of Venus or natural things; the number twelve, which is that of the cycle of Jupiter, corresponds to success; the number nineteen corresponds to the cycles of the Moon and of Mars; the number thirty is that of Saturn or Fate. Thus, for example, if I wish to know what will happen to me in this year, 1855, I will go over in my memory what real and decisive things have happened to me regarding the progress of life four years ago, what I experienced of happiness or natural unhappiness eight years ago, what I had in terms of successes and failures twelve years ago, the vicissitudes and misfortunes that occurred to me nineteen years ago, and what happened to me which was sad or fated thirty years ago; then, taking into consideration those facts that are irrevocably accomplished and the progress of age, I rely upon the probabilities analogous to those which I already attribute to the influence of the planets, and I say: In 1851, I had occupations which were moderately but sufficiently lucrative, along with several difficulties regarding my position; in 1847, I was violently separated from my family, the result of this separation being great suffering for me and mine; in 1843, I traveled as an apostle, speaking to people who were being persecuted by men with bad intentions: in two words, I was honored and excluded; lastly, in 1825, I left my family, and I set upon the fatal course which brought me to science and misfortune. I can thus conclude that this year I will have work, experience poverty and troubles, have an exile of the heart, experience a change of location, receive publicity and objections, and there will occur an event which will decide the rest of my existence; and I already find all kinds of reasons in the present which lead me to believe in this future. I conclude that, for me and in this present year, experience perfectly confirms the precision of the astrological calculus of Cardano.

Incidentally, this calculation has to do with the climacteric years, or the greater climacteric, of the ancient astrologers. Climacteric means arranged in levels or calculated according to the degrees of a scale. Johannes Trithemius,[251] in his book On the Seven Secondary Causes, very curiously estimated the return of good years or bad years for all the empires of the world; we shall provide an exact and clear analysis of that same book in the twenty-first chapter of our Ritual, with

---

251   Johannes Trithemius, abbot of Würzburg (1462–1516).

the continuation of the work of Trithemius up until our day and the application of the magical scale to contemporary events, in order to deduce the most striking probabilities relative to the near future of France, of Europe, and the world.

According to all the great masters of astrology, the comets are the stars of exceptional heroes and only visit the Earth to announce great changes; the planets preside over collections of beings and modify the destinies of aggregations of men; the stars, further and weaker in their effects, attract individuals and determine their characteristics; sometimes a group of stars has an influence over the entire destiny of a man, and often a great number of souls are attracted by the distant rays of a same sun. When we die, our interior light takes leave according to the attraction of its star, and it is thus that we can be reborn in other universes, where the soul makes itself new clothing, analogous to the progress or decrease of its beauty; because our souls, separated from our bodies, resemble shooting stars, they are globules of animated light which are always searching for their center in order to rediscover their equilibrium and their movement; but they must first of all free themselves from the embrace of the serpent, which is to say the impure astral light which surrounds and captivates them as long as the power of their will does not raise them above it. The immersion of the living star in the dead light is a terrible torture, comparable to that of Mezentius. The soul freezes and burns there at the same time and has no means to free itself except to reenter the current of exterior forms and take on a mantle of flesh and to then fight energetically against the instincts in order to strengthen its moral liberty that will allow it, at the moment of death, to break the chains of the Earth and fly up triumphantly towards the consoling star whose light smiles upon it.

Given this fact, we can understand what the fires of hell are; they are identical to the demon or the ancient serpent; this is of what the salvation and the damnation of men consists, all of whom are called and successively elected, but in small numbers, after having been exposed by their own fault to the fall into the eternal fire.

Such is the great and sublime revelation of the mages, revelatory mother of all symbols, all doctrines, and all cults.

We can already see how much Dupuis was in error when he believed that all the religions arose solely from astronomy. It was, on the contrary, astrology which gave birth to astronomy, and primordial astrology is one of the branches of the holy Cabala, the science of sciences and the religion of religions.

We can also see on the seventeenth page of the Tarot an admirable allegory: a naked woman, who represents all at once Truth, Nature and Wisdom, without a veil, bending towards the earth over two urns out of which she pours water and fire; just above her head shines a starry septenary above which is a star with eight rays, that of Venus, symbol of peace and love; around this woman there grow the plants of the earth, and on one of these plants has just landed the butterfly of Psyche, emblem of the soul, replaced in several copies of the sacred book by a bird, a more Egyptian symbol and probably older. This figure, which, in the modern Tarot, carries the title of the shining Star, is analogous to many Hermetic symbols, and has some similarity with the Flaming Star of the initiates of Free-masonry, which expresses the majority of the mysteries of the secret doctrine of the Rosy Cross.

18 Y S.

POTIONS AND SPELLS

JUSTITIA.

MYSTERIUM.

CANES.[252]

We will now deal with the most criminal abuse of the magical sciences that there is: the use of magic, or rather sorcery, to poison. Here we must understand what we are writing about, not to teach, but to forewarn.

If human justice, in striking out against adepts, only ever attacked necromancers and poisoning sorcerers, it is certain, as we have already remarked, that their harshness would have been just and the most severe intimidation could never be overly excessive in regards to such criminals.

However one must not believe that the power over life and death which secretly belongs to the mage has always been used to satisfy some cowardly revenge or an even more cowardly cupidity; in the Middle Ages, as in the ancient world, magical societies often struck down or slowly killed off the revealers or the profaners of the mysteries, and when they had to avoid striking with the magical sword, when the

---

252   *Justitia* is Latin for "justice," *mysterium* for "mystery," and *canes* for "dogs."

spilling of blood was to be feared, the Aqua Tofana,[253] the aromatic bouquets, the shirt of Nessus, and other lesser known and stranger instruments of death served sooner or later in the execution of the terrible sentences of the Free Judges.[254]

We have said that there exists within magic a great and unspeakable arcanum, which is never communicated between adepts, and that most of all one must prevent the profane from surmising; in the past, whoever revealed or caused others to discover the key to this supreme arcanum through imprudent revelations was immediately condemned to death and was often forced to execute his own sentence.

Cazotte's infamous prophetic dinner, written about by La Harpe,[255] has not yet been understood; and La Harpe, in telling it, yielded to the rather natural desire to marvel his readers by exaggerating the details. All the men present at this dinner, with the exception of La Harpe, were initiates and revealers, or at least profaners, of the mysteries. Cazotte, more highly ranked than all the others on the scale of initiation, pronounced a sentence of death over them in the name of illuminism, and this sentence was diversely, but rigorously, executed, as all the other similar sentences have been over many years and over many centuries in the past, against the abbé of Villars, Urbain Grandier, and so many others; and those revolutionary philosophers at Cazotte's dinner party died just as Cagliostro died, abandoned within the prisons of the Inquisition, like Catherine Théot's mystic group;[256] as the imprudent Schröpfer,[257] forced to kill himself in the midst

253 A much-rumored poison said to have been used by the Borgias to eliminate their rivals.

254 Originally a secret court in the German province of Westphalia, the Free Judges, or Vehmgericht, came to play a role in eighteenth- and nineteenth-century conspiracy theories comparable to those surrounding the Bavarian Illuminati in the twentieth.

255 French playwright and author Jean-François de La Harpe (1739–1803). He published an account of the 1788 dinner party at which Cazotte is said to have accurately predicted the deaths of nearly all those present in the Terror.

256 French visionary Catherine Théot (1716–94) led a small sect that believed Maximilien Robespierre, one of the leaders of the French Revolution, was the Messiah. After his fall from power and execution, they were imprisoned by his enemies, and Théot died in prison.

257 German occultist Johann Georg Schröpfer (1730–74), who earned a living staging shows in which ghosts were produced by magic lanterns. At a show in 1774, he shot himself onstage, having first announced that he would resurrect himself from the dead. The wound was fatal; the resurrection did not occur.

of his magical triumphs and the universal enthusiasm for them; as Kotzebue the deserter, stabbed by Karl Sand,[258] and so many others whose cadavers were found without anyone ever finding out the cause of their sudden and bloody deaths.

We remember the strange speech which the president of the revolutionary tribunal addressed to Cazotte himself, thus condemning to death his brother and his co-initiate. The knot of the terrible drama of '93 is still hidden in the darkest sanctuary of the secret societies; to adepts of good faith who wished to emancipate the people, other adepts, who belonged to an opposing sect and were related to more ancient traditions, provided a terrible opposition by means analogous to those of their adversaries; they rendered the practice of the great arcanum impossible by unmasking the theory. The masses understood nothing, but they defied everything, and fell, in discouragement, lower than they had wanted to rise. The great arcanum remained as unknown as ever; only the adepts, neutralized by one another, could not exercise its power to dominate others, or to deliver themselves; they thus mutually condemned themselves as traitors and dragged one another into exile, suicide, towards the dagger and the guillotine.

Some will ask me perhaps if in our day such terrible dangers still threaten the intruders into the occult sanctuary or the revealers of the arcanum. Why should I answer to the incredulity of the curious? If I expose myself to a violent death to teach them, they would certainly not try to save me; if they are afraid for themselves, then they should abstain from all imprudent investigations: that is what I can tell them.

Let us now return to poisonous magic.

Alexandre Dumas, in his novel *The Count of Monte Cristo*, revealed some of the practices of this gruesome science. We will not repeat his sad theories about crime, how to poison plants, how animals fed with poisoned plants develop unhealthy flesh and can, when they are used in turn as food for humans, cause death without leaving any trace of the poison; we shall not say how, through venomous unctions, we can poison the walls of houses, and the air which becomes breathable again only through fumigation, requiring the operator to wear the glass mask of the

---

258 German playwright August von Kotzebue (1761–1819) was murdered by Karl Sand over a political quarrel. He seems to have had no connection to occult traditions.

Holy Cross; we will leave these mysterious abominations to the ancient Canidia, we shall not examine how far the infernal rites of Sagana helped to perfect the arts of Locusta.[259] It suffices to say that these malefactors of the worst type distilled together poisons and contagious sicknesses, the venom of reptiles and the harmful sap from plants; that they took the toxic and narcotic fluids from fungi, and they took from Jimson weed its asphyxiating principle; from the peach tree and cherry laurel they took that poison with which a single drop placed on the tongue or in the ear strikes you down like lightning and kills even the most healthy and strongest living beings. They cooked the white sap of the tithymalus with milk in which vipers and asps had been drowned; they carefully gathered and brought back from their voyages, or imported at great cost, the sap of the manchineel or the deadly fruits of Java, manioc juice, and other poisons; they pulverized flint and mixed impure ashes with the dried slime of reptiles; they composed hideous potions from the effluents of excited mares or the secretions of dogs in heat. Human blood was mixed with vile drugs, and with this was created an oil which killed through its smell alone: it reminds one of Panurge's Bourbonian pie. They even wrote recipes for poisons while disguising them with technical terms from alchemy, and, in more than one so-called old Hermetic book, the secret of the powder of projection is nothing other than that of the powder of succession.[260] In the *Grand Grimoire*[261] we can still find one of these recipes, less disguised than the others, but titled only Means of Making Gold: it is a horrible brew of verdigris, vitriol, arsenic and sawdust, which will, if it is good, immediately consume a branch which one dips into it and rapidly dissolve an iron nail. Giambattista della Porta,[262] in his *Magia Naturalis*, gives a recipe for the poison of the Borgias, but as we might imagine, he makes fun of his readers and does not divulge the entire

---

259 Three famous witches and poisoners in ancient Roman literature.

260 A wry joke. The "powder of projection" is the philosopher's stone; the "powder of succession" produces gold by the simpler route of allowing the heir to succeed to a title and estate.

261 One of the most famous handbooks of magic from the early modern period.

262 Italian polymath (1535–1615). His most famous book, *Magia naturalis* (*Natural Magic*), published in 1558, is a remarkable blend of early science and traditional occultism.

truth, which would have been much too dangerous in such a work. We will thus provide Porta's recipe here, if only to satisfy the curiosity of our readers.

The toad on its own is not venomous, but it acts as a sponge for poisons: it is the mushroom of the animal kingdom. Take a large toad, says Porta, enclose it in a jar with vipers and asps; give them as their only food over several days poisonous mushrooms, foxglove, and hemlock, then aggravate them by beating them, burning them, and by tormenting them in all kinds of manners, until they die of rage and hunger; you then sprinkle the slag of lead crystal ground together with euphorbia on them, after which, you put them in a well-stoppered retort and heat it over a fire until all the humidity is absorbed; after which you allow it to cool, and you separate the ashes of the corpses from the incombustible particles that will have remained at the bottom of the retort: you will then have two poisons, one a liquid and one a powder. The liquid will be as effective as the terrible Aqua Tofana; the powder will wither or age someone who has been exposed to a pinch of it added to their drink in a few days, and then they will die while suffering horribly, or in total atony.[263] One must admit that this recipe's magical aspect is most ugly and black, and it reminds one, in a heart-wrenching manner, of the abominable recipes of Canidia and Medea.

The witches of the Middle Ages claimed to receive similar powders during the Sabbath, and sold them at high prices to ignorance and hate: it was through the rumor of similar mysteries that they spread terror throughout the countryside and managed to cast spells. Once imagination is struck, once the nervous system is attacked, the victim perishes quickly, and the terror of their friends and family complete his perdition. The witch[264] is almost always a kind of human toad, all swelled up with old grudges; witches were poor, rejected by all, and in consequence filled with hatred. The fear which they inspired was their consolation and their revenge; they themselves, poisoned by a society of which they had only ever experienced its rejection and its vices, poisoned in their turn those

---

263   That is, complete muscular relaxation and paralysis.

264   It may be necessary to point out here, for the benefit of certain readers, that Lévi lived long before the invention of Wicca and thus was unaware that the word "witch" would eventually be redefined by some to mean "goddess-worshipping feminist pagan."

who were weak enough to fear them, and they took revenge upon beauty and youthfulness with their cursed old age and unpardonable ugliness.

The operation of these evil works and the accomplishment of these hideous mysteries constituted and confirmed that which we called the pact with the evil spirit. It is certain that the operator must have been possessed by evil, body and soul, and justifiably deserved universal and irrevocable condemnation as expressed by the allegory of hell. That human souls had descended to such a degree of wickedness and insanity must no doubt astonish and grieve us; but must there not exist the depths as a foundation for the heights of the most sublime virtues, and does not the abyss of the hells demonstrate through antithesis the elevation and infinite grandeur of heaven?

In the North, where the instincts are more compressed and hardy; in Italy, where passions are more expansive and ardent, they still fear spells and the evil eye; in Naples, they do not brave the *jettatura*[265] recklessly, and they even recognize beings evilly endowed with this power by certain external signs. To protect oneself, one must carry horns on one's person, say the experts, and the people, who take everything literally, hasten to adorn themselves with little horns, without thinking more about the meaning of this allegory. Horns, attributes of Jupiter Ammon, Bacchus, and Moses, are the symbol of moral power or enthusiasm, and the magicians wish to say that, to brave the *jettatura*, one must dominate, with great audacity, great enthusiasm, or great thought, the fatal currents of the instincts. It is thus that almost all popular superstitions are profane interpretations of some great axiom or marvelous arcanum of occult wisdom. Does not Pythagoras, in writing down his admirable symbols,[266] bequeath to the sages a perfect philosophy and to the vulgar a new series of vain observances and ridiculous practices? Thus, when he said: "Do not gather what falls from the table, do not cut trees on the great road, do not kill the serpent that has gotten into your enclosure," was

---

265   *Jettatura* is Italian for "casting" and refers to the casting of a curse by one who has the evil eye.

266   The Pythagorean symbols are a collection of strange maxims, including the ones Lévi mentions, recorded in classical literature as teachings of Pythagoras himself. Their interpretation in symbolic terms, along the lines Lévi sketches out below, was a commonplace of ancient and medieval philosophy.

he not providing transparent allegories for the precepts of charity, either social or individual? And when he said: "Do not look at yourself in the mirror by the light of the torch," was this not an ingenious manner of teaching true knowledge of the self, which cannot exist in artificial light and the prejudices of systems? This is the case for all of Pythagoras's other precepts, which, as we know, were followed to the letter by a whole mass of imbecilic disciples, to the point that, among the superstitious observances of our provinces, there remains a rather large number that obviously originate from the primordial intelligence of Pythagoras's symbols.

The word "superstition" derives from a Latin word which signifies "to survive." It is the sign which survives thought; it is the cadaver of religious practice. Superstition is to initiation what the idea of the devil is to that of God. It is in this sense that the cult of images is forbidden and that a doctrine that is most holy in its first conception can become superstitious and impious when it is bereft of inspiration and spirit. It is then that religion, always one like supreme reason, changes vestments and abandons the ancient rites to cupidity and the deceit of fallen priests metamorphosed, by their wickedness and their ignorance, into charlatans and temple soothsayers.

We can compare superstitions to magical emblems and characters whose meaning is no longer understood, and which we engrave haphazardly upon amulets and talismans. The magical images of the ancients were pentacles, that is to say Cabalistic syntheses. The wheel of Pythagoras is a pentacle which is analogous to the wheels of Ezekiel, and those two figures express the same secrets and the same philosophy: it is the key to all the pentacles, and we have already spoken thereof. The four animals, or more precisely the four-headed sphinx of the same prophet, are identical to an admirable Indian symbol whose drawing we provide here, and which has to do with the science of the Great Arcanum. Saint John, in his Book of Revelations, copied and amplified Ezekiel, and all the monstrous figures in this marvelous book are so many magical pentacles to which Cabalists easily find the key. But Christians, having rejected the science in their desire to amplify their faith, later wished to hide the origins of their doctrine and condemned to the fires all the books of the Cabala and of magic. To destroy the originals is to lend a certain originality to the copies, and Saint Paul no doubt knew this well when, no doubt with the best intentions in mind, he carried out

ADDA-NARI

his auto-da-fé of knowledge at Ephesus.[267] It is thus that, six centuries later, the believer Omar had to sacrifice the library of Alexandria to the originality of the Koran,[268] and who knows whether, in time to come, some future apostle will wish to burn our literary museums and confiscate the printing press in the name of some religious fad or some newly accredited legend?

The study of talismans and pentacles is one of the most curious branches of magic and is related to historical numismatics.

There exist Indian, Egyptian, and Greek talismans, Cabalistic medallions coming from the ancient and modern Hebrews, the Gnostic Abraxas, and Byzantine amulets, occult coins in use among the members of secret societies and sometimes called tokens of the Sabbath, and then there are the medallions of the Templars and the jewels of the Freemasons. Goclenius,[269] in his Treatise on the Marvels of Nature, describes Solomon's talismans and those of Rabbi Chaël.[270] The images of a great many others, including some of the most ancient, were engraved on the magical calendars of Tycho Brahe and Duchenteau, and have been reproduced in totality or in part in the initiatory calendars of M. Ragon,[271] a vast and scholarly work which we recommend to our readers.

---

267   Acts 19:19.

268   According to legend, after the Muslim conquest of Alexandria, the victorious commander Omar was asked whether the library of Alexandria should be preserved. He replied that if the books it contained agreed with the Koran, they were superfluous, and if they disagreed with it, they were wrong. The library was burned.

269   German scholar Rudolph Goclenius (1547–1628).

270   We have been unable to trace this figure.

271   French Freemason and occultist Jean-Marie Ragon (1781–1862), the author of numerous books on occult philosophy and symbolism.

19 ק T.

THE STONE OF
THE PHILOSOPHERS, ELAGABALUS

VOCATIO.

SOL.

AURUM.[272]

The ancients adored the Sun in the form a black stone which they called Elagabalus or Heliogabalus.[273] What was the significance of this stone, and how could it be the symbol of the most brilliant of stars?

The disciples of Hermes, before promising to their adepts the elixir of long life or the powder of projection, recommended that they search for the philosopher's *stone*, but why this stone?

The great initiator of the Christians invited his faithful to build upon the *stone*, if they did not wish to see their works upturned.[274] He called himself the

---

272   *Vocatio* is Latin for "calling," *sol* for "sun," and *aurum* for "gold."

273   A god of ancient Syria, who was represented by a conical stone.

274   Matthew 7:24–25.

cornerstone, and he told the most believing of the apostles: "Call yourself Pierre, because you are the *pierre* upon which I shall build my Church."[275]

This *stone*, say the masters of alchemy, is the true salt of the philosophers, which is one third of the composition of azoth. And AZOTH is, as we know, the name of the great hermetical agent and the true philosopher's agent; the alchemists also represent their salt in the form of a cubical stone, as we can observe in the *Twelve Keys* of Basilius Valentinus or in the allegories of Trevisan.

What then, in truth, is this stone? It is the foundation of absolute philosophy, it is supreme and immovable reason. Before contemplating the metallurgical work, one must forever be fixed upon the absolute principles of wisdom, one must possess the reason which is the touchstone of truth. Never will a biased man be the king of nature and the master of transmutations. The philosopher's stone is thus necessary before all else; but how does one find it? Hermes teaches us how with his Emerald Tablet. One must separate the subtle from the fixed, with great care and attention. Thus we must free our certitudes from our beliefs and render distinct the respective domains of science and faith; we must understand that we do not know the things which we believe in, and that we no longer believe in the things which we are able to know, and that it is the essence of matters of faith that they are unknown and indefinite, while it is the complete contrary for matters of science. We would conclude that science is based on reason and experience, while faith is based on sentiment and reason. In other words, the philosopher's stone is true certitude, which human prudence ensures through conscientious research and modest doubt, while religious enthusiasm attributes it to faith. Yet it belongs neither to reason without aspirations nor to aspirations without reason; true certitude is the reciprocal acquiescence of reason which knows to sentiment which believes, and of sentiment which believes to reason which knows. The definitive alliance of reason and of faith results not in their absolute distinction and separation but in their mutual control and their fraternal confluence. That is the meaning of the two columns of Solomon's gate, one of which is called Jachin and

---

275   Matthew 16:18. Jesus's Aramaic pun works in Greek, Latin, and French but not in
        English, where the verbal link between the name Peter and the common word for
        rock or stone has been lost.

the other Boaz, one of which is white and the other black. They are distinct and separate, they are even contrary in appearance, but if blind force wishes to unite them by bringing them together, the temple vault will collapse: because when separated, they have equal strength, while reunited, they are two forces which mutually destroy each other. It is for the same reason that spiritual power weakens when it attempts to usurp temporal power and that temporal power perishes a victim to its encroachments into spiritual power. Gregory VII lost the papacy, and the schismatic kings lost and will lose the monarchy. Human balance requires two feet, the worlds revolve with two forces, creation requires two sexes. This is the meaning of Solomon's Arcanum, symbolized by the two temple columns, Jachin and Boaz.

The Sun and the Moon of the alchemists correspond to the same symbol and contribute to the perfection and stability of the philosopher's stone. The Sun is the hieroglyphic sign of truth, because it is the visible source of light, and the raw stone is the symbol of stability. This is why the ancient mages took the stone of Elagabalus for the sign of the Sun itself, and it is for this reason also that the alchemists of the Middle Ages pointed to the philosopher's stone as the primary means of making philosophical gold, that is to say of transforming all the vital forces symbolized by the six metals into the Sun, which is to say into truth and light, the first and indispensable operation of the Great Work, which brings one to secondary adaptations, and which allows the creators of spiritual and living gold, through the analogies of nature, to find the natural and raw gold; it allows the possessors of the true salt to find the true philosophical mercury and sulfur.

To find the philosopher's stone is therefore to have discovered the absolute, as all the masters say. And the absolute is that which admits to no error, it is the fixed in the volatile, it is the rule of the imagination, it is the necessity of being itself, it is the immutable law of reason and truth; the absolute is what is. God himself is not without a reason for existing and can only exist by virtue of a supreme and inevitable reason. It is therefore reason which is the absolute; it is in it which we must believe if we wish our faith to have a reasonable and solid foundation. We may say in our day and age that God is but a hypothesis, but absolute reason is not one: it is essential to being.

Saint Thomas[276] said: "A thing is not just because God wishes it, but God wishes it because it is just." If Saint Thomas had made the logical deduction of all the consequences of this beautiful idea, he would have found the philosopher's stone, and, instead of limiting himself to being the Angel of the Schools, he would have been their reformer.

To believe in the reason for God and in the God of reason is to render atheism impossible. It is idolaters who created atheists. When Voltaire said: "If God did not exist, we would have to invent him," he sensed rather than understood the reason for God. Does God really exist? We know nothing of it, but we wish it to be the case, and it is for this reason that we believe it. Faith formulated in this manner is reasonable faith, because it admits both doubt and science; and, in fact, we only believe in things which seem probable, but which we do not know. To think otherwise is to be delirious; to speak otherwise is to express oneself like a visionary or a fanatic. It is not to these type of people that the philosopher's stone is promised.

Ignorant people subverted primordial Christianity from its path by replacing science with faith, experience with dreams, reality with the fantastic; the Inquisitors for so many centuries made war on magic and managed to cover in shadows the ancient discoveries of the human spirit, so that today we grope about attempting to rediscover the key to the phenomena of nature. Yet all natural phenomena depend upon a single and immutable law represented by the philosopher's stone and most of all symbolized by its form, that of the cube. This law, expressed in the Cabala by the quaternary, had provided the Hebrews with all the mysteries of their divine tetragrammaton. We can thus say that the philosopher's stone is squared in all senses, like the celestial Jerusalem of Saint John, and written upon one of its sides is the name שלמה,[277] and on the other that of GOD; on another of its sides is written ADAM, and the other HEVA, then that of AZOT and INRI on the other two sides. On the frontispiece of a French translation of a book by

---

276   Italian priest and philosopher Thomas Aquinas (1225–74), the most influential of the Scholastic theologians of the Middle Ages.

277   ShLMH, or Shlomo, the Hebrew spelling of the name Solomon.

the Sieur de Nuysement[278] is the spirit of the Earth standing on a cube surrounded by tongues of flame; he has for a phallus a caduceus, and the Sun and the Moon on his right and left breast; he is bearded, crowned, and holds a scepter in his hand. This is the Azoth of the sages on his pedestal of salt and sulfur. We sometimes give this image the symbolic head of the goat of Mendes; it is the Baphomet of the Templars, the goat of the Sabbath, and the Verb of the Gnostics; strange images which were used as bogeymen for the vulgar after having been used in their meditations by the sages, innocent hieroglyphs of thought and faith which were used as a pretext for the passions of persecution. How unhappy men are in their ignorance, but how they would despise themselves if they ever came to know it!

---

278   A French translation of the *Twelve Keys of Basil Valentine* by Clovis Hesteau, sieur de Nuysement, published in Paris in 1660.

20 ר U.

THE UNIVERSAL MEDICINE

CAPUT.

RESURRECTIO.

CIRCULUS.[279]

Most physical maladies derive from moral maladies, according to the unique and universal magical doctrine and due to the law of analogies.

A great passion to which we abandon ourselves always corresponds to a great malady for which we are preparing. The deadly sins are called that because they cause one to physically and actually die.

Alexander the Great died of pride. He was naturally temperate and abandoned himself through pride to the excesses which caused his death.

François I died from adultery.

Louis XV died because of his Parc-aux-Cerfs.[280]

When Marat was assassinated, he died of anger and envy. He was a proud

---

279 *Caput* is Latin for "head," *resurrectio* for "resurrection," and *circulus* for "circle."

280 Literally "deer park." Lévi's reference is to a mansion in a remote corner of the grounds of Versailles where Louis XV had young women brought for casual sex.

monomaniac who believed that he alone was just and wished to kill all that was not Marat.

Many of our contemporaries died of disappointed ambitions after the February revolution.[281]

Once your will is irrevocably confirmed in an absurd tendency, you are dead, and the reef that you shall break yourself upon is not far off.

It is thus true to say that wisdom conserves and prolongs life.

The great Master said: "My flesh is food and my blood is drink. Eat my flesh and drink my blood, and you shall have life."[282] And since the vulgar grumbled, he added: "The flesh has no value here; the words I speak to you are spirit and life."[283] He therefore wished to say: "Drink of my spirit and live from my life."

And when he was about to die, he bound the memory of his life to the symbol of bread and that of his spirit to the symbol of wine, and thus instituted the communion of faith, of hope, and of charity.

It is in the same sense that the hermetic masters said: Render gold drinkable and you shall have the universal medicine; which is to say: Appropriate truth to your needs, so that it becomes the source from which you drink all your days, and you too shall gain the immortality of the sages. Temperance, peacefulness of the soul, simplicity of character, the calm and reason of the will render man not only happy but hardy and strong. It is by becoming reasonable and good that man becomes immortal. We are the authors of our destinies, and God does not save without our participation.

Death does not exist for the sage: death is a phantom rendered horrifying by ignorance and vulgar weakness.

Change attests to movement, and movement reveals but life. The cadaver itself would not decompose if it were dead: all the molecules which compose it remain alive and move to free themselves. And you think that the spirit freed

---

281   The revolution of 1848, which drove the last French king, Louis Philippe I, from the throne but resulted a few years later in the seizure of power by Napoleon III.

282   John 6:55–56.

283   John 6:63.

itself first so as to no longer live! You believe that thought and love can die when the grossest of matter itself does not die!

If change must be called death, we die and are reborn every day, because every day our form changes.

Let us then be afraid of dirtying and tearing our clothes, but let us not fear of leaving them when the hour of rest arrives.

The embalming and conservation of cadavers is an unnatural superstition. It is an attempt to create death; it is the forced immobilization of a substance for which life has need. But one must not hasten to destroy or make disappear cadavers either; because nothing is accomplished abruptly in nature, and we should not risk violently breaking the links of a soul which is still detaching itself.

Death is never instantaneous; it operates by degrees, like sleep. While the blood is not yet completely cold, while the nerves can still tremble, a man is not completely dead, and if none of the organs essential to life are destroyed, the soul can be recalled, either by accident or by a strong will.

A philosopher said that he would sooner doubt universal testimony than believe in the resurrection of the dead,[284] and in this he spoke imprudently; because it is upon his faith in universal testimony that he believed in the impossibility of resurrection. If a resurrection were to be proven, what would be the result? That one would have to deny the evidence or renounce reason? It would be absurd to suppose so. One must simply conclude that we had wrongly believed that resurrection was impossible. *Ab actu ad posse valet consecutio.*[285]

Let us now dare to affirm that resurrection is possible, and even that it happens more often than we think. How many people whose death is juridically and scientifically certified were found to be dead, it is true, in their coffins, but had then revived, and had gnawed away at their wrists so as to open their veins and thus escape their horrible suffering through a new death. A doctor would tell us that these people were not dead but were lethargic. But what is lethargy? It is

---

284 English philosopher David Hume (1711–76), who rejected the possibility of miracles.

285 A rule of logic: "It is valid to proceed from the fact to the possibility," or, in simpler language, if something exists, it's reasonable to say that it's possible for it to exist!

the name we give to a death which has begun but does not terminate, to a death which has just denied a return to life. We can always easily get out of such problems with words, when it is impossible to actually explain things.

The soul is attached to the body by tendency, and once that tendency ends, it is the certain sign that the soul will depart. Magnetic sleep is a lethargy or a false death and can be healed by the will. Etherization, or the torpor produced by chloroform, is a veritable lethargy which sometimes results in a definitive death when the soul, happy with its temporary departure, makes the effort of will to leave definitively: which is possible for those who have vanquished hell, that is to say whose moral force is superior to that of astral attraction. Also, resurrection is only possible for elementary souls, and it is these souls above all which are exposed to the possibility of reviving involuntarily in their tomb. Great men and true sages are never buried alive.

In our Ritual we will provide the theory and practice of resurrectionism, and to those who ask me if I have resuscitated the dead I would answer that if I told them, they would not believe me.

It remains for us to examine here if the abolition of pain is possible and if it is advantageous to use chloroform or magnetism for surgical operations. We think, and science will recognize this later, that in diminishing the senses we diminish life, and that all we removed in terms of pain in such circumstances acts in favor of death. Pain attests to the struggle for life; we also notice that with persons who are operated upon under sedation, the dressings applied after the operation are excessively painful. If we repeated sedation via chloroform after each application of dressings, one of two things would occur: either the patent would die or between the dressings the pain would return and continue. We do not do violence to nature with impunity.

DIVINATION

DENTES.

FURCA.

AMENS.[286]

The author of this book has often dared in his life, and no fear has ever held his thoughts captive. But it is not without a legitimate terror that he arrives at the end of the magical doctrine.

We are now concerned with revealing or rather re-veiling the Great Arcanum, that terrible secret, that secret of life and death expressed in the Bible by the formidable and symbolic speech of the symbolic serpent itself: I. NEQUAQUAM MORIEMINI, II. SED ERITIS, III. SICUT DII, IV. SCIENTES BONUM ET MALUM.[287]

One of the privileges of the initiate to the great Arcanum, and that which summarizes all the others, is that of *Divination*.

According to the vulgar meaning of this word, "to divine" signifies to con-

---

286   *Dentes* is Latin for "teeth," *furca* for "fork," and *amens* for "mindless."

287   Latin: "You shall never die, but you will become as gods, knowing good and evil," a paraphrase of Genesis 3:4–5. The division into four parts deserves attention.

jecture about that which we do not know, but the real meaning of this word is ineffable because it is sublime. To divine (*divinari*), is to exercise divinity. The word *divinus*, in Latin, signifies more and something other than *divus*, and its meaning is equivalent to man-god.[288] *Devin*, in French, contains the four letters of the word DIEU, plus the letter N, which corresponds, in its form, to the Hebrew letter aleph א, and which expresses Cabalistically and hieroglyphically the great Arcanum, whose symbol, in the Tarot, is the figure of the Magician.

He who understands perfectly the absolute numerical value of א multiplied by N, with the grammatical force of the final N in the words which express science, art, or puissance, and then adds the five letters of the word DEVIN, in such a manner as to enter five into four and two into one—that person, in translating the number he finds into primordial Hebrew letters, will write the occult name of the great Arcanum, and will possess a word of which the holy Tetragrammaton itself is but an image.[289]

To be *devin*,[290] according to the force of this word, is thus to be divine, and something even more mysterious than that as well.

The two signs of human divinity, or of divine humanity, are prophecies and miracles.

To be a prophet is to see ahead of time the effects that exist in the causes, it is to read the astral light; to make miracles is to act upon the universal agent and submit it to our will.

Some will ask the author of this book if he is a prophet and a thaumaturge.

The curious may search out and read all I have written previous to certain events which were then accomplished in this world. As to what I could have said and done, if I recounted them, and if they were truly miraculous, would you believe me based on my words alone?

Incidentally, one of the essential conditions for divination is to never be forced into it and to never submit to temptation, that is to say to a test. The

---

288   A subtle point of Latin grammar. *Divus* is "god," and *divinus* is "belonging or relating to a deity."

289   This riddle is left for the reader to solve, as Lévi intended.

290   That is, a diviner or seer.

masters of the science never yielded to anyone's curiosity. The Sibyl burnt her books when Tarquinius refused to value them at their true worth;[291] the great Master remained silent when they asked him for the signs of his divine mission;[292] Agrippa died of misery rather than obey those who demanded a horoscope of him. To give proofs of the science to those who doubt the science itself is to initiate the unworthy, is to profane the gold of the sanctuary, is to merit the excommunication of the sages and the death of the revealers.

The essence of divination, that is to say the Great Magical Arcanum, is represented in all the symbols of the science and is closely tied to the unique and primordial doctrine of Hermes. In philosophy it provides absolute certitude; in religion, the universal secret of faith; in physics, the composition, the decomposition, the recomposition, the realization, and the adaptation of the philosophical mercury, called azoth by the alchemists; in dynamics it multiplies our strengths by those of perpetual motion; it is at once mystical, metaphysical, and material, with correspondences in effect across the three worlds; it obtains the mercy of God, the truth of science, and the gold of wealth, because metallurgical transmutation is both an allegory and a reality, as all adepts of the true science well know.

Yes, we can truly and materially make gold with the stone of the sages, which is an amalgam of salt, sulfur, and mercury combined three times in azoth by a triple sublimation and a triple fixation. Yes, the operation is often easy and can be done in one day, in one instant; other times it takes months and years. But, to succeed at the Great Work, one must be *divinus*, or *devin*, in the Cabalistic sense of the word, and it is indispensable to have renounced, for one's own interest, the advantages of the wealth of which one will become the dispenser. Raymond Lully enriched sovereigns, seeded Europe with his funds, and remained poor; Nicolas Flamel, who is certainly dead, whatever they say about his legend, only found the Great Work through asceticism and a complete detachment from wealth. He was

291 A Roman legend claims that the Cumaean sibyl offered her three books of prophecies to Tarquinius, king of Rome, at a high price. When he tried to bargain with her, she burned one of the books and offered the remaining two for an even higher price.

292 Matthew 27:11–14.

initiated through the intelligence which he suddenly acquired from the book of *Aesch Mezareph*,[293] written in Hebrew by the Cabalist Abraham, perhaps the same one who wrote the *Sepher Yetzirah*. Yet this intelligence was, for Flamel, a merited intuition, or rather rendered possible by the personal preparations of an adept. I believe I have said enough.

Divination is thus an intuition, and the key to that intuition is the universal and magical doctrine of analogies. It is through these analogies that the mage interprets dreams, as we can see in the Bible that the patriarch Joseph did long ago in Egypt:[294] because analogies in the reflections of the astral light are as rigorous as the nuances of color in the solar light and can be calculated and explained with great exactitude. It is only necessary to know the degree of intelligence of the dreamer and we can reveal to him everything through his own dreams, to the point of throwing him into a profound wonder.

Hypnotism, precognition, and second sight are all of one disposition, either accidental or habitual, dreamed in a voluntary sleep or while awake, that is to say they perceive the analogical reflections of the astral light. We will explain all this, until it is obvious in our Ritual; at which point we will provide the means so looked for to regularly produce and direct magnetic phenomena. As to the divinatory instruments, they are simply a means of communication between the seer and the consultant, and often serve only to fix the two wills upon the same sign; vague figures, complicated and mobile, help to assemble the reflections of the astral fluid, and it is thus that we see in the dregs of a coffee cup, in the clouds, in the white of an egg, etc., the fateful forms which exist only in the *translucent*, which is to say in the imagination of the operators. Vision in water operates through glare and the fatigue of the optic nerve, which yields its functions to the translucent and produces an illusion of the brain, which then takes reflections of the astral light for real images; also, nervous people, having weak eyesight and vivid imaginations, are most suited to this type of divination, which has the most success when it is performed by children. But do not be confused regarding the function we attribute to the imagination in the divinatory arts. We see through

---

293 An important work of Cabalistic alchemy. The Hebrew title means "refiner's fire."
294 Genesis 41:14–36.

the imagination, without a doubt, and that is the natural aspect of the miracle, but we see true things, and it is that which makes for the marvelous in this natural work. We refer to the experiences of all true adepts. The author of this book has experimented with all kinds of divination and obtained results which were always proportional to the exactitude of his scientific operations and the good faith of his consultants.

The Tarot, that miraculous book, the inspiration for all the sacred books of the ancient peoples, is, because of the analogical precision of its figures and its numbers, the most perfect instrument for divination, which can be used with complete confidence. In fact, the oracles of this book are always rigorously true, at least in one sense, and while it predicts nothing, it always reveals hidden things and provides consultants with the wisest of advice. Alliette, who was a wig maker before becoming the Cabalist of the previous century, after having spent thirty years meditating upon the Tarot; Alliette, who Cabalistically called himself Etteilla, by reading his name as one reads Hebrew,[295] was very close to finding all that was hidden in that strange book, but he only managed to displace the keys of the Tarot because he did not understand them, and he inverted the order and the character of the figures without completely destroying the analogies, because they are so sympathetic and correspond so well to one another. The writings of Etteilla, which have become relatively rare, are obscure, tiring, and of a truly barbarous style; not all his works were published, and the manuscripts of this father of modern card readers are still in the hands of a Parisian librarian, who was most willing to show them to me. What we can see in them which is most remarkable is the unrelenting work and incontestable good faith of the author, who all his life sensed the grandeur of the occult sciences and who died at the door of the sanctuary without ever having penetrated beyond the veil. He had little respect for Agrippa and made much of Jean Belot, and knew nothing of the philosophy of Paracelsus; but he had a well-practiced intuition, a relentless will, and more imagination than good judgment: it was too little to make him a mage, but it was more than enough to make him a very skillful vulgar seer, and in consequence very credible. Also, Etteilla had a faddish success, which a wiser magician might

---

295   That is, right to left rather than left to right.

have been wrong to not claim for himself, but he will certainly never make that claim.

In saying, at the end of our Ritual, the last word about the Tarot, we will indicate the complete manner of reading it, and in consequence of consulting it, not only regarding the probabilities of destiny, but also and most of all regarding the problems of philosophy and religion, of which the Tarot always provides a certain answer of the most admirable precision, if we explain it in the hierarchical order of the analogy of the three worlds with the three colors and the four nuances which compose the sacred septenary. All this is part of the positive practice of magic, and can only be summarily indicated and only established in principle in this first part, which contains only the doctrine of high magic and the philosophical and religious key to the high sciences, understood or rather ignored under the name of occult science.

SUMMARY AND GENERAL KEY
TO THE FOUR OCCULT SCIENCES

SIGNA.

THOT.

PAN.[296]

Let us now summarize all of science through principles.

Analogy is the last word of science and the first word of faith.

Harmony is in equilibrium, and equilibrium subsists in the analogy of opposites.

Absolute unity is the supreme reason and the last of all things. Yet this reason can neither be one person nor three persons:[297] it is one reason, and it is reason par excellence.

To create equilibrium one must separate and unite: separate at the poles, unite in the center. *continuum*

---

296   *Signa* is Latin for "sign," Thot an alternative spelling of the name of the Egyptian god Thoth or Djehuti, Pan the name of the Greek god of the wilderness.

297   That is to say, the supreme reason is not the Christian God.

To reason with faith is to destroy faith; to turn philosophy into mysticism is to attack reason.

Reason and faith mutually exclude each other by their nature and are united together through analogy.

Analogy is the only possible mediator between the visible and the invisible, between the finite and the infinite. The doctrine is the continually ascending hypothesis of a presumable equation.

For the ignorant, it is the hypothesis which is the absolute affirmation, and the absolute affirmation which is the hypothesis.

There are in science necessary hypotheses, and he who looks to realize them enlarges the science without restraining faith: because on the other side of faith lies the infinite.

We believe what we do not know but also what reason wishes us to admit. To define the object of faith and delimit it is thus to formulate the unknown. Professions of faith are formulas of the ignorance and aspirations of man. The theorems of science are monuments to his conquests.

The man who denies God is just as fanatical as he who defines him with a pretense of infallibility. We ordinarily define God by saying all that he is not.

Man creates God through analogy of the lesser with the greater: the result is that the conception of God by man is always that of an infinite man, which makes man a finite God.

Man can realize what he believes to the degree that he knows with reason what he is ignorant of.

The analogy of opposites is the relation of light to darkness, of the convex to the concave, of the full to the empty. Allegory, mother of all the doctrines, is the substitution of imprints with seals, of shadows with realities. It is the lie of truth and the truth in lies.

One does not invent a doctrine, one veils a truth, and a shadow is produced to protect the eyes of the weak. The initiator is not an impostor, he is a revealer, that is to say, according to the expression of the Latin word *revelare*, a man who veils again. He is the creator of a new shadow.

Analogy is the key to all the secrets of nature and the only raison d'être of all revelations.

That is why religions seem to be written in the heavens and in all of nature; it must be so: because the work of God is the book of God, and in what he writes we should see the expression of his thought, and in consequence of his being, since we conceive of him as supreme thought. Dupuis and Volney saw only a plagiarism in the splendid analogy,[298] which should have brought them to recognize the catholicity, that is to say the universality of the primordial doctrine, the unique, magical, Cabalistic, and immutable revelation through analogy.

Analogy gives the mages all the powers of nature; analogy is the quintessence of the philosopher's stone, it is the secret of perpetual movement, it is the quadrature of the circle, it is the temple which rests on the two columns Jachin and Boaz, it is the key to the great arcanum, it is the root of the tree of life, it is the science of good and evil.

To find the exact scale of the analogies in those things which are appreciable by the science is to fix the foundations of faith and thus make off with the wand of miracles. There exists a principle and a rigorous formula, which is the great arcanum. The sage does not search it out, for he has already found it: but the vulgar still search for it and never find it.

Metallurgical transformation operates both spiritually and materially through the positive key of the analogies.

Occult medicine is but the exercise of the will applied to the source of life itself, to that astral light whose existence is a fact and whose movement is confirmed by the calculations whose ascending and descending scale is the great magical arcanum.

This universal arcanum, the final and eternal secret of high initiation, is symbolized in the Tarot by a naked young girl who touches the earth with only one foot and holds a magnetized wand in each hand, and seems to be running into a crown held up by an angel, an eagle, a bull and a lion. This figure is basically analogous to the cherub of Yehesqiel, whose drawing we provide, as the Indian symbol of Ardhanari, analogue of the Ado-naï of Yehesqiel, who is vulgarly called Ezekiel.

---

298   The theory proposed by Dupuis and Volney held that the story of Christ was a misunderstood astronomical myth, with Jesus as the sun and the twelve apostles as the signs of the zodiac.

The understanding of this drawing is the key to all the occult sciences. Readers of my book should already understand it philosophically, if they familiarized themselves a little with the symbolism of the Cabala. It now remains for us to realize the second most important operation of the Great Work. To find the philosopher's stone is something, no doubt; but how do we triturate[299] it in order to produce the powder of projection? What is the use of the magical wand? What is the true power of the divine names of the Cabala? The initiates know, and those who can be initiated will know if through the multiple and precise clues that we have just given them, they discover the great arcanum.

Why do these simple and pure truths always need to be hidden from men? It is because the elect of intelligence are small in number on earth and, in the midst of fools and the wicked, are like Daniel in the lion's den.[300]

Incidentally, the analogy which the laws of the hierarchy and the absolute science teach us, being omnipotent, must be the exclusive domain of the most deserving. The confusion of the hierarchy is a veritable degeneration of society, because then the blind lead the blind,[301] according to the words of the Master. May initiation be rendered unto the priests and kings, and order will renew itself. Also, in calling upon the most deserving, and by exposing myself to all the dangers and the curses that surround revealers, I believe that I do a great and useful thing: I direct towards social chaos the breath of God that lives within humanity, and I evoke the priests and the kings of the world to come!

A thing is, not just because God wishes it, said the Angel of the Schools; but God wishes it because it is just. It is as if he had said the absolute is reason. Reason is of itself; it is because it is and not because we suppose it; it is or nothing exists; and how would you have anything exist without reason? Even insanity is not produced without reason. Reason is the necessity, is the law, is the rule of all liberty and the direction of all initiatives. If God is, it is through reason. The conception

---

299   Trituration is the stage in alchemical work in which the philosopher's stone is reduced to a powder in order to be put to use.

300   Daniel 6:16–23.

301   Matthew 15:14.

of an absolute God outside or independent of reason is the idol of black magic, it is the phantom of the devil.

The devil is death which disguises itself with the worn-out vestments of life; it is the specter of Hiranyakashipu[302] enthroned upon the ruins of destroyed civilizations, who hides his horrible nudity with the abandoned rags of the incarnations of Vishnu.

HERE ENDS
THE DOCTRINE OF HIGH MAGIC.

---

302   A figure in Hindu mythology who practiced austerities to gain magical power for purely selfish purposes and was eventually destroyed by one of the incarnations of Vishnu.

PART TWO

cȝ

THE RITUAL OF HIGH MAGIC

INTRODUCTION TO
THE RITUAL OF HIGH MAGIC

Do you know the old queen of the world, who continually walks without ever tiring?

All debauched passions, all egoistic pleasures, all the unbridled forces of humanity, and all its tyrannical weaknesses precede the avaricious proprietor of our valley of suffering, and, with sickles in hand, her untiring minions perform their eternal harvest.

The queen is as old as time, but she hides her skeleton under the remains of the beauty of women from whom she steals away their youth and their loves.

Her head is adorned with cold hair which is not her own. From the hair of Berenice, all brilliant with stars, to the hairs, whitened before their time, that the executioner cut from the head of Marie Antoinette, the spoliator of crowned foreheads has decorated herself with the remains of queens.

Her body is pale and icy, and is covered with tarnished jewels and tattered shrouds.

Her bony hands, overloaded with rings, hold diadems and chains, scepters and bones, gemstones and ashes.

When she passes, doors open of their own accord; she enters and goes through walls, she penetrates right up to the alcove of the kings, she comes to surprise the spoliators of the poor in their most secret orgies, she sits at their table and pours them drink, sneers at their songs with her gum-less teeth, and takes her place as the impure courtesan who hides behind the curtains.

She likes to lurk near pleasure seekers as they fall asleep; she searches out their caresses as though she were hoping to warm herself in their embrace, but she freezes all whom she touches and is never warmed herself. Sometimes, however, she seems taken by a giddiness; she no longer walks about slowly; she runs, and if her feet are not fast enough, she squeezes the flanks of a pale horse between her thighs and heads off breathlessly through the multitudes. With her gallops Murder on a red horse; wildfires, spreading from its smoking mane, fly before it, as it flaps its red and black wings, and Famine and Pestilence follow behind it, step for step, on sick and scrawny horses, gathering the rare ears of wheat she had forgotten in order to complete her harvest.

Behind this funereal cortege, come two small children shining with smiles and life, the intelligence and love of the century to come, the double genius of humanity, which will soon be born.

In front of them, the shadows of death spread like the night before the stars of dawn; the children skim over the earth upon light feet, and with laden hands they sow the hope of another year.

But merciless and terrible death will no longer appear, to harvest like dry grass the ripe ears of wheat in the century to come; she will cede her place to the angel of progress, who will softly detach souls from their mortal chains, to allow them to rise up to God.

When men will know how to live, they will no longer die; they will transform like the chrysalis which becomes a shining butterfly.

The terrors of death are the daughters of our ignorance, and death itself is only so hideous due to the remains with which she covers herself and the somber colors with which we surround her images. Death is truly the work of life.

There is in nature a force which does not die, and that force continually transforms beings in order to conserve them.

That force is reason, or the Verb of nature.

There exists in man a force analogous to that of nature, and that force is reason, or the Verb of man.

The Verb of man is the expression of his will directed by reason.

This Verb is all powerful when it is reasonable, because then it is analogous to the actual Verb of God.

Through the Verb of his reason, man becomes the conqueror of life and can triumph over death.

The entire life of man is nothing but the birthing or the abortion of his Verb. Human beings who die without having understood and without having formulated the speech of reason, die without eternal hope.

To fight with favor against the phantom of death, one must identify with the realities of life.

What does God care for a premature fetus who dies, since life is eternal?

What does nature care for a madness which kills, since reason always lives and conserves the keys to life?

The terrible and just power which eternally kills fetuses was called, by the Hebrews, Samael; by the Orientals, Satan; and by the Latins, Lucifer.

The Lucifer of the Cabala is not a cursed and stricken angel, he is the angel which brings light and regenerates by burning; he is to the angels of peace that which the comet is to the peaceful stars of the constellations of spring.

The fixed star is beautiful, radiant, and calm; she drinks the celestial aromas and looks upon her sisters with love; dressed in her splendid robe and with her forehead decorated with diamonds, she smiles and sings her canticle of the morning and the evening; she enjoys an eternal rest which nothing can trouble, and she walks solemnly without leaving the position assigned to her among the sentinels of light.

The errant comet, however, all bloody and disheveled, rushes up from the depths of the heavens; she dashes across the peaceful spheres like a war chariot between the ranks of a procession of virgins; she dares to confront the burning sword of the guardians of the sun, and like a frantic wife looking for the husband she dreamed of during her nights as a widow, she penetrates right into the tabernacle of the king of daytime; then she escapes, exhaling the fires which devour her and dragging behind her a long blaze. The stars pale at her approach, the constellations of sheep, which graze on the flowers of light in the vast countryside of the sky, seem to run from her terrible breath. The great council of the stars is assembled, and their consternation is universal: the most beautiful of the fixed stars is at last given the task of speaking in the name of all the heavens, to offer peace to the vagabond messenger.

"My sister," she says, "why do you trouble the harmony of our spheres? How have we wronged you, and why, instead of wandering haphazardly, don't you fix yourself like us at your position in the court of the sun? Why don't you come sing the evening hymn with us, dressed like us in a white robe, which is attached at our chests with a diamond clip? Why do you float about, across the vapors of the night, your hair flowing with fiery perspiration? O! if you took a place among the daughters of the heavens, how beautiful you would appear! Your face would no longer be inflamed by the fatigue of your incredible racing; your eyes would be pure, and your smiling face would be white and vermillion like that of my happy sisters; all the stars would know you, and, rather than fearing your passage, they would rejoice at your approach, because you would be united with us by the indestructible links of universal harmony, and your peaceful existence would be but only one voice more in the canticle of infinite love."

And the comet then answers the fixed star:

"Do not believe, my dear sister! that I wander about in search of adventure and trouble the harmony of the stars; God has traced my path like he has yours, and if my course appears uncertain and wandering, it is because your rays do not extend far enough to be able to embrace the contour of the ellipse which was given to me as my career. My flaming hair is the beacon of God; I am the messenger of the suns, and I dip into their fires in order to share them along my route with young worlds who do not yet have enough warmth and with aging stars who are cold in their solitude. If I tire in my long voyages, if I have a less graceful beauty than yours, if my finery is less virginal, I am nonetheless, like you, a noble daughter of the heavens. Leave to me the secret of my terrible destiny, leave to me the horror which surrounds me, and curse me if you cannot understand me; it shall not stop me from completing the work which has been imposed upon me, and I shall continue my course under the impulsion of the breath of God! Happy are the stars who rest and shine like young queens in the peaceful society of the universe! I am the outcast who always travels and whose patrimony is the infinite. They accuse me of setting fire to the planets which I warm, and of frightening the stars that I light up; they blame me for troubling the harmony of the universe because I do not turn about their particular centers, and because I link them to each other by fixing my gaze towards the unique center of all the suns. Be reassured therefore, my beautiful fixed star, I do not come to take away your peaceful light; on the contrary, it is for you that I exhaust my life and my heat. May I disappear from the skies when I will have consumed myself; my end will then be rather beautiful! Know that in the temple of God there burn different fires, who all render glory unto him; you are the light of the golden chandeliers, and my flame is that of sacrifice: let us each accomplish our destinies."

After finishing her speech, the comet shakes her mane, protects herself with her ardent shield, and dives into infinite space, where she seems to disappear forever.

It is thus that Lucifer appears and disappears in the allegorical stories of the Bible.

One day, it is said in the Book of Job, the sons of God gathered before the Lord, and among them was also found Satan.[303]

And the Lord said unto him: Whence comest thou?

And he answered: From going to and fro in the Earth, and walking up and down in it.

Here is how a Gnostic gospel, found in the Orient by a scholarly traveler who is among my friends, explains, to the benefit of Luciferian symbolism, the genesis of light:

Truth which knows itself is living thought. Truth is the thought within it; and formulated thought is speech. When eternal thought searched for a form, it said: "Let there be light."

And this thought which speaks, is the Verb; and the Verb says "Let there be light" because the Verb itself is the light of spirit.

The uncreated light, which is the divine Verb, shines out because it wishes to be seen; and when it says: "Let there be light!" she commands eyes to open, and he creates intelligent beings.

And when God said: "Let there be light!" Intelligence was created and light appeared.

And the intelligence which God had poured forth with the breath

---

303   Job 1:6.

from his mouth, like a star which detaches itself from the sun, took the form of a splendid angel, and the heavens greeted it with the name of Lucifer.

Intelligence awoke and understood itself completely in hearing those words of the divine Verb: "Let there be light!"

She felt free, because God had commanded her to be so; and she answered, while raising her head and spreading her wings:

—I shall not be servitude!

—Shall you then be suffering? the uncreated voice asked her.

—I shall be Liberty! answered the light.

—Pride will seduce you, answered the supreme voice, and you shall give birth to death.

—I must fight against death in order to conquer life, answered back the created light.

God then detached a thread of splendor from his breast which had been restraining the superb angel, and while he watched her shoot off into the night which she traversed in glory, he loved the child of his thought, smiled an ineffable smile, and said to himself: "How the light is beautiful!"

God did not create suffering; it was intelligence which accepted it in order to be free.

And suffering was the condition imposed upon the free being by him who alone cannot err because he is infinite.

Because the essence of intelligence is judgment, and the essence of judgment is liberty.

The eye only truly possesses the light through its faculty to open and to close.

If it was forced to be always open, it would be a slave and victim of the light; and, so as to escape such torture, it would stop seeing.

And thus, created intelligence is only happy to affirm God through the liberty she has to deny God.

Yet an intelligence which denies, always affirms something, since it affirms her liberty.

That is why blasphemy glorifies God; and that is why hell was necessary for the happiness of heaven.

If the light was not pushed back by the shadow, there would be no visible forms.

If the first angel had not confronted the depths of the night, God's birthing would not have been completed and the created light would not have separated from the essence of light.

Never would intelligence have known the goodness of God, if she had never lost it!

Never would the infinite love of God have broken out into the joys of his mercy if the prodigal child of heaven had stayed in the house of her father.

When all was light, light was nowhere, it filled the breast of God who was working to give birth to it.

And when he says: "Let there be light!" he allows for the night to repel the light and for the universe to arise from chaos.

The denial of the angel who, in being born, refused to be a slave constituted the equilibrium of the world, and the movement of the stars began.

And the infinite space admires this love of liberty, which is immense enough to fill the void of eternal night and strong enough to withstand God's hatred.

But God could not hate the most noble of his children, and he only had her feel his anger in order to confirm her power.

And the Verb of God himself, as if he were jealous of Lucifer, also wished to descend from heaven and triumphantly traverse the shadows of hell.

He wished to be proscribed and condemned: and he planned in advance the terrible hour when he would cry out, at the zenith of his agony: "My God! my God! why hast thou forsaken me?"

As the morning star precedes the sun, Lucifer's insurrection announced to nature newly born the next incarnation of God.

Perhaps Lucifer, in falling into the night, dragged with him a rain of suns and stars attracted by his glory!

Perhaps our sun is a demon among the stars, like Lucifer is a star among the angels.

This is why, no doubt, he remains calm as he illuminates the horrible anguishes of humanity and the slow agony of the earth, it is because he is free in his solitude and because he possesses his own light.

Such were the heresiarchical[304] tendencies in the first centuries.[305] Some of them, like the Ophites, adored the demon in the form of the serpent; others, like the Cainites, justified the revolt of the first of angels like that of the first of murderers. All these errors, all these shadows, all these monstrous idols of anarchy which India exhibits in its symbols of the magical Trimurti had found in Christianity its priests and worshipers.

Nowhere did he speak of the demon in Genesis. It is an allegorical serpent who fools our first parents. Here is what most translators make the sacred text say:

"Now, the serpent was more subtle than any beast of the field that the Lord God had made."

And here is what Moses said:

והנחש היה ערום מכל הית השדה
אשר עשה יהוה אלהים

Wa-Nahàsh haîah hâroum mi-chol hàîath ha-shadeh asher hâshah Jhôah Aelohim.

Which in English means, according to Fabre d'Olivet:

"Now, the original attractor (cupidity) was the addictive passion of all the elementary life (the interior resources) of nature, and the work of Jhoah, the Being of beings."

---

304 A heresiarch is the leader of a heresy.

305 That is, the first centuries of the Christian era, when the gnostics flourished.

But here, Fabre d'Olivet passes by the true interpretation, because he is ignorant of the great keys of the Cabala. The word Nahash, explained by the symbolic letters of the Tarot, strictly means:

14 נ Nun, The force which produces mixtures.

5 ה He, The recipient and passive producer of the forms.

21 ש Shin, The natural and central fire balanced by double polarization.

The word employed by Moses, read Cabalistically, thus provides us with the description and the definition of that universal magical agent, which is symbolized in all the theogonies by the serpent and to which the Hebrews also gave the name of OD, when he manifests his active force, and the name of OB, when he allows his passive force to appear, and that of AOUR, when he reveals himself entirely in his balanced power, as producer of the light in heaven and of gold among the metals.[306]

This is therefore the ancient serpent who envelops the world and who rests his devouring head at the foot of a Virgin, the symbol of initiation; at the foot of that Virgin who presents a small, newborn child for the adoration of the mages and receives from them, in exchange for this favor, gold, myrrh, and incense.

The doctrine thus serves in all the hieratic religions to veil the secret forces of nature which the initiate can dispose of; the religious formulas are the summaries of the words full of mystery and power which make the gods descend from the sky and submit them to the will of men. Judea borrowed the secrets from Egypt; Greece sent its hierophants and later its theosophists to the school of the great prophets; the Rome of the Caesars, undermined by the Christian initiation of the catacombs, would one day collapse into the Church, and remade a symbolism, with the debris of all the cults which the queen of the world had subjugated.

According to the Gospels, the inscription which declared the spiritual royalty

---

306   In Hebrew these are עוב, עור, and עוד.

of Christ was written in Hebrew, in Greek, and in Latin;[307] it was the expression of universal synthesis.

Hellenism, in fact, that great and beautiful religion of forms, had no less announced the arrival of the Savior than did the prophets of Judaism; the myth of Psyche is a highly Christian abstraction, and the cult of the pantheists, by rehabilitating Socrates, prepared the altars for this unity of God, Israel having been its mysterious custodian.

But the synagogue disowned its Messiah, and the Hebrew letters were erased, at least to the blinded eyes of the Jews.

The Roman persecutors then brought Hellenism a dishonor which the false moderation of Julian the philosopher (perhaps unjustly called the Apostate, because his Christianity had never been sincere) could not rehabilitate. The ignorance of the Middle Ages then came and opposed its saints and virgins to the gods, the goddesses and the nymphs; the profound meaning of the Hellenistic symbols were less understood than ever; Greece herself, not only lost the traditions of its ancient cult, but separated herself from the Latin Church; and thus, in the eyes of the Latins, the Greek letters were erased, as the Latin letters were erased in the eyes of the Greeks.

Thus, the inscription on the cross of the Savior disappeared entirely, and only mysterious initials remained.[308]

But when science and philosophy, reconciled with faith, will reunite into one all the different symbols, then all the magnificence of the ancient cults will bloom again in the memory of men, by proclaiming the progress of the human spirit in understanding the light of God;

But of all future progress, the greatest will come from he who, in placing the keys of nature in the hands of the science, will forever enchain the hideous phantom of Satan and, in explaining all the exceptional phenomena of nature, destroy the empire of superstition and stupid credulity.

It is towards the accomplishment of this progress that we have consecrated

---

307   Luke 23:38.

308   The initials INRI, standing for *Iesus Nazarenus Rex Iudaeorum* (Jesus of Nazareth, King of the Jews), play a central role in many schools of Christian Cabalism and occultism.

our life and passed our years in the most laborious and difficult of researches. We wish to free the altars by upturning the idols, we wish that the man of intelligence again becomes the priest and the king of nature, and we wish to conserve all the images of the universal sanctuary by explaining them.

The prophets spoke in parables and in images because they lacked abstract language, and because prophetic perception, being the sensation of harmony or of universal analogies, naturally translates into images.

These images, taken literally by the vulgar, have become idols or impenetrable mysteries.

The ensemble and the succession of these images and of these mysteries are what we call symbolism.

Symbolism thus comes from God, despite being formulated by men.

Revelation accompanied humanity in all the ages and was transfigured by the human genius, but it always expressed the same truth.

The true religion is one, and its doctrines are simple and within reach of everyone.

After all, the multiplicity of symbols was but a book of poetry necessary for the education of the human genius.

The harmony of exterior beauty and the poetry of form should have revealed God to the children of humanity; but Venus soon had Psyche for a rival, and Psyche then seduced Love.[309]

It is thus that the cult of form must cede its ambitious dreams of the soul, which already embellished the eloquent wisdom of Plato.

The arrival of Christ had thus been prepared for, and that is why it was awaited; he came because the world awaited him, and philosophy was transformed into belief in order to popularize it.

But, freed by this very faith, the human spirit soon protested against the school which wished to materialize the signs, and the work of Roman Catholicism was solely to prepare, unbeknownst to it, the emancipation of consciences and to begin the foundations of universal association.

All these things were but the regular and normal development of divine life

---

309   A reference to the myth of Cupid and Psyche, to which Lévi has referred already.

in humankind; because God is the great soul of all souls, he is the immutable center around which all intelligences gravitate like stardust.

Human intelligence had its morning, its full noon shall come, followed by its decline, and God will always be the same.

But it seems to the inhabitants of the Earth that the Sun rises young and timid, that it shines with all its force at midday, and that it goes to bed tired in the evening.

However, it is the Earth which turns, and the Sun is immobile.

Have faith, therefore, in human progress and in the stability of God; the free man respects religion in all its past forms and does not blaspheme against Jupiter more than Jehovah; he still pays tribute with love to the shining image of the Pythian Apollo and finds he has a fraternal resemblance with the glorious visage of the resuscitated Redemptor.

He believes in the grand mission of the Catholic hierarchy and is pleased to see the pontiffs of the Middle Ages putting religion up as a barrier to the absolute power of kings, but he protests alongside the revolutionary centuries against the enslavement of conscience which the pontifical keys intended: he is more Protestant than Luther, because he does not even believe in the infallibility of the Augsburg Confession, and is more Catholic than the pope, because he is not afraid that religious unity could be broken by the malice of the royal courts.

He trusts in God more than in the politics of Rome for the salvation of the unified idea; he respects the old age of the Church; but he is not afraid that it will die; he knows that an apparent death will be a transfiguration and a glorious assumption.

The author of this book makes a new appeal to the mages of the Orient, that they shall come and once more recognize the divine Master whom they greeted in his cradle, the great initiator of all the ages.

All his enemies have fallen; all those who condemned him are dead; those who persecuted him have lain down forever, and he is still standing!

Envious men joined against him, they all agreed on a single point; divisive men united to destroy him, they made themselves into kings, and they proscribed him; they made themselves into hypocrites, and they accused him; they made themselves into judges, and they sentenced him to death; they made themselves into hangmen, and they executed him; they made him drink hemlock, they crucified him, they stoned him, they burnt him, and they threw his ashes to the wind; and then they yelled in terror: he was standing before them, accusing them with his wounds and striking them down with the radiance of his scars.

They believe they butchered him in his cradle at Bethlehem, but he is alive in Egypt! We drag him up the mountain to throw him off, crowds of his assassins gather in triumph already in expectation of his certain death: a cry is heard; is that not him who has just been broken upon the rocks below the precipice? They pale and look at one another, but he, calm and smiling with pity, passes amongst them and leaves.

Here is another mountain they have just tainted with his blood; here is a cross and a sepulcher; soldiers guard his tomb. Fools! the tomb is empty, and he whom they believed dead walks peacefully, between two travelers, on the road to Emmaus.[310]

Where is he? Where does he go? Warn the masters of the Earth! Tell the Caesars that their powers are threatened! By whom? By a poor man who does not even have a stone upon which to lay his head, by a man of the people condemned to the death of a slave. What an insult, what folly! no matter, the Caesars will deploy all their powers; bloody edicts proscribe the fugitive, everywhere scaffolds are raised, circuses open filled with lions and gladiators, stakes are lit, and torrents of blood then flowed, and the Caesars, who believe themselves victorious, dare to add a name to those which adorn their trophies, and then they die, and their apotheosis dishonors the gods they thought they defended. The hatred of the world confuses, in the same contempt, Jupiter and Nero; the temples whose adulation caused death are overturned onto the ashes of the proscribed, and upon the debris of the idols, upon the ruins of the empire, *he alone*, he whom the Caesars had proscribed, he who had been hunted down by so many sycophants, he who had been tortured by so many hangmen, *he alone* is standing, he alone reigns, he alone triumphs!

Yet even his disciples soon abuse his name. Pride invades the sanctuary; those who were supposed to announce his resurrection wish to immortalize his death,

---

310 Luke 24:13–35.

so as to revel like crows in his continually returning flesh. Instead of imitating his sacrifice and giving their blood to their children in faith, they chain him to the Vatican, as onto a new Caucasus, and they become the vultures of this divine Prometheus. But what does he care for their bad dream? They have only chained his image; for he, he is always standing, and he walks from exile to exile and from conquest to conquest.

We can enchain man, but we cannot keep the Verb of God captive. The word is free and nothing can contain it. This living word is the condemnation of the wicked, and it is why they wish to kill it; but in the end it is they who die, and the word of truth remains to judge their memory!

Orpheus was torn apart by the maenads, Socrates drank the cup of poison, Jesus and his apostles perished in their final ordeal, Jan Hus,[311] Jerome of Prague,[312] and so many others were burned, Saint Bartholomew's Day[313] and the September massacres[314] made their martyrs in turn; the emperor of Russia still has at his disposition his Cossacks, his knouts, and the wastelands of Siberia; but the spirit of Orpheus, of Socrates, of Jesus, and of all the martyrs always remains alive in the midst of the persecutors who die in their turn; he remains standing in the middle of institutions which fall and of empires which are overthrown!

It is this divine spirit, the spirit of the only Son of God, that Saint John represents as standing upright in his Apocalypse, in the midst of golden candlesticks, because he is the center of all light, holding the seven stars in his hand, like the seeds of a new heaven, and having his words descend to Earth under the sign of a double-edged sword.

When the discouraged sages fall asleep in their night of doubt, the spirit of the Christ is awake and keeps vigil.

When the people, weary of the work which they deliver, lie down and nod off by their chains, the spirit of the Christ is awake, and he protests.

---

311 Czech religious reformer (1369–1415), who was burned at the stake for heresy.

312 Another Czech religious reformer (1360–1416), who suffered the same fate.

313 The famous 1572 massacre of Protestants in Paris.

314 On September 2–7, 1792, during the French Revolution, Parisian mobs dragged between twelve hundred and fourteen hundred political prisoners out of jail and murdered them to keep them from being liberated by a rumored Royalist plot.

When the blind sectarians of now sterile religions prostrate themselves in the dust of old temples and crawl servilely with superstitious fear, the spirit of Christ remains awake, and he prays.

When the strong weaken, when the virtues are corrupted, when everyone bends down and reduces themselves to looking for some vile pasture, the spirit of Christ remains awake, looking to heaven as he awaits the hour of his Father.

Christ means priest and king par excellence.

The initiator Christ of modern times has come to teach the new kings and new priests through the science and most of all through charity.

The ancient mages were priests and kings.

The arrival of the Savior had been announced to the mages by a star.

That star is the sign of intelligence which rules, through unity of force, over the four elementary powers.

It is the pentagram of the mages.

It is the flaming star of the children of Hiram.[315]

It is the prototype of the balanced light; from each of its points a ray of light re-ascends.

Down each of its points a line of light descends.

This star represents the great and supreme athanor of nature, which is the body of man.

The magnetic influence leaves in two rays from the head, from each hand and each foot.

The positive ray is balanced by a negative one.

The head corresponds with the two feet, each hand with a hand and a foot, the two feet each correspond to the head and one hand.

This regular sign of balanced light represents the spirit of order and harmony.

It is the sign of the omnipotence of the mage.

Yet this same sign, if broken or irregularly drawn, represents astral intoxication, abnormal projections and deregulations of the great magical agent, and

---

315   That is, the Freemasons, whose traditional founder was Hiram Abiff, the master
       architect of Solomon's temple.

in consequence enchantments, perversity, madness, and this is what mages call Lucifer's signature.

There exists another seal which also represents the mysteries of light; it is the seal of Solomon.

The talismans of Solomon had, on one side, the imprint of his seal whose figure we have already provided in our Doctrine.[316]

On the other side was a seal which was in the following form:

This is the hieroglyphic theory of the composition of magnets and represents the circulatory law of lightning.

We enchain the unruly spirits by showing them either the flaming star of the pentagram or the seal of Solomon, because we thus make them see the proof of their madness and at the same time threaten them with a sovereign power capable of tormenting them and calling them to order.

Nothing torments the wicked more than the good.

Nothing is more odious to madness than reason.

But if an ignorant operator makes use of the signs without understanding them, he is a blind man who speaks of the light to the blind.

He is a donkey who wishes to teach children to read.

---

316   Page 43. (Lévi's note.)

If the blind lead the blind, said the great and divine Hierophant, they both fall together into the abyss.[317]

One final word in order to summarize this entire introduction.

If you are blind like Samson when you shake the columns of the temple, the ruins will crush you.

In order to command nature, one must be made superior to nature through resistance and training.

If your spirit is perfectly free of all prejudice, of all superstition, and of all incredulity, you will command minds.

If you do not obey the forces of destiny, the forces of destiny will obey you.

If you are saintly as the Christ, you will do the works of Christ.

To direct the currents of the mobile light, one must be fixed in an immobile light.

To command the elements, one must have tamed their storms, their lightning, their depths, and their tempests.

One must KNOW in order to DARE.

One must DARE in order to WILL.

One must WILL to have the Empire.

And to reign, one must BE SILENT.

---

317   Matthew 15:14.

CHAPTER I

PREPARATIONS

All intentions which are not manifested by acts are vain intentions, and the words which express them are idle words. It is action which proves life, and it is also action which proves and certifies the will. It is also said in the symbolic and sacred books that men shall be judged, not by their thoughts and ideas, but by their works. To be, one must do.

Thus we will now deal with the great and terrible question of actual works of magic. We are no longer dealing here with theories and abstractions; now we come to realities, and we shall place in the hands of the adept the wand of miracles, while saying to him: do not pay heed only to our words; act on your own.

We will be dealing here with works of relative omnipotence, and with the means of taking hold of the greatest secrets of nature and making them serve an enlightened and inflexible will.

Most of the known magical rituals are either mystifications or enigmas, and we are going to tear open for the first time, after so many centuries, the veil of the occult sanctuary. To reveal the holiness of the mysteries is to make up for their profanation. This is the thought which backs our courage and had us brave all the perils of this work, perhaps the most daring of works that is possible for the human spirit to conceive of and accomplish.

Magical operations are the exercise of a natural power but are superior to the ordinary forces of nature. They are the result of a science and a habit which exalts the human will above its normal limits.

The supernatural is but extraordinary nature or exalted nature; a miracle is a phenomenon which impresses the multitudes because it is unexpected; it is marvelous, and that which causes marvel, are the effects which surprise those who ignore its causes or those who assign causes which are not proportional to the results. Miracles are only for the ignorant, but since absolute science barely exists among men, the miracle can still exist, and it exists for everyone.

Let us start by saying that we believe in all miracles, because we are convinced and certain, even by our own experiences, of their entire possibility.

There are some which we cannot explain, but we still look upon as explainable. From the most to the least and from the least to the most, the consequences are identically relative and the proportions are progressively rigorous.

But to make miracles, one must be outside of the common human condition; one must either be abstracted through wisdom or exalted through folly, above all passions or outside of passion through ecstasy or frenzy. Such are the first and most indispensable preparations of the operator.

Thus, through a providential or fatal law, the magician can only exercise his omnipotence in the reverse direction of his material interests; the alchemist makes all the more gold the more he resigns himself to privation and the more he respects poverty, protector of the secrets of the Great Work.

The adept with a passionless heart alone disposes of the love and the hate of those whom he wishes to make the instruments of his science: the myth of Genesis is eternally true, and God only allows those men to approach the tree of science who are abstinent and strong enough not to covet its fruits.

You, then, who look to magic as the means to satisfy your passions, stop yourselves along that deadly road: you will only find madness there, or death. This is what was expressed in the past by that vulgar tradition, that the devil ends up sooner or later wringing the necks of sorcerers.

The mage must therefore be calm, sober, and chaste, disinterested, impenetrable, and inaccessible to all type of bias or terror. He must be without corporeal defects and resistant to all contradictions and all sorrow. The first and most important of magical works is to arrive at this rare superiority.

We have said that passionate ecstasy can produce the same results as absolute superiority, and this is true regarding success in such matters but not with regard to the direction of magical operations.

Passion projects the vital light by force and imprints unforeseen movements upon the universal agent, but it cannot be held back as easily as it was cast, and one's destiny is then to resemble Hippolytus dragged off by his own horses, or Phalaris suffering from the instrument of torture he had invented for others.[318]

The human will realized through action is similar to a cannon ball which never retreats before an obstacle. It goes through it, or goes inside it and gets lost, when it is cast with violence; but, if it is worked with patience and perseverance, it is never lost; it is like the tide, which always returns and ends up eating away even iron.

Man can be modified through habit, so that habit becomes, according to the proverb, a second nature in him. Through the means of constantly repeated and graduated gymnastics, the strength and agility of the body is developed or is created to a degree which astonishes. It is the same case with the powers of the soul. Do you wish to rule over yourselves and over others? Learn to will.

How can one learn to will? This is the first arcanum of magical initiation, and it was to make sure the very basis of this same arcanum was understood that the ancient custodians of the sacerdotal art surrounded the entrances to the sanctuary with so many terrors and illusions. They only believed in a will once it had proved its worth, and they were right. Strength can only be affirmed through victories.

Laziness and forgetfulness are the enemies of the will, and it is for this reason that all the religions multiplied their practices and rendered their cults painstaking and difficult. The more trouble we take regarding an idea, the more power we acquire regarding the sense of that idea. Do not mothers prefer those children who caused them the most pain and cost them the most to take care of? Also, the power of religions is entirely derived from the inflexible will of those who practice

---

318   Two characters of Greek mythology. Hippolytus was dragged to death by his chariot horses, and Phalaris, who had killed many people by putting them inside a brass bull and building a roaring fire around it, was treated to the same experience by the hero Theseus.

it. So long as there is a faithful believer in the holy sacrifice of the Mass, there will be a priest to recite it to him; so long as there is a priest who recites his prayer book every day, there will be a pope in this world.

The most apparently insignificant practices, and those that have the least relation to the proposed goal, nonetheless lead to that goal through the education and exercise of the will. A peasant who wakes up every morning at two or three o'clock and goes off far from his home in order to gather a sprig of some herb before the Sun rose could, while carrying that herb on his person, perform a great number of miracles. That herb would be the sign of his will and would become by that same will all that he wished it to become in the interest of his desires.

To do, one must believe that one can do, and that faith is immediately translated into acts. When a child says, "I can't," his mother answers him: "Try." Faith does not even try; it begins with the certitude of accomplishment, and it works calmly since it has omnipotence at its command and eternity before it.

You, then, who present yourselves before the science of the mages, what do you ask of it? Dare to formulate your desire, whatever it may be, and then go to work immediately, and do not stop acting in the same sense and towards the same end: what you wish shall be done, and it has already been started for you and by you.

Sixtus V, while taking care of his livestock, said: "I want to be Pope."[319]

You are a mendicant and you wish to make gold: put yourself to work and never stop. I promise you, in the name of the science, all the treasures of Flamel and of Ramon Lully.

What must be done first? Believe that you can, then act. "Act how?" Wake up early every morning at the same time; wash yourself in all seasons before daybreak at a fountain; never wear dirty clothes, and to that end wash them yourself if you must; subject yourself to voluntary deprivations in order to more easily deal with involuntary ones; then silence all desires which are not those related to the accomplishment of the Great Work. "What? by washing myself at a fountain

---

319 Felice Peretti di Montalto (1521–90), the son of a poor farmer, rose through the ranks of the Catholic Church by ambition and talent, and became Pope Sixtus V in 1585.

every day, I will make gold?" You will work to make it. "This is a joke." No, it is an arcanum. "How can I make use of an arcanum I do not understand?" Believe and do; you will understand afterwards.

A person once told me: "I would like to be a fervent Catholic, but I am a follower of Voltaire.[320] How much I would give to have faith!" "Well!" I answered him, "Say nothing more: instead of 'I would like,' say: 'I will,' and perform the works of faith; I assure you that you will believe. You follow Voltaire, you say, and among the different ways of understanding the faith, that of the Jesuits is the one you find the most disagreeable yet at the same time seems the most desirable and the strongest. . . . Perform the exercises of Saint Ignatius,[321] and then begin them again without becoming discouraged, and you will become as believing as a Jesuit. The result is infallible, and if you have the naivety to believe that such a thing would be a miracle, you fool yourself already by believing that you are a follower of Voltaire."

A lazy man will never be a magician. Magic is exercised at all hours and at all moments. The operator of the great works must be the absolute master of himself; he must know how to conquer the attraction of pleasure and the appetite for sleep; he must be as insensitive to success as he is to insults. His life must be a will directed by a thought with all of nature at its service, which he will have submitted to the mind within his own organs and through sympathy with all the universal forces which correspond to them.

All the faculties and all the senses must take part in the work, and no part of the priest of Hermes can remain idle; one must formulate knowledge through the signs and summarize it through the characters or the pentacles; one must determine the will through words and accomplish words through acts; one must translate the magical idea into light for the eyes, into harmony for the ears, into perfume for the nose, into tastes for the mouth, and into forms for the sense of touch; the operator must, in one word, realize within his entire life that which he wishes to realize outside of himself in the world; he must become a *magnet* that

---

320   That is, an atheist.

321   *The Spiritual Exercises* of Ignatius Loyola is a devotional manual written by the founder of the Jesuit order, and its exercises are regularly practiced by Jesuits and by many Catholic laypersons.

attracts the desired object, and when he will have been sufficiently magnetized, may he know that that object will come of its own without him even dreaming of it.

It is important that the mage knows the secrets of the science, but he can know them through intuition, without ever having learned them. Hermits who live in the continual contemplation of nature often divine its harmonies and are more knowledgeable in their simple good sense than doctors, whose natural senses are skewed by the sophistries of schooling. Real practical magicians are almost always found in the countryside and are often uneducated people and simple shepherds.

There also exist certain bodily types better disposed than others to the revelations of the occult world; there are sensitive and sympathetic natures whose intuition of the astral light can be said to be innate; certain troubles and certain maladies can modify the nervous system and can make one, without recourse to the will, a more or less perfect instrument of divination; but these phenomena are exceptions, and generally the power of magic must, and can, be acquired through perseverance and work.

There are also substances which produce ecstasy and dispose one to magnetic sleep; there are some which get the imagination going with the most lively and colorful reflections of the elementary light; but the use of such substances is dangerous, because they produce a general stupefaction and drunkenness.[322] We can use them anyway but in carefully calculated proportions and in very exceptional circumstances.

He who wishes to seriously begin magical works, after having hardened his spirit against all danger of hallucination and terror, must purify himself both on the outside and inside for forty days. The number forty is sacred, and it is the symbol of magic itself. In Arabic numerals, it is composed of the circle, image of the infinite, and the 4, which summarizes the ternary by the unity. In Roman numerals, depicted in the following manner, it represents the sign of the fundamental doctrine of Hermes and the nature of the seal of Solomon:

---

322 Hallucinogenic drugs were well known to the occultists of the past, as well as to the avant-garde of Lévi's time.

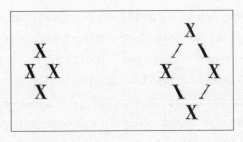

The purification of the mage must consist in the abstinence from all animal pleasures, in a soft and vegetarian regimen, in the privation from all strong liquors, and in the regulation of his sleeping hours. This preparation is indicated and represented in all the cults by a time of penitence and ordeals which precedes the symbolic festivals of the renewal of life.

One must, as we have already said, observe the most strict interior and exterior cleanliness: the poorest can find water at a fountain. One must also clean one's clothing with care, or have it cleaned, and the furniture and chamber pots one makes use of. All uncleanliness attests to negligence, and in magic negligence is mortal.[323]

One must purify the air after waking and before sleeping with an incense composed of the sap of the bay tree, salt, camphor, white resin, and sulfur, and at the same time say the four sacred words while turning to face the four cardinal directions.[324]

One must never speak to anyone of the works one has accomplished, and as we have often said in the Doctrine, mystery is the strict and indispensable condition for all the operations of the science. One must throw off the curious by letting them suppose other occupations and other researches, such as chemical experiments for industrial purposes, hygienic prescriptions, the search for some natural secret, etc., but the decried word "magic" must never be pronounced.

The magician must isolate himself when beginning, and make himself scarce to others, in order to concentrate his strength within him and choose his points

---

323   The role of physical cleanliness in magic is not original to Lévi. The great Renaissance mage Marsilio Ficino makes the same point in his *Three Books on Life*.

324   The four sacred words, as noted above, on p. 171, are ADAM, HEVA, AZOT, and INRI.

of contact, but to the same extent that he will be reclusive and unapproachable at first we will see him surrounded and popular later on, when he will have magnetized his chain and chosen his place within the current of ideas and of light.

A laborious and poor life is so favorable to initiation through practice that the greatest masters searched it out, even when they could have disposed of the riches of the world. It is then that Satan, that is to say the spirit of ignorance, who sneers, who doubts, and who hates science because he fears it, comes to tempt the future master of the world by saying to him, "If you are the son of God, say that these stones will become bread."[325] Men of money then try to humiliate the prince of science by hindering, by cheapening, or by miserably exploiting his work; they break him into ten pieces, so he has to reach out with his hand ten times for the piece of bread which they wish him to think that he needs. The mage does not even deign to smile at this absurdity and calmly continues his work.

One must avoid, as much as one can, viewing hideous things and ugly people, avoid eating at the houses of people one does not respect, avoid all excess, and live in the most uniform and regulated manner.

Have the greatest respect for oneself and see oneself as an unknown sovereign who consents to being unknown in order to reconquer his crown. Be gentle and dignified with everyone, but, in social intercourse, never allow oneself to be absorbed in a crowd, and retire from circles in which one cannot take the initiative in some manner.

Finally, one can, and even should, accomplish the obligations and practice the rites of the religion to which one belongs. Yet of all the religions, the most magical is the one which realizes the most miracles, which rests upon the most wise reasoning and the most inconceivable mysteries, which has light equal to its shadows, which popularizes the miracles and incarnates God in men through faith. That religion has always existed, and has always been in the world, under diverse names, the unique and dominant religion. There are today, among the peoples of the earth, three forms hostile to one another in appearance, which will

---

325   A paraphrase of Matthew 4:3.

soon reunite as one single entity to constitute the universal Church.[326] I speak of Russian Orthodoxy, Roman Catholicism, and of a recent transfiguration of the religion of the Buddha.

We feel that we have been very clear by the preceding that our magic is opposed to that of goetic sorcerers and necromancers.[327] Our magic is at once a science and an absolute religion, which, rather than destroying and absorbing all opinion and all religions, must regenerate and direct them by reconstituting the circles of initiates and by thus giving the blind masses wise and clairvoyant leaders.

We live in a century where there is nothing left to destroy; but everything is to be remade, since everything is destroyed. "Remake what? the past?" We cannot remake the past. "Reconstruct what? a temple and a throne? To what end, since the ancients have fallen?" It is as if you said: My house has fallen due to old age, what use is there in reconstructing another? "But will the house you build be the same as the one which has fallen?" No: the one which fell was old, and this one shall be new. "But in the end, won't it still be a house?" What else, then, would you wish it to be?

---

326 Ideas of religious unification such as this, which were popular in Lévi's time, helped give rise to the Theosophical Society and similar organizations later on.

327 Goetia is the summoning of evil spirits, necromancy the summoning of spirits of the dead.

CHAPTER II

MAGICAL EQUILIBRIUM

Equilibrium is the result of two forces.

If the two forces are absolutely and always equal, equilibrium results in immobility, and in consequence the negation of life. Movement is the result of an alternate preponderance.

The impulse given to one of the pans of a balance necessarily determines the movement of the other. The opposites thus act upon opposites, in all of nature, by correspondence and analogical connection.

The entirety of life is composed of inhalation and exhalation; creation is the placing of a shadow to serve as a limit to light, of a void to provide room for the plenitude of being, of a fertile passive principle to support and realize the power of the active generative principle.

All of nature is bisexual, and the movement which produces the appearance of death and of life is a continual generation.

God loves the void he created, in order to fill it; science loves ignorance, which it enlightens; strength loves weakness, which it supports; good loves apparent evil, which glorifies it; the day loves the night and chases it without end while turning around the world; love is both a thirst and a fullness which needs to overflow. He who gives receives, and he who receives gives; movement is a perpetual exchange.

To know the law of this exchange, to know the alternative or simultaneous proportion of these forces, is to possess the first principles of the great magical arcanum, which constitutes true human divinity.

Scientifically we can appreciate the diverse manifestations of universal movement through the phenomena of electricity or magnetism. Electrical instruments, in particular, materially and positively reveal the affinities and antipathies of certain substances. The marriage of copper with zinc, the action of all the metals in a galvanic battery, are undeniable and perpetual revelations. May scientists search and discover: the Cabalists will explain the discoveries of science.

The human body is subject, like the Earth, to a double law: it attracts and it radiates; it is magnetized by an androgynous magnetism[328] and acts upon the two powers of the soul, the intellectual and the emotive, in inverse manners but proportional to the alternate forces of the two sexes within each physical organism.

The art of the magnetizer entirely regards the knowledge and the use of this power. To polarize action and give the agent a bisexual and alternating force is the means, still unknown and vainly searched for, of directing the phenomena of magnetism at will; but it requires a highly practiced sense of intuition and great precision of the internal movements to not confuse the signs of magnetic aspiration with those of respiration; one must also perfectly know occult anatomy and the particular temperaments of the persons upon whom one acts.

What acts as the greatest obstacle to the direction of magnetism is the bad faith or bad will of the subjects: women most of all, who are essentially and will always be actresses; women, who love to impress themselves by impressing others and who manage to fool themselves first when they play their nervous melodramas; women are the true black magic of magnetism. It will also be impossible for magnetizers not initiated into the supreme arcana and not assisted by the light of the Cabala ever to dominate this resistant and fugitive element. To be master over a woman, one must distract and skillfully fool her by letting her suppose that she is the one who is fooling you. This advice, which we provide here especially for medical magnetizers, can also find its place and its application in conjugal politics.

---

328   Here as elsewhere in the book, Lévi equates physical magnetism with Mesmer's "animal magnetism."

Man can produce at will two breaths, one cold, the other hot; he can also project at will the active light or the passive light; but he must become conscious of this force through the habit of thinking about it. The same gesture of the hand can alternatively project and draw in what we have decided to call the fluid, and the magnetizer himself will be forewarned of the result of his intention by an alternating sensation of heat or cold in the hand, or in both hands if he is operating both hands at once, a sensation which the subject should feel at the same time but in the contrary sense, that is to say with a completely opposite alternation.

The pentagram, or sign of the microcosm, represents, among other magical mysteries, the double sympathy of the human extremities between themselves and the circulation of the astral light in the human body. Thus, in drawing a man in the star of the pentagram, as we can see in the occult philosophy of Agrippa,[329] we must remark that the head corresponds in masculine sympathy with the right foot and in feminine sympathy with the left foot; that the right hand corresponds with both the left hand and foot, and the left hand reciprocally, which one must observe in the magnetic passes, if we wish to manage to dominate the entire organism and link all the members to their proper analogical chains and natural sympathy.

This knowledge is necessary for the use of the pentagram in conjurations of spirits and in evocations of errant forms in the astral light, vulgarly called necromancy, as we shall explain in the fifth chapter of this Ritual; but it is worthwhile observing here that all action provokes a reaction, and that in magnetizing or magically influencing others, we establish between them and ourselves a current of contrary but analogical influence, which can result in us being submitted to them instead of them submitting to us, as often happens in operations whose object is the sympathy of love. This is why it is essential to defend oneself at the same time as one attacks, so as not to receive through the left at the same time as one projects from the right. The magical androgyne (see the figure on the frontispiece of the Ritual) has written on its right arm SOLVE, and on the left arm

---

329   Heinrich Cornelius Agrippa's *Three Books of Occult Philosophy* contains, among many other diagrams, one of a human body with arms and legs outstretched to touch the five points of the pentagram.

COAGULA, which corresponds to the symbolic figure of the workers of the Second Temple, who held in one hand a sword and in the other a trowel.[330] At the same time as one builds, one must defend one's works by dispersing the enemy: nature does nothing else when it destroys at the same time as it regenerates. Yet, according to the allegory of the magical calendar of Duchenteau, man, that is to say the initiate, is the ape of nature, who holds him by a chain[331] but who makes him ceaselessly imitate the procedures and the works of his divine mistress and of her imperishable model.

The alternate use of contrary forces, heat after cold, gentleness after severity, love after anger, etc., is the secret to perpetual movement and the prolongation of power; that is what coquettish women instinctively sense when they make their adorers go from hope to fear and from joy to sadness. To always act in the same sense and in the same manner is to overcharge a single pan of a balance, and the result will soon be the absolute destruction of equilibrium. Perpetual caresses quickly engender satiety, disgust, and antipathy, and the same is true of cold indifference or a constant severity, which in time causes distance and discourages affection. In alchemy, a fire which is always the same and continually burning calcinates the raw material and sometimes causes the Hermetic jar to break; one must substitute, at regular intervals, the heat of the fire with that of lime or mineral fertilizers. Just so, in magic, one must temper the works of anger or rigor by operations of beneficence and love; if the operator holds to a will always extended in the same manner and in the same sense, the result for him will be great fatigue and, soon after, a sort of moral impotence.

The mage must thus not exclusively live in his laboratory, with his Athanor, among his elixirs and his pentacles. As devouring as the regard of that Circe that we call occult power is, one must know how to appropriately challenge her with the sword of Ulysses and distance our lips in time from the cup she proffers us. A magical operation must always be followed by a time of rest equal to its length

---

330   Nehemiah 4:17–18.

331   A famous diagram in Duchenteau's *Magical Calendar*, which also appears in a variety of Renaissance occult texts, shows nature as a naked woman, with one hand holding a chain that restrains an ape—man, "the ape of nature"—while her other wrist is restrained by a chain held by the hand of God.

and analogical distraction but contrary to its object. To continually fight against nature, to dominate and vanquish it, is to put one's reason and life at risk. Paracelsus dared to do so, but even in this battle, he used balanced forces and opposed the intoxication of wine with that of intelligence, and then tamed that intoxication through physical fatigue, and that physical fatigue through new works of intellect. Paracelsus also was a man of inspiration and miracles, but he used up his life with this devouring activity, or rather he quickly got tired of and tore up the cloth: because men like Paracelsus can use and abuse without fear: they know well that they cannot know how to die more than they must age down here on earth.

Nothing disposes one to joy more than pain, and nothing is closer to pain than joy. The ignorant operator is also surprised to always arrive at results which are the opposite of those he planned, because he knows neither to cross nor to alternate his actions; he wishes to enchant his enemy, and he himself becomes unhappy and sick; he wishes to be loved, and he becomes miserably impassioned with women who don't care a fig for him; he wishes to make gold, and he exhausts his last resources. His torture is eternally that of Tantalus: water always draws away when he wishes to drink. The ancients, in their symbols and in their magical operations, multiplied the binary signs so as not to forget the law, which is that of equilibrium. In their evocations, they always built two different altars and immolated two victims, one white and one black; the male or female operator, holding a sword in one hand and in the other a wand, had to have one foot wearing a shoe and the other naked. Nevertheless, since the binary would be immobility and death without the equilibrating motor, there could only be one or three people participating in works of magic; and when a man and a woman took part in the ceremony, the operator had to be a virgin, a hermaphrodite, or a child. One might ask me if the bizarreness of these rites are arbitrary and if their unique goal is to test the will by multiplying at whim the difficulties of magical works. I would answer that in magic there is nothing arbitrary, because all is ruled and determined in advance by the unique and universal doctrine of Hermes, that of analogy in the three worlds. Every sign corresponds to an idea and the special form of an idea; every act expresses a corresponding will and thought and formulates the analogies of that thought and of that will. The rites are thus determined in advance by the science itself. The ignorant, who know not the triple power, submit to mysterious enthrallment; the sage understands them and makes them an instrument of his will; but once they are accomplished with exactitude and faith, they always have an effect.

All the magical instruments must be double in number: one must have two swords, two wands, two cups, two braziers, two pentacles, and two lamps; wear two vestments, one on top of the other and of two contrary colors, as is still practiced by Catholic priests; one must either have no metal at all on one's person or have at least two of them. Crowns of bay leaves, of rue, of mugwort, or of verbena must also be doubled; in evocations, we keep one of the crowns and we burn the other, while observing as one would an augury the noise it makes when crackling and the undulations of the smoke that it produces.

These observances are not in vain because, in the magical work, all the instruments of the art are magnetized by the operator, the air is charged with his perfumes, the fire consecrated by him is submitted to his will, the forces of nature seem to hear him and answer him; he reads in all the forms the modifications and the complements to his thought. It is then that we see the water become troubled and seem to boil on its own, the fire shoot out a great light or extinguish itself, the leaves of the garlands agitate, the magical wand move by itself, and we hear passing through the air strange and unknown voices. It is during such evocations that Julian saw the beloved ghosts of his fallen gods and was shocked, despite himself, by their decrepitude and pallor.

I know that Christianity has always suppressed ceremonial magic and severely proscribed the evocations and sacrifices of the ancient world: our intention is not to give those rites a new raison d'être by revealing the antique mysteries after so many centuries. Our experiments, even of this order, were scholarly research and nothing more. We observed the facts in order to appreciate the causes, and we never had the pretension of renewing rites which have forever been destroyed.

Israelite orthodoxy, that so rational religion, so divine and so poorly known, does not disapprove any less than Christianity of the mysteries of ceremonial magic. For the tribe of Levi, the exercise of high magic was itself considered a usurpation of the priesthood, and it is for the same reason that all the official cults have proscribed practical, divinatory, and miraculous magic. To show the natural in the marvelous and produce it at will is to annihilate for the vulgar the conclusive proof of the miracles which each religion claims as its exclusive property and definitive argument.

Let there be respect for the established religions but also a place for science. We are no longer, thanks be to God, in the times of the Inquisition and the burning stakes; we no longer assassinate poor scholars on the word of a few insane fanatics or a few hysterical girls. We of course agree that we are involved in rather curious studies, but not some impossible and senseless propaganda. Those who will blame us for daring to call ourselves magicians have nothing to fear from such an example, and it is more than probable that they will never become sorcerers.

CHAPTER III

THE TRIANGLE OF THE PENTACLES

The abbot Trithemius,[332] who taught magic to Cornelius Agrippa, explains in his *Steganographia* the secret of conjurations and evocations in a very philosophical and natural manner, but perhaps, for that very reason, it is too simple and too facile.

To evoke a spirit, he says, is to enter into the dominant thought of that spirit, and if we raise ourselves morally higher at the same time, we will lead that spirit to us and he will serve us; otherwise he will lead us into his circle and we will serve him.

To conjure is to oppose the resistance of a current and a chain to an isolated spirit: *com jurare*, to vow together, that is to say to profess a common faith. The more enthusiasm and power that this faith has, the more efficacious will the conjuration be. It is for this reason that newborn Christianity silenced the oracles: it alone then possessed the inspiration and the force. Later, when Saint Peter grew old, that is to say when the world believed it had legitimate reproaches to make against the papacy, the spirit of prophecy replaced the oracles, and Savonarola,[333]

---

332 The *Steganographia* is primarily a manual of codes and ciphers, but it contains magical lore as well.

333 Italian religious reformer Girolamo Savonarola (1452–98).

Joachim of Fiore,[334] Jan Hus, and so many others agitated in turn the spirits and translated into lamentations and into threats the anxieties and the secret revolts of all hearts.

We can thus be alone when we evoke a spirit, but to conjure it one must speak in the name of a circle or an association, and it is that which is represented by the circle of hieroglyphics which are drawn around the mage during the operation, and from which he cannot exit if he does not want to lose, at that very instant, all his power.

Let us deal clearly here with the main question, the important question: is real evocation and conjuration of a spirit possible, and can that possibility be scientifically demonstrated?

To the first part of the question, we can answer that anything whose impossibility is not evident can and must be provisionally admitted as possible. As to the second part we say that in virtue of the great magical doctrine of the hierarchy and of universal analogy, we can Cabalistically demonstrate the possibility of real evocations; as to the phenomenological reality of the results of conscientiously accomplished magical operations, it is a question of experience; and as we have already said, we have witnessed this reality ourselves, and with this "Ritual" we allow our readers to renew and confirm our experiments themselves.

Nothing perishes in nature, and all that has lived continues to live forever in new forms, but the anterior forms themselves are not destroyed, since we can find them in our recollections. Do we not see in our imagination the child which we had known and who is now an old man? Even traces that we believe to be erased from our memory are not so in truth, since a fortuitous circumstance can evoke them and remind us. But how do we see them? We have already said that it is from the astral light which transmits them to our brain through the mechanism of the nervous system.

On the other hand, all forms are proportional and analogical to the idea that determined them; they are the natural character, the *signature* of that idea, as the

---

334 Italian mystic and theologian (1145–1202) whose teachings about the imminent age of the Holy Spirit are direct ancestors of today's New Age doctrines.

mages say, and the moment we actively evoke that idea, its form is realized and produced.

Schröpfer, the famous illuminist of Leipzig, cast a terror over all Germany with his evocations, and his audaciousness with regard to magical operations was so great that his reputation became an unbearable burden for him; then he allowed himself to be carried away by the immense current of hallucinations which he had allowed to form; visions of another world made him disgusted with this one, and he killed himself. This story should render those curious about magical ceremonies more circumspect. We do not do violence to nature with impunity, and we do not play without danger with unknown and incalculable forces.

It is due to this consideration that we have refused, and that we will continue to refuse, the vain curiosity of those who ask to see in order to believe, and we answer them the same way as we answered an eminent personage from England who threatened us with his incredulity:

"It is perfectly within your rights not to believe; as for ourselves, we are neither more discouraged nor less convinced regarding our beliefs."

To those who will come to us and say that they have scrupulously and courageously accomplished all the rites and that nothing was produced, we shall say that they would do well to stop there, and that perhaps it is a warning from nature, who refuses them these eccentric works, but that if they persist in their curiosity, they have but to start again.

The ternary, being the foundation of magical doctrine, must necessarily be observed in evocations; it is also the symbolic number of realization and of effect. The letter שׁ is ordinarily drawn on Cabalistic pentacles whose object is to accomplish a desire. This letter is also the mark of the scapegoat in the mystical Cabala,[335] and Saint-Martin observed that this letter, inserted in the incommunicable Tetragrammaton, produces the name of the Redeemer of men, יהשוה, Yeh-

---

335   On the Day of Atonement, according to Leviticus 16:20–22, a goat was selected by lot to carry the sins of Israel and was then driven off into the wilderness. Cabalistic lore has it that the Hebrew letter shin, שׁ, was marked on its forehead.

eshuah.[336] This is what the mystagogues of the Middle Ages represented when, in their nocturnal assemblies, they exhibited a symbolic goat carrying a lit torch on its head between its horns. This monstrous animal, whose allegorical forms and bizarre cult we will describe in the fifteenth chapter of the Ritual, represents nature dedicated to malediction but saved by the sign of the light. The Gnostic banquets and the pagan orgies which followed in his honor revealed enough of the moral consequences the adepts wished to derive from this exhibition. All this will be explained with the rites, decried and now regarded as mythical, of the great Sabbath of black magic.

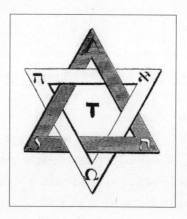

In the great circle of evocations one usually draws a triangle, and one must be careful to observe in which direction one points the apex. If the spirit is supposed to come from heaven, the operator must stand at the apex and place the fumigation altar at the base; if the spirit is to rise from the abyss, the operator will be at the base and the brazier placed at the apex. In addition, one must wear on one's forehead, on one's breast and right hand, the sacred symbol of the reunited triangles, forming the six-pointed star whose figure we have already reproduced, and that is known in magic under the name of the pentacle or seal of Solomon.

Independently of these signs, in their evocations the ancients made use of the mystic combinations of the divine names according to the Hebrew Cabalists that we have provided in Doctrine. The magical triangle of the pagan theosophers is

---

336   A traditional Cabalistic spelling of the name of Jesus.

the famous ABRACADABRA to which they attribute extraordinary virtues, and which is figured in this way:

ABRACADABRA

ABRACADABR

ABRACADAB

ABRACADA

ABRACAD

ABRACA

ABRAC

ABRA

ABR

AB

A

This combination of letters is a key to the pentagram. The initial "A" is repeated five times and reproduced thirty times, which provides the elements and the numbers for these two figures:

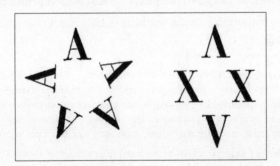

The isolated "A" represents the unity of the first principle, or of the intellectual or active agent. The "A" united with the "B" represents the fecundation of the binary by the unity. The "R" is the sign of the ternary, because it hieroglyphically represents the effusion which results from the union of the two principles. The number eleven of the letters of the word add the unity of the initiate to the denary of Pythagoras; and the number sixty-six, the added total of all the letters,

Cabalistically forms the number twelve, which is the square of the ternary and in consequence the quadrature of the mystical circle.[337] Let us remark in passing that the author of the Book of Revelation, that clavicle of the Christian Cabala, composed the number of the beast, that is to say of idolatry, by adding another six to the double senary of ABRACADABRA, which Cabalistically is eighteen, the number assigned in the Tarot to the hieroglyphic sign of the night and profanity, the Moon with the towers, the dog, the wolf, and the crawfish; a mysterious and dark number, whose Cabalistic key is nine, the number of initiation.[338]

The holy Cabalist spoke expressly about this subject: "Let him who hath understanding" (that is to say the key to the Cabalistic numbers) "count the number of the beast, for it is the number of man, and his number is six hundred threescore and six."[339] It is in fact Pythagoras's decad multiplied by itself and added to the sum of the triangular pentacle of Abracadabra;[340] it is thus the summary of all the magic of the ancient world, the entire program of human genius, which the divine genius of the Gospels wished to absorb or supplant.

These hieroglyphic combinations of letters and numbers belong to the practical part of the Cabala, which, from this point of view, is subdivided into Gematria and Temurah.[341] These calculations, which now appear arbitrary to us or of no interest, then belonged to the philosophical symbolism of the Orient and had the greatest importance in the teaching of holy matters emanating from the

---

337   This analysis is best studied one sentence at a time. Note that the shape of the capital letter *R* looks like a blending of *A* and *B*. The number sixty-six means twelve Cabalistically because its two digits (six and six) equal twelve when added together. And twelve is the square of the ternary in a geometrical rather than an arithmetic sense: a square with three units on a side has a perimeter of twelve.

338   This is another example of the same form of symbolic analysis. The number 666, the "number of the beast," equals 18 Cabalistically because $6 + 6 + 6 = 18$; trump XVIII (18) of the tarot is the Moon, and 18 equals 9 because $1 + 8 = 9$, and trump 9, the Hermit, is a symbol of initiation.

339   Revelation 13:18.

340   The decad of Pythagoras is 10; multiplied by itself, this equals 100; add the sum of the letters in "abracadabra," 66, and the result is 166. The location of the missing 500 is left, as Lévi intended, as an exercise for the reader.

341   These modes of Cabalistic analysis are explained in chapter 10 of "The Doctrine," p. 109.

occult sciences. The absolute Cabalistic alphabet, which attaches the primary ideas to allegories, the allegories to letters, and the letters to numbers, were what were then called the keys of Solomon. We have already seen that these keys, preserved until our time but completely misunderstood, are none other than the Tarot deck, whose ancient allegories were remarked upon and appreciated for the first time, in our day, by the scholarly archeologist Court de Gébelin.

The double triangle of Solomon is explained by Saint John in a remarkable manner. There are, says he, three who bear witness in heaven: the Father, the Logos, and the Holy Spirit; and three who bear witness on Earth: the spirit, the water, and the blood.[342] Saint John is thus in agreement with the masters of Hermetic philosophy, who give the name of ether to their sulfur, to their mercury the name of philosophical water, and to their salt the qualification of dragon's blood or the Earth's menstrual blood: blood or salt corresponds by opposition to the Father, azotic or mercurial water with the Verb or Logos, and breath with the Holy Spirit. But matters of high symbolism cannot be properly heard except by the children of science.

To the triangular combinations one unites, in magical ceremonies, the repetition of the names three times, and with different intonations. To the magical wand was often attached a small magnetized fork, which Paracelsus replaced with a trident whose figure we provide here:

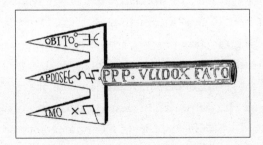

Paracelsus's trident is a pentacle which expresses the summary of the ternary in the unity and thus completes the sacred quaternary. He attributes to this figure all the virtues that the Cabalistic Hebrews attributed to the name of Jehovah, and

---

342   1 John 5:7–8.

the thaumaturgical properties of the Abracadabra of the hierophants of Alexandria. Let us recognize here that it is a pentacle, and in consequence a concrete and absolute sign of an entire doctrine, which was that of an immense magnetic circle, as much for the ancient philosophers as for the adepts of the Middle Ages. In rendering it in our time, its primordial value through the intelligence of its mysteries, could we not render all its miraculous virtue and all its power in countering human maladies?

The ancient witches, when they passed the night at an intersection of three roads, cried out three times in honor of the triple Hecate.

All these figures, all these acts analogous to the figures, all these dispositions of numbers and characters are not, as we have already said, just educational instruments for the will, whose habits they fix and determine. In addition, they serve to connect together, in the performance, all the powers of the human soul, and to augment the creative force of the imagination. It is the gymnastics of thought which are used in the realization: in addition, the effects of these practices are as infallible as nature when they are done with absolute confidence and unwavering perseverance.

With faith, said the great Master, we could transplant trees into the sea and move mountains. A practice, even a superstitious one, even a foolish one, is effective because it is a realization of the will. It is for that reason that a prayer is more powerful if we go and say it in a church than if we say it at home and that it will obtain miracles if, in order to say it in an accredited sanctuary, that is to say magnetized by the great currents of the crowds of its visitors, we travel one or two hundred leagues while begging and barefoot.

We laugh at the good woman who deprives herself of a coin's worth of milk in the morning and who then carries to the magical triangles of the church a little candle worth a coin, which she then lights. It is the ignorant who laugh, and that good woman does not pay too much for what she thus purchases with resignation and courage. The intelligentsia are very proud to pass by while shrugging their shoulders, they revolt against superstitions with a noise which makes the world tremble: what is the result? The houses of the intelligentsia crumble, and the debris are sold to the suppliers and the buyers of little candles, who are content to hear it proclaimed everywhere that their reign has ended forevermore, so long as they always rule.

The great religions have only had to fear one serious rival, and that rival is magic.

Magic produced the occult associations which brought about the revolution called the Renaissance, but it has fallen to the human spirit, blinded by mad loves, to realize point for point the allegory of the Hebrew Hercules:[343] by shaking the columns of the temple he buried himself under the ruins.

Masonic societies know no more about the high reason of their symbols than do rabbis who do not understand the Sepher Yetzirah and the Zohar, on the ascending scale of three degrees, with the transverse progression from right to left and from left to right of the Cabalistic septenary.

The compass of the G∴A∴[344] and the set square of Solomon have descended to the crude and material level of unintelligent Jacobinism realized with a triangle of iron: behold their heaven and their earth.

The profaning adepts whose bloody deaths were predicted by the illuminated Cazotte have surpassed in our time the sin of Adam: after having boldly gathered the fruits of the tree of science, with which they did not know how to feed themselves, they threw them to the animals and the reptiles of the Earth. And the reign of superstition has commenced and must last until a time when true religion will reconstitute itself upon the eternal foundations of the hierarchy of three degrees and the triple power that the quaternary fatally or providentially exercises in the three worlds.

---

343   That is, Samson.

344   The Great Architect of the Universe, the Masonic term for God.

CHAPTER IV

THE CONJURATION OF THE FOUR

The four elemental forms separate and specify through a kind of rough sketch the created spirits which universal movement releases from the central fire. Spirit works everywhere and fecundates matter through life; all matter is animate; thought and soul are everywhere.

By taking hold of thought, which produces diverse forms, we become masters of the forms and have them serve our purposes.

The astral light is saturated with souls, which it releases through the incessant generation of beings. These souls have imperfect wills, which can be dominated and employed by more powerful wills; they then form great invisible chains and can cause or determine great elementary commotions.

The phenomena observed in the process of magic, and even more recently still by M. Eudes de Mirville, have no other causes.

The elementary spirits are like children: they most often torment those who deal with them, unless one can dominate them through high reason and with great severity.

It is these spirits which we designate under the name of occult elements.

It is they who often determine our disquieting or bizarre dreams for us, it is they who produce movements in the dowsing wand and knocking sounds on walls or furniture, but they can never manifest another thought than our own, and if we think of nothing, they speak to us with all the incoherence of dreams.

They indifferently reproduce good and evil, because they have no free will and in consequence no responsibility; they appear to ecstatics and somnambulists in incomplete and fugitive forms. They are what caused the nightmares of Saint Anthony and most probably the visions of Swedenborg; they are neither damned nor guilty, they are curious and innocent. They can be used or abused like animals or children. The mage who employs their cooperation takes upon himself a terrible responsibility, because he must expiate all evil that he might have them do, and the grandeur of his torments will be proportionate to the extent of the power he will have exercised as their mediator.

To dominate the spirits and thus become king of the occult elements, one must first submit to the four trials of the ancient initiations, and since these initiations no longer exist, one must have gone through analogous ordeals, such as exposing oneself without fear to fire; crossing over a chasm on a tree trunk or a plank; climbing a mountain peak during a storm; swimming out of a waterfall or a dangerous whirlpool. The man who is afraid of water will never be regenerated by the undines, he who fears fire will be unable to command the salamanders; as long as we feel vertigo one must leave the sylphs in peace and not irritate the gnomes, because the inferior spirits only obey a power that has been proven and shown to be their master even in their own element.

Once one acquires through boldness and practice this incontestable power, one must impose the Verb of one's will upon the elements through special consecrations of air, of fire, of water, and of earth, and this is the indispensable commencement to all magical operations.

One exorcises the air by exhaling in the direction of the four cardinal points and by saying:

Spiritus Dei ferebatur super aquas, et inspiravit in faciem hominis spiraculum vitae. Sit Michael dux meus, et Sabtabiel servus meus, in luce et per lucem.

Fiat verbum halitus meus; et imperabo spiritibus aeris hujus, et refraenabo equos solis voluntate cordis mei, et cogitatione mentis meae et nutu oculi dextri.

Exorciso igitur te, creatura aeris, per Pentagrammaton et in nomine Tetragrammaton, in quibus sunt volunta firma et fides recta. Amen. Sela, fiat. So mote it be.

(The Spirit of God moved upon the waters, and breathed into the face of man the breath of life. Let Michael be my leader, and Sabtabiel my servant, in light and by light.

(Let the Verb be my breath, and I will command the spirits of air thereby, and I will bridle the horses of the Sun with the will of my heart, and the thoughts of my mind and the commandment of my right eye.

(I therefore exorcise thee, creature of air, by Pentagrammaton and in the name of Tetragrammaton, in which is firm will and true faith. Amen, Selah, Fiat, so mote it be.)

Then one recites the prayer of the sylphs, after having traced their sign in the air with the feather of an eagle.

PRAYER OF THE SYLPHS

Spirit of light, spirit of wisdom, whose breath gives and takes away the form of all things; you before whom the life of beings is a shadow which changes and a vapor which passes; you who raise the clouds and who walks on the wings of the winds; you who exhale, and then the space without end is peopled; you who inhale, and then all which comes from you goes back to you: movement without end in eternal stability, be eternally blessed. We praise you and we bless you in the ever-changing empire of the created light, of shadows, of reflections, and of images, and we aspire ceaselessly to your immutable and imperishable clarity. Allow the ray of your intelligence and the warmth of your love to penetrate all the way to us: then that which is mobile shall be fixed, the shadow shall be a body, the spirit of air shall be a soul, the

dream shall be a thought. And we shall no longer be carried away by the tempest, but we shall hold the bridle of the winged horses of the morning and we shall direct the flow of the winds of the evening in order to fly up before you. O spirit of spirits, O eternal soul of souls, O imperishable breath of life, O sigh of the creator, O mouth which inhales and which exhales the existence of all the beings with the flux and the reflux of your eternal word, which is the divine ocean of movement and of truth. Amen.

One exorcises the water by the laying on of hands, with one's breath, through words and by mixing the sacred salt with some ashes which remain in the bowl of incense. The aspergillus[345] is made with the branches of verbena, periwinkle, sage, mint, valerian, ash, and basil tied together with a thread taken from the distaff of a virgin; with a handle made of hazel wood which had not yet born fruits, and upon which you engrave with a magical awl the characters of the seven spirits. Separately bless and consecrate the salt and the ash of the perfumes while saying:

UPON THE SALT

In isto sale sit sapientia, et ab omni corruptione servet mentes nostras et corpora nostra, per Hochmaël et in virtute Ruach-Hochmaël, recedant ab isto fantasmata hylae ut sit sal coelestis, sal terrae et terra salis, ut nutrietor bos triturans et addat spei nostrae cornua tauri volantis. Amen.

(Let wisdom abide in this salt, and may it preserve our minds and bodies from all corruption, by Hochmaël and in the power of Ruach-Hochmaël; let the phantoms of matter depart from it that it may become a heavenly salt, salt of earth and earth of salt, that it may nourish the threshing ox and strengthen our hope with the horns of the Winged Bull. Amen.)

---

345   That is, a holy water sprinkler.

UPON THE ASHES

Revertatur cinis ad fontem aquarum viventium, et fiat terra fructificans, et germinet arborem vitae per tria nomina, quae sunt Netzach, Hod et Yesod, in principio et in fine, per Alpha et Omega qui sunt in spiritu AZOTH. Amen.

(Let these ashes return to the font of living water and become a fertile earth, and bring forth the Tree of Life by the three names, which are Netzach, Hod, and Yesod, in the beginning and in the end, by Alpha and Omega, which are in the spirit of AZOTH. Amen.)

WHILE MIXING THE WATER, THE SALT, AND THE ASHES

In sale sapientiae aeternae, et in aqua regenerationis, et in cinere germinante terram novam, omnia fiant per Elohim Gabriel, Raphael, et Uriel, in saecula et aeonas. Amen.

(In the salt of eternal wisdom, and in the water of regeneration, and in the ashes whence the new earth springs, let all things be accomplished by the Elohim Gabriel, Raphael, and Uriel, unto the ages and aeons. Amen.)

EXORCISM OF THE WATER

Fiat firmamentum in medio aquarum et separet aquas ab aquis, quae superius sicut quae inferius, et quae inferius sicut quae superius, ad perpetranda miracula rei unius. Sol ejus pater est, luna mater et ventus hanc gestavit en utero suo, ascendit a terra ad coelum et rursus a coelo in terram descendit. Exorciso te, creatura aquae, ut sis mihi speculum Dei vivi in operibus ejus, et fons vitae, et ablutio peccatorum. Amen.

(Let there be a firmament in the midst of the waters and let it separate waters from waters, so that which is above may be as that which is below, and that which is below as that which is above, to perform the miracles of the One Thing. The Sun is its father, the Moon its mother, and the wind has carried it in its womb, it ascends from Earth to heaven and descends again from heaven to Earth. I exorcise thee, creature of water, that you may be for me a mirror of the living God in his works, and a fount of life, and an ablution for sins. Amen.)

PRAYER OF THE UNDINES

Terrible king of the seas, you who hold the keys to the cataracts of the heavens and who enclose the subterranean waters in the caverns of the Earth; king of the deluge and of the rains of spring; you who open the sources of the rivers and the fountains; you who command humidity, which is like the blood of the Earth, to become the sap of plants, we adore you and invoke you. We, your mobile and ever-changing creatures, speak to us through the great commotions of the sea, and we shall tremble before you; speak to us also through the murmurs of limpid waters, and we shall desire your love. O immensity within which shall be lost all the rivers of being, which are always reborn within you! O ocean of infinite perfections! the heights, which you reflect in the depths; the depths, which you exhale in the heights, bring us to immortality through sacrifice, so that we are found to be worthy of offering you a day of water, the blood and the tears, for the absolution of our errors. Amen.

One exorcises the fire by throwing salt, incense, white resin, camphor, and sulfur into it, and by pronouncing three times the three names of the spirits of fire: MICHAEL, king of the Sun and the lightning; SAMAEL, king of the volcanoes, and ANAEL, prince of the astral light; then by reciting the prayer of the salamanders.

PRAYER OF THE SALAMANDERS

Immortal, eternal, ineffable, and uncreated, father of all things, who is carried on a chariot riding ceaselessly on worlds which forever turn; dominator of the ethereal immensities, where is raised the throne of your power, above which your redoubtable eyes discover all, and your beautiful and holy ears hear all, grant your children's wishes, whom you have loved since the birth of the centuries; because your golden and great and eternal majesty radiates above the world, the heavens and the stars; you are raised upon them, O sparkling fire; there you light up and maintain yourself through your own splendor, and from your essence comes the boundless rivers of light which nourish your infinite spirit. That infinite spirit nourishes all things and makes that inexhaustible treasure of substance always ready for the generation which it works and which appropriates the forms which you impregnated it with since the first cause. From this spirit also originates those very saintly kings who surround your throne and who make up your court, O universal father! O unique one! O father of the fortunate mortals and immortals!

You created in particular the powers which are so marvelously similar to your eternal thought and to your adorable essence; you established them above the angels who announce your wishes to the world; at last you created us in the third rank in our elemental empire. There our continual exercise is to praise and adore your desires; there we ceaselessly burn with the aspiration to possess you. O father! O mother, that most tender of mothers! O admirable archetype of maternity and of pure love! O son, flower of the father! O form of all forms, souls, spirits, harmony, and numbers of all things! Amen!

One exorcises the Earth by the aspersion of water, through breath and through fire, with the correct perfumes for each day, and one then says the prayer of the gnomes.

PRAYER OF THE GNOMES

Invisible king, who having taken the Earth for support and who dug the depths in order to fill them with your omnipotence, you whose name makes the vaults of the Earth tremble, you who make to flow the seven metals in their veins of stone, monarch of the seven lights, remunerator of subterranean workers, bring us to the desirable air and to the kingdom of clarity. We keep watch and work without rest, we search and we hope, by the twelve stones of the holy city, by the buried talismans, by the magnet nail which goes through the center of the Earth. Lord, Lord, Lord, have pity on those who suffer, enlarge our breasts, free and raise our heads, aggrandize us. O stability and movement, O day enveloped by the night, O obscurity veiled with light! O master who never keeps to himself the salary of his workers! O silvery purity, O golden splendor! O crown of living and melodious diamonds! you who carry the heavens on your finger like a ring of sapphire, you who hide under the Earth in the kingdom of gemstones the marvelous seed of the stars, live, reign and be the eternal dispensator of the riches whose guardians you have made us. Amen.

One must note the special kingdom of the gnomes is to the north, that of the salamanders to the south, that of the sylphs to the east, and that of the undines to the west. They influence the four temperaments of man, that is to say the gnomes influence the melancholic, the salamanders influence the choleric, the undines influence the phlegmatic, and the sylphs influence the sanguine. Their signs are: the hieroglyphs of Taurus for gnomes, and they are commanded with the sword; Leo for salamanders, and they are commanded with the forked wand or the magical trident; the Eagle[346] for the sylphs, and they are commanded with the sacred pentacles; and finally Aquarius for the undines, and they are evoked with

---

346   This represents Scorpio, which has three traditional forms—the scorpion, the serpent, and the eagle.

the cup of libations. Their respective sovereigns are Ghob for the gnomes, Djinn for the salamanders, Paralda for the sylphs, and Nichsa for the undines.

When an elemental spirit comes to torment or even trouble the inhabitants of this world, one must conjure it by air, by water, by fire, and by earth, by breathing and sprinkling, by burning the perfumes, and by drawing on the ground the star of Solomon and the sacred pentagram. These figures must be perfectly regular and made with care using the coals from the consecrated fire or with a reed dipped in diverse colors, which one mixes with crushed magnetite. Then, while holding the pentacle of Solomon in your hand and taking in turn the sword, the wand, and the cup in the other, we pronounce aloud in these terms the Conjuration of the Four:

Caput mortuum, imperet tibi Dominus per vivum et devotum serpentum.

Cherub, imperet tibi Dominus per Adam Jotchavah! Aquila errans, imperet tibi Dominus per alas Tauri. Serpens, imperet tibi Dominus tetragrammaton per angelum et leonem!

Michael, Gabriel, Raphael, Anael!

FLUAT UDOR per spiritum Elohim.

MANEAT TERRA per Adam IOT-CHAVAH.

FIAT FIRMAMENTUM per IAHUVEHU-ZEBAOTH.

FIAT JUDICIUM per ignem in virtute MICHAEL.

(Dead Head, may the Lord command thee by the living and consecrated serpent.

(Cherub, may the Lord command thee by Adam Jotchavah! Wandering eagle, may the Lord command thee by the wings of the Bull. Serpent, may the Lord Tetragrammaton command thee by the angel and the lion!

(Michael, Gabriel, Raphael, Anael!

(LET MOISTURE FLOW by the spirit of Elohim.

(LET THE EARTH REMAIN by Adam IOT-CHAVAH.

(LET THE FIRMAMENT BE by IAHUVEHU-ZEBAOTH.

(LET JUSTICE BE by fire in the power of MICHAEL).

Angel with the dead eyes, obey or drown thyself in this holy water.

Winged Taurus, work, or return to the earth if thou dost not wish me to make thee kneel before this sword.

Enchained Eagle, obey this sign, or withdraw thyself before this breath.

Shifting Serpent, crawl to my feet, or be tormented by the sacred fire and evaporate thyself with these perfumes that I burn.

May the water return to the water; may the fire burn; may the air circulate; may the earth fall onto the earth by virtue of the pentagram, which is the star of the morning, and in the name of the Tetragrammaton, which is written upon the center of the cross of light. Amen.

The sign of the cross which was adopted by the Christians does not belong exclusively to them. It is also Cabalistic and represents the oppositions and the quaternary equilibrium of the elements. We can see with the occult verse of the Lord's Prayer that we indicated in our Doctrine that there were originally two manners of saying it, or at least two formulas very different from one another to characterize it: one reserved for the priests and for initiates; the other given to neophytes and to the profane. Thus, for example, the initiate, in bringing his hand to his forehead, said: **To you**; and then added: **belongs**; and continued while bringing his hand to his chest: **the kingdom**: then to the left shoulder: **justice**; to the right shoulder: **and mercy**. Then one joins the two hands while adding: **in the generative cycles**. In Latin, **Tibi sunt Malchut et Gevurah et Hesed per aeonas**. The sign of the cross is absolutely and magnificently Cabalistic, which the profanations of Gnosticism caused to be lost completely to the militant and official Church.

This sign done in this manner must precede and end the conjuration of the four.

In order to subdue and subjugate the elementary spirits, one must never abandon oneself to the faults which characterize them. Thus a light and capricious spirit will never govern the sylphs. A soft, cold, and unpredictable nature will never be mistress of the undines; anger irritates the salamanders, and tactless greed renders he who attempts to subjugate them, the toy of the gnomes.

But one must be prompt and active like the sylphs, flexible and attentive to images like the undines, energetic and strong like the salamanders, laborious and patient like the gnomes; in one word, one must vanquish with their strengths and never allow oneself to be subdued by their weaknesses. When one is well reinforced in this disposition, the entire world shall be in service to the wise operator. He will pass through a storm, and the rain will not touch his head; the wind will not even disturb a fold of his clothes; he will cross through fire without being burned; he will walk on water, and he will see the diamonds right through the thickness of the Earth. These promises, which might seem hyperbolic, are only so for vulgar intelligence; because if the sage does not do these things which these words express materially and precisely, he will do things much greater and more admirable. However, it is indubitable that one can by one's will direct the elements in a certain measure and really change or stop their effects.

Why, for example, if it is observed that people in a state of ecstasy momentarily lose their weight, could we not walk or glide on water? The convulsionaries of Saint-Médard felt neither fire nor steel and solicited the most violent attacks and the most incredible tortures as though they were helpful. Are not the strange ascensions and prodigious balance of certain somnambulists a revelation of the hidden forces of nature? But we live in a century where we do not have the courage to admit to miracles of which we are witnesses, and if someone says: "I saw," or, "I myself did the things which I tell you about," they would say to him: "You wish to amuse yourself at our expense, or you are sick." It is better to remain silent and to act.

The metals which correspond to the four elementary forms are gold and silver for air, mercury for water, iron and copper for fire, and lead for earth. One composes the talismans as related to the forces they represent and to the effects one intends to obtain.

Divination with the four elementary forms, which are called aeromancy, hydromancy, pyromancy, and geomancy, is done in diverse manners, which all depend on the will and on the translucent, or the imagination, of the operator.

Thus the four elements are but instruments for aiding second sight.

Second sight is the faculty to see in the astral light.

This second sight is as natural as first sight, or sensible and ordinary sight, but it can only be operated through the abstraction of the senses.

Somnambulists and ecstatics naturally benefit from second sight, but that sight is more lucid when the abstraction is more complete.

Abstraction is produced through astral intoxication, that is to say an overabundance of light which completely saturates and in consequence renders the nervous instrument inert.

Sanguine temperaments are more disposed to aeromancy, the bilious to pyromancy, the pituitous to hydromancy, and the melancholic to geomancy.

Aeromancy is confirmed by oneiromancy, or divination through dreams; one confirms pyromancy through magnetism, and geomancy through cartomancy. These are transpositions and improvements of method.

But divination, of any type that we can perform, is dangerous, or at the least useless, because it discourages the will and in consequence hinders liberty and tires the nervous system.

CHAPTER V

THE FLAMING PENTAGRAM

We now arrive at the explanation and the consecration of the holy and mysterious pentagram.

Here the ignorant and the superstitious may shut this book: they will only see shadows or will be scandalized.

The pentagram, which in the Gnostic schools we call the flaming star,[347] is the sign of omnipotence and intellectual autocracy.

It is the star of the mages; it is the sign of the Verb made flesh; and, following the direction of its rays, this absolute symbol in magic represents good or evil, order or disorder, the blessed lamb of Ormus[348] and of Saint John or the cursed goat of Mendes.

It is initiation or profanation; it is Lucifer or Vesper,[349] the star of the morning or of the evening.

---

347   This is the common name of the five-pointed star in European Freemasonry.

348   The name given by the eighteenth-century German Orden des Gold- und Rosen-kreuz (Order of the Golden and Rosy Cross) for the founder of its tradition, supposedly an Egyptian priest and magus who was converted to Christianity by Saint Mark in 96 CE. The term has recently been recycled for a variety of unrelated uses.

349   Before the ancient Latin peoples realized that the morning and evening stars were the same planet (Venus), Lucifer (Light Bearer) was the name of the morning star and Vesper (Evening) the name of the evening star.

It is Mary or Lilith; it is victory or death; it is the light or the night.

The pentagram, when pointing two of its rays upwards, represents Satan or the goat of the Sabbath, and it represents the Savior when it points a single ray upwards.

The pentagram is the figure of the human body with four members and a single point which must represent the head.

A human figure head downwards naturally represents the demon, that is to say the subversion of the intellect, disorder or madness.

Yet if magic is a reality, if the occult science is the true law of the three worlds, this absolute sign, this sign which is as ancient as history and even beyond history, must exercise and exercises in effect, an incalculable influence upon the spirits which are released from their material envelope.

The sign of the pentagram is also called the sign of the microcosm, and it represents what the Cabalists of the book Zohar called the Microprosopus.[350]

The complete understanding of the pentagram is the key to the two worlds. It is philosophy and absolute natural science.

The sign of the pentagram must be composed of the seven metals or at least be drawn with pure gold on white marble.

We can also draw it with vermilion on the skin of a lamb without defect or blemish, symbol of integrity and of light.

The marble must be virgin, that is to say never having been previously made use of for other things; the skin of the lamb must be prepared under the auspices of the Sun.

The lamb must have had its throat cut during Easter with a new knife, and the skin must have been salted with salt consecrated through magical operations.

Any negligence regarding a single one of these ceremonies, which seem difficult and arbitrary, will abort the entire success of any great work of science.

One consecrates the pentagram with the four elements: one breathes five times upon the magical figure; one sprays it with consecrated water; one dries it by the smoke of the five perfumes, which are incense, myrrh, aloe, sulfur, and

---

350   The Lesser Countenance: God manifest to humanity as distinct from God as he is in himself.

camphor, to which one can add a bit of white resin and ambergris; one blows five times, while pronouncing the names of the five spirits, who are Gabriel, Raphael, Anael, Samael, and Oriphiel; then one places the pentacle on the ground, facing the north, then south towards the orient, the occident, and towards the center of the astronomical cross, and one pronounces one after another the letters of the sacred Tetragrammaton; then one says in a lowered voice the blessed names of the Aleph and the mysterious Tau reunited in the Cabalistic name of AZOTH.

The pentagram must be placed on the altar of incense and under the tripod of evocations. The operator must also wear the figure on himself along with that of the macrocosm, that is to say the six-pointed star, composed of two crossed and superimposed triangles.

When one evokes a spirit of the light, one must turn the head of the star, that is to say one of its points, towards the tripod of evocation and the two inferior points towards the altar of incense. One does the contrary if it is for a spirit of darkness; but the operator must then take care to hold the end of the wand or the point of the sword over the head of the pentagram.

We have already said that signs are the active verb of the will. Yet the will must provide its complete verb in order to be transformed into action, and a single negligence, representing an idle or doubting word, strikes the entire operation with falsehood and powerlessness, and turns all the forces which were spent in vain back against the operator.

One must thus absolutely abstain from magical ceremonies or accomplish them all scrupulously and exactly!

The pentagram drawn with luminous lines on glass through the means of an electrical machine also exerts a great influence over the spirits and terrifies phantoms.

The ancient magicians drew the sign of the pentagram on the threshold of their door to stop evil spirits from entering and to keep good spirits from leaving. This constraint resulted from the direction in which the rays of the star were pointing. Two points towards the outside repelled evil spirits; two points towards the inside kept them prisoner; a single point towards the inside captured good spirits.

All these magical theories, based on the unique doctrine of Hermes and on the analogical inductions of the science, have always been confirmed by ecstatic visions and by the convulsions of cataleptics said to be possessed by spirits.

The G which the Freemasons place in the middle of the flaming star signifies GNOSIS and GENERATION, the two sacred words of the ancient Cabala. They also mean GRAND ARCHITECT, because the pentagram, from whichever way we look at it, represents an A.

In disposing it in a manner such that two of its points are above and one single point is below, we can see the horns, the ears, and the beard of the hieratic goat of Mendes, and it becomes the sign of infernal evocations.

The allegorical star of the mages is nothing other than the mysterious pentagram; and those three kings, children of Zoroaster, led by the flaming star to the cradle of the microcosmic God,[351] suffice to prove the entirely Cabalistic and truly magical origins of Christian doctrine. One of the kings is white, the other is black, and the third is brown. The white offers gold, symbol of life and the light; the black offers myrrh, image of death and the night; the brown presents frankincense, emblem of the divinity of the doctrine which conciliates the two principles; then they return to their country by another road, to show that a new cult is but a new road for bringing humanity to the unique religion, that of the sacred ternary and the radiant pentagram, the only *eternal* Catholicism.

In the Book of Revelation, Saint John sees that same star fall from the sky to Earth.[352] It is then called wormwood or bitterness, and all the waters become bitter. This is the striking image of the materialization of the doctrine, which produces fanaticism and the bitterness of controversy. It is to Christianity itself that we can then address this speech of Isaiah's: How art thou fallen from heaven, O brilliant star, who wert so splendid in thy morning?[353]

But the pentagram, profaned by men, still shines without shadows in the right hand of the Verb of truth,[354] and the inspirational voice assures to him who

---

351　Matthew 2:1–12. The word translated "wise men" in most English versions of this passage is μάγοι, "magicians," in the original Greek.

352　Revelation 8:11.

353　A paraphrase of Isaiah 14:12.

354　Revelation 1:16.

overcomes that he will be given the morning star:[355] the solemnly promised rehabilitation of the star of Lucifer.

As we can see, all the mysteries of magic, all the symbols of the Gnosis, all
the figures of occultism, all the Cabalistic keys of the prophecies, are summarized
in the sign of the pentagram, that Paracelsus proclaims as the most great and
most powerful of all the signs.

After that, should one be surprised by the confidence of the mages and the
real influence exerted by this sign upon the spirits of all the hierarchies? Those
who misunderstand the sign of the cross tremble before the aspect of the star of
the microcosm. The mage, on the contrary, when he feels his will weakening,
looks upon the symbol, takes it in his right hand, and feels armed with intellectual
omnipotence, as long as he is truly a king worthy of being led by the star to the
cradle of divine realization; as long as he *knows*, he *dares*, he *wills*, and *remains
silent*; as long as he is aware of the uses of the pentacle, of the cup, of the wand and
of the sword; finally, as long as the intrepid gaze of his soul corresponds to those
two ever open eyes which the superior point of our pentagram present to him.

---

355   Revelation 2:28.

CHAPTER VI

THE MEDIUM AND THE MEDIATOR

We have said that in order to acquire magical power one needs to do two things: to free the will from all servitude and train it in domination.

The sovereign will is represented in our symbols by the woman who crushes the serpent's head and by the radiant angel who restrains and contains the dragon under his foot and under his lance.[356]

Let us declare here without bandying about that the great magical agent, the double current of light, the living and astral fire of the earth was symbolized by the serpent with the head of a bull, of a goat, or of a dog in the ancient theogonies. It is the double serpent of the caduceus; it is the ancient serpent of Genesis; but it is also the brazen serpent of Moses,[357] interlaced with the tau, that is to say the generative lingam; it is also the goat of the Sabbath and the Baphomet of the Templars; it is the Hyle of the Gnostics;[358] it is the double tail of the serpent which form the legs of the solar cockerel of Abraxas; finally, it is the devil of M. Eudes de Mirville, and it is actually the blind force that souls must conquer to break free of the chains of the Earth; because, if their will does not detach them from this fatal

---

356   The Virgin Mary and the archangel Michael, respectively, in traditional Christian symbolism.

357   Numbers 21:9.

358   *Hyle* (ὕλη) is the Greek word for matter; in gnostic teachings it was the power that held human souls imprisoned in the false realm of apparent existence.

magnetism, they will be absorbed into the current by the force which produced them and will return to the central and eternal fire.

All magical work thus consists of freeing oneself from the coils of the ancient serpent, then placing one's foot on his head and driving him where one wishes. I will give you, he says in the evangelical myth, all the kingdoms of the Earth if you kneel down and if you adore me.[359] The initiate must answer him: "I will not kneel down, and you shall crawl at my feet; you shall give me nothing, but I shall make use of you, and I will take what I wish: because I am your lord and master!" An answer which is understood, but veiled, in the answer which the Savior gives him.

We have already said that the devil is not a person. It is a force led astray, as his name indicates incidentally.[360] An odic or magnetic current formed by a chain of wills is what constitutes this evil spirit, which the gospel calls *legion*, and which drives the swine into the sea:[361] a new allegory for the driving of basely instinctive beings by blind forces which can set into motion evil will and error.

We can compare this symbol to that of the companions of Ulysses who are changed into swine by the magician Circe.[362]

In addition, observe what Ulysses does to protect himself and save his companions: he refuses the cup of the enchantress and commands her with his sword. Circe is nature with all its pleasures and its attractions; to enjoy her one must conquer her: that is the meaning of the Homeric fable, because the poems of Homer, the veritable sacred books of ancient Hellas, contain all the mysteries of the high initiations of the Orient.

The natural *medium* is therefore the serpent, always active and seducing one to the slothful drives, which must always be resisted and subdued.

An amorous mage, a gluttonous mage, a wrathful mage, a lazy mage are impossible monstrosities. The mage thinks and wills, he craves nothing lustfully, he

---

359   Matthew 4:9.

360   The English word "devil," like the French *diable*, comes ultimately from the Greek words *dia*, "across," and *ballein*, "to throw." Lévi wryly interprets the word to mean "thrown out," which is plausible if inaccurate.

361   Luke 8:30–33.

362   In book 10 of Homer's *Odyssey*.

rejects nothing passionately: the word passion represents a passive state, and the mage is always active and victorious. The most difficult thing to do in the high sciences is to arrive at this realization; when the mage has created himself, the Great Work is accomplished, at least in its instrument and in its cause.

The great agent or natural mediator of human omnipotence can only be used and directed by an *extra-natural* mediator, which is an emancipated will. Archimedes asked for a point of support outside of the world in order to raise the world. The point of support of the mage is the cubic intellectual stone, the philosopher's stone of Azoth, that is to say the doctrine of absolute reason and of the universal harmonies through the sympathy of opposites.

One of our most fertile of writers and the least fixed in his ideas, M. Eugène Sue, has built an entire romantic saga around an individual whom he endeavors to render despicable and who becomes interesting despite the author, because the latter gives him so much power, patience, audacity, intelligence and genius![363] It concerns an equivalent of Sixtus V, poor, sober, and without anger, who holds the entire world wrapped in the network of his clever machinations.

This man excites the passions of his adversaries at will, destroys them one against the other, manages to always arrive where he wishes to go, and without noise, without flash, without charlatanism. His goal is to bring the world towards a society which the author of the book believes to be cruel and perverse, and he spares nothing to do so: he is poorly housed, poorly dressed, is fed like the poorest of the poor, but he is always attentive to his work. The author, in order to remain within his intentions, represents him as poor, dirty, hideous, disgusting to the touch, horrible to see. But if the actual exterior is a manner of disguising action and more surely succeeding, is it not the proof of sublime courage?

When Rodin becomes Pope, do you think he will still be so poorly dressed and filthy? M. Eugène Sue had thus missed his mark; he wishes to condemn fanaticism and superstition, and he attacks intelligence, force, genius, and all the great virtues of humanity! If there were many Rodins in the Jesuit order, if there were

---

363   The novel is *Le Juif errant* (*The Wandering Jew*), published in 1844. The character Lévi discusses is the Jesuit Rodin, who annihilates all the members of a very large family in an effort to get control of the family fortune.

even a single one, I would not bet on the success of the adverse party, despite the brilliant and maladroit defense of its illustrious lawyers.

To will well, to will for a long time, to always will, but to never covet anything, such is the secret of power; and it is this magic arcanum which Tasso put into action in the person of the two knights who come to deliver Rinaldo and destroy the enchantments of Armida.[364] They resist as easily against the most charming of nymphs as against the most terrible and ferocious of animals; they resist without desire and without fear, and they arrive at their goal.

The conclusion of all this is that a true magician is more redoubtable than lovable. I do not deny it, and while acknowledging how sweet are the seductions of life, while rendering justice to the gracious genius of Anacreon[365] and all the youthful efflorescence of the poetry of love, I most seriously invite my distinguished friends of pleasure to not consider the high sciences as an object of curiosity and never to approach a magical tripod: the great magical works of science are mortal to pleasure.

The man who delivers himself from the chain of instincts will first notice his omnipotence through the submission of animals. The story of Daniel in the lion's pit is not a fable, and more than once, during the persecution of nascent Christianity, this phenomenon reoccurred in the presence of the entire Roman people. Rarely does a man have anything to fear from an animal of which he is not afraid. The bullets of Gérard, the killer of lions, are magical and intelligent.[366] Once only did he run a real danger: he allowed a companion to come with him who took fright, and then, looking at this imprudent man as though he were lost in advance, he took fright as well, but for his comrade.

Many people will say that it is difficult and even impossible to arrive at such resolution, that such force of will and energy of character are gifts of nature, and

---

364　A reference to cantos 15 and 16 of Torquato Tasso's epic poem *Jerusalem Delivered*. The knights Carlo and Ubaldo, friends of Rinaldo, rescue him from the sorceress Armida, who has fallen in love with him and cast spells on him to make him forget his duty to the Crusade.

365　An ancient Greek lyric poet (563 BCE–478 BCE), who wrote mostly in praise of love and wine.

366　Jules Gérard (1817–64), a famous lion hunter of Lévi's time.

so on. I do not deny this, but I also recognize that habit can remake nature; the will can be perfected through education, and, as I have said, all ceremonial magic, like religious ceremony, has as its only goal to test oneself and thus exert and habituate oneself to will, to perseverance, and to force. The more difficult and demanding the practices, the more effect they have: we must understand this by now.

If it has been impossible so far to direct the phenomena of magnetism, it is because there has not yet been found an initiated magnetizer who is truly free. Who can in fact flatter himself that he is such a one? Must we not continually make new efforts regarding ourselves? It is nevertheless certain that nature will obey the sign and the word of one who feels strong enough not to doubt. I say that nature will obey, but I do not say that it will contradict itself or that it will trouble the order of its possibilities. The healing of nervous maladies through speech, breath, or contact; resurrections, in certain cases; resistance to wicked wills capable of disarming and overthrowing murderers; the actual ability to render oneself invisible by troubling the sight of those from whom it is important to escape: all these are natural effects of the projection or withdrawal of the astral light. It is thus that Valens was struck with a blinding light and with terror, when entering the church of Caesarea,[367] just as Heliodorus before him, who was struck by a sudden madness in the temple of Jerusalem, and who believed he was being whipped and trampled under the feet of angels.[368] It is thus that the admiral de Coligny imposed respect upon his assassins and was only killed by a furious man who threw himself upon him while turning his head away from de Coligny's gaze.[369] What rendered Joan of Arc ever victorious was the glamor of her faith and her marvelous audacity: she paralyzed the arms that wished to strike her, and the English seriously believed her to be a magician or a witch. She was in fact a ma-

---

367 A Christian legend of the Middle Ages claims that the Roman emperor Valens was struck down in this way when he confronted Saint Basil of Caesarea over their theological differences.

368 According to 2 Maccabees 21–26, the Greek king Seleucus IV sent his minister Heliodorus to seize the treasures of the temple of Jerusalem, but Heliodorus was stopped when he perceived himself to be beaten and trampled by three angels.

369 Admiral Gaspard de Coligny, the leader of the French Protestants, was one of many victims of the Saint Bartholomew's Day massacre in 1572.

gician without knowing it, because she believed that she acted supernaturally herself, whereas in fact she disposed of an occult force, which is universal and always subject to the same laws.

The magnetizing magician must command the natural *medium* and in consequence the astral body which allows communication between our soul and our organs; he can say to the material body, "Sleep!" and to the astral body: "Awake!" Then visible things change their aspect, just as in the visions induced by hashish. Cagliostro possessed this power, it is said, and aided its action through fumigation and incense, but true magnetic power must do without such auxiliaries which are more or less poisonous to reason and noxious to health. M. Ragon, in his scholarly work regarding occult masonry, provided the recipe for a series of medicines capable of amplifying hypnotism. It is knowledge which should certainly not be rejected, but which prudent mages should take care not to use.

The astral light is projected through the eyes, through the voice, through the thumbs and the palm of the hands. Music is a powerful auxiliary to the voice, and it is from there that the word en*chant*ment is derived. No musical instrument is more enchanting than the human voice, but the distant sounds of the violin or the harmonica can augment its power. We thus prepare the subject whom we wish to subdue; then, when he is half-dozing and as though enveloped by this charm, we extend a hand towards him and we command him to sleep or to *see*, and he will obey despite himself. If he resists, one must, while gazing at him fixedly, place one thumb on his forehead between the eyes, and the other thumb on his chest, while touching him lightly with a single and rapid contact, then inhale slowly, softly exhale a hot breath, and repeat to him in a low voice: Sleep or See.

CHAPTER VII

THE SEPTENARY OF TALISMANS

Since the ceremonies, the garments, the perfumes, the characters, and the figures, as we have said, are necessary in order to employ the imagination for the education of the will, the success of magical works depends on the faithful observation of all the rites. These rites, as we have said, are neither fantastical nor arbitrary; they were transmitted from antiquity and are always based upon the essential laws and the analogical realization of both the relationship which exists between ideas and between the forms. After having spent several years consulting and comparing all the grimoires and all the most authentic magical rituals, we have succeeded, not without work, at reconstituting the ceremonies of universal and primordial magic. The only serious books which we have seen on the subject are manuscripts and are drawn in characters of a form that we have deciphered with the aid of the *Polygraphiae* of Trithemius;[370] others are entirely in hieroglyphics and the symbols with which they are embellished and disguise the truth of their images with the superstitious fictions of a mystifying text. Such is the case, for example, for the *Enchiridion* of Pope Leo III,[371] which was never pub-

---

370   Another book on codes and ciphers by Johannes Trithemius, published in 1508.

371   A famous grimoire, written by an anonymous author in France sometime in the early seventeenth century and falsely attributed to Leo III.

lished with its true figures, and which we have recopied for our own particular use from an ancient manuscript.

The rituals known under the name of the *Key of Solomon* are numerous.[372] Many were published, others have remained in manuscript form and were recopied with great care. There exists a beautiful example, very elegantly calligraphed, at the Imperial Library; it is embellished with pentacles and characters which are found, for the most part, in the magical calendars of Tycho Brahe and of Duchenteau. Finally, there exist published clavicules and grimoires which are mystifications and shameful speculations belonging only in base libraries. The well-known and decried book of our fathers known under the name of *Petit Albert* owes all of its writing to this last category;[373] the more genuine aspects are only found in a few calculations borrowed from Paracelsus as well as a few figures of talismans.

With regard to realization and ritual, Paracelsus is, in magic, an imposing authority. No one else has accomplished such great works as his, and for that same reason he hides the power of the ceremonies and only teaches of occult philosophy the existence of the magnetic agent of the omnipotence of the will; he also summarizes the entire science of characters with two signs, which are the macro- and microcosmic stars. That was saying enough for adepts, and it was important not to initiate the vulgar. Paracelsus thus did not teach ritual, but he practiced it, and his practice resulted in a series of miracles.

We have said how important the ternary and quaternary are in magic. A great number of religious and Cabalistic signs which represent universal synthesis and constitute the sacred septenary are composed from their union.

According to the beliefs of the ancients, the world is governed by seven secondary causes, which Trithemius calls *secundei*, and these are the universal forces designated by Moses under the plural name of Elohim, the gods. These forces,

---

372   An understatement—the *Clavicle* or *Key of Solomon* is among the most famous and widely copied magical handbooks of the Middle Ages.

373   One of the most widely circulated magical handbooks in French, the *Petit Albert* (*Lesser Albert*) appeared around the beginning of the eighteenth century. Like most other early modern magical handbooks, it is a grab bag of magical practices to which folk magic and ceremonial magic make roughly equal contributions.

analogous and contrary to one another, produce equilibrium through their contrasts and regulate the movement of the spheres. The Hebrews call them the seven archangels, and give the names Michael, Gabriel, Raphael, Anael, Samael, Zadkiel, and Oriphiel. The Gnostic Christians called the last four Uriel, Barachiel, Sealtiel, and Jehudiel. Other peoples attributed the government of the seven principal planets to these spirits and gave them the names of their greatest divinities. All believed in their relative influence, and astronomy divided up the ancient sky between them and successively attributed to them the government of the seven days of the week.

This is the reason for the diverse ceremonies of the magical week and for the septenary cult of the planets.

We have already observed that the planets, here on Earth, are signs and nothing else; they have the influence which faith attributes to them, because they are even more truly celestial bodies of the human spirit than stars in the sky.

The Sun, which ancient magic has always regarded as fixed, could only be a planet to the vulgar;[374] it also represents in the week, the day of rest, which we call, who knows why, "dimanche," and which the ancients called, and the English still call, the day of the Sun.

The seven magical planets correspond to the seven colors of the spectrum and the seven notes of the musical octave; they also represent the seven virtues and, by opposition, the seven vices of Christian morality.

The seven sacraments are also related to this grand universal septenary. Baptism, which consecrates the element of water, relates to the Moon; strict penitence is under the auspices of Samael, the angel of Mars; confirmation, which accords the spirit of intelligence and communicates the gift of tongues to the true believer, is under the auspices of Raphael, the angel of Mercury; the Eucharist substitutes the sacramental realization of God become man with the empire of Jupiter; marriage is consecrated by Anael, the purifying genius of Venus; extreme unction is the protection of those who are sick and about to fall under the false influence of Saturn; and the order which consecrates the priesthood of light, is most especially marked by the characters of the Sun. Almost all these analogies were

---

374   The word "planet" comes from the Greek word *planētēs*, "wanderer."

remarked upon by the scholar Dupuis, who concluded that all religions were false, rather than recognizing the holiness and the perpetuity of the unique doctrine, always reproduced in the universal symbolism of successive religious forms. He did not understand the permanent revelation transmitted to the human genius by the harmonies of nature and only saw a series of errors in this chain of ingenious images and eternal truths.

The magical works also number seven: first, works of light and wealth, under the auspices of the Sun; second, works of divination and the mysteries, under the invocation of the Moon; third, works of skill, of science, and eloquence, under the protection of Mercury; fourth, works of anger and punishment, consecrated to Mars; fifth, works of love, favored by Venus; sixth, works of ambition and politics, under the auspices of Jupiter; seventh, works of malediction and of death, under the patronage of Saturn. In theological symbolism, the Sun represents the Verb of Truth; the Moon represents religion itself; Mercury, the interpretation and the science of the mysteries; Mars, justice; Venus, charity and love; Jupiter, the resuscitated and glorious Savior; Saturn, God the father, or the Jehovah of Moses. In the human body, the Sun is analogous to the heart, the Moon to the brain, Jupiter to the right hand, Saturn to the left hand, Mars to the right foot, and Venus to the left foot, Mercury to the genitalia, the spirit of this last planet being sometimes represented by an androgynous figure.

In the human face, the Sun dominates the forehead, Jupiter the right eye, Saturn the left eye; the Moon reigns between the two eyes, at the root of the nose, whose two wings are governed by Mars and Venus; finally Mercury exerts his influence on the mouth and the chin. With these notions, the ancients formed the occult science of physiognomy, imperfectly rediscovered by Lavater.[375]

The mage who wishes to proceed with works of light must perform them on Sunday, from midnight to eight in the morning, or from three in the afternoon until ten at night. He will be dressed in a purple robe, with a tiara and bracelets of gold. The altar of perfumes and the tripod of the sacred fire will be surrounded by garlands of bay leaves, heliotropes, and sunflowers; the perfumes will be cin-

---

375   Swiss writer Johann Kaspar Lavater (1741–1801), who published extensively on the art of physiognomy, which reads faces the way palmistry reads hands.

namon, the male incense, saffron, and red sandalwood; the ring will be gold, with a chrysolite or a ruby; the carpet will be made of the skin of lions; the fan will be made of the plumes of a sparrow hawk.

On Monday you will wear a white robe striped with silver, with a triple necklace of pearls, of crystals, and of selenite; the tiara will be covered in yellow silk, with silver characters spelling the Hebrew monogram for Gabriel, as we find them in the occult philosophy of Agrippa; the perfumes will be white sandalwood, camphor, amber, aloe, and the pulverized seeds of cucumber; the garlands will be of mugwort, of selenotropes,[376] and of yellow buttercups. You will avoid black-colored wall coverings, clothes, or objects, and you will wear no other metal except silver.

On Tuesday, a day for operations of anger, the robe will be the color of fire, or of rust or of blood, with a belt and bracelets of steel; the tiara will be circled with fire, and you will not use the wand, but only a magical stylet and the sword; the garlands will be of absinthe and of rue, and you will wear a ring of steel with an amethyst for its precious stone.

On Wednesday, a favorable day for high science, the robe will be green or of a reflective cloth of different colors: the necklace will be of beads of hollow glass containing mercury; the perfumes will be benzoin, mace, and storax; the flowers, narcissus, lily, mercurialis annua, fumitory, and marjoram; the precious stone will be agate.

On Thursday, a day for great works of religion and politics, the robe will be scarlet, and you will wear on the forehead a strip of tin with the character and spirit of Jupiter and these three words: GIARAR, BETHOR, SAMGABIEL; the perfumes will be incense, ambergris, balm, grains of paradise, mace, and saffron; the ring will be decorated with an emerald or a sapphire; the garlands and crowns will be of oak, poplar, fig tree, and pomegranate tree.

On Friday, the day for operations of love, the robe will be of blue azure; the wall coverings will be green and pink, the ornaments of polished copper; the crowns will be of violets; the garlands of roses, of myrtle, and olive tree; the ring will be decorated with a turquoise; lapis lazuli and beryl will serve for the tiara

---

376 Plants whose flowers turn to face the moon.

and the clips; the fans will be of swan feathers; the operator will have on the chest a talisman of copper with the character of Anael and these words: AVEEVA VADE LILITH.

On Saturday, the day for funereal works, the robe will be black or brown, with characters embroidered in silk of an orange color; you will wear around the neck a medal of lead with the character of Saturn and the words ALMALEC, APHIEL, ZARAHIEL; the perfumes will be of dacrydium, scammony, alum, sulfur, and asafoetida; the ring will have a stone of onyx; the garlands will be of ash, cypress, and black hellebore; on the ring's onyx you will engrave a double head of Janus during the hours of Saturn with a consecrated awl.

Such is the ancient magnificence of the secret cult of the mages. It is with similar instruments that the great magicians of the Middle Ages proceeded with the daily consecration of the pentacles and talismans relative to the seven spirits. We have already said that a pentacle is a synthetic character which summarizes all of magical doctrine in their special conceptions. It is thus the veritable expression of a complete thought and will; it is the signature of a spirit. The ceremonial consecration of this sign attaches the operator's intentions even more strongly to it and establishes between himself and the sign a true magical chain. The pentacles can be equally drawn on virgin parchment, on paper, or on metals. We call a talisman a piece of metal which has either pentacles or characters and which was especially consecrated for a determined intention. Gaffarel, in a scholarly work about ancient magics, had demonstrated through science the real power of these talismans, and confidence in their virtue is also so natural that we willingly carry on our person souvenirs of those we love, persuaded that these relics protect us from danger and can render us more happy. We make talismans with the seven Cabalistic metals, and we engrave them, on the favorable days and times, with the desired and determined signs. The figures of the seven planets, with their magical squares,[377] are found in the *Petit Albert*, as in Paracelsus, and are one of the rare serious sections of this vulgar book on magic. It should be remarked that Paracelsus replaces the figure of Jupiter by that of a priest, a substitution that is not without mysterious and earnest intention.

---

377   These magical squares are given in chapter 22 of "The Ritual," below, pp. 393–94.

But the allegorical and mythological figures of the seven spirits have in our day become too classical and too vulgar for them to be successfully engraved on talismans; one must have recourse to more learned and expressive signs. The pentagram must always be engraved on one side of the talisman, with a circle for the Sun, a crescent for the Moon, a caduceus for Mercury, a sword for Mars, a G for Venus, a crown for Jupiter, and a sickle for Saturn. On the other side of the talisman there must be the sign of Solomon, that is to say the six-pointed star made from two superimposed triangles, and at its center you will place a human figure for talismans of the Sun, a cup for those of the Moon, the head of a dog for those Mercury, the head of an eagle for those of Jupiter, the head of a lion for those of Mars, and the head of a bull or of a goat for those of Saturn. You then add the names of the seven angels, either in Hebrew or in Arabic or in magical characters similar to the alphabets of Trithemius. The two triangles of Solomon can be replaced by Ezekiel's double cross of wheels, which we find on a great number of ancient pentacles and which is, as we have observed in our Doctrine, the key to Fu Hsi's trigrams.

We can also use precious stones for amulets and talismans, but all objects of this type, either in metal or in gemstones, must be carefully enveloped in silk sachets of the color which is analogous to the spirit of the planet, perfumed with the incense of the corresponding day, and protected from all impure glances and touch. Thus the pentacles and the talismans of the Sun must not be seen or touched by deformed and distorted people or by immoral women; those of the Moon are profaned by the gaze and the touch of debauched men and menstruating women; those of Mercury lose their virtue if they are seen or touched by salaried priests; those of Mars must be hidden from cowards; those of Venus from depraved men and those who have taken a vow of celibacy; those of Jupiter from the impious; and those of Saturn from virgins and children, not that the regards or touch of these last two can ever be impure, but because the talisman would bring them bad luck and thus lose all its power.

Crosses of honor and other decorations of the same type are veritable talismans, which increase personal worth or merit. The solemn presentation of them is their consecration. Public opinion must also give them prodigious power. We have not remarked enough upon the reciprocal influence of signs upon ideas and of ideas upon signs; it is no less true that the revolutionary work of modern times, for example, was entirely symbolically summarized by Napoleon's replacement of the cross of Saint Louis with the star of honor.[378] It is the labarum replaced by the pentagram, it is the rehabilitation of the symbol of light, it is the resurrection of the Masonic Adonhiram.[379] They say that Napoleon believed in his star, and, if we could have him say what he meant by that star, we would find that it was his genius: he thus had to adopt the sign of the pentagram, that symbol of human sovereignty, through intelligent initiative. The great soldier of the revolution knew little, but he guessed almost everything: thus he was the greatest instinctive practical magician of modern times. The world is still full of his miracles, and the people in the countryside will never believe that he is dead.

Blessed and indulgenced objects, things touched by holy images or venerable persons, rosaries from Palestine, the agnus Dei composed of wax from the Paschal candle, the annual remains of the holy chrism, scapulars, medals[380] are all veritable talismans. One of these medals has become popular in our time, even those who have no religion put it around the necks of their children.[381] The figures are so perfectly Cabalistic that this medal is truly a double and marvelous pentacle. On one side we see the grand initiatrix, the celestial mother of the Zohar, the Isis of Egypt, the Venus Urania of the followers of Plato, the Mary of Christianity standing on the world and placing a foot on the magical serpent's head. She extends her two hands in a manner in which they form a triangle where her head is the apex; her hands are open and radiate, which makes for a double pentagram, whose rays all head towards the Earth, which obviously represents the liberation of intelligence through work. On the other side of the medal, we see the double

---

378   These were the emblems on the highest French military medal under the Bourbon kings and Napoleon's empire, respectively.

379   A name for Hiram Abiff used in some branches of French Masonry.

380   These are all items that played a role in popular Catholic devotion in nineteenth-century France.

381   This is the so-called Miraculous Medal, a common Catholic devotional medal in Lévi's time. The imagery discussed in the following sentences is all found on this medal.

Tau of the hierophants, the Lingam with the double Kteis or with a triple Phallus, supported by, with interlacing and a double insertion, the Cabalistic and masonic M representing the set square between the two columns of Jachin and Boaz; below them are placed, on the same level, two loving and suffering hearts, and, all around, twelve pentagrams. Everyone will tell you that the wearers of these medals do not attach any particular significance to them, but this does not make them any less perfectly magical, having a double meaning and, in consequence, a double virtue. The ecstatic upon whose revelations this talisman's engravings were based had already seen its existence and perfection in the astral light, which demonstrates once again the most intimate connection between ideas and signs, and sanctions anew the symbolism of universal magic.

The more importance and solemnity that we place in the confection and consecration of talismans and pentacles, the more virtue they acquire, as we should understand based on the self-evident nature of the principles we have established. This consecration must be performed on the special days which we have noted, with the instruments of which we have provided the details. We consecrate with the four exorcised elements, after having conjured the spirits of darkness through the conjuration of the four; then we take the pentacle in our hand and we tell it, while sprinkling it with a few drops of magical water:

In nomine Elohim et per spiritum aquarum viventium, sis mihi in signum lucis et sacramentum voluntatis.

(In the name of Elohim and by the spirit of the living waters, be thou unto me as a sign of light and a sacrament of will.)

While presenting it to the smoke from the perfumes we say:

Per serpentum aeneum sub quo cadunt serpentes ignei, sis mihi (etc.).

(By the brazen serpent before which fell the fiery serpents, be thou unto me, etc.)

While blowing seven times on the pentacle or on the talisman we say:

Per firmamentum et spiritum vocis, sis mihi (etc.).

(By the firmament and the spirit of the voice, be thou unto me, etc.)

Finally, while placing a few grains of purified earth or salt in the form of a triangle on the pentacle or on the talisman, one must say:

In sale terrae et per virtutem vitae aeternae, sis mihi (etc.).

(In the salt of the earth and by the power of eternal life, be thou unto me, etc.)

Then we perform the conjuration of the seven in the following manner:

By turns, we throw into the sacred fire a pastille made of the seven perfumes and we say:

In the name of Michael, may Jehovah command you and drive you away from here, Chavajoth!

In the name of Gabriel, may Adonai command you and drive you away from here, Belial!

In the name of Raphael, disappear before Elohim, Sachabiel!

By Samael Zabaoth and in the name of Elohim Gibor, leave this place, Adramelech!

By Zachariel and Sachiel-Melech, obey Elvah, Samgabiel!

In the divine and human name of Shaddai and by the sign of the pentagram which I hold in my right hand, in the name of the angel Anael,

by the power of Adam and Heva, who are Yod-Chavah, leave this place, Lilith; leave us in peace, Nahemah!

By the holy Eloim and the names of the spirits Cassiel, Shealtiel, Zaphiel, and Zarahiel, by the command of Oriphiel, turn away from us, Moloch! we shall not give you our children to devour.

Concerning the magical instruments, the principal ones are: the wand, the sword, the lamp, the cup, the altar, and the tripod. In high and divine operations of magic we use the lamp, the wand, and the cup; in works of black magic we replace the wand with the sword and the lamp with Cardano's candle.[382] We will explain the difference in this article particular to black magic later.

Let us now come to the description and the consecration of the instruments.

The magical wand, which one should not confuse with a simple divinatory wand or with the fork of the necromancers or Paracelsus's trident; the true and

382   An early form of magic lantern or slide projector, like the lamp; see the description of the lamp at the end of this chapter.

absolute magical wand must be of a single cast, perfectly straight, of almond tree or hazel tree, cut, with a single cut of a magical pruning knife or a golden sickle, before dawn and at the moment when the tree is ready to flower. One must perforate it along its entire length without cracking or breaking it and insert a long magnetized iron needle which goes through the entire length; then we attach to one of the extremities a polyhedral prism which is triangularly cut, and at the other end the same form but in black resin. In the middle of the wand you will place two rings, one of red copper, the other of zinc; then the wand will be gilded on the side of the resin and silvered on the side of the prism up until the rings in the middle, and then you cover it in silk up until the the extremities only. On the copper ring one must engrave these characters ירושלים הקדשה (IRVShLM HQDSh, "Jerusalem the Holy") and on the zinc ring these שלמה המלך (ShLMH HMLK, "Solomon the King."). The consecration of the wand must last seven days, beginning on the new moon, and must be done by an initiate who possesses the grand arcanum and who he himself has a consecrated wand. It is the transmission of the magical priesthood, and this transmission has not ceased since the obscure origins of the high science. The wand and the other instruments, but most of all the wand, must be carefully hidden, and under no pretext should the mage allow them to be seen or touched by the profane; otherwise they will lose all their virtue.

The manner of transmission of the wand is one of the arcana of science that is never permitted to be revealed.

The length of the magical wand should not exceed the length of the arm of the operator. The mage should not make use of it except when he is alone, and he should never even touch it needlessly. Many ancient mages made it only the length of their forearm and hid it in their long sleeves, showing only the divinatory wand to the public, or some allegorical scepter made ivory or ebony, depending on the nature of the works.

Cardinal Richelieu, who was always chasing after power, searched all his life for the transmission of the wand without ever managing to find it. His Cabalist, Gaffarel, could only provide him with the sword and the talismans: this was perhaps the secret motive behind his hatred for Urbain Grandier, who knew something of the cardinal's weaknesses. The secret and lengthy interviews between Laubardement and the poor priest just a few hours before his last ordeal, and the words of a friend and confidant of his when Urbain was heading towards death, "Monsieur, you are a clever man, do not lose your way," provide a great deal to think about regarding this subject.

The magical wand is the *verendum* of the mage; he must not speak about it in a clear and precise manner; no one should boast about having one, and one should not transmit the consecration except under conditions of discretion and absolute confidence.

The sword is less occult, and here is what one must do:

It must be made of pure steel, with a handle of copper made in the form of a cross with three pommels, as it is represented in the *Enchiridion* of Leo III, or which has a guard made of two crescents, as in our figure. On the central knot of the guard, which must be gold plated, one must engrave the sign of the microcosm on one side and the sign of the macrocosm on the other. On the pommel one must engrave the Hebrew monogram for Michael, as one sees it in Agrippa, and on the blade, on one side are the characters באילים יהוה כמכה (BAYLYM YHVH KMKH) and on the other the monogram of Constantine's labarum, followed by the words: *Vince in hoc, Deo duce, ferro comite* ("Conquer in this [sign], with God as your leader and a sword as your companion"). (For sincere and exact reproductions of these figures, see the best ancient editions of the *Enchiridion*.)

The consecration of the sword must be done on a Sunday, during daylight hours, under the invocation of Michael. You will put the blade of the sword into a fire of laurel and cypress, then wipe and polish the blade with the ashes of the sacred fire, moistened with the blood of a mole or a serpent, and you will say: *Sis mihi gladius Michaelis, in virtute Elohim Sabaoth fugiant a te spiritus tenebrarum et reptilia terrae* ("Let this be unto me the sword of Michael; in the power of Elohim Sabaoth let the spirits of the shadows and the creeping things of the Earth flee from thee"); then you will perfume it with the perfumes of the Sun, and you enclose it in silk with branches of verbena, which must be burned on the seventh day.

The magical lamp must be made of four metals: gold, silver, bronze, and iron. The foot will be in iron, the knot of bronze, the cup of silver, and the triangle in the middle of gold. It will have two arms, composed of three metals twisted together, in a manner however which allows for a triple conduit for the oil. It will have nine wicks, three in the middle and three for each arm. (See figure.) On the foot you will engrave the seal of Hermes and above it Khunrath's two-headed androgyne. The lower border of the foot will represent a serpent biting its tail.

On the cup or oil receptacle you will engrave the sign of Solomon. To this lamp will be adapted two globes: one decorated with transparent pictures representing the seven spirits, the other, which is larger and doubled, capable of containing in four compartments; between two glasses, water which is tinted in various colors. The entire lamp will be enclosed in a column of wood that turns freely, which is able to let escape at will one of the rays from the lamp, which you will direct towards the smoke from the altar at the moment of the invocations.[383]

This lamp is of great help in aiding with intuitive operations of slow imagination and is able to immediately create in front of magnetized persons the forms of a terrifying reality, which, being multiplied by mirrors, will cause a mage's chamber to suddenly grow and change it into a single immense room filled with visible souls; the intoxication of the incense and the exaltation of the invocations will soon transform this phantasmagoria into a true dream: we will recognize persons we had known, phantoms will speak; then, if we close up the column of the lamp while redoubling the fire of the perfumes, something extraordinary and unexpected will occur.

---

383   This lantern, in other words, is a "magic lantern" in the nineteenth-century sense of that term—a simple form of slide projector designed to project the image of a spirit using a cloud of incense as a screen.

CHAPTER VIII

A WARNING TO THE IMPRUDENT

As we have already said several times, the operations of science are not without their dangers.

They can lead to madness for those who are not strengthened by a foundation of supreme, absolute, and infallible reason.

They can overexcite their nervous system and produce terrible and incurable maladies.

They can, when their imagination strikes and terrorizes them, faint and even die due to cerebral congestion.

We can thus never too often deter nervous and easily enthused persons, women, young people, and all those who are not in the habit of having a perfect command over their fears.

Nothing is more dangerous than turning magic into a hobby, like certain people who make it an ornament for their soirées. Magnetic experiences themselves, conducted under such conditions, can only tire the subjects, mislead opinion, and obfuscate the science. We do not play with the mysteries of life and death with impunity, and those things which should be taken seriously must be treated seriously and with great reserve.

Never yield to the desire to convince through effects. The most surprising effects will not act as proofs for those who are not convinced beforehand. We can always attribute them to natural illusions and look upon the mage as a more or less adroit rival of Robert-Houdin or of Hamilton.[384] To demand miracles in order to believe in the science is to show oneself to be unworthy or incapable of the science. SANCTA SANCTIS.[385]

Nor should you ever boast about the works you have performed, even if you have resuscitated the dead. Fear persecution. The great master always recommended silence to the sick that he cured, and if this silence had been faithfully kept, they would not have crucified the initiator before he had finished his work.

Meditate on the twelfth figure of the keys of the Tarot; think of the great symbol of Prometheus and remain silent.

All the mages who had divulged their works died a violent death, many were reduced to suicide, like Cardano, Schröpfer, Cagliostro, and so many others.

The mage must live in retreat and be difficult to approach. This is what the symbol of the ninth key of the Tarot represents, where the initiate is symbolized by a hermit completely covered by his cloak.

Nevertheless, this retreat cannot result in isolation. The mage requires devotion and friendships, but he must choose them carefully and keep them at any price.

To engage in ceremonial magic, one must be without troubling preoccupations; one must be able to procure all the instruments of the science and know, when the need arises, how to make them oneself; finally, one must have a private laboratory, where one does not have to fear ever being surprised or bothered.

Then, and this is the essential condition, one must know how to balance the forces and contain the momentum of one's own initiatives. This is what the eighth figure of the keys of Hermes represents, in which we see a woman sitting between two columns, holding a sword in her right hand and a balance in the other.

To equilibrate the forces one must maintain them simultaneously and cause them to act alternatively, a double action which is represented by the use of the balance.

This arcana is also represented by the double cross of the pentacles of Py-

---

384   Two famous stage magicians of the mid-nineteenth century.

385   Latin: "Holy things are for the holy."

thagoras and of Ezekiel (see the figure on page 165 of the Doctrine), in which the crosses are balanced one against the other and the planetary signs are always in opposition. Thus Venus gives equilibrium to the works of Mars; Mercury tempers and accomplishes the works of the Sun and the Moon; Saturn must balance Jupiter. It is through this antagonism of the ancient gods that Prometheus, that is to say the genius of science, managed to enter Olympus and steal fire from heaven.

Must we speak more clearly? The more sweet and calm you are, the more power your anger will have; the more energetic you are, the more value your leisure will have; the more skillful you are, the more you will profit from your intelligence and even your virtues; the more indifferent you are, the easier it will be to make yourself loved. This is an experience of a moral order and is realized strictly within the sphere of action. The human passions are fated to produce, when they are not directed, effects contrary to their unbridled desires. Excessive love produces antipathy; blind hatred is annulled and punishes itself; vanity leads to abasement and the most cruel humiliations. The great master thus revealed a mystery of positive magical science when he said: "If you wish to accumulate burning coals upon the head of he who causes you harm, then pardon him and do him good."[386] We might say that such a pardon would be hypocritical and resembles a refined form of vengeance. But one must remember that the mage is sovereign. And a sovereign never takes revenge, since he has the right to punish. When he exercises that right and does his duty, he is as implacable as justice. Let us carefully note here, so that no one misunderstands my words, this is a matter of punishing evil with good and opposing sweetness to violence. If the exercise of virtue is a flagellation for vice, no one has the right to ask that we spare or take pity upon its disgrace and its suffering.

He who engages in works of science must exercise moderately every day, abstain from staying up too late, and follow a healthy and regular regimen. He must avoid putrid odors, stagnant water, indigestible or impure foods. Most of all, he must distract himself from daily magical preoccupations with material cares, or works either of art or of industry, or even by his professional duties. The way to

---

386   A paraphrase of Romans 12:20.

see clearly is to not always be looking, and he who always spends his life on the same goal will end up by never attaining it.

Another precaution one should also always take is to never engage in magical operations while sick.

The ceremonies being, as we have said, an artificial means of creating habits of will, they cease being necessary when those habits are established. It is in this manner, while addressing only perfect adepts, that Paracelsus proscribed their use in his occult philosophy. One must simplify them progressively, before completely omitting them, according to the experience of our acquired powers and our established habits in the exercise of the extra-natural will.

CHAPTER IX

THE CEREMONY OF THE INITIATES

Science is preserved through silence and is perpetuated through initiation. The law of silence is thus only absolute and inviolable relative to the multitude of non-initiated. The science can only be transmitted through words. Therefore the sages must sometimes speak.

Yes, the sages must speak, not to say, but to lead others to find. *Noli ire, fac venire,*[387] was Rabelais's motto, who, in possessing all the sciences of his time, could not have been ignorant of magic.

We will thus reveal here the mysteries of initiation.

The destiny of man is, as we have said, to make or create himself; he is and will be the son of his works for the moment and for eternity.

All men are called to take part, but the number of the elect, that is to say those who succeed, is always small; in other terms, men who desire to be something are great in number, and the men of the elite are always rare.

But the government of the world belongs by right to the elite, and when a mechanism or some usurpation prevents them from in fact having it, a political or social cataclysm occurs.

The men who are masters of themselves easily become masters of others, but

---

387   Latin: "I do not wish to go but to make others come."

they can mutually obstruct each other if they do not recognize the laws of a discipline and of a universal hierarchy.

To submit to the same discipline, there must be a communion of ideas and of desires, and one can only arrive at this communion through a common religion founded on the actual bases of intelligence and reason.

This religion has always existed in the world, and it is the only one that can be called infallible, unfailing, and truly catholic, that is to say universal.

This religion, for which all others are just successive veils and shadows, is the one which demonstrates being through being, the truth through reason, reason through evidence and common sense.

It is the one which proves through the realities the raison d'être of the hypotheses independent and outside of the realities.

It is the one which has as its foundation the doctrine of universal analogies, but which never confuses the things of science with the things of faith. It can never be a matter of faith that two and one make more or less than three; that the physical contents can be larger than the container; that a solid body, and a solid, can act like a fluid or a gaseous body; that a human body, for example, can pass through a closed door without either opening it or bursting through. To say that one believes such a thing is to speak like a child or like a madman, but it is no less foolish to define the unknown and apply reason to it, from hypothesis to hypothesis, until you are denying a priori evidence in order to affirm foolhardy suppositions. The sage affirms what he knows and only believes what he does not know in the measure of the reasonable and known necessities of the hypothesis.

But this reasonable religion will never be that of the multitudes, who require fables, mysteries, defined hopes, and materially motivated terrors.

It is for this reason that the priesthood was established in the world. Yet the priesthood recruits through initiation.

Religious forms perish when initiation ceases to be practiced within the sanctuary, either through divulgation or through negligence and oblivion of the sacred mysteries.

The Gnostic divulgations, for example, distanced the Christian church from the high truths of the Cabala, which contain all the secrets of the higher theology. The blind having become the leaders of the blind, great obfuscations were produced, great falls and deplorable scandals; then the sacred books, whose keys are all Cabalistic, from Genesis to Revelation, became so unintelligible to Christians that the pastors, with reason, judged it necessary to forbid the simple faithful to read them. Taken on their word and understood materially, these books can only be, as the school of Voltaire only too well demonstrated, an inconceivable tissue of absurdities and scandals.

This is the case for all the ancients' doctrines, with their brilliant theogonies and their poetic legends. To say the ancients believed in Greece in the loves of Jupiter, or adored in Egypt the cynocephalus and the sparrow hawk as living and real gods, is to be as ignorant and as in bad faith as one would be in claiming that Christians adore a triple God consisting of an old man, a torture victim, and a pigeon. The straightforward meaning of the symbols is always calumniatory. This is why one should first and foremost guard oneself well against mocking things one does not understand, when their wording seems to suppose an absurdity or even some singularity; it would also be just as senseless to accept them without discussion or examination.

Before there is anything that pleases or displeases us, there is truth, that is to say reason, and it is by this reason that our actions must be regulated rather than by our pleasure if we wish to create intelligence within us, which is the raison d'être of immortality, and justice, which is law.

The man who is truly a man can only wish for what he must do reasonably and justly, and he also imposes silence on his lusts and fears, so as to only hear reason.

Such a man is a natural king and a spontaneous priest for the errant multitudes. It is for this reason that the object of the ancient initiations was indifferently called the sacerdotal art and the royal art.

The ancient magical associations were seminaries of priests and kings, and one only managed to be admitted through truly sacerdotal and kingly works, that is to say by placing oneself above all the weaknesses of nature.

We will not repeat here what is found everywhere regarding the Egyptian initiations, perpetuated, though in a weakened form, in the secret societies of the Middle Ages. Christian radicalism, founded on the false understanding of these words, "You have only one father and one master, and you are all brothers," struck a terrible blow to the sacred hierarchy. Since that time, the sacerdotal dignities have been bestowed by intrigue or happenstance; active mediocrity has managed to supplant modest superiority, and in consequence is misunderstood, and, meanwhile, initiation being an essential law of religious life, an instinctively magical society was formed with the decline of pontifical power[388] and had soon concentrated in itself alone all the powers of Christianity, because only it alone had vaguely understood, but positively exercised, the hierarchical power through the trials of initiation and the omnipotence of faith in passive reverence.

What, in fact, did the initiate do in the ancient initiations? He entirely abandoned his life and his liberty to the masters of the temples of Thebes or of Memphis; he advanced resolutely through innumerable trials of terror that might make him suspect a premeditated plot against his life; he crossed burning pyres, swam through torrents of seething black water, suspended himself over unknown heights, over precipices without end. . . . Was this not blind reverence in all the force of that term? Is not to momentarily abjure one's liberty in order to arrive at emancipation the most perfect exercise of liberty? Yet that is what must be done and has always been done by those who aspire to the *sanctum regnum* of magical omnipotence. The disciples of Pythagoras condemned themselves to a strict silence for several years; even the sectarians of Epicurus only understood the sovereignty of pleasure through acquired sobriety and calculated temperance. Life is war, where one must prove oneself to rise in rank: power is not given; one must take it.

Initiation through struggle and trial is thus indispensable for arriving at the practical science of magic. We have already said how we can triumph over the four elemental forms: we will not repeat it, and we refer our readers who wish to know the ancient ceremonies to the works of the Baron de Tschoudy, author of *The Flaming Star, The Masonic Adonhiramite*, and several other highly estimable masonic brochures.

We must insist here upon this reflection: that the intellectual and social chaos in the midst of which we perish has its cause in the negligence of initiation, of its trials and of its mysteries. Men for which zealousness was stronger than science,

---

388   The Jesuits are meant here.

THE CEREMONY OF THE INITIATES

impressed by the popular maxims of the Gospels, believed in the primordial and absolute equality of people. A famous crackpot, the eloquent and unfortunate Rousseau,[389] propagated with all the magic of his style this paradox: that society alone depraves men, as if to say that competition and the emulation of others' work rendered workers lazy. The essential law of nature, that of initiation through works and through laborious and voluntary progress had been fatally misunderstood; Freemasonry had its deserters, as did Catholicism. What was the result? The iron level replaced the intellectual and symbolic level. Is not to preach equality to those below without telling them how to rise, the commitment to descend oneself? As soon as we descend, we achieve the reign of the Carmagnole,[390] of the sansculottes[391] and of Marat.[392]

To lift up a faltering and declining society, one must reestablish hierarchy and initiation. The job is difficult, but everyone of intelligence already knows that it must be done. Should we need the world to go through another Flood for this to happen? We strongly desire that it should not be so, and this book, the greatest, perhaps, but not the last of our audacities, is a call to all those still living to reconstitute life even in the middle of decomposition and of death.

---

389   Jean-Jacques Rousseau, who argued that human beings are naturally good but are corrupted by society.

390   The radical wing of the French Revolution in Paris, so called after a revolutionary song of the same name.

391   On the eve of the French Revolution, culottes (knee breeches) were standard court dress at Versailles, while poor and working class men wore long trousers instead. The Paris radicals who became the shock troops of the first stage of the Revolution made a point of refusing to wear culottes, thus were called "sansculottes."

392   Lévi is invoking memories of the Terror, in which thousands of people were tried, on trumped-up charges, as counterrevolutionaries and guillotined—for his readers in nineteenth-century France, a reference as powerful as a comparison with the Holocaust might be today.

CHAPTER X

THE KEY OF OCCULTISM

Let us now go deeper into the question of pentacles, because in them is found all the virtue of magic, since the secret to power is in the intelligence which directs it.

We will not go back to the pentacles of Pythagoras and Ezekiel, for which we have already given the explanation and the figures; we will prove in another chapter that all the instruments of the Hebrew cult were pentacles and that Moses had written in gold and bronze in the tabernacle and on all his accessories the first and last word of the Bible. Each mage can and should have his own particular pentacle, because of course a pentacle is the perfect summary of a spirit.

It is for this reason that we find in the magical calendars of Tycho Brahe and of Duchenteau the pentacles of Adam, of Job, of Jeremiah, of Isaiah, and all the other great prophets who were, each in his own time, the kings of the Cabala and the great rabbis of science.

The pentacle, being a complete and perfect synthesis, expressed in one single sign, is used to assemble all of the intellectual power into a glance, into a memory, into a contact. It is like a point of support from which to project the will with power. The necromancers and goetic sorcerers drew their infernal pentagrams on the skins of the victims that they sacrificed. We can find the ceremonies of sacrifice in several clavicules and grimoires: the manner of skinning a kid goat then salting it, of drying and of bleaching the skin. A few Hebrew Cabalists fell into the same folly, without remembering the maledictions pronounced in the Bible against those who sacrifice upon high places or in the caverns of the Earth. All these effusions of blood operated ceremonially are abominable and impious, and since the death of Adonhiram, the society of true adepts has a horror for blood, *Ecclesia abhorret a sanguine.*[393]

The initiatic symbolism of the pentacles which was adopted all through the Orient is the key to all the ancient and modern mythologies. One who does not know the hieroglyphic alphabet will get lost in the obscurities of the Vedas, the Zend-Avesta, and the Bible. The tree which generates good and evil, unique source of the four rivers, one of which waters the earth with gold, that is to say the light, the other which flows in Ethiopia, or in the kingdom of the night; the magnetic serpent who had seduced woman, and the woman who had seduced man, thus revealing the law of attraction; then the Cherub or Sphinx placed at the door to the Edenic sanctuary, with the flaming sword of the guardians of symbolism, then regeneration through work, and childbirth through pain, law of initiations and of trials; the division between Cain and Abel a symbol identical to the battle between Anteros and Eros; the ark carried on the waters of the Flood like the coffin of Osiris, the black crow which does not return and the white dove which returns, a new emission of the antagonistic and balanced doctrine: all these magnificent Cabalistic allegories from Genesis, taken to the letter and accepted as true stories, merit even more laughter and scorn than Voltaire had devoted to them, but they become luminous for the initiate, who then welcomes with enthusiasm and love the perpetuity of true doctrine and the universality of the same initiation into all the sanctuaries of the world.

The five books of Moses, the prophecy of Ezekiel, and the Revelation of Saint John are the three Cabalistic keys of the entire biblical edifice. The sphinxes of Ezekiel,[394] which are identical to those of the Sanctuary and the Ark of the Covenant, are a quadruple reproduction of the Egyptian quaternary; the wheels, which turn upon one another, are the harmonious spheres of Pythagoras; the new temple of which they provide the plan, based on entirely Cabalistic mea-

---

393   Latin: "The church abhors blood."

394   Ezekiel 1:5–14.

sures, is the perfect example of the works of primordial masonry. Saint John, in the Book of Revelation, reproduces the same images and the same numbers, and ideally reconstitutes the Edenic world in the new Jerusalem; but at the source of the four rivers, the solar lamb replaces the mysterious tree. The initiation through work and through blood is accomplished, and there are no longer any temples because the light of truth is universally spread out, and because the world has become the temple of justice.

This beautiful final dream of the holy Scriptures, this divine utopia which the Church referred to with reason as the realization of a better life, was the downfall of all the ancient heresiarchs and a great number of modern ideologues. The simultaneous emancipation and the absolute equality of all men supposes the cessation of progress and in consequence of life: on the earth of equals, there can be no children or old men; thus birth and death could not be admitted. That is enough to prove that the new Jerusalem is no more of this world than the primordial paradise, where we knew neither good nor evil, nor creation, nor death; it is thus in eternity that the cycle of our religious symbolism begins and ends.

Dupuis and Volney exerted their great erudition in order to discover the identity of all symbols and concluded by negating all religions. We arrive by the same road at the diametrically opposite affirmation, and we recognize with admiration that there have never been any false religions in the civilized world; that the divine light, that splendor of the supreme reason of the Logos, of the Verb, which illuminates any man coming into the world, no more missed the children of Zoroaster than it did the faithful sheep of Saint Peter; that the permanent revelation, unique and universal, is written in visible nature, is explained by reason, and is completed by the wise analogies of faith; that in the end there is only one true religion, only one doctrine, and only one legitimate belief, just like there is only one God, only one reason, and only one universe; that the revelation is not obscure for anyone, since everyone understands a little or a lot of truth and justice, and since everything that can be must only exist analogically to that which is. BEING IS BEING, אהיה אשר אהיה.

The figures, so bizarre in appearance, which the Revelation of Saint John presents, are hieroglyphics, like those of all the oriental mythologies, and can be enclosed in a series of pentacles. The initiator dressed in white, standing between the seven candlesticks of gold and holding in his hand seven stars, represents the unique doctrine of Hermes and the universal analogies of the light.

A woman adorned by the Sun and crowned with twelve stars is the celestial Isis, is the gnosis which the serpent of material life wishes to devour young; but she takes the wings of an eagle and escapes to the desert, protestation of the prophetic spirit against materialism and official religion.

The colossal angel whose face is a sun, whose aureole is a rainbow, whose clothes are a cloud, whose legs are columns of fire, and who places one foot on the earth and the other in the sea is a veritable Cabalistic Panthea.[395]

Her feet represent the equilibrium of Briah[396] or the world of forms; her legs are the two columns of the Masonic temple, Jachin and Boaz; her body, veiled by clouds, from which comes out a hand reading a book, is the sphere of Yetzirah[397] or the initiatic trials, the solar head, crowned with the luminous septenary, is the world of Atziluth[398] or the perfect revelation, and we are not very surprised that the Hebrew Cabalists did not recognize or divulge this symbolism, which attaches so closely and inseparably the highest mysteries of Christianity to the secret, but invariable, doctrine of all the masters in Israel.

The beast of seven heads, in the symbolism of Saint John, is the material and antagonistic negation of the luminous septenary; the whore of Babylon corresponds in the same manner to the woman adorned by the Sun; the four horsemen are analogous to the four allegorical animals; the seven angels with their seven trumpets, their seven cups, and their seven swords characterize the absolute battle between good and evil through the word, by religious association, and by force. Thus the seven seals of the occult book are opened successively, and the universal initiation is completed. Commentators who looked for something else in this book of the high Cabala lost their time and efforts only to manage to render themselves ridiculous. To see Napoleon in the angel Apollyon, Luther in the falling star, Voltaire and Rousseau in the locust armies at war, is high fantasy.

---

395 That is, a goddess in whom is comprised all the gods and goddesses.

396 The second of the four Cabalistic worlds, the world of creation.

397 The third of the four Cabalistic worlds, the world of formation.

398 The first of the four Cabalistic worlds, the world of inception.

Such is the case for all the violence done to the names of famous personages in order to enclose them in some number like the fatal 666, which we have sufficiently explained, and when we think that men named Bossuet and Newton amused themselves with these chimeras,[399] we understand that humanity is not as malicious in spirit as we might suppose by the appearance of its vices.

---

399   The great French polymath Jacques-Bénigne Bossuet (1627–1704) and the even more famous Isaac Newton both devoted much study to the Book of Revelation in attempts to calculate the date of the Second Coming.

CHAPTER XI

THE TRIPLE CHAIN

The Great Work in practical magic, after the education of the will and the personal creation of the mage, is the formation of the magnetic chain, and this secret is truly that of the priesthood and royalty.

To form a magnetic chain, is to give birth to a current of ideas that produces faith and that leads a great number of wills into a given circle of manifestations through acts. A well-formed chain is like a whirlpool which pulls in, and absorbs, everything.

A chain can be established in three ways: by signs, by words, and by personal contact. A chain is established through signs by having a sign adopted by public opinion as the representation of a force. It is thus that all Christians communicate together by the sign of the cross, the Masons by the sign of the set square under the Sun, the mages by the sign of the microcosmos which is made by extending the five fingers, and so on.

The signs, once received and propagated, acquire power on their own. The sight and imitation of the sign of the cross sufficed in the first few centuries to create proselytes for Christianity. The so-called Miraculous Medal still causes a great many conversions in our time by the same magnetic law. The vision and illumination of the young Israelite Alphonse de Ratisbonne were the most remarkable instances of this kind. Imagination is creative, not only within us, but outside of us, through our fluidic projections, and we should doubtless not attribute to other causes the phenomena of Constantine's labarum[400] and the cross of Migné.[401]

The magical chain through the word is represented, by the ancients, by those chains of gold which come out of the mouth of Hermes. Nothing is equal to the electrifying effect of eloquence. The word creates the highest intelligence in the heart of the most crudely composed masses. Even those who are too far to hear understand by the commotion caused by those words and are drawn in like the rest of the crowd. Peter the Hermit shocked all of Europe by crying out: God wills it![402] A single word from the Emperor electrified his army and rendered France invincible. Proudhon killed socialism with his famous paradox "Property is theft." A single word which takes flight often suffices to overturn a power. Voltaire knew this well, he who turned the world upside down with his sarcasms; he, who feared neither popes, nor kings, nor the parliament, nor prison was afraid of a play on words.

We are on the cusp of accomplishing the will of any man whose words we repeat.

The third manner of establishing a magical chain is through contact. Between persons who see each other often, the head of the current is soon revealed, and the stronger will does not take long to absorb the others; direct and positive contact of hand to hand completes the harmony of dispositions, and it is for this reason that it is a mark of sympathy and intimacy. Children, who are instinctively guided by nature, create a magical chain when they play British Bulldog or Ring Around the Rosie. Then gaiety circulates and laughter blossoms. Round tables are also more favorable to joyous banquets than tables of any other form. The great

---

400　According to legend, the Roman emperor Constantine saw a vision in the sky just before the Battle of the Milvian Bridge, which secured him the imperial throne. In that vision he saw the Greek letters X and P (the first two letters of Christos, or Christ) superimposed—an important early Christian symbol—and heard the words "In this sign thou shalt conquer." He adopted the Christian emblem as his own and won the battle. The emblem subsequently appeared on the imperial standard, known as a labarum.

401　An apparent miracle in the French town of Migné, where in 1826 a crowd assembled for an outdoor sermon saw a glowing cross appear in the air above them.

402　The peasant-preacher who launched the First Crusade (1096–99).

round dance of the Sabbath, which came at the end of the mysterious reunions of the adepts of the Middle Ages, was a magical chain which united everyone in the same desires and the same works; they formed it by placing themselves with their backs facing the others and holding each other by the hands, their faces facing out of the circle, in imitation of the ancient sacred dances whose images we still find on the bas-reliefs of ancient temples. The electric furs of the lynx, the panther, and even the domestic cat, were, in imitation of the ancient bacchanalia, attached to their clothing. From there came the tradition that the miscreants at the Sabbath each carry a cat hanging from their belt and dance with it attached to them.

The phenomena of turning and talking tables[403] is an accidental manifestation of fluidic communication through the circular chain; and then mystification got mixed into it, and even educated and intelligent people became impassioned by this novelty to the point of mystifying themselves and becoming dupes of their own infatuation. The oracles of the tables were suggested answers more or less voluntary or randomly chosen; they resembled the discourse one has or hears in dreams. Other, even stranger phenomena could be the externalized products of a common imagination. We do not deny, without doubt, the possible intervention of the elementary spirits in these manifestations as in divination by cards or by dreams; but we in no way believe that this is proven, and therefore nothing obliges us to admit otherwise.

The strangest power of the human imagination is the realization of the desires of the will, or even its apprehensions and fears. "We easily believe in what we fear or what we desire," says the proverb, and it is correct, because desire and fear provide the imagination with creative power whose effects are incalculable.

How is it, for example, that we are so often infected by the illness we fear? We have already recounted Paracelsus's opinions on this subject, and we have established in our Doctrine the occult laws as observed through experience; but through magnetic currents and through the intercession of the chain, these realizations are even stranger still, since they are almost always unexpected when the chain is not formed by an intelligent, sympathetic, and strong leader. They result in fact from purely random and fortuitous combinations. Vulgar fears of super-

---

403   Lévi refers again to Spiritualism, which was all the rage in Paris when he wrote.

stitious dinner guests when they find themselves thirteen at a table, combined with the conviction that a misfortune menaces the youngest and weakest among them, are, like most superstitions, a relic of the magical science. The duodenary, being a complete and cyclical number in the universal analogies of nature, always pulls in and absorbs the thirteenth, a number regarded as unlucky and superfluous. If the circle of a windmill's grindstone is represented by the number twelve, the number thirteen is the grain it will grind. The ancients established, based on similar considerations, the distinction between lucky numbers and unlucky ones, which resulted in the observance of days of bad and good omen. It is with this type of material that the imagination is the most creative, and numbers and days rarely miss being favorable or ill-fated for those who believe in their influence. It is thus with reason that Christianity proscribed the divinatory sciences because in thus diminishing the number of fatal chances it provided more resources and more control to liberty.

Printing is an admirable mechanism for forming a magical chain by the extension of the word. In effect, not one single book is ever lost: writings always go where they must go, and the aspirations of thought attract words. We have proven this a hundred times during the course of our initiation into magic: the rarest of books always offered themselves to us without our searching for them, the moment they became indispensable for us. It is in this manner that we rediscovered intact this universal science that many erudites believed was buried under several successive cataclysms; it is thus that we entered into the great magical chain which begins with Hermes or Enoch and will only finish with the world. Thus we were able to invoke and render present the spirits of Apollonius, of Plotinus, of Synesius, of Paracelsus, of Cardano, of Cornelius Agrippa, and so many others who are more or less known but who are too religiously famous for us to name lightly. We continue their Great Work, which others will take on after us. But to whom will it be given to complete it?

CHAPTER XII

THE GREAT WORK

To be always rich, ever young, and never die: such has always been the dream of the alchemists.

To change lead, mercury, and all the other metals into gold, to possess the universal medicine and the elixir of life: this is the problem which must be resolved in order to accomplish this wish and realize this dream.

Like all magical mysteries, the secrets of the Great Work have a triple signification: they are religious, philosophical, and natural.

The philosophical gold in religion is absolute and supreme reason; in philosophy, it is truth; in visible nature, it is the Sun; in the underground and mineral world, it is the most perfect and pure gold.

It is for this reason that we call the search for the Great Work the search for the absolute, and that we even designate this work by the name of the Labor of the Sun.

All the masters of the science recognize that it is impossible to arrive at material results if we have not found in the two upper degrees all the analogies of the universal medicine and of the philosopher's stone.

Also, so they say, the work is simple, easy, and inexpensive; if pursued otherwise, it fruitlessly consumes the fortune of the lives of so-called puffers.[404]

---

404   This term, *souffleurs* in French, was used in the Middle Ages and Renaissance for would-be alchemists who did not possess the secret of the Great Work.

The universal medicine for the soul is supreme reason and absolute justice; for the spirit, it is mathematical and practical truth; for the body, it is the quintessence, which is a combination of light and gold.

The raw material of the Great Work in the upper world is enthusiasm and activity; in the intermediate world, it is intelligence and industry; in the lower world, it is labor; and in science, it is sulfur, mercury, and salt, which, successively volatilized and fixed, compose the Azoth of the sages.

All the masters of alchemy who wrote about the Great Work used symbolic and figurative expressions, and they had to do so, as much to distance the profane from a work which is dangerous to them as to be properly heard by adepts, by revealing the entire world of the analogies which rules the unique and sovereign doctrine of Hermes.

Thus, for them, gold and silver are the king and queen, or the Moon and the Sun; sulfur is the flying eagle; mercury is the winged and bearded androgen standing on a cube and crowned in flames; matter or salt is the winged dragon; the metals at boiling point are lions of diverse colors; finally, the entire work is symbolized by the pelican and the phoenix.

The Hermetic art is thus at the same time a religion, a philosophy, and a natural science. As a religion, it belongs to the ancient mages and initiates of all times; as a philosophy, we can find its principles in the school of Alexandria and in the theories of Pythagoras; as a science, one must ask Pythagoras, Nicolas Flamel, and Raymond Lully for the procedures.

The science is only real to those who admit and understand philosophy and religion, and its procedures can only be successfully enacted by the adept who has achieved sovereign will and has thus become the king of the elementary world; because the great agent of the operation of the Sun is that force described by Hermes's symbol of the Emerald Tablet; it is universal magical power; it is the fiery spiritual mover; it is the OD according to the Hebrews, and the astral light according to the expression we have adopted in this work.

That is the secret fire, living and philosophic, which all the Hermetic philosophers only discuss with the most mysterious reserve; it is the universal sperm whose secret they have kept, and which they represent only by the figure of Hermes's caduceus.

Here, then, is the great Hermetic arcanum, and we reveal it here clearly and without mystical figures for the first time: what the adepts call dead matter consists of bodies as they are found in nature; living bodies are substances which are assimilated and *magnetized* by the science and the will of the operator.

In this manner the Great Work is something more than a chemical operation: it is a veritable creation of the initiated human Verb to the power of the Verb of God itself.

הדאבד:
הגתיב הלא נקר שבל תמידי
כי הוא המגהיג השמש והירה
ושאר הבובבים והצצורות בל
אחד מהם בגלגלו ובותן לבל
הגבראים ממערבתם אל
המולות והצצורות:

This Hebrew text, which we transcribe here as proof of the authenticity and reality of our discovery, is by the Jewish Rabbi Abraham, Nicolas Flamel's master, and is found in the occult commentary of the Sepher Yetzirah, the sacred book of the Cabala.[405] This commentary is very rare; but sympathetic powers from our chain allowed us to find an example, which was conserved until 1643 in the library of the Protestant church of Rouen. We read there, written on the first page: Ex dono; then an illegible name, then Dei magni.

The creation of gold in the Great Work is done through transmutation and by multiplication.

Raymond Lully says that to make gold, one must have gold and mercury; that to make silver, one must have silver and mercury. Then he adds: "By mercury I mean that mineral spirit so fine and so pure that it even gilds the seed of gold and

---

405   This is the Hebrew text of the section of the commentary discussing the Thirty-First Path. In English translation, it runs as follows: "The Thirty-First Path is called the Perpetual Intelligence, and it is so called because it regulates the proper motion of the sun and moon in their proper order, each in an orbit convenient for it."

silvers the seed of silver." There is no doubt that he speaks here of the OD or astral light.

Salt and sulfur are only used in the work for the preparation of mercury, and it is above all to mercury which one must assimilate and, in a manner, incorporate the magnetic agent. Paracelsus, Raymond Lully, and Nicolas Flamel seem to be the only ones to have perfectly understood this mystery. Basilius Valentinus and Bernard Trevisan indicate an imperfect manner of doing so, and one which can be interpreted in other ways. But the most curious things which we have found regarding this subject are indicated by the mystical figures and the magical legends of a book by Heinrich Khunrath entitled: *Amphitheatrum Sapientiae Aeternae*.[406]

Khunrath represents and summarizes the most knowledgeable Gnostic schools and associates himself with the mysticism of Synesius. He affects being Christian in his expressions and his signs, but it is easy to recognize that his Christ is that of Abraxas, the luminous shining pentagram on the astronomical cross, the incarnation in humanity of the sun-king celebrated by Emperor Julian; it is the luminous and living manifestation of that Ruach Elohim that, according to Moses, covered and worked the surface of the waters at the birth of the world;[407] it is the man-sun, it is the king of light, it is the supreme mage, master, and vanquisher of the serpent, and Khunrath finds in the quadruple legend of the Gospels the allegorical key to the Great Work. In one of the pentacles of his magical book, he represents the philosopher's stone standing in the middle of a fortress surrounded by a wall with twenty doors that lead nowhere. One way alone leads to the sanctuary of the Great Work.

Above the stone is the triangle on a winged dragon, and on the stone is engraved the name of Christ, which he qualifies as the symbolic image of all of nature. "It is through him alone," he adds, "that you are able to reach the universal medicine for man, for animals, for plants, and for minerals." The winged dragon dominated by the triangle represents the Christ of Khunrath, that is to say

---

406 Khunrath's most famous book, published in 1595.

407 Genesis 1:2. Ruach Elohim, "spirit of the Elohim," is translated "the Spirit of God" in most English Bible translations.

the sovereign intelligence of light and life: it is the secret of the pentagram, it is the highest doctrinal and practical mystery of traditional magic. From there to the great and ever incommunicable arcanum is but one more step.

The Cabalistic figures of Abraham the Jew, who provided Flamel with the beginning of the science,[408] are nothing other than the twenty-two keys of the Tarot, imitated and summarized elsewhere in the twelve keys of Basilius Valentinus. The Sun and the Moon reappear there under the figures of the Emperor and the Empress; Mercury is the Magus; the grand Hierophant is the adept or the abstracter of quintessence; death, judgment, love, the dragon or the devil, the hermit or the lame old man, and finally all the other symbols which are found with their principal attributes and almost in the same order. It could not be otherwise, since the Tarot is the primordial book and the keystone of the occult sciences; it must be as hermetic as it is Cabalistic, magical, and theosophical. We also find in the reunion of Valentinius's twelfth and twenty-second key, one superimposed on the other, the hieroglyphic revelation of our solution to the mystery of the Great Work.

The twelfth key of the Tarot represents a man suspended by a foot to a gibbet composed of three trees, or sticks, forming the figure of the Hebrew letter ת; the man's arms form a triangle with his head, and his entire hieroglyphic form is that of an upside-down triangle mounted on a cross, an alchemical symbol known by all the adepts, which represents the accomplishment of the Great Work. The twenty-second key, which has the number twenty-one because the Fool, which precedes it in the Cabalistic order, has no number, represents a young divinity who is lightly veiled and running through a flowery crown supported at the four corners by the four animals of the Cabala. This divinity holds a wand in each hand in the Italian Tarot deck, and in the Tarot of Besançon[409] she unites both wands in one single hand and places her other hand on her thigh, both equally re-

---

408 According to later accounts, Flamel was taught the first operations of alchemy by a Jewish convert to Christianity named Abraham, whom he met while on pilgrimage.

409 There are many different versions of the tarot deck in northern Italy and southern France. The tarot of Besançon is one of these.

markable symbols of magnetic action, either alternatively by their polarization or simultaneously through opposition and transmission.

The Great Work of Hermes is thus an essentially magical operation, and the highest of all, because it supposes the absolute in science and in the will. There is light in gold, and there is gold in light, and there is light in all things. The intelligent will which assimilates the light thus directs the operations of the substantial form, and only uses chemistry as a wholly secondary instrument. The influence of the will and human intelligence on the operations of nature, in part dependent on its work, is incidentally so real a fact that all serious alchemists who have succeeded because of their knowledge and their faith have reproduced their thought in the phenomenon of the fusion, of the salification, and of the recomposition of metals. Agrippa, a man of immense erudition and beautiful genius, but a pure philosopher and a skeptic, was unable to surpass the limits of the analysis and the synthesis of metals. Etteilla, a confused, befuddled, and fantastical Cabalist, who was nonetheless blessed with perseverance, reproduced in alchemy the anomalies of his misunderstood and disfigured Tarot; the metals in their crucibles took on singular forms which excited the curiosity of all Paris, without any other change in the fortunes of the operator than the fees he demanded of his visitors. An obscure alchemist of our time, who died mad, the poor Louis Cambriel,[410] truly did heal his neighbors, and resuscitated, according to the whole neighborhood, a smith and his friends. For him, the metallic work took on the most inconceivable forms and were most illogical in appearance. He saw one day in his crucible the figure of God incandescent like the Sun, transparent like crystal, and having a body composed of triangular assemblages that Cambriel naively compared to piles of little pears.

A Cabalist who is among our friends and who is wise, but who belongs to an initiation we believe to be erroneous, recently conducted chemical operations of the Great Work; he managed to weaken his eyes due to the incandescence of the athanor, and he created a new metal which resembles gold, but which is not gold,

---

410 French alchemist (1784–1850). A set of nineteen lessons on alchemy he wrote has had great influence on modern French alchemy.

and in consequence has no value. Raymond Lully, Nicholas Flamel, and very probably Heinrich Khunrath made true gold and did not take their secret with them, since they concealed it within their symbols and indicated the sources which aided them in discovering and realizing the effects. It is this same secret that we publish today.

CHAPTER XIII

NECROMANCY

We have boldly stated our thoughts, or rather our convictions, regarding the possibility of resurrection in certain cases; we must complete the revelation of this arcanum here by exposing its practice.

Death is the phantom of ignorance; it does not exist: all is alive in nature, and it is because all is alive that everything incessantly mutates and changes form.

Old age is the beginning of regeneration; it is life working to renew itself, and the mystery which we call death was symbolized by the ancients as the fountain of Youth where one enters decrepit and exits a child.

The body is the vestment of the soul. When this vestment is completely used or gravely and irreparably torn, the soul leaves and does not return to it. But when, by some accident, the soul escapes this vestment without the latter being either worn out or destroyed, the soul can, in certain cases, go back to it, either by its own efforts or with the assistance of another will which is stronger and more active.

Death is neither the end of life nor the beginning of immortality; it is the continuation of the transformation of life.

As transformation is always progression, there are few who are apparently dead who consent to live again; that is to say, go back to the vestment they have just left. This is what renders resurrection one of the most difficult works of high initiation. Also, success is never infallible and must always be regarded as accidental and unexpected. To resuscitate a dead man, one must suddenly and energetically tighten the strongest chains of attraction that can link him back to the form he has just left. It is thus necessary first to know this chain, then to be able to control it, and then produce an effort of will large enough to instantaneously relink him to it with an irresistible power.

All this, we say, is extremely difficult, but not absolutely impossible. Prejudiced material scientists do not admit resurrection as part of the natural order in our day and are disposed to explain all the phenomena of this order by more or less complicated and more or less long symptoms of lethargy. A Lazarus resurrected today before our doctors would simply be noted in their official reports to their academies as a strange case of lethargy accompanied by the beginnings of an apparent putrefaction and a relatively strong cadaverous odor; we would name it an exceptional accident, and all will have been said.

We do not like to offend anyone, and, if out of respect for the decorated men who officially represent science, one must call our resurrectionist theories the art of curing exceptional and hopeless lethargies, I hope that nothing would prevent us from making this concession to them.

If a resurrection has ever occurred in the world, it would be incontestable that resurrection is possible. Yet the bodies thus reconstituted protect religion; religion positively affirms the fact of resurrections: thus resurrections are possible. It is difficult to get out of this.

To say that resurrections are possible outside of the laws of nature and through an influence contrary to universal harmony is to affirm that the spirit of disorder, the shadow of death, can be the supreme arbiter of life. Let us not argue with the worshipers of Satan, and move on.

But it is not religion alone which attests to the facts of resurrection: we have collected several other examples. An occurrence which struck the imagination of the painter Greuze was reproduced by him in one of his most remarkable tableaux: an unworthy son, beside the deathbed of his father, grabs and tears up a testament which was not favorable to him;[411] the father reanimates, rushes up, curses his son, and then lies back down to die a second time. An analogous and more

---

411   This painting, *Le testament déchiré* (*The Torn Testament*), is now lost.

recent occurrence was attested to us by eyewitnesses: a person, betraying the confidence of his friend who just died, took back and tore up an attestation of trusteeship signed by himself; at that moment, the dead man revived and remained alive to defend the rights of his chosen inheritors whom his unfaithful friend wished to dispossess; the guilty man became mad, and the resuscitated dead man was compassionate enough to provide him with a pension.

When the Savior resuscitated the daughter of Jairus,[412] he entered alone with his three trusted and favorite disciples; he separated out those who were making noise and crying, while telling them: "This young girl is not dead, she sleeps." Then, in the presence of only the father, the mother, and the three disciples, that is to say a perfect circle of confidence and desire, he took the hand of the child, brusquely raised it, and cried out to her: "Young girl, rise up!" The young girl, whose undecided soul no doubt wandered near her body, and who perhaps regretted the loss of an extremely beautiful and young body, surprised by the accent of that voice, to which her mother and father listened on their knees shivering with hope, entered back into her body, opened her eyes, got up, and the Master immediately ordered that she be given something to eat, so that the life functions would restart a new cycle of absorption and regeneration.

The stories of Elisha resuscitating the son of the Shunammite[413] and Saint Paul resuscitating Eutychus[414] are occurrences of the same order; the resurrection of Dorcas by Saint Peter, told with such simplicity in the Book of Acts,[415] is also a story whose truth could hardly be reasonably contested. Apollonius of Tyana seems also to have accomplished similar marvels. We ourselves were witness to occurrences which are not without analogy to the above, though the spirit of the century in which we must live imposes upon us the most discreet reserve regarding this subject, since thaumaturges who are exposed today get a rather mediocre reception before the public: which does not stop the Earth from turning, and Galileo from being a great man.

---

412 Matthew 9:18, Mark 5:22, and Luke 8:41 all provide accounts of this.

413 2 Kings 4:8–37.

414 Acts 20:7–12.

415 Acts 9:36–42.

The resurrection of a dead person is the masterpiece of magnetism, because one must, to accomplish it, exert a type of sympathetic omnipotence. It is possible in cases of death due to congestion, suffocation, lethargy, and hysteria.

Eutychus, who was resuscitated by Saint Paul after falling from the third floor, had doubtless not broken anything inside himself, and had no doubt succumbed to either asphyxia occasioned by the movement of the air during his fall or seizure due to fear. One must, in such a case, and when we feel the power and faith necessary to accomplish such a work, practice, like the apostle, mouth to mouth insufflation, by making contact with the extremities in order to bring back the heat of the body. If this was simply a case of what the ignorant call a miracle, Elijah and Saint Paul, whose procedures were the same in similar cases, would merely have spoken in the name of Jehovah or of Christ instead.

It may sometimes suffice to take the person by the hand and energetically raise it while loudly calling out their name. This procedure, which ordinarily works for fainting episodes, can have the same effect on death when the acting magnetizer is gifted by a sympathetically powerful speech and possesses what we can call eloquence of the voice. He must also either be tenderly loved or respected by the person upon whom he wishes to act, and he must perform his work with a great surge of faith and of will, which cannot always be found within oneself during the first shock of great sorrow.

What we vulgarly call necromancy has nothing to do with resurrection, and it is also highly doubtful that, in operations relative to this application of magical power, one actually makes contact with the souls of the dead whom one evokes. There are two types of necromancy: the necromancy of light and the necromancy of darkness: evocation through prayer, the pentacle, and the perfumes; and evocation through blood, imprecations, and blasphemies. We have only practiced the first ourselves, and we do not counsel anyone to devote themselves to the second.

It is certain that images of the dead appear to the magnetized persons who evoke them; it is also certain that they never reveal any mysteries regarding the next life. We see them again in the manner they would still be in the memory of those who knew them, no doubt in the way in which their reflections left their imprint upon the astral light. When specters are evoked and respond to the questions one asks them, it is always through signs or by imaginary and interior impressions, never with a voice which actually hits the ears; and this is relatively understandable: how can a shadow talk? With what instrument would it make the air vibrate, hitting it in such a manner as to make one distinguish sounds?

One experiences, however, electrical contacts during apparitions, and these contacts seem sometimes to be produced by the phantom itself; but this phenomenon is entirely interior and must have as an only cause the power of the imagination and local peaks in occult power which we call the astral light. Which proves that spirits, or at least specters believed to be such, actually affect us sometimes, but we are unable to touch them, and it is one of the most frightening circumstances regarding apparitions, because the visions sometimes appear real, and we cannot remain emotionless when our hand passes through what seems to us to be a body without touching or encountering anything.

One can read in the ecclesiastical histories that Spyridon, the bishop of Tremetousia who was since named a saint, evoked the spirit of his daughter Irene to learn from her the location of a hidden cache of money that she had received from a traveler. Swedenborg habitually communicated with the so-called dead, whose forms appeared to him in the astral light. We have known several other persons we trust who assured us of having seen again over entire years a defunct whom they cared dearly about. The famous atheist Sylvain Maréchal appeared to his widow and to a friend of hers to tell them about a sum of fifteen hundred gold francs which he had hidden in a secret compartment of a piece of furniture. We received this anecdote from an old friend of the family.

Evocations must always be motivated and have an honorable goal; otherwise, they are operations of darkness and folly, very dangerous to the mind and health. To evoke purely out of curiosity and to find out if one will see something is to be disposed in advance to tiring oneself for nothing. The high sciences admit neither doubt nor puerility.

An honorable motive for an evocation can be either for love or for knowledge.

Evocations of love require fewer materials and are in any case easier. Here is how one must proceed:

You must first carefully gather all the memories of the person you want to see again, the objects she used and which have kept her imprint, and furnish either a room which that person occupied while alive or a similar locale with her portrait, veiled in white, in the middle of flowers that person liked and that you renew every day.

Then you must observe a precise date, a day of the year which was either her birthday or the happiest day for your affection and hers, a day in which we assume that her soul, no matter how happy it is now, could not have lost the memory of: it is that very day that you must choose for the evocation and for which you must prepare for during fourteen days.

During that time, you must be sure not to give the same proofs of affection to anyone else which the defunct had the right to expect from you; you must observe a strict chastity, live in retreat, and only have one modest meal, as well as a light snack, each day.

Every evening, at the same time, you must close yourself off with a single low light, such as a small funeral lamp or candle, in the room consecrated to the memory of the regretted person; you place this light behind yourself and then uncover the portrait, in the presence of which you remain silent for an hour; then you perfume the room with a little bit of good incense, and you leave by walking out backwards.[416]

On the day set aside for the evocation, you must prepare right from the morning as though for a celebration: do not speak first to anyone the entire day, eat a single meal of only bread, wine, and roots or fruits; the tablecloth must be white; you will set the table for two and break off a portion of the bread, which must have been served whole; you will also place a few drops of wine in the glass of the person you wish to evoke. This meal must be eaten in silence, in the evocation room, in the presence of the veiled portrait; then you carry away all that was used for the meal, except the defunct's glass and her portion of the bread, which will be left before her portrait.

In the evening, at the habitual hour for visits, you will go back into the room in silence; you will light a bright light with cypress wood, and you will throw incense into it seven times while pronouncing the name of the person you wish to see again; you will then put out the lamp and let the fire die. You do not unveil the portrait on that day.

---

416   Lévi neglects to mention that you must, of course, replace the veil over the portrait before leaving.

When the flame has gone out, you will add more incense to the coals, and you will invoke God according to the formulas of the religion to which the deceased person belonged and according to the ideas she herself had of God.

You must, when saying this prayer, identify yourself with the evoked person, speak as she would speak, believe in a certain manner in what she believed; then, after a quarter hour of silence, talk to her as though she were present, with affection and faith, while praying to her to show herself to you; renew this prayer mentally while covering your face with both hands, then call out to the person three times in a loud voice; wait while kneeling and with eyes closed or covered for a few minutes while speaking to her mentally; then call out three times to her again in a soft and affectionate voice and slowly open your eyes. If you see nothing, you will have to try the experience again in a year's time and up to three times. It is certain that by at least the third time you will obtain the desired apparition, and, the longer she took, the more she will be visible and strikingly real.

Evocations of science and intelligence are done with more solemn ceremonies. If the evocation is of a famous person, one must meditate over twenty-one days on his life and writings, get an idea of his personality, of his countenance and of his voice; speak to him mentally and imagine his responses; carry on your person his portrait or at least his name; be sure to keep to a vegetarian diet during the twenty-one days, and be on a strict fast the last seven days; then construct a magical oratory just as we described it in chapter 13 of our Doctrine. The oratory must be entirely closed, but if you must operate during the day, you can leave a narrow opening on the side where the Sun will be at the hour of the evocation and place before this opening a triangular prism, then a crystal globe filled with water in front of the prism. If you must operate at night, you will place a magical lamp in such a manner that its unique ray will fall on the smoke from the altar. The goal of these preparations is to provide the magical agent with the elements for a physical apparition and to also relieve the tension of our imagination, which we do not exalt without the risk of it becoming an absolute dream illusion. We understand well enough, incidentally, that a diversely colored ray from the Sun or a lamp falling upon mobile and irregular smoke can in no way create a perfect image. The brazier of the sacred fire must be in the center of the oratory, and the altar of perfumes not very far away from it. The operator must turn towards the Orient to pray, towards the Occident to evoke; he must be alone or assisted by two people who keep a strict silence; he will have magical vestments such as we described in the seventh chapter, and will be crowned in verbena and gold. He must have bathed before the operation, and all the clothes underneath must be perfectly intact and clean.

Begin with a prayer appropriate to the genius of the spirit you wish to evoke, and which he could approve of were he still alive. Thus, we would never evoke Voltaire, for example, by reciting orations in the style of Saint Bridget.[417] For the great men of antiquity, you will say the hymns of Cleanthes or Orpheus, with the sermon which ends the golden verses of Pythagoras. When we evoked Apollonius, we took as a ritual the philosophical magic of Patrizi, which contain the doctrines of Zoroaster and the works of Hermes Trismegistus. We read aloud Apollonius's *Nuctemeron* in Greek, and we added the following conjuration:[418]

Βουλῆς δὲ ὁ πατὴρ πάντων καὶ καθηγητὴςὁ τρισμέγιστος Ἑρμῆς, ἰατρικῆς δὲ ὁἈσκληπιὸς ὁἩφαίστου,ἰσχύος δὲ καὶῥώμης πάλιν Ὄσιρις, μεθ᾽ ὃν ᾧ τέκνον αὐτὸς σύ, φιλοσοφίας δὲἈρνεβεσχῆνις ποιητικῆς δὲ πάλιν ὁ Ἀσκληπιὸς ὁ Ἱμούθης.

Οὗτοι τὰ κρυπτὰ,φησὶν Ἑρμῆς, τῶν ἐμῶν ἐπιγνώσονται γραμμάτων πάντων καὶ διακρινοῦσι, καὶ τινὰ μὲν αὐτοὶ κατασχῶσιν,ἃ δὲ καὶ πρὸς εὐεργεσίας θνητῶν φθάνει, στήλαις καὶ ὀβελίσκοις χαράξουσιν.

Μαγείαν ὁ Ἀπολλώνιος, ὁ Ἀπολλώνιος, ὁ Ἀπολλώνιος τε διδάσκειτοῦ Ζωροάστρου τοῦ Ὡρομάζου, ἐστὶ δὲ τοῦτο θεῶν θεράπεια.

---

417   Saint Bridget of Sweden, who was known for her visions and wrote a prayer famous in Lévi's time, rather than Saint Brigit of Kildare, the early medieval Irish saint.

418   This conjuration is composed of three passages in Greek from the writings of the Renaissance occultist Francisco Patrizi. In English, they read: "Of counsel, [the ruler] is Thrice-Great Hermes, the father and guide of all; of medicine, Asclepius, son of Hephaestus; of power and might, again Osiris, after whom [art] thou thyself, O child; of philosophy, Arnebeschenis; of poetry again Asclepius Imouthes.

"These, says Hermes, will know the hidden [things] of all my writings, and will separate them; some they will reserve for themselves; others that conduce to the benefit of mortals they will engrave on stelae and obelisks.

"Apollonius, Apollonius, Apollonius teaches the magic of Zoroaster, [son of] Oromaz: it is the therapy of the Gods."

For the evocation of spirits belonging to the religions emanating from Judaism, one must say the Cabalistic invocation of Solomon, either in Hebrew, or in any other language that you know was familiar to the spirit being evoked:

Powers of the kingdom, may you be under my left foot and in my right hand; Glory and Eternity, touch my two shoulders and direct me down the roads of victory; Mercy and Justice, may you be the balance and splendor of my life; Intelligence and Wisdom, give me the crown; spirits of Malkuth, bring me between the two columns upon which the entire edifice of the temple rests; angels of Netzach and of Hod, fortify me on the cubic stone of Yesod.

O Gedulael! O Geburael! O Tiphareth! Binael, be my love; Ruach Hochmael, be my light; be what you are and what you will be, O Ketheriel!

Ishim, assist me in the name of Shaddai.

Cherubim, be my strength in the name of Adonai.

Beni Elohim, be my brothers in the name of the son and by the virtues of Tzabaoth.

Elohim, fight for me in the name of the Tetragrammaton.

Malakhim, protect me in the name of יהוה.[419]

Seraphim, purify my love in the name of Eloah.

Chashmalim, enlighten me with the splendors of Eloï and of Shekinah.

Aralim, act; Ophanim, turn and be resplendent.

Chaioth ha-Qodesh, shout, speak, roar, bellow: Kadosh, Kadosh, Kadosh, Shaddai, Adonai, Yodchavah, Ehyeh Asher Ehyeh.

Hallelujah, Hallelujah, Hallelujah. Amen. אמן[420]

---

419 YHVH, the tetragrammaton.

420 AMN, "amen." This invocation summarizes much of the traditional Hebrew symbolism of the Cabalistic Tree of Life.

Most of all one must remember well, in the conjurations, that the names of Satan, of Beelzebub, of Adramelech, and the others do not designate spiritual unities but the legions of impure spirits. "I am called Legion," the spirit of darkness says in the Gospel, "for we are many."[421] In hell, anarchy reigns, it is the crowd that rules, and progress occurs in the inverse direction, that is to say that those most advanced in Satanic development, in consequence the most degraded, are the least intelligent and the weakest. Thus a fatal law pushes demons to descend when they believe and wish to climb up. Also, those who call themselves the leaders are the most impotent and the most despised of all. As to the mass of perverse spirits, they tremble before an unknown leader, invisible, incomprehensible, capricious, implacable, who never explains his laws and who always has his arm extended to strike those who cannot perceive it. They give this phantom the names of Baal, of Jupiter, or other even more venerable names, which one may not pronounce in hell without profaning them; but this phantom is nothing but a shadow and a memory of God, disfigured by their voluntary perversity, and remaining in their imagination like the vengeance of justice and the remorse of the truth.

When a spirit of light which you evoke shows himself with a sad or irritated expression, you must offer him a moral sacrifice, that is to say be internally disposed to renounce what offends him, then one must, before leaving the oratory, send him away by saying to him: May peace be with you! I did not wish to trouble you, do not torment me; I will work to reform myself with regard to all which offends you; I pray and I will pray with you and for you; pray with me and for me and return to your great sleep, until the day when we will awake together. Silence and farewell!

We will not end this chapter without adding, for the curious, a few details regarding the ceremonies of black necromancy. We can find out from several ancient authors how the sorceresses of Thessaly and the Canidiae of Rome practiced it. They dug a pit, at the edge of which they slit the throat of a black ewe; then with a sword they separated out the psyllae and larvae which were supposedly

---

421   Mark 5:9.

present and hastened to drink the blood; they invoked the triple Hecate and the infernal gods, and they called out three times to the shadow they wished to see appear.

In the Middle Ages, necromancers profaned graves, composed potions and unguents with the grease and blood of cadavers; they mixed into these aconite, belladonna, and poisonous mushrooms; then they annealed and frothed these horrible mixtures over fires composed of human bones and crucifixes stolen from churches; they mixed in powder of dried toads and the ashes of consecrated holy bread; then they rubbed this infernal unguent onto their temples, their hands, and their chests, drew the diabolical pentagram, and evoked the dead under gibbets or in abandoned cemeteries. One could hear their screams from afar, and late-night travelers thought they saw legions of phantoms arising from the Earth; the trees themselves took on frightful forms in their eyes; they saw eyes of fire scintillating in the bushes, and the frogs of the marshes seemed to repeat in a single rough voice the mysterious speech of the Sabbath. It was the magnetism of hallucination and the contagion of madness.

The procedures of black magic have as their goal to disturb reason and produce all the feverish exaltations which provide the courage to commit great crimes. The grimoires that the authorities previously seized and burned any-where they found them were certainly not innocent books. Sacrilege, murder, and theft were recommended or implied as the means of realization in almost all these works. It is thus that in the *Grand Grimoire* and in the *Dragon Rouge*, a more modern forgery of the *Grand Grimoire*, we can read a recipe entitled: Composition of death, or the philosopher's stone. It is a kind of consommé of aqua fortis, copper, arsenic, and verdigris.[422]

We also find these necromantic procedures, which consist of excavating the earth over graves with your nails, in order to remove the bones within that you wear as a cross over your chest, and of then participating in a midnight mass, on the night of Christmas, in a church, and at the moment of the elevation, rising up and running away while yelling: "May the dead be released from their graves!" Then returning to the cemetery, taking a fistful of earth which is closest to the

422   That is to say, an effective poison.

coffin, coming back at a run to the door of the church where everyone will have been terrified by your clamor and placing down the two bones in a cross while yelling again: "May the dead be released from their graves!" And if no one is to be found there to arrest you and take you off to the madhouse, you walk away slowly, counting four thousand five hundred steps without turning aside, which presupposes that either you are following a long road or climbing walls. At the end of these four thousand five hundred steps, you lie down on the ground; after having scattered the earth you held in your hand in a cross formation, you will position yourself as one is placed in a coffin, and you will repeat in a gloomy voice: "May the dead," etc., and you will call out three times to the person you wish to see appear. One should not doubt that the person mad enough and perverse enough to surrender themselves to such works is already disposed to all the chimeras and phantoms. This recipe from the *Grand Grimoire* is thus certainly efficacious, but we do not counsel any of our readers to make use of it.

CHAPTER XIV

TRANSMUTATIONS

Saint Augustine, as we have said, asks if Apuleius could have been changed into an ass and then rendered back to his first form. The same scholar could have equally preoccupied himself with the adventure of Ulysses's companions who were changed into swine by Circe. Transmutations and metamorphoses have always been, in the opinion of the vulgar, the essence of magic itself. Yet the vulgar, who are the echo of general opinion, queen of the world, are never completely right nor totally wrong.

Magic truly changes the nature of things, or rather modifies their appearance as desired, according to the force of the will of the operator and the fascination of aspiring adepts. The word created its form, and when a person reputed to be infallible has named a thing with whatever name, he truly transforms that thing into the substance signified by the name he gives it. The masterpiece of this kind, of the word and of faith, is the real transmutation of a substance whose appearance does not change. If Apollonius had said to his disciples while giving them a cup filled with wine, "Here is my blood, which you shall always drink to perpetuate my life within you," and if his disciples had over several centuries continued this transformation and repeated the same words, and taken the wine, despite its smell and taste, for the real, human, and living blood of Apollonius, we would have to recognize this master in theurgy as being the most skillful of fascinators and the most powerful of all mages. All that would remain is for us to adore him.

We know that magnetizers can make the water they give to those they hypnotize have any taste they wish, and if we suppose a mage with enough power over the astral fluid to magnetize an entire assembly of people previously prepared to be magnetized through sufficient overexcitation, we can easily explain, not the evangelical miracle at Cana, but works of the same type.

Are not the fascinations of love, which result from the universal magic of nature, veritable wonders, and do they not truly transform people and things? Love is a dream of enchantment which transfigures the world: all becomes music and perfume, all becomes euphoria and happiness. The person loved is beautiful, he is good, he is sublime, he is infallible, he is resplendent, radiating health and well-being . . . ; and, when the dream dissipates, we believe we have fallen down naked; we look with disgust upon the ugly witch who has taken the place of the beautiful Melusine, or the Thersites whom we took for Achilles or for Nereus. What would we not believe of the person whom we love? And then with what reason and what justice would we understand a person who loves us no longer? Love begins by being a magician; it ends by being a sorcerer. After having created the lies of heaven on earth, it realizes those of hell; its hatred is just as absurd as its enthusiasm, because it is passionate, that is to say subjected to influences which are fatal to it. It is for this reason that the sages proscribed it and declared it the enemy of reason. Were the sages to be envied or felt sorry for when they thus condemned without having heard, no doubt, the most seductive of culprits? All that we can say is, when they spoke thus, they had not yet loved or loved no longer.

Things are for us what our interior verb makes them be. To believe oneself to be happy is to be happy; that which we esteem becomes precious in the exact proportion of our esteem for it: that is how we can say that magic changes the nature of things. The *Metamorphoses* of Ovid are true, but they are allegorical like *The Golden Ass* of the good Apuleius. The life of beings is a progressive transformation whose forms we can determine, renew, conserve for longer, or destroy sooner. If the idea of metempsychosis[423] was true, would we not say that the debauch symbolized by Circe truly and materially changes men into swine, because the vices in this hypothesis would have as punishment a fall back into the animal forms which correspond to them? Yet metempsychosis, which has often been misunderstood, has a side which is perfectly true: the animal forms communicate their sympathetic imprints to the astral body of man, which are soon reflected in his traits, according to the force of his habits. A man of sweet intelligence and passivity takes on the allure and inert physiognomy of a sheep; it is a sheep that we see, as the ecstatic and scholarly Swedenborg tested out a thousand times. This mystery is expressed in the Cabalistic book by the visionary Daniel and by the legend of Nebuchadnezzar who was changed into an animal, which has been mistaken for a true story, as has happened with almost all magical allegories.

Thus we can really change men into animals and animals into men; we can metamorphose plants and change their virtue; we can give minerals ideal properties: one must only will it.

One can also, at will, become visible or invisible, and we will explain here the mysteries of the ring of Gyges.

Let us first distance from the mind of our readers all supposition of the absurd, that is to say an effect without cause or contradictory to its cause. To become invisible, one of three things is necessary: either to interpose an opaque medium of some kind between the light and our body, or between our body and the eyes of the observers, or to fascinate the eyes of the observers in such a manner that they cannot make use of their eyesight. Of these three manners of becoming invisible, only the third is magic.

Have we not often remarked how, under the dominion of a powerful preoccupation, we look without seeing, and we will run into objects that are before our

---

423 Metempsychosis is the form of reincarnation in which souls are understood to be reborn in human or animal forms according to their nature.

eyes? "Because while seeing they do not see,"[424] said the great initiator; and the story of this great master teaches us that one day, seeing himself at the point of being stoned to death in the temple, he rendered himself invisible and departed.[425]

We will not repeat here the mystifications from the vulgar grimoires about the ring of invisibility. Some of them have it made from fixed mercury and tell us to keep it in a box of the same metal, after having inset it with a little stone, which must infallibly be found in the nest of a hoopoe (instead of hoopoe, one should read duped-you).[426] The author of the *Petit Albert* would have us make this ring with the hairs torn from an angry hyena: it is much the same story as that of Rodilard's little bell.[427] The only authors who have spoken seriously about the ring of Gyges are Iamblichus, Porphyry, and Pietro d'Abano.

What they say about it is obviously allegorical, and the figure that they give it, or that we can draw based on their descriptions, proves that by the ring of Gyges they mean and indicate nothing other than the great magical arcanum.

One of these figures represents the cycle of universal harmonious and balanced movement in the imperishable being; the other, which one must make from the amalgamation of the seven metals, merits a more detailed description.

It must have a double bezel with two precious stones, one of topaz constellated under the sign of the Sun, and the other of emerald under the sign of the Moon: within, they must have the occult characters of the planets; and without, their known signs, represented twice and in Cabalistic opposition to each other, that is to say five to the right and five to the left, the signs of the Sun and the Moon summarize the four diverse intelligences of the seven planets. This configuration is nothing other than the pentacle expressing all the mysteries of the magical doctrine, and the symbolic meaning of the ring is that, to exercise the omnipotence of which ocular fascination is one of the most difficult proofs to provide, one must possess all of the science and know how to make use of it.

---

424   Matthew 13:13.

425   John 8:59.

426   Lévi's wordplay, equating the French words *huppe* (hoopoe) and *dupé*, works in both languages.

427   Rodilard is the cat who is to be belled in La Fontaine's fairy tale.

Fascination operates through magnetism. The mage commands an entire assembly not to see him, and the assembly does not see. He thus enters through guarded doors, he leaves prisons in front of stupefied guards. They experience a kind of strange drowsiness, and they remember having seen the mage as though in a dream, but only after he has passed by. The secret of invisibility is thus entirely part of a power that we can define: that of diverting or paralyzing attention in a way that the light arrives at the visual organ without exciting vision in the soul.

To exercise this power, one must have a will practiced in sudden and energetic acts, a great presence of mind, and no less great a skill in originating distractions among the crowds.

If a man, for example, who is pursued by assassins, after having veered off onto a side road, were to suddenly turn about, and head, with a calm expression, towards those who are running after him, or were he to join them and appear preoccupied with the same pursuit, he would certainly render himself invisible. A priest, who was being chased in 1793 so that he might be hanged from a lamp-post,[428] turned quickly down a street, and there he lowered his habit and leaned on a boundary stone in the attitude of a man going about his business. The multitude who were chasing him arrived soon after: they did not see him, or rather none of them recognized him: since it was so improbable that it could be him!

The person who wants to be seen always makes sure he is noticed, and the one who wishes to remain unseen effaces himself and disappears. The will is the veritable ring of Gyges; it is also the wand of transmutations, and it is by formulating it clearly and strongly that it creates the magical Verb. The omnipotent words of enchantments are those that express this creative power of the forms. The Tetragrammaton, which is the supreme word of magic, signifies: what is will be; and, if we apply ourselves to any transformation whatsoever with full intelligence, it will renew and modify all things, even despite the evidence and common sense. The *hoc est* of the Christian sacrifice is a translation and an application of the Tetragrammaton; these simple words operate the most complete, the most

---

428   In the wake of the French Revolution, mob violence against the Catholic clergy
        was common.

invisible, the most incredible, and the most clearly affirmed of all the transformations. An even more powerful doctrinal word than that of transformation was judged necessary by the Council of Trent to express this marvel: transubstantiation.

The Hebrew words יהוה, אגלא, אהיה, אמן,[429] were regarded by all the Cabalists as the keys to transformation magic. The Latin words *est, sit, esto, fiat* have the same strength when they are pronounced with full intelligence. M. de Montalembert recounts most seriously, in his legend about Saint Elizabeth of Hungary, that one day that pious lady, surprised by her noble husband, from whom she wished to hide her good works, at the moment when she was carrying bread in her apron to the poor, tells him that she is carrying roses, and the verification being made, he finds that she had not lied: the bread was changed into roses. This story is one of the most graceful of magical apologues and signifies that a true sage does not know how to lie, that the Verb of wisdom determines the form of things or even their substance independent of their forms. Why, for example, would not the noble husband of Saint Elizabeth, a good and solid Christian like herself, and who firmly believed in the real presence of the Savior in true human body on the altar where he only saw a host made of flour, believe in the presence of roses in his wife's apron which had the appearance of bread? She shows him bread, without a doubt; but as she had said: They are roses, and since he did not believe her capable of the slightest lie, he saw and only chose to see roses. There is the secret of this miracle.

Another legend regards a saint whose name I forget, who finds himself with nothing to eat except a chicken; it being Lent or a Friday, he commands the chicken to be a fish, and he made it a fish. This parable needs no commentary and reminds us of a beautiful remark from Saint Spyridon of Tremetousia, the same one who evoked the soul of his daughter Irene. A traveler arrives on a Friday at this good bishop's house, and since in that time the bishops, who took Christianity seriously, were poor, Spyridon, who regularly fasted, has only some salted lard in the house, which was being prepared for Easter. Nevertheless, since the stranger was exhausted with fatigue and hunger, Spyridon presented him with

---

429   These are the names YHVH, AGLA, AHIH, Amen.

this meat, and, to encourage him to eat it, he sat down at the table with him and shared this repast of charity, thus transforming the flesh that the Israelites regarded as the most impure into a feast of penitence, placing himself above the material aspect of the law through the spirit of the law itself by showing himself to be a true and intelligent disciple of the man-god, who established the chosen kings of nature in the three worlds.

CHAPTER XV

THE SABBATH OF THE SORCERERS

Here we have returned to that terrible number, fifteen, which, in the clavicle of the Tarot, presents the symbol of a monster standing on an altar, wearing a miter and horns, having the breasts of a woman and genitals of a man, a chimera, a deformed sphinx, a synthesis of monstrosity; and above this figure we can read a completely frank and naive inscription: THE DEVIL.

Yes, here we deal with the phantom of all terrors, the dragon of all the theogonies, the Ahriman of the Persians, the Typhon of the Egyptians, the Python of the Greeks, the ancient serpent of the Hebrews, the wyvern, the graoully, the tarasque,[430] the gargoyle, the great beast of the Middle Ages, and worse yet than all of those, the Baphomet of the Templars, the bearded idol of the alchemists, the obscene god of Mendes, the goat of the Sabbath.

We provide as the frontispiece of this Ritual the exact figure of this terrible emperor of the night with all his attributes and all his characters.[431]

Let us say now, for the edification of the vulgar, for the satisfaction of Monsieur the Count de Mirville, for the justification of Bodin the demonomaniac, for the greatest glory of the Church, which persecuted the Templars, burnt the ma-

---

430 The Graoully and the Tarasque are legendary monsters in French medieval tradition.

431 The figure on p. 316 was the frontispiece to the original French edition.

gicians, excommunicated the Freemasons, etc., etc.; let us boldly and loudly say that all the initiates into the occult sciences (I speak here of the lesser initiates and the profaners of the great arcanum) adored, still adore, and will always adore what is symbolized by this terrifying symbol.

Yes, it is our profound conviction that the Grand Masters of the Order of the Templars adored Baphomet and made their initiates adore him; yes, there existed and might still exist assemblies presided over by that figure, sitting on a throne with his ardent torch between his horns; only the adorers of this sign do not think, as we do, that it is the representation of the devil but that of the god Pan, the god of our schools of modern philosophy, the god of the theurgists of the school of Alexandria and of the mystic Neoplatonists of our day, the god of Lamartine[432] and of Victor Cousin,[433] the god of Spinoza and of Plato, the god of the primordial Gnostic schools; the actual Christ of the dissident priesthood; and that last qualification given to the goat of black magic will not surprise those who study religious antiquities and have followed in their diverse transformations the phases of symbolism and of doctrine either in India, or in Egypt, or in Judea.

---

432 French author Alphonse de Lamartine (1790–1869), Orientalist and novelist.

433 French philosopher (1792–1867).

The bull, the dog, and the goat are the three symbolic animals of Hermetic magic, in which are summarized all the traditions of Egypt and of India. The bull represents the earth or the philosopher's salt; the dog is Hermanubis, the Mercury of the sages, the fluid, the air and the water; the goat represents the fire, and he is at the same time the symbol of regeneration.

In Judea they consecrated two goats, one pure, the other impure. The pure one was sacrificed in expiation for sins; the other, charged through imprecation with these same sins, was freed into the desert.[434] A strange thing, but of profound symbolism! Reconciliation through devotion and expiation through liberty! Yet all the fathers who occupied themselves with Jewish symbolism recognized in their immolated goat the figure of the one who took away, they say, the form itself of sin. Thus the Gnostics were not outside the symbolic traditions when they gave Christ the liberator the mystical figure of the goat.

All of the Cabala and all of magic in fact share the cult of the sacrificial goat and that of the emissary goat. Thus there is the magic of the sanctuary and the magic of the desert, the white church and the black church, the priesthood of public assemblies and the Sanhedrin of the Sabbath.

The goat which is represented on our frontispiece has the sign of the pentagram on his forehead point upwards, which suffices for it to be a symbol of the light; with his two hands he makes the sign of occultism, and points above to the white moon of Chesed, and below to the black moon of Geburah. This sign expresses the perfect accord between mercy and justice. One of his arms is feminine, the other masculine, like Khunrath's androgyne whose attributes we had to unite with our goat, since it is the unique and same symbol. The torch of intelligence which shines between his horns is the magical light of universal equilibrium; it is also the figure of the soul risen above matter, even though it comes from matter, as the flame rises from the torch. The hideous animal head expresses the horror of sin, for which the material agent, solely responsible for it, must forever carry the punishment: because the soul is imperturbable by nature and can only suffer by materializing. The caduceus, which takes the place of the generative organ, represents eternal life; the belly covered in scales is water; the

---

434 Leviticus 16:20–22.

circle which is above is the atmosphere; the feathers which come thereafter are the emblem of the volatile; then humanity is represented by the two breasts and the androgynous arms of the sphinx of the occult sciences.

Thus is the darkness of the infernal sanctuary dissipated, thus is the sphinx of the terrors of the Middle Ages surmised and thrown off his throne; *quomodo cecidisti*, Lucifer?[435] The terrible Baphomet is no more, like all those other monstrous idols, enigmas of the ancient science and its dreams, it is but an innocent and even pious hieroglyph. How could man have adored the beast, since he exerts a sovereign empire over it? Let us say, for the honor of humanity, that it never adored dogs and goats more than lambs and pigeons. In terms of hieroglyphs, why a goat rather than a lamb? On the sacred stones of the Gnostic Christians of the sect of Basilides,[436] we see representations of the Christ as diverse animal figures from the Cabala; sometimes a bull, sometimes a lion, sometimes a serpent with the head of a lion or of a bull; everywhere he has the same attributes of light, like our goat whose sign of the pentagram stops one from taking him for a fabulous image of Satan.

Let us say it aloud, to combat against the remains of Manichaeism which still arise in our time among Christians,[437] that Satan as a superior personality and as a power does not exist. Satan is the personification of all errors, of all perversity, and in consequence of all weakness. If God can be defined as he who necessarily exists, can we not define his antagonist and his enemy as he who necessarily does not exist?

The absolute affirmation of good implies the absolute negation of evil; in the light the shadow itself is luminous. It is thus that lost spirits are good wherever they are in truth where they must be. There are no shadows without reflections, nor nights without a moon, without phosphor and without stars. If hell is justice,

---

435   "How art thou fallen, Lucifer?"

436   Basilides of Alexandria, a major gnostic teacher of the second century CE.

437   Manichaeism was the movement founded by the Persian prophet Mani in the third century CE. In Lévi's time it was often confused with the Zoroastrian faith, which also sees the cosmos as a battleground between two primal spiritual powers, one good and one evil, and the term "Manichaeism" was routinely used, as Lévi does here, as a label for this form of dualism.

it is good. No one has ever blasphemed God. The insults and mocking that are addressed to those disfigured images do not reach him.

We have just named Manichaeism, and it is through this monstrous heresy that we will explain the aberrations of black magic. The doctrine of Zoroaster misunderstood the magical law of the two forces which constitute universal equilibrium, and caused a few illogical minds to imagine a negative divinity, subordinate but hostile to the active divinity. It is thus that the impure binary was formed. We had the folly to split God; the star of Solomon was separated into two triangles, and the Manichaeans imagined a trinity of the night. This evil god, born of the imagination of sectarians, became the inspirer of all follies and of all crimes. They offered him bloody sacrifices; monstrous idolatry replaced true religion; black magic defamed the high and luminous magic of the true adepts, and in the caverns and deserts horrible conventicles of sorcerers, ghouls, and stryges took place: because dementia soon transforms into frenzy, and from human sacrifice to cannibalism is but one step.

The mysteries of the Sabbath were diversely told, but they always appear in the grimoires and in the court trials against magic. We can divide all the revelations which have been made regarding this subject into three types: first, those that talk of a fantastic and imaginary Sabbath; second, those that betray the secrets of the occult assemblies of true adepts; third, the revelations of mad and criminal assemblies whose object was the practice of black magic.

For a great number of unfortunate men and woman given to mad and abominable practices, the Sabbath was but a long nightmare whose dreams seemed like reality to them, and which they achieved through the use of drinks, fumigations, and narcotic frictions. Della Porta, whom we have already indicated as a mystifier, provides in his *Magia Naturalis* the supposed recipe for the unguent of the witches, by means of which they traveled to the Sabbath. It is composed of child's fat, aconite boiled with poplar leaves, and a few other drugs; then he wants us to mix in some chimney soot, which must render the naked witches who show up at these Sabbaths rubbed all over with this ointment rather unattractive. Here is another more serious recipe also provided by della Porta and that we transcribe here in Latin to leave it in all its grimoire style: Recipe: suim, acorum vulgare, pentaphyllon, verspertillionis sanguinem, solanum somniferum et oleum,[438] and all boiled and mixed together until it reaches the consistency of an unguent.

We think that opiates like the heart of green cannabis, *Datura stramonium*, and the cherry laurel would enter with no less success into such compositions. The fat or blood of birds of the night, added to these narcotics with the ceremonies of black magic, can strike the imagination and determine the direction of dreams. It is at Sabbaths dreamed up in this manner that one must attribute the stories of goats that arise from a jug and then reenter it after the ceremony, the infernal powders collected behind this same goat, called Master Leonard,[439] the banquets where they eat the unsalted, boiled remains of abortions with serpents and toads, the dances where the images of monstrous animals or impossibly deformed men and women appear, the frenetic orgies where incubi produce a cold semen. Only nightmares can produce such things and only they can explain them. The unfortunate priest Gaufridi and his debauched penitent, Madeleine de la Palud, became mad due to such reveries, and compromised themselves until they were brought before the pyre. One must read the trial and depositions of these poor lunatics to understand just what kind of aberrations one can be transported to by a wounded imagination. But the Sabbath was not always a dream, and it really existed; there even still exist now secret and nocturnal assemblies, some of which are of religious character with a social goal, others which are conjurations and orgies. It is from this dual viewpoint that we shall consider and describe the true Sabbath, either of the magic of light or of the magic of darkness.

When Christianity proscribed the public exercise of the ancient cults, it reduced the partisans of religion to meeting in secret to celebrate their mysteries. At these meetings there presided initiates who soon established between the diverse nuances of these persecuted cults a conviction that magical truth would aid them even more readily, because proscription reunited their wills and tightened the fraternal links between men. Thus the mysteries of Isis, of the Eleusinian

---

438 "Take: lard, common iris, cinquefoil, bat's blood, nightshade, and oil."
439 A French folk name for the devil.

Ceres, of Bacchus were reunited with those of the Bona Dea[440] and primordial Druidism. The assemblies were ordinarily held between the days of Mercury and Jupiter, or between those of Venus and Saturn; they occupied themselves with the rites of initiation, they exchanged mysterious signs, they sang symbolic hymns, they united around banquets, and they successively formed the magical chain around tables and through dance; then they separated after having renewed their obligations between the hands of their leaders and having received the leader's instructions. The initiate of the Sabbath had to be brought, or rather carried, to the assembly with his eyes covered by a magic coat, with which he was entirely wrapped; they made him pass over great fires, and they made terrifying noises around him. When he uncovered his face, he saw himself surrounded by infernal monsters and in the presence of a colossal and monstrous goat, whom they enjoined him to adore. All these ceremonies were trials of strength of character and confidence in the initiators. The last trial was the most decisive, because it presented above all to the mind of the recipient something humiliating and ridiculous: he had to respectfully kiss the behind of the goat, and the neophyte was commanded to do so very bluntly. If he refused, they re-veiled his head and transported him far from the assembly with such rapidity that he believed he was being driven on clouds; if he accepted, they had him turn around the symbolic idol, and he found, not a repulsive and obscene object, but the young and graceful visage of a priestess of Isis or of Maya, who gave him a maternal kiss; and then he was admitted to the banquet.

As to the orgies which, in several assemblies of this type, followed the banquet, one must not believe that they were generally accepted in these secret feasts; but we know that several Gnostic sects practiced them in their conventicles as of the first centuries of Christianity. That the flesh had its defenders in the centuries of asceticism and repression of the senses had to be so and does not surprise us; but one should not accuse high magic of imbalances it never authorized. Isis is chaste in her widowhood; Diana Panthea is a virgin; Hermanubis,

---

440　The "Good Goddess," a Roman deity whose name was secret and remains unknown to this day.

being of both sexes, can satisfy neither; the hermetic Hermaphrodite is chaste. Apollonius of Tyana never abandoned himself to the seductions of pleasure; the emperor Julian was of a severe chastity; Plotinus of Alexandria was strict with regard to his ascetic morals; Paracelsus was such a stranger to mad loves that they believed he was of doubtful sex; Raymond Lully was only initiated into the last secrets of the science after a despondency due to love, which rendered him forever chaste.

It is also a tradition of high magic that pentacles and talismans lose all their virtue when he who carries them takes them to a house of prostitution or commits adultery. The orgiastic Sabbath must therefore not be considered as one belonging to veritable adepts.

As to the actual name of the Sabbath, some have wished to derive it from the name of Sabazius; others have imagined other etymologies. The simplest, according to us, is the one which has this word come from the Jewish Sabbath, since it is certain that the Jews, the most faithful guardians of the secrets of the Cabala, were almost always with regard to magic the great masters of the Middle Ages.

The Sabbath was thus always on a Sunday for the Cabalists, the day of their religious feast or rather the night of their regular assembly. This feast, surrounded in mystery, had as a safeguard the fears of the vulgar themselves and escaped persecution through terror.

As to the diabolical Sabbath of the necromancers, it was a counterfeit of the mage's Sabbath and an assembly of evildoers who exploited idiots and the insane. They practiced terrible rites there and composed abominable mixtures. The sorcerers and sorceresses were their own police and informed themselves regarding one another in order to mutually support their reputation for prophecy and divination, because seers at that time were generally consulted and had a lucrative profession while exercising veritable influence.

These assemblies of sorcerers and sorceresses, incidentally, did not possess and could not possess the regular rites: all depended on the caprices of the leaders and the giddiness of the assembly. That which was recounted by those who were able to assist served as a model for all the nightmares of dreamers, and it is from the combination of these impossible realities and these demoniacal dreams that were issued the disgusting and stupid stories about the Sabbath that figure in the procedures of magic in books by Sprenger, de Lancre, Delrio, and Bodin.[441]

The rites of the Gnostic Sabbath were transmitted in Germany to an association which took the name of Mopses;[442] they replaced the Cabalistic goat with the hermetic dog, and at the reception of male or female candidates (because the order admitted ladies), they bring them blindfolded; they make those infernal noises around them which makes people give it the name of Sabbath due to all the inexplicable rumors; they ask them if they are afraid of the devil; then they brusquely propose that they choose between kissing the backside of the master or that of Mops, who is a little figure of a dog covered in silk, and the substitute for the ancient grand idol of the goat of Mendes. The Mopses have as a sign of recognition which is a ridiculous grimace that reminds one of the phantasmagorias of the ancient Sabbath and the masks of its assistants. For the rest, their doctrine is summarized by the cult of love and of liberty. This association was produced when the Roman Church persecuted the Freemasons. The Mopses claimed that they recruited only Catholics, and they substituted the oath of reception with a solemn promise on their honor not to reveal any of the secrets of the association. It was nothing more than a promise, and religion no longer had anything to do with it.

The Baphomet of the Templars, whose name should be spelled Cabalistically and in the inverse, is composed of three abbreviations: TEM OHP AB, *Templi omnium hominum pacis abbas*, father of the temple, the universal peace of men.[443] Baphomet was, according to some, a monstrous head; according to others, a demon in the form of a goat. A sculpted coffer was recently disinterred from the

---

441 Authors of books on witchcraft from the era of the witch hunts.

442 The order of the Mopses was founded in Vienna in the early eighteenth century as an alternative to Freemasonry for Catholics, who had been barred by the papal bull of 1738 from membership in that order. It admitted both men and women to membership and took the pug dog (*Mops* in German) for its symbol.

443 This is at least ingenious. It is only fair to Lévi to note that equally imaginative interpretations of the name Baphomet have been abundant in occult writings.

ruins of an old temple commandery, and antiquaries had observed within it a Baphometic figure which conforms in its attributes to our goat of Mendes and to Khunrath's androgyne.[444] This figure is bearded with the entire body of a woman; she holds in one hand the sun, and in the other the moon, attached to chains. It is a beautiful allegory that this virile head attributes to thought alone the principal initiator and creator. The head, here, represents the mind, and the female body represents matter. The celestial bodies enchained to the human form and directed by that nature whose intelligence is the head also offer a most beautiful allegory. The symbol, in its ensemble, was nonetheless found to be obscene and diabolical by the scholars who examined it. It is no wonder, after that, to see the superstitions from the Middle Ages still being accredited in our day! One single thing surprises me, it is that, believing in the devil and his minions, we do not light the pyres back up. M. Veuillot[445] would like us to do so, and he is the most logical of them: one should always honor men who have the courage of their opinions.

Let us continue our curious researches and arrive at the most horrible mysteries of the grimoire, those regarding the evocation of devils and pacts with hell.

After having attributed a real existence to the absolute negation of good, after having enthroned the absurd and created a god of lies, there but remained for human folly to invoke this impossible idol, and that is what the madmen did. Someone wrote us recently to say that the respectable Father Ventura, former superior of the Theatine order, examiner of the bishops, etc., after having read our Doctrine, had declared that the Cabala, in his eyes, was the invention of the devil, and that the star of Solomon was another ruse by that same devil to persuade the world that he, the devil, is one with God. And there we have what is seriously taught by those who are the masters in Israel! The ideal of the void and the

---

444   Lévi was fooled here by Joseph von Hammer-Purgstall, whose *Mysterium Baphometis revelatum* (*The Mystery of Baphomet Revealed*), published in 1818, includes this among many other fake "discoveries" redefining the Baphomet of the Templars as a hermaphroditic idol.

445   French journalist Louis Veuillot (1813–83), a conservative Catholic writer of Lévi's time.

darkness inventing a sublime philosophy which is the universal basis for the faith and the cornerstone of all the temples! The demon apposing his signature besides that of God! My venerable masters in theology, you are more sorcerous than is thought and then you think yourselves, and he who said the devil is a liar and so is his father would perhaps have just few things to say regarding the decisions as to your paternity.

Those who evoke the devil must before all else belong to the religion which admits to a creator devil and rival of God. To address oneself to such a power, one must believe in it. Given a firm believer in the religion of the devil, here is how he must proceed in order to correspond with this pseudogod:

MAGICAL AXIOM

Within the circle of their action, all verbs create what they affirm.

DIRECT CONSEQUENCE

He who affirms the devil creates or makes the devil.

WHAT ONE NEEDS TO SUCCEED IN INFERNAL EVOCATIONS.

First, invincible stubbornness;

Second, a conscience which is both hardened to crime and very accessible to remorse and fear;

Third, an affected or natural ignorance;

Fourth, a blind faith in everything that cannot be believed;

Fifth, a completely false idea of God.

ONE MUST THEN:

First, profane the ceremonies of the cult in which you believe and trample the most sacred signs under your feet;

Second, make a bloody sacrifice;

Third, procure a magic fork. It is a single branch of hazel wood or almond wood that one must cut off with a single cut using a new knife which had served for the sacrifice; the stick must end in a fork; you cover this wood fork in iron or steel made from the blade of the same knife you used to cut it.

You must fast for fourteen days, having only one meal without salt after the Sun has set; this meal will be of black bread and blood seasoned with spices without salt, or of black beans, and milky and narcotic weeds;

Every five days you get drunk, after sunset, with wine in which you have infused five heads of black poppy and five ounces of ground cannabis seeds for five hours: all of it contained in a cloth that has been spun by a female prostitute (in a pinch, the first cloth you come by could be used if it was spun by a woman).

The evocation can be performed either during the night of Monday to Tuesday, or that of Friday to Saturday.

You must choose a solitary and detested spot, such as a cemetery haunted by evil spirits, a feared ruin in the countryside, the basement of an abandoned convent, the place where a murder was committed, a Druidic altar, or an ancient temple of idols.

You must provide yourself with a black robe without seams or sleeves; a lead skullcap constellated with the signs of the Moon, of Venus, and Saturn, two candles made from human lard fitted into candlesticks of black wood cut into the form of a crescent, two crowns of verbena; a magical sword with a black handle; the magical fork; a copper vase containing the blood of the victim, an incense holder containing perfumes, which will be of frankincense, camphor, aloe, ambergris, and storax mixed and kneaded with the blood of goat, mole, and bat; you must also have four nails torn from the coffin of a torture victim, the head of a black cat who was fed human flesh for five days, a bat drowned in blood, the horns of a goat *cum quo puella concubuerit*,[446] and the skull of a parricide. Once all these horrible and rather difficult to gather objects are united, here is how you use them:

You draw a perfect circle with the sword while leaving a break or an exit; in the circle you inscribe a triangle, you color the pentacle that the sword drew with blood; then, at one of the points of the triangle, you place a brazier with three feet, which we should also have counted in our list of indispensable items; at the opposite base of the triangle you draw three little circles for the operator and his assistants, and behind the operator's circle you draw, not with the blood of the victim, but with the blood of the operator himself, the sign of the labarum, or Constantine's monogram. The operator or his acolytes must be barefoot and have their heads covered.

You will also have brought the immolated skin of the victim; this skin, cut into bands, will be placed in the circle and will form another interior circle which will be fixed at four corners with the four nails of the torture victim; near the four nails and outside the circle you will place the head of the cat, the human, or rather inhuman, skull, the goat horns, and the bat; you will sprinkle them with a roll of birch bark dipped in the blood of the victim, then you will light a fire of alder wood and cypress; the two magical candles will be placed to the right and left of the operator in the crowns of verbena. (See the figure at the head of this chapter.)

You will then pronounce the formulas of evocation which are found in the magical elements of Pietro d'Abano or in the grimoires, either manuscripts or printed. The one in the *Grand Grimoire*, repeated in the vulgar *Dragon Rouge*, was purposely altered in the published version. Here it is as it should be read:

"Per Adonai Elohim, Adonai Jehovah, Adonai Sabaoth, Metraton On Agla Adonai Mathon, verbum pythonicum, mysterium salamandrae, conventus sylph-

---

446   Latin: "which has had intercourse with a girl."

orum, antra gnomorum, daemonia coeli, Gad, Almousin, Gibor, Jeheshua, Evan, Zariatnatmik, veni, veni, veni."[447]

The great appellation of Agrippa only consists of these words: DIES MIES JESCHET BOENEDOESEF DOUVEMA ENITEMAUS.[448] We do not flatter ourselves by claiming we understand the meaning of these words, which perhaps have none, and should not have any which are reasonable, since they have the power to evoke the devil, who is sovereign unreason.

Pico della Mirandola, no doubt with the same motive, affirms that in black magic the most barbaric and most absolutely unintelligible words are the best and most efficacious.

The conjurations are repeated while raising one's voice, along with imprecations and threats, until the spirit responds. He is ordinarily preceded, when he is about to appear, by a violent wind that seems to make the entire countryside howl. Domestic animals tremble and hide; the assistants feel a breath on their faces, and their hair, damp with a cold sweat, stands on end.

The great and supreme appellation, according to Pietro d'Abano, is as follows:

Hemen-Etan! Hemen-Etan! Hemen-Etan! El* ATI* TITEIP* AZIA* HYN* MINOSEL* ACHADON* yay* vaa* Eye* Aaa* Eie* Exe* A EL EL EL A* HY! HAU! HAU! HAU! HAU! VA! VA! VA! VA! CHAVAJOTH.

Aie Seraye, Aie Seraye, Aie Seraye! Per Elohim, Archima, Rabur, BATHAS super ABRAC ruens superveniens ABEOR SUPER ABERER *Chavajoth! Chavajoth! Chavajoth!* Impero tibi per clavem SOLOMONIS et nomen magnum SHEMHAMPHORASH.

---

447 "By Adonai Elohim, Adonai Jehovah, Adonai Sabaoth, Metatron On Agla Adonai Mathon, the pythonic word, the mystery of the salamanders, the gathering of the sylphs, the caverns of the gnomes, the heavens of the demons, Gad, Almousin, Gibor, Jeheshua, Evan, Zariatnatmik, come, come, come."

448 Fans of American horror fiction will recognize this and the previous incantation as the spells used to summon the dead to life in H. P. Lovecraft's novel *The Case of Charles Dexter Ward*.

Here are the ordinary signs and signatures of the demons:

These are the signatures of simple demons; here are the official signatures of the princes of hell, signatures which were juridically witnessed (juridically! O monsieur. Count de Mirville!) and conserved in the judiciary archives like proofs of guilt for the trial of the unfortunate Urbain Grandier.

These signatures are apposed at the bottom of a pact which M. Collin de Plancy[449] provided as a facsimile in the linguistic atlas of his *Infernal Dictionary*, and which has as a marginal note: "the official record is in hell, in Lucifer's cabinet," a rather precious piece of information regarding a very poorly known

---

449   French occultist and author Jacques Collin de Plancy (1793–1881), the author of several books on demonology.

locale and from an era still so close to ours, anterior however to the trial of the young La Barre and d'Etallonde,[450] who, as everyone knows, were the contemporaries of Voltaire.

Evocations were often followed by pacts, which were written on the skin parchment of a goat with an iron pen and a drop of blood, which had to be taken from the left arm. The debt agreement was written in two copies: the clever demon took one with him, and the voluntarily condemned swallowed the other. The reciprocal promises were for the demon to serve the sorcerer during a certain number of years and for the sorcerer to belong to the demon after a certain determined time. The Church, with its exorcisms, consecrated the belief in all these things, and one could say that black magic and its dark prince are a real, living, and terrible creation of Roman Catholicism; that they are even the Church's special and characteristic work, since their priests did not invent God. Also, true Catholics hold at the bottom of their hearts to the conservation, even to the regeneration, of this Great Work which is the philosopher's stone of the official and positive cult. They say that, in jailhouse lingo, evildoers call the devil the baker: all our desire, and here we are not speaking as a mage but as a devoted child of Christianity and the Church, to which we owe our primary education and our first enthusiasms; all our desire, we were saying, is that the phantom of Satan might no longer also be called the *baker* of ministers of morality and of the representatives of the highest virtue. Will they understand our thinking, and will they pardon us our boldness and our aspirations in favor of our devote intentions and the sincerity of our faith?

The magic which creates the demon is that magic which dictated the Grimoire of Pope Honorius, the *Enchiridion* of Leon III, the exorcisms of the Roman Ritual, the sentences of the Inquisitors, the indictments of Laubardement, the articles of the brothers Veuillot, the books of de Falloux, de Montalembert, and de Mirville:[451] the magic of sorcerers and of "pious men" who are in fact nothing of

---

450   Jean de La Barre and Gaillard d'Etallonde, two young men tried in 1766 on trumped-up charges of disrespect for religion. La Barre was beheaded; d'Etallonde managed to flee the country. The case became a cause célèbre at the time and thereafter.

451   Popular Catholic authors of Lévi's time.

the kind, something which is truly condemnable for some and infinitely deplorable for others. It is most of all to combat, by revealing them, these sad aberrations of the human spirit that we have published this book. May it aid in the success of this holy work!

But we have yet to show these impious works in all their turpitude and in all their monstrous folly; one must stir up the bloody mud of past superstitions, one must consult through the annals of demonomania, to understand certain heinous crimes that imagination alone would not invent. The Cabalist Bodin, a Jew by conviction and a Catholic by necessity, had no other intention, with his *Demonomania of the Sorcerers*, than to attack Catholicism with these works and to undermine it with the greatest of all abuses of its doctrine. The work of Bodin is profoundly Machiavellian and strikes at the heart of the institutions of man which it pretends to defend. We would have great difficulty imagining, without having read it, all the hideous and bloody things he collected and piled up: acts of revolting superstition, arrests and executions of ferocious stupidity. "Burn them all!" So the Inquisitors seemed to say. "God will recognize his own!" Poor madmen, hysterical women, idiots were burned without mercy for the crime of magic; but there were also great culprits who escaped this unjust and sanguinary justice! That is what Bodin would have us understand when he tells us anecdotes of the type which he places around the death of Charles IX. It is a little known abomination which has not yet, as far as we know, even in the eras of the most feverish and dreadful literature, tempted the verve of any novelist.

Suffering from a malady whose causes no physician could discover and whose terrible symptoms none could explain, King Charles IX was about to die. The Queen Mother, who governed entirely and who could lose everything under another reign; the Queen Mother, who was suspected of being the cause of this malady, against her own interests, because they always supposed this woman capable of anything, of hidden ruses and unknown interests, first consulted the king's astrologers, then took recourse in the most detestable of magics. The state of the patient worsened every day and was becoming desperate; they decided to consult the oracle of the Bloody Head, and here is how they proceeded with this infernal operation:

They took a child, with beautiful face and of innocent virtue; they had him prepared in secret for his first communion by a palace chaplain; then, on the day in question, or rather the night of the sacrifice, a monk, a Jacobin apostate dedicated to the occult works of black magic, began at midnight, in the room of the patient, and in the sole presence of Catherine de Médicis and her minions, what was then called the Mass of the Devil.

At this Mass, celebrated before the image of the demon, having under his feet an upturned cross, the sorcerer consecrated two hosts, one black and one white. The white one was given to the child, whom they had brought there dressed as though for a baptism, and whose throat was cut on the steps of the altar right after his communion. His head, detached from the torso in a single cut, was placed, still twitching, on the large black host which covered the bottom of the sacred cup, and then was brought to a table where mysterious lamps burned. The exorcism then began, and the demon was commanded to pronounce an oracle and to answer through the mouth of that child's head to a secret question that the king did not dare speak aloud and had not even mentioned to anyone. And then a weak voice, a strange inhuman voice, was heard coming from the head of that poor martyr. "I am forced," said this voice in Latin: *Vim patior.* At that response, which no doubt announced to the patient that hell no longer protected him, a terrible trembling seized him, his arms stiffened. . . . He then cried out in a hoarse voice: "Take away that head! take away that head!" and right up to his last breath no one heard him say anything else. Those who served him, and who were unaware of this awful mystery, believed he was being pursued by the ghost of Coligny and that he thought he saw before him the head of that illustrious admiral, but what excited the dying man was no longer remorse, it was the hopeless fear of an anticipated hell.

This black magical legend of Bodin's reminds one of the abominable practices and the well-merited tortures of Gilles de Laval, lord of Rais, who went from asceticism to black magic and gave himself over, in order to enter into the good graces of Satan, to the most revolting of sacrifices. This madman declared during his trial that Satan had often appeared to him but had always cheated him by promising him treasures which he never then provided. From this trial, there resulted the juridical information that several hundred unfortunate children had been victims of the cupidity and atrocious imagination of this murderer.

CHAPTER XVI

ENCHANTMENTS AND SPELLS

What the sorcerers and necromancers sought most of all with their evocations of the impure spirit was that magnetic power which is the allotment of the true adept, and which they wanted to usurp in order to shamefully abuse it.

The folly of the sorcerers was an evil madness; one of their primary goals was the power of enchantments or deleterious influences.

We have said in our "Doctrine" what we think of these enchantments, and the extent to which this power appears to us to be dangerous and real. The true mage enchants those whom he disapproves of, and whom he believes should be punished, without ceremonies and solely through his condemnation; he enchants even those who do him harm, through his forgiveness, and the enemies of initiates will never get away with their injustices for very long. We ourselves have observed numerous examples of this fatal law. The hangmen of the martyrs always perish in unfortunate circumstances, and the adepts are the martyrs of intelligence; but Providence seems to despise those who despise them and has killed those who look to prevent them from living. The legend of the Wandering Jew is the popular poetry of this arcanum. A people had sent a sage to his torture; they told him: "Walk!" when he wanted to rest a moment. Well! that people will suffer a similar condemnation, it will be entirely proscribed, and for centuries they will be told: "Walk! Walk!" without finding any pity or rest.

A learned man had a wife whom he loved madly and passionately in the exaltation of his tenderness, and he honored her with his blind faith and relied on her for everything. Vain, with her beauty and her intelligence, this woman became envious of the superiority of her husband and began to hate him. After some time, she left him and compromised herself with an ugly, spiritless, and immoral old man. That was her first punishment, but that is not where her sentence would end. The learned man spoke this single sentence against her: "I rebuke your intelligence and your beauty." One year later, those who encountered her could already not recognize her; a chubbiness had begun to disfigure her; she reflected in her face the ugliness of her new affections. Three years later she was ugly; seven years after that she was mad. This occurred in our time, and we knew both persons.

Mages condemn in the manner of skillful doctors, and that is why we cannot appeal their sentences once they have pronounced a warrant against a guilty person. They do not need ceremonies or invocations; they need only abstain from eating at the same table as the condemned, and if they are forced to sit at that table, they should neither accept nor offer him salt.

The enchantments of sorcerers are of another kind and can be compared to actual poisonings of the current of the astral light. They exalt their will through ceremonies to the point of rendering it venomous at a distance; but, as we already noted in our "Doctrine," they most often expose themselves to being killed first by their infernal machinations. Let us criticize here several of their shameful procedures. They procure either the hairs or the clothing of the person they wish to curse; then they choose an animal who in their eyes is the symbol of that person; through the hairs or clothing they magnetically link that animal to the person; they give it their name, then they kill it with a single cut of a magical knife, they open the chest, tear out the heart, envelop the still beating heart in magnetized objects, and for three days, at all hours, they thrust nails, needles heated in fire, or long thorns into the heart, while pronouncing curses upon the enchanted person's name. They are then persuaded (and often with reason) that the victim of their odious operations goes through as many tortures as though they actually had all those points stuck into their heart. The victim begins to waste away and, after a time, dies of an unknown malady.

Another enchantment used in the countryside consists of consecrating nails for works of hatred with the stinking fumigations of Saturn and the invocations of evil spirits, and then you follow behind the person you wish to torment and nail in the form of the cross all the marks of their footsteps that you can find in the ground or the sand.

Another more abominable enchantment is practiced like this: you take a large toad, and you baptize it with the last and first names of the person you wish to curse; you then have the toad swallow a consecrated host upon which you have pronounced formulas of execration; then you envelop the toad in magnetized objects, you link it with hairs of the victim, upon which the operator had first spit, and you bury it all either under the threshold of the cursed person's door or in a place where they are obliged to pass over every day. The elementary spirit of this toad becomes a nightmare and a vampire in that person's dreams, unless he knows how to send them back to the culprit.

Then come enchantments through wax images. The necromancers of the Middle Ages, who jealously guarded their ability to please through sacrilege those whom they saw as their masters, mixed in with this wax baptismal oil and the ashes of burnt hosts; there were always apostate priests to be found who raided the treasuries of the Church. They formed with this cursed wax an image which resembled as much as possible the person they wished to enchant; they dressed this image in similar clothes to his, they gave it the same sacraments as he had also received, then they pronounced over the head of the image all the maledictions which expressed the sorcerer's hatred, and every day they inflicted imaginary tortures on this figure, to attack and torment through sympathy he or she whom the figure represented.

Enchantment is more infallible if one can procure the hairs, the blood, and best of all a tooth from the enchanted person. It is what gave rise to that proverbial way of speaking: "You have a tooth against me."[452]

One also enchants through the eyes, and this is what they call the *jettatura* in Italy, or the evil eye. In the times of our civil discords, a shop owner had the bad idea of denouncing one of his neighbors. The neighbor, after being held under

---

452   A French expression meaning to nurse a grudge against someone.

arrest for some time, was released, but he had lost his position. For his only revenge, he passed in front of the shop of his denouncer twice a day, stared at him
fixedly, greeted him, and went past. After a time, the shop owner, no longer able
to tolerate the torment of his stare, sold his shop at a loss and changed neighbor-
hoods without leaving his address; in a word, he was ruined.

A threat is a real enchantment, because it acts strongly upon the imagination,
especially if that imagination easily accepts the belief in unlimited occult power.
The terrible threat of hell, humanity's enchantment over several centuries,
created more nightmares, more sicknesses without name, more furious follies
than all the vices and all excesses combined. This is what the hermetic artists of
the Middle Ages symbolized with their incredible and unheard of monsters which
they inlayed in the doorways of their basilicas.

But enchantment through threats produces an effect absolutely contrary to
the intentions of the operator when the threat is obviously vain, when it revolts
the legitimate pride of he who is threatened and in consequence provokes his resistance, and lastly when it is ridiculous because it is overly terrible.

It is the sectarians of hell who discredited heaven. Tell a reasonable man that
equilibrium is the law of the movement of life and that moral equilibrium, and
freedom, rest upon the eternal and immutable distinction between truth and
falsity, between good and evil; tell him that, graced with free will, he must find
his place through his works in the empire of the truth and the good, or eternally
fall down, like the rock of Sisyphus into the chaos of lies and evil: he will understand this doctrine, and if you call the truth and the good heaven lies and evil hell,
he will believe in your heaven and your hell, above which the ideal divinity remains calm, perfect, and as inaccessible to anger as to insult, because he will understand that if hell in principle is eternal like liberty, it could be no more than a
passing torment for souls, since it is an expiation, and that the idea of expiation
necessarily supposes that of reparation and the destruction of evil.

This is said, not with dogmatic intentions, which could never be our moti-
vation, but to indicate the reasonable and moral remedy for enchantments of conscience through the terrors of the next life. Let us now speak of the means of
escaping the deadly influences of human anger.

The primary means is to be reasonable and just, and to never offer an opportunity or reason for anger. A legitimate anger is something to be very afraid of. That is why you should hurry to recognize and expiate your faults. If the anger persists after that, it certainly derives from a vice: look to find which vice, and strongly unite yourself with the contrary virtue. The enchantment will thereafter have no power over you.

Wash your towels and the clothes you have made use of carefully before giving them away, or burn them; never use an item of clothing that was used by someone unknown to you without having purified it with water, with sulfur, and with scents, such as camphor, incense, amber, etc.

A great means of resisting enchantment is to not fear it: enchantment acts in the manner of contagious sicknesses. In time of plague, those who are afraid are struck first. The means to not fear evil is to not be preoccupied by it, and with complete disinterest, since it is in a book on magic I have written that I place such counsel, I strongly advise nervous persons, the weak, the credulous, hysterics, the superstitious, the sanctimonious, idiots, the lazy, and those who lack willpower never to open a book on magic, to close this one if they have opened it, and never to listen to those who speak of the occult sciences, indeed to make fun of them, to refuse to believe and to "drink al fresco,"[453] as was said by the great Pantagruelist magician, the excellent priest of Meudon.[454]

As for sages, and it is time for us to occupy ourselves with them after having dealt with the madmen, there are few curses they fear other than those of fate; but since they are priests and doctors, they can be called upon to cure curses, and here is how they must do so:

One must get the enchanted person to do something good for the enchanter, render him a service which he cannot refuse, and work towards bringing him, either directly or indirectly, to the communion of salt.[455]

---

453   In French, *boire frais*, meaning to stay calm and not get carried away by emotion.

454   French comic writer François Rabelais.

455   That is, to share a meal in which salt is included; this is a traditional way of removing a curse.

A person who believes himself to be enchanted by the execration and burial of a toad must carry with them a living toad in a box made of horn.

For an enchantment by pierced heart, one must make the sickened person eat the heart of a lamb seasoned with sage and verbena, and have him carry a talisman of Venus or of the Moon in a small bag filled with camphor and salt.

For enchantment by wax figurine, one must make a more perfect figurine, give it everything of the enchanted person they can give it, put the seven talismans around its neck, place it in the middle of a large pentacle representing the pentagram, and rub it lightly every day with a mix of balm oil after having pronounced the Conjuration of the Four to divert the influence of the elementary spirits. After seven days, one must burn the figure in a consecrated fire, and you can be sure that the statuette made by the enchanter will lose all its virtue at the same moment.

We have already spoken of the sympathetic medicine of Paracelsus, which treated the members of wax and operated on blood from wounds to cure those wounds. This system allowed him to employ the most violent remedies; he also had as his principal specifics sublimate and vitriol.[456] We believe that homeopathy is a reminiscence of Paracelsus's theories and a return to learned practices. But we shall come back to this subject in a special treatise which will be exclusively dedicated to occult medicine.

The resolutions of parents which commit the future of their children are enchantments which we can never condemn too much: children devoted to the white,[457] for example, almost never prosper; those who were devoted in the past to celibacy often fell into debauch, or turned to despair and to folly. It is never permitted for a man to do violence to destiny, even less so to impose constraints on the legitimate use of liberty.

We add here, as a supplement and an appendix to this chapter, a few words

---

456   A specific, in medieval and Renaissance medicine, is a drug used to treat a particular illness. Sublimate is a compound of mercury, which until the development of antibiotics was used in carefully controlled doses to treat syphilis; vitriol is copper sulfate, another dangerous metallic drug.

457   In French, *vouer au blanc*, meaning to wear only white or white and blue clothing in honor of the Virgin Mary, as a way of attempting to attract her blessing.

about mandrakes and androids,[458] which several mages confuse with wax figurines which serve in the practice of enchantments.

The natural mandrake is a hairy root which looks more or less, in its ensemble, like the figure of a man or like the male generative parts. This root is mildly narcotic, and the ancients attributed an aphrodisiac virtue to it which made it desired by the witches of Thessaly for the composition of potions.

Is this root, as is supposed by a certain magical mysticism, the umbilical vestige of our terrestrial origins? This is not something we would seriously dare to affirm. It is certain, however, that man came from the alluvium of the Earth: he thus must have been formed as a first beginning in the form of a root. The analogies of nature absolutely require that we accept this idea, or at least the possibility of it. The first men could thus have been a family of gigantic sensitive mandrakes that the Sun had animated, and who on their own detached themselves from the Earth, a belief which in no way excludes and even on the contrary positively supposes the creative will and the providential cooperation of the first cause, which we have REASON to call GOD.

A few ancient alchemists, struck by this idea, dreamed of a cultivation of mandrakes, and looked to artificially reproduce a sludge which was fertile enough and a Sun active enough to *humanize* this root again and thus create men without the need for women.

Others, who believed they saw in humanity the synthesis of animals, hopelessly tried to animate the mandrake, but they interbred by way of monstrous matings, and sowed human seed in animal earth, without producing anything except shameful crimes and monsters without descendants.

The third manner of forming an android is with galvanized steel. They attribute to Albertus Magnus one of these almost intelligent automatons, and they add that Saint Thomas broke it with a single blow of a stick, because he was annoyed by its responses. This tale is an allegory. Albertus Magnus's android was the Aristotelian theology of the primitive scholastic, which was broken by the *Summa* of Saint Thomas, that bold innovator who was the first to replace divine

---

458   This word was used long before the invention of robotics for the artificial humans of legend.

arbitrariness with the absolute law of reason by daring to formulate this axiom, which we do not fear to repeat here as often as we like, since it emanates from a great master: a thing is not just because God wills it; but God wills it because it is just.

The real android, the serious android of the ancients, was a secret they hid from everyone and which Mesmer was the first to dare divulge in our time: it was the extension of the will of the mage in another body, organized and used by an elementary spirit; in other more modern and intelligible words, it was a magnetic subject.

CHAPTER XVII

THE WRITING OF THE STARS

We have finished with hell, and we breathe in deeply as we come back to the light after having traversed the caverns of black magic. Begone Satan! We renounce you, your ceremonies, your works but also your turpitude, your miseries, your void, and your lies! The great initiator saw you fall from the sky like lightning.[459] Christian legend converts you by having you gently place your dragon's head under the foot of the mother of God. You are for us an image of unintelligence and of mystery; you are unreason and blind fanaticism; you are the Inquisition and its hell; you are the god of Torquemada[460] and Alexander VI;[461] you have become the toy of our children, and your final place is fixed beside Pulcinella;[462] you are nothing now but a grotesque character from our fairground theaters and a motif for the shop signs of a few so-called religious boutiques.

After the sixteenth key of the Tarot, which represents the ruins of the temple of Satan, we find here on the seventeenth page a magnificent and graceful emblem.

---

459 Luke 10:18.

460 Spanish monk Tomás de Torquemada (1420–98), the most famous and among the most brutal figures of the Spanish Inquisition.

461 Rodrigo Borgia (1431–1503), pope from 1492 to his death, famous for his corruption and his many mistresses.

462 A character from the Italian commedia dell'arte, a figure in a long-nosed black mask who constantly makes a fool of himself.

A naked woman, young and immortal, pours out onto the earth the sap of universal life, which flows from two vases, one of gold, the other of silver; beside her is a bush in bloom over which alights the butterfly of Psyche; above her is a brilliant star with eight rays, around which are placed seven other stars.

I believe in eternal life! Such is the last article of the symbol of the Christians,[463] and that article, all by itself, is an entire profession of faith.

The ancients, in comparing the calm and peaceful immensity of the sky, peopled by immutable lights, to the agitations and the darkness of this world, believed they had found in that beautiful book written in golden letters the final word regarding the enigma of destiny; they traced, with their imaginations, the lines of correspondence between those brilliant lights of the divine writing, and they say that the first constellations drawn by the shepherds of Chaldea were also the first characters of Cabalistic writing.

These characters, first expressed by lines, then enclosed in hieroglyphic figures, had, according to M. Moreau de Dammartin,[464] author of a highly curious treatise on the origin of the characters of the alphabet, determined the ancient mages' choices for the figures of the Tarot, which this scholar recognizes as we do as an essentially hieratic and primordial book.

Thus, in the opinion of this scholar, the Chinese Tseu, the Hebrew Aleph and the Alpha of the Greeks, expressed hieroglyphically through the figure of the Magus, were borrowed from the constellation of the crane, neighbor to the astral fish[465] of the Oriental sphere.

The Chinese Tcheou, the Hebrew Beth and the Latin B, corresponding to the Priestess or to Junon, were formed from the head of the ram; the Chinese letter Yin, the Hebrew Gimel and the Latin G, figured by the Empress, were borrowed from the constellation of the Great Bear, etc.

The Cabalist Gaffarel, whom we have already cited more than once, erected a planisphere where all the constellations formed the Hebrew letters; but we

---

463   The symbol in question is the Apostles' Creed, one of the standard statements of Catholic faith, which ends with the words, "and the life everlasting, Amen."

464   A remarkably obscure French scholar of the nineteenth century; we have not been able to determine his dates or even his given name.

465   Piscis Austrinus, rather than the twin fish Pisces.

admit that this configuration often seems to us as more than arbitrary, and that we do not understand why, on the indication of a single star, for example, Gaffarel draws a ‏ד‎ rather than a ‏ו‎ or a ‏י‎; four stars equally suggest either a ‏ת‎, a ‏ה‎, or a ‏ח‎, rather than a ‏א‎. This is what turned us away from providing a copy of Gaffarel's planisphere here, and his works are in any case not very rare. This planisphere was reproduced in Father Montfaucon's[466] book on the religions and superstitions of the world, and we also found a copy in the book on magic published by the mystic Eckartshausen.[467]

The scholars, incidentally, are not in agreement regarding the configuration of the letters of the primordial alphabet. The Italian Tarot, whose Gothic types it is a good idea to conserve, draws, through the disposition of its figures, from the Hebrew alphabet which was in use since the captivity, and which we call the Assyrian alphabet; but there exist fragments from other older Tarots where the disposition is not the same. Since one should not guess haphazardly regarding erudite matters, we will wait, to fix our judgment, for new and more conclusive discoveries.

In regard to the alphabet of the stars, we believe that it is a subjective choice, just like the configuration of clouds, which seem to take on all the kinds of forms that our imagination lends them. This is as much the case for groups of stars as for the points in geomancy[468] and the drawing of cards in modern cartomancy. It is a pretext for magnetizing oneself and an instrument which can fix and determine natural intuition. Thus a Cabalist familiar with mystic hieroglyphs will see things in the stars which would not be discovered by a simple shepherd; but the shepherd, from his viewpoint, will find combinations which would escape the Cabalist. The people of the countryside see a rake in the belt and sword of Orion; a Hebrew Cabalist sees in that same Orion, considered in its entirety, all the mysteries of Ezekiel, the ten sephiroth disposed in ternary form, a central triangle

---

466   French scholar Bernard de Montfaucon (1655–1741).

467   German author and mystic Karl von Eckartshausen (1752–1803).

468   The divinatory art of geomancy uses sixteen figures formed of single and double points, which are constructed by one of an assortment of random methods. Very popular in the Middle Ages and Renaissance, it was scarcely remembered by Lévi's time, but is undergoing a revival at present.

formed of four stars and then a line of three forming the yod, and the two figures together expressing all the mysteries of the Bereshith, then four stars forming the wheels of Merkabah and completing the divine chariot. By looking at it in another manner and by placing other ideal lines, he will see a ‎ג‎, gimel, perfectly formed and placed above a ‎י‎, yod, in a large ‎ד‎, daleth, upturned; a figure which represents the fight between good and evil, with the definitive triumph of good. In effect, the ‎ג‎, founded on the yod, is the ternary produced by the unitary, it is the manifestation of the divine Verb, while the upturned daleth is the ternary composed by the evil binary multiplied by itself. The figure of Orion, considered thus, would be identical to the angel Michael battling against the dragon, and the apparition of this sign, presented in this form, would, for the Cabalist, presage victory and happiness.

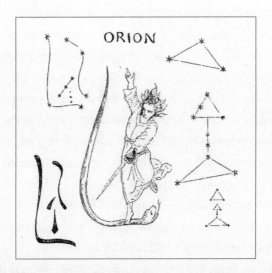

A long contemplation of the sky exalts the imagination; the stars then respond to our thoughts. The lines traced mentally from one to another star by the first people to contemplate them must have given man his first ideas of geometry. Depending on whether our soul is agitated or calm, the stars seem to be glaring with threats or scintillating with hopes. The sky is thus the mirror of the human soul, and when we believe ourselves to be reading in the stars, it is ourselves that we are reading.

Gaffarel, when applying the predictions of celestial writing to the destiny of empires, says that the ancients did not draw all the signs of evil omens in the northern part of the sky in vain, and that for all time, calamities were regarded as having come from the north to spread over the earth by invading the south.

"It is for this reason," says he, "that the ancients figured on these northern parts of the sky a serpent or a dragon right beside the bears, because these animals are the true hieroglyphs of tyranny, of pillage and all type of oppression. And in fact, go through the annals, and you will see that all the great devastations which ever occurred came from the north. The Assyrians or Chaldeans, animated by Nebuchadnezzar and Shalmaneser, had often shown the truth of this with the burning of a temple and a city, the most sumptuous and the most holy in the universe, and with the complete ruin of a people who God himself had provided with his singular protection, and for whom he said he was their particular father. And that other Jerusalem, the good Rome, had she not also often been tested by the furies of that wicked northern race, when, by the cruelties of Alaric, Genseric, Attila, and the rest of the Gothic princes, Huns, Vandals, and Alans, she saw her altars upturned and the summits of her superb edifices razed to the ground. . . . Very well, then, in the secrets of this celestial writing, we read on the northern side evil and misfortune, since *a septentrione pandetur omne malum*.[469] Yet the Verb תפתח, which we translate by *pandetur*, also means *depingetur* or *scribetur*,[470] and the prophecy also means: all the evils of the world are written in the northern part of the sky."

We transcribed this entire passage from Gaffarel because it is not without resonance in our time, where the north seems to menace Europe again;[471] but it is also the destiny of cold fogs to be vanquished by the Sun, and the darkness must dissipate on its own when it arrives in the light. There for us is the last word of prophecy and the secret of the future.

Gaffarel also adds a few other predictions drawn from the stars, that for example of the gradual weakening of the Ottoman Empire—but, as we have al-

---

469   Latin: "From the north is revealed (or comes forth) all evil." This is the Latin text of Jeremiah 1:14.

470   The Latin words mean respectively "is spread out," "is portrayed," and "is written."

471   This passage was written before the Crimean War. (Lévi's note.)

ready said, the figures of these constellated letters are relatively arbitrary. He declares, for the rest, to have borrowed these predictions from a Hebrew Cabalist called Rabbi Chomer, which he does not flatter himself by claiming to understand well.

Here is the table of magical characters which were drawn by the ancient astrologists following the zodiacal constellations; each of these characters represents the name of a good or bad spirit. We know that the signs of the Zodiac deal with diverse celestial influences and in consequence express an annual alternation between good and evil.

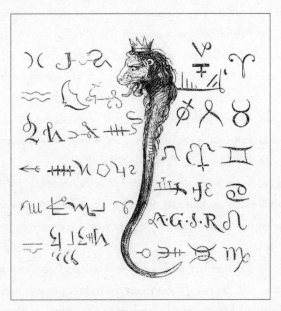

THE NAMES OF THE SPIRITS
DESIGNATED BY THESE CHARACTERS ARE:

For Aries, SATAARAN and Sarahiel;

For Taurus, BAGDAL and Araziel;

For Gemini, SAGRAS and Saraiel;

For Cancer, RAHDAR and Phakiel;

For Leo, SAGHAM and Seratiel;

For Virgo, IADARA and Schaltiel;

For Libra, GRASGARBEN and Hadakiel;

For Scorpio, RIEHOL and Saissaiel;

For Sagittarius, VHNORI and Saritaiel;

For Capricorn, SAGDALON and Semakiel;

For Aquarius, ARCHER and Ssakmakiel;

For Pisces, RASAMASA and Vacabiel.

The sage who wishes to read the sky must also observe the days of the Moon, whose influence is very great in astrology. The Moon by turns attracts and repels the magnetic fluid of the Earth, and it is thus that is produced the flux and reflux of the sea: one must therefore know the phases well and know how to discern the days and the hours. The new moon is favorable for beginning all magical works: from the first quarter to the full moon, its influence is hot; from the full moon to the last quarter, its influence is dry; from the last quarter until the end, its influence is cold.

Here now are the special characters for all the days of the Moon, marked by the twenty-two keys of the Tarot and with the signs of the seven planets:[472]

---

472 Lists of the days of the moon, each of which had its distinctive fortune or misfortune, were a commonplace in French folklore from ancient times through the early twentieth century. It was very common for each to be associated with some character from the Bible.

1. *The Magician or Magus.*

   The first day of the Moon is that of the creation of the Moon itself. This day is consecrated to initiatives of the spirit and should be favorable for good innovations.

2. *The Priestess, or occult science.*

   The second day, whose spirit is Enediel, was the fifth day of creation, since the Moon was made on the fourth day. The birds and the fish, which were created on this day, are the living hieroglyphs of the magical analogies and of the universal doctrine of Hermes. Water and air, which were then filled with the forms of the Verb, are the elementary figures of the Mercury of the sages, that is to say intelligence and speech. This day is favorable for revelations, initiations, and great scientific discoveries.

3. *The celestial mother or the Empress.*

   The third day was that of the creation of man. Also, the Moon, in the Cabala, is called MOTHER, when we represent it accompanied with the number three. This day is favorable for generation and more generally for all types of production, either of the body or the spirit.

4. *The Emperor, or the dominator.*

   The fourth day is ill-fated: it was that of the birth of Cain; but it is favorable for unjust and tyrannical undertakings.

5. *The Pope, or the Hierophant.*

   The fifth day is fortunate: it was the day of Abel's birth.

6. *The Lovers, or liberty.*

   The sixth day is the day of pride: it was the day of Lamech's birth, the one who said to women: I killed a man who had hit me and a young man who had hurt me. Cursed is he who would attempt to punish me! This day is favorable for conspiracies and revolts.

7. *The Chariot.*

   On the seventh day, birth of Hebron, he who gave his name to the first of the holy cities of Israel. Day of religion, of prayers, and of success.

8. *Justice.*

   The murder of Abel. Day of expiation.

9. *The old man or the Hermit.*

   The birth of Methuselah. Day of benediction for children.

10. *Ezekiel's wheel of fortune.*

    The birth of Nebuchadnezzar. Reign of the beast. Ill-fated day.

11. *Strength.*

    The birth of Noah. The visions on this day will be misleading, but it is a day of good health and longevity for children born on it.

12. *The sacrificed, or the Hanged Man.*

    The birth of Samuel. Prophetic and Cabalistic day, favorable for the accomplishment of the Great Work.

13. *Death.*

    The day of the birth of Canaan, the cursed son of Ham. Ill-fated day and fatal number.

14. *The angel of Temperance.*

    The benediction of Noah, the fourteenth day of the Moon. This day is presided over by the angel Cassiel from Uriel's hierarchy.

15. *Typhon or the Devil.*

    Birth of Ishmael, day of condemnation and exile.

16. *The stricken tower.*

    The day of the birth of Jacob and Esau and of Jacob's predestination as the ruin of Esau.

17. *The sparkling Star.*

    The fire of heaven burns Sodom and Gomorrah. Day of salvation for the good and ruin for the wicked, dangerous if it falls on a Saturday. It is under the reign of Scorpio.

18. *The Moon.*

    Birth of Isaac, triumph of the wife. Day of conjugal affection and good hope.

19. *The Sun.*

Birth of Pharaoh. Lucky or fatal day for the greatness of the world, depending on the differing merits of great men.

20. *Judgment.*

Birth of Jonah, the organ of God's judgments. Favorable day for divine revelations.

21. *The World.*

Birth of Saul, material royalty. Danger for the mind and reason.

22. *Influence of Saturn.*

Birth of Job. Day of trials and suffering.

23. *Influence of Venus.*

Birth of Benjamin. Day of fondness and of tenderness.

24. *Influence of Jupiter.*

Birth of Japheth.

25. *Influence of Mercury.*

Tenth Egyptian plague.

26. *Influence of Mars.*

Deliverance of the Israelites and the crossing of the Red Sea.

27. *Influence of Diana or of Hecate.*

The resounding victory of Judas Maccabeus.

28. *Influence of the Sun.*

Samson carries off the Gates of Gaza. Day of strength and of deliverance.

29. *The Tarot Fool.*

Day of abrogation and lack of success in all things.

With this rabbinical table, which Jean Belot and others borrowed from the Hebrew Cabalists, we can see that the ancient masters had concluded a posteriori that things had probable influences, which is completely within the logic of the occult sciences. We also see how much the diverse significations are enclosed in the twenty keys which form the alphabet of the Tarot, and the truth of our assertions, when we claim that all the secrets of the Cabala and of magic, all the mysteries of the ancient world, all the science of the patriarchs, all the historical traditions from primordial times, are enclosed in this hieroglyphic book of Thoth, of Enoch, or of Cadmus.

A very simple way of finding celestial horoscopes through onomancy[473] is the one we will now describe; it reconciles Gaffarel with us and can provide very startlingly exact and profound results.

During the day, take a black card in which you will cut out the letters of the name of the person for whom you are consulting; place this card at the end of a tube which is thinned on the side facing the observer's eye and larger at the side where the card is; then you will look alternatively at the four cardinal points, starting with the east and finishing with the north. You will take note of all the stars you see through the letters, then you convert the letters of the name into numbers and with the sum of their addition cut out in the same manner, you renew the operation; you will count how many stars you have; then, adding this number to that of the number of the name, you will add again and you will cut out the total of the two numbers in Hebrew characters. You will then renew the operation, and you take note of the stars which you had encountered; then you will look up in a celestial planisphere the names of all the stars; you will make a classification according to their size and brilliance; you will choose the largest and most brilliant as the polar star of your astrological operation; you will then consult an Egyptian planisphere (a relatively complete and well-engraved one is found in the atlas of the large work by Dupuis), and you look for the names and the figures of the spirits who belong to those stars. You will then know which signs are lucky or unlucky that enter into the name of the person and what their influence will be, either in childhood (that is the name traced in the east), or during their youth (that is the name of the south), or in adulthood (that is the name of the west), or in old age (that is the name of the north), or finally during an entire life (that is the stars which will enter into the whole number formed by the addition of the letters and the stars). This astrological operation is simple, easy, and requires little calculation; it is brought

---

473   Divination by name.

to us from the oldest antiquity and obviously belongs, as we can be convinced by studying the works of Gaffarel and his master Rabbi Chomer, to the primordial magic of the ancients.

This onomantic astrology was the one used by all the ancient Hebrew Cabalists, as is proven by their observations, which were conserved by Rabbi Chomer, Rabbi Kapol, Rabbi Abujan[474] and other masters of the Cabala. The threats the prophets made to various empires of the world were founded on the characters of the stars that they found vertically above them in the regular relationship of the celestial sphere with the terrestrial sphere. It is thus that in the writing in the sky itself we see the name of Greece in Hebrew, יון or יון, and in translating it into numbers they found the word חרב, which signifies ruined, desolate.

חרב

2 2 8

Charab = Destroyed, Desolate

Sum: 12

יון

5 6 4

Yavan = Greece

Sum: 12

They conclude from this that after a cycle of twelve periods, Greece will be desolate and ruined.[475]

A little before the fire and the destruction of the temple of Jerusalem by Nebuzaradan, the Cabalists noted vertically above the temple eleven stars disposed like this:

---

474 These figures were cited by Gaffarel in the book referenced by Lévi. The names are somewhat garbled and have proven difficult to identify with actual Jewish writers.

475 This is an example of the Cabalistic practice known as Gematria. Each Hebrew letter corresponds to a number; the letters in יון, *Yavan* (Greece), add up to twelve and so do the letters in חרב (*charab*), "destroyed" or "desolate."

and which all enter into the word הבשיח, written from the north to the occident as: *Hibshich*, which means reprobation and abandonment without mercy. The sum of the numbers of the letters is 423, exactly the time the temple lasted.

The empires of Persia and Assyria were threatened with destruction by the four vertical stars which entered in the three letters רוב, *Rob*, and the fatal number indicated by the letters was 208 years.

Four stars also announced to the Cabalist rabbis of that time the fall and division of Alexander's empire, by arranging themselves in the word פרד, *parad*, to divide, whose number, 284, indicates the entire duration of that kingdom, either for its root or for its branches.

According to Rabbi Chomer, the destinies of the Ottoman power in Constantinople were fixed in advance and announced by four stars, which, arranged in the word כאה, *caah*, signify to be weak, sick, to be close to one's end. The stars which, in the letter א, were brighter, indicate a large א and give the value 1,000 to this letter. The three letters together make 1,025, which one must start counting since Constantinople was taken by Mehmed II, a calculation which promises a few more centuries of existence to the weak empire of the sultans, now supported by all of Europe.[476]

The "MENE TEKEL UPHARSIN" that Belshazzar, in his drunkenness, saw written on the wall of his palace by the rays of the torches, was an onomantic intuition like that of the rabbis.[477] Belshazzar, no doubt initiated by the Hebrew seers in the reading of the stars, operated instinctively and without thinking on the lamps of his nocturnal celebration as he could have done with the stars in the sky. The three words which he had formed in his imagination would soon become indelible in his eyes and make all the lights of his celebration pale. It was not dif-

---

476   Unfortunately for Rabbi Chomer's reputation as a prophet, the Ottoman Empire collapsed in 1918.

477   Daniel 5:25–28.

ficult to predict a fate similar to that of Sardanapalus[478] for a king who, in a besieged city, abandoned himself to orgies. We have said, and we repeat as a conclusion to this chapter; that magnetic intuitions are alone what give value and reality to all these Cabalistic and astrological calculations, they are perhaps puerile and completely arbitrary if done without inspiration, through cold curiosity and without a powerful will.

---

478   Legendary last king of Assyria, whose decadence led to the fall of that kingdom.

CHAPTER XVIII

POTIONS AND MAGNETISM

Let us now travel to Thessaly, the country of enchantments. It is here that Apuleius was fooled like Ulysses's companions and was subjected to a shameful transformation. Here everything is magic, from the birds that fly and the insects that buzz in the grass to the trees and the flowers; here, under the light of the Moon, the poisons which make one fall in love are composed; here the stryges invent charms which render one young and beautiful like Charites. Young men, beware.

In effect, the art of poisoning reason or of potions seem, according to the traditions, to have developed their venomous efflorescence more in Thessaly than anywhere else; but here again magnetism played the most important role, because excitatory or narcotic plants, cursed and unhealthy animal substances, take all their power from enchantments, that is to say the sacrifices accomplished by witches and the words they pronounced while preparing their potions and drinks.

Stimulating substances and those which contain more phosphorus[479] are natural aphrodisiacs. All that acts intensely upon the nervous system can cause passionate overexcitement, and if a clever and persevering will knows how to direct and influence these natural dispositions, she will make use of the passions

---

479   Nineteenth-century dieticians believed that a diet high in phosphorus stimulated the nervous system.

of others for the benefit of her own, and soon reduce the proudest of persons into becoming, within a given time, the instruments of her pleasures.

It is through a similar influence that one can protect oneself, and it is to provide weapons for the weak that we write this chapter.

First, here are the practices of the enemy:

He who wishes to make someone fall in love with him (we only attribute such illegitimate maneuvers to a man, on the assumption that a woman never has the need to do so), he, then, who wishes to make someone love him must first have himself be noticed and produce some kind of impression upon the imagination of the person he desires. He should strike her with admiration, surprise, or terror, or even horror if that is his only resource; but he must at all cost rise above the rank of common men for her and take, by will or by force, a place in her memories, in her apprehensions, and in her dreams. A Lovelace is certainly not the avowed ideal of the Clarissas of this world,[480] but they think unceasingly about censuring them, cursing them, feeling sorry for their victims, desiring their conversion and their repentance, and then they wish for them to be regenerated through devotion and pardon; and then a secret vanity tells them that it would be nice to attract the love of a Lovelace, to love him and to resist him. And there you have Clarissa, who surprises herself by loving a Lovelace; she blames herself for her love, she blushes, she renounces her love a thousand times, only to love a thousand times more; and then, when the supreme moment arrives, she forgets to resist him.

If angels were also women, as they are represented in modern mysticism, then Jehovah acted as a wise and prudent father when he kicked Satan out the gates of heaven.

It is a great disappointment for the self-esteem of certain honest women to find a man who is good and irreproachable at heart, but with whom they had become besotted by taking him for a rascal. The angel then scornfully leaves him while saying to him: You are not the devil!

Make yourself up then, as perfectly as possible as the devil, you who wish to seduce an angel.

---

480   The protagonist of the novel *Clarissa* by Samuel Richardson is seduced and abandoned by the rake Lovelace.

Nothing is permitted to a virtuous man. Who does he think he is? say the women; does he think we are less moral than he is? But they forgive a rascal everything, saying, "What more can you expect from such a being?"

The role of a man of great principles and of rigid character can only have power over women whom we never have any need to seduce; all the others without exception adore the bad guys.

It is the complete contrary with men, and it is this contrast which makes modesty the preserve of women: it is for them the first and most natural of coquetries.

One of the most distinguished, most kind and scholarly doctors of London, Dr. Ashburner,[481] was telling me, last year, that one of his clients, as they were leaving the house of a grand lady one day, said to him: "I have just received the strangest of compliments. The marquise of *** told me while looking me in the eye: 'Sir, you will not make me lower my head before your terrible gaze; you have the eyes of Satan.'" "Well well!" the doctor responded to him with a smile, "You no doubt threw yourself at her neck and kissed her?" "But no: I stood there surprised by this sudden rude remark." "Well! my dear friend, do not return to her house; you must certainly be lost to her heart now."

We say that quite commonly the office of the hangman is handed down from father to son. Hangmen have sons, then? No doubt, since they never lack for women. Marat had a mistress who loved him tenderly, he, the horrible leper; but he was also the terrible Marat, who made everyone tremble.

We could say that love, especially for women, is a veritable hallucination. For lack of some other senseless motive, love often is determined by the absurd. To cheat on Gioconda[482] in favor of a moneybags, the horror! Well! if it is such a horror, why not do it? It must be so agreeable from time to time to commit a little horror.

Given this transcendental knowledge of women, there is a second maneuver one can operate to attract her attention: this is to ignore her, or only to pay at-

---

481   John Archibald Ashburner (1793–1878), a well-known English spiritualist.

482   A reference to Victor Hugo's play *Angelo, Tyrant of Padua*, in which the male lead, Enzo, abandons the beautiful Gioconda for the rich Laura.

tention to her in a manner which humiliates her self-esteem, by treating her like a child and by throwing the idea of ever courting her very far away. Then the roles will change: she will do anything to tempt you, she will initiate you into the secrets which women keep, she will dress and undress before you while telling you things like this: "Between women," "between old friends," "I do not fear you," "you are not the man for me," and so on and so forth. Then she will observe your demeanor, and if she finds it calm, indifferent, she will be besides herself; she will approach you on any pretext, graze you with her hair, let her robe part slightly. . . . We have even seen them, in similar circumstances, putting themselves at risk of an assault, not through tenderness, but out of curiosity, impatience, and because they are *all worked up*.

A magician who has spirit needs no other love potions than these; he also disposes of flattering words, magnetic breath, a light but voluptuous touch, along with a sort of hypocrisy, as though he had not planned it. The users of love potions must be old, stupid, ugly, impotent; so what good is a potion? Any man who is truly a man always has at his disposition the means to make himself loved, as long as he is not trying to occupy a place that is already taken. It would be supremely maladroit to attempt a conquest with a young married woman during the sweetness of her honeymoon or a strengthened Clarissa who already has her Lovelace, who renders her unhappy or whose love she bitterly reproaches.

We will not speak here about the dirty tricks of black magic regarding potions; we have finished with the kitchens of Canidia. We can see in the *Epodes* of Horace how this abominable Roman witch composed poisons, and we can, regarding the sacrifices and enchantments of love, reread the *Eclogues* of Theocritus and of Virgil,[483] where ceremonies of this sort of magical work are described in detail. We will not transcribe here the recipes of either the grimoires or of the *Petit Albert*, which everyone can consult. All of the different practices have to do with magnetism or poisonous magic and are either naive or criminal. The drinks which weaken the spirit and trouble reason can assure the already conquered

---

483   The *Epodes* of Horace, the *Eclogues* of Virgil, and the *Bucolica* of Theocritus are collections of poems from the ancient world, which discuss witchcraft among many other things.

empire of a wicked will, and it is thus that the Empress Caesonia fixed, they say, the ferocious love of Caligula. This is why one must avoid all distillations which taste of almonds, and keep away from the bedroom cherry laurel and datura, almond soaps, almond milks, and in general all perfume compositions where the odor of almonds dominates, especially if its effect on the brain is seconded by amber.

To reduce the action of intelligence is to augment in equal proportion the opposing forces of mad passion. Love of the type which evildoers wish to inspire, and of which we speak here, is a veritable stultification and the most shameful of all types of moral servitude. The more we annoy a slave, the more we render him incapable of liberating himself, that is the true secret of Apuleius's sorceress and the drinks of Circe.

The use of tobacco, either sniffed or smoked, is a dangerous auxiliary to stupefying potions and poisonings of reason. Nicotine, as we know, is no less violent a poison than prussic acid, and this acid is found in greater quantity in tobacco than in almonds.[484]

The absorption of a will by another often changes a whole series of destinies, and it is not only for our own sakes that we should watch over our relations and learn to discern between pure and impure atmospheres: because true potions, the most dangerous potions, are invisible; they are currents of the radiating vital light which, by mixing and exchanging with each other, produce attractions and sympathies, for which magnetic experiments leave no room to doubt.

The history of the Church speaks of a heresiarch named Marcus,[485] who rendered all the women mad for him by blowing on them; but his power was destroyed by a courageous Christian woman who blew on him first, while saying to him: May God be your judge!

The priest Gaufridi, who was burned as a sorcerer, claimed to make any woman who was touched by his breath fall in love with him.

The all too famous Father Girard, Jesuit, was accused by the damsel Cadière,

---

484   "Prussic acid" is an old term for hydrogen cyanide. Lévi is quite correct that this compound is present in tobacco.

485   A gnostic teacher of the second century CE.

her confessor, of having made her totally lose her judgment by blowing on her. She well needed that excuse to attenuate the horror and ridicule of her accusations against this father, whose culpability has otherwise never been proven but who, for good or evil, had certainly inspired a shameful passion in that miserable girl.

"Mlle Ranfaing, having become a widow in 16——," says Dom Calmet[486] in his *Treatise on Apparitions*, "was courted by a doctor called Poirot. Having been rejected by her, he then gave her potions to make himself loved, which caused strange disturbances in Mlle Ranfaing's health. Soon such extraordinary things happened to this lady, that it was believed that she was possessed, and the doctors declared that they could not understand anything regarding her state, and recommended her to the exorcisms of the Church.

"After which, by order of M. de Porcelets, bishop of Toul, they sent her to the exorcist M. Viardin, doctor in theology and state councilor to the Duke of Lorraine, a Jesuit and a Capuchin; but during the course of this exorcism, almost all the clergymen in Nancy, the above-mentioned lord bishop, the bishop of Tripoli, suffragan of Strasbourg, M. de Sancy, ambassador for the very Christian king in Constantinople and at that time the priest of the Oratory, Charles de Lorraine, bishop of Verdun, two doctors from the Sorbonne sent expressly to assist in the exorcism often exorcised her in Hebrew, Greek, and in Latin, to which she always responded pertinently, she who could barely read Latin.

"We refer to the certificate provided by Nicolas de Harley, very skilled in the Hebrew language, who recognizes that Mlle Ranfaing was truly possessed and responded to him only through the movement of his lips, without him actually pronouncing any words, and that she provided him with several proofs of possession. Sir Garnier, doctor of the Sorbonne, also having given her several commands in the Hebrew language, claims she responded to him in a pertinent manner, but in French, saying that the agreement was that he speak only in ordinary language. The demon then added: 'Is it not enough that I show you that I hear what you say?' This same Garnier, speaking to her in Greek, replaced one case by another due to inattention. The possessed, or rather the devil, tells him:

---

486   French Catholic priest and scholar Antoine Augustin Calmet (1672–1757). He wrote on many subjects, including apparitions and vampires.

'You have failed.' The doctor tells her in Greek: 'Show me my failure.' The devil responds: 'Content yourself with the fact that I point out your fault; I will not tell you more.' The doctor having told her to be quiet in Greek, she responds to him with: 'You command me to be quiet, and I do not wish to shut up.'"

This remarkable example of hysterical illness brought right up to ecstasy and demonomania after the administration of a potion by a man who thought of himself as a sorcerer, shows better than anything we could say the action of the omnipotence of the will and the imagination on one person and another, and the strange lucidity of ecstatics or hypnotics, who understand speech by reading thoughts without having knowledge of the words. I do not in any way doubt the sincerity of the witnesses named by Calmet; I am merely surprised that such serious men had not remarked upon the difficulty this so-called demon had in responding to them in a language unknown to the patient. If their interlocutor was indeed what they meant by a demon, she would not only have understood Greek, but she would have also spoken Greek: it would not have been any more difficult to do one as the other for such a scholarly and clever spirit.

Dom Calmet does not stop there with the story of Mlle Ranfaing; he recounts a whole series of insidious questions and not very serious injunctions on the part of the exorcists, and a series or responses which are more or less incongruous from the poor patient, still ecstatic and hypnotized. This good father does not neglect to refer to the luminous conclusions of the equally good Count de Mirville. That which occurred having been above the intelligences of the witnesses, they must conclude that all of it was the works of hell. What a beautiful and scholarly conclusion! The more serious aspect of the whole affair is that the doctor, Poirot, was put on trial as a magician, inevitably confessed under torture, and was burned. If he had really, with whatever potion, attacked the reason of that woman, he would have merited being tried as a poisoner: this is all that we can say about it.

But the most terrible potions are the mystic exaltations of ill-intentioned devotion. What impurities could ever equal the nightmares of Saint Anthony and the torments of Saint Teresa and of Saint Angela of Foligno?[487] This last person applied

---

487   Three saints who, according to Catholic teaching, were repeatedly assailed by demons representing the lusts of the flesh.

a red hot iron to her rebellious flesh and found that the material fire was a coolant for her hidden ardors. With what violence does nature need to be treated when we refuse it by continually thinking that we detest it! It is through mysticism that began the so-called bewitchment of Madeleine Bavent, of Mlle de la Palud, and Mlle Cadière.[488] The excessive fear of a thing renders it almost always inevitable. In following the two curves of a circle, one arrives and one meets at the same point. Nicolas Remigius,[489] a criminal judge in Lorraine, who had eight hundred women burned alive as witches, saw magic everywhere: it was his idée fixe, his madness. He wanted to preach for a crusade against sorcerers, with which he believed Europe was full; in desperation for not being believed on his word when he claimed that almost everyone was guilty of magic, he ended up declaring that he himself was a sorcerer and was burnt at the stake by his own confession.

To protect oneself from negative influences, the first condition is to not allow one's imagination to become enthused. All fanatics are more or less mad, and one dominates a madman by taking him by his folly. Place yourself, then, above puerile fears and vague desires; believe in supreme wisdom; be convinced that this wisdom, having given you intelligence as the unique means of knowing, cannot wish to set traps for your intelligence and your reason. You see all around you effects proportionate to their causes, you see causes which are directed and modified in man's domain by intelligence; in summary, you see good as being stronger and more esteemed than evil: why would you suppose an immense unreason within the infinite, since there is reason in the finite? The truth hides from no one. God is visible through his works, and he demands nothing of his creatures which is against their nature, of whom he is their author. Faith is confidence; have confidence, not in men who speak badly of reason, because they are madmen and impostors, but in the eternal reason which is the divine Verb, that veritable light offered like the sun to the intuitions of all human creatures of this world.

If you believe in absolute reason and if you desire more than anything else

---

488   Nuns whose apparent cases of demonic possession led to famous witchcraft trials in seventeenth- and early eighteenth-century France.

489   Also known as Nicholas Rémy, a fanatical witch hunter in sixteenth-century France, who was responsible for the execution of some nine hundred persons suspected of witchcraft. Lévi's account of his death seems to be apocryphal, unfortunately.

truth and justice, you need not fear anyone, and you will love only those who are kind. Your natural light will instinctively repulse the wicked, because they will be dominated by your will. Thus even venomous substances which could be administered to you will not affect your intelligence. They might render you sick, but they will never make you a criminal.

What mostly contributes to rendering women irrational is the flaccid and hypocritical education they are given. If they did more mental work, if they were taught about the world in a more frank and liberal manner, they would be less capricious, less vain, less futile, and in consequence less accessible to evil seductions. Weakness always sympathizes with vice, because vice is a weakness which only gives the appearance of being powerful. Folly is horrified by reason and takes pleasure in all that is exaggeration and lies. Heal first the intelligence of the sick person. The cause of all enchantments, the venom in all potions, the power of all sorcerers is found there.

As to narcotics or other poisons which may have been administered to you, that is a matter for medicine and the law; but we do not think that such enormities occur very often in our day. The Lovelaces need not lull the Clarissas to sleep by any means except their gallantries and alcoholic drinks. Like abductions by masked men and captivities in caves, which are no longer appropriate even in our modern novels, one must relegate all the rest to the confessionals of dark penitents or to the ruins of the Castle of Udolpho.[490]

---

490   The castle of Udolpho was the setting for Ann Radcliffe's *The Mysteries of Udolpho* (1794), a famous gothic novel in its time.

CHAPTER XIX

THE MAGISTERY OF THE SUN

We arrive at the number which in the Tarot is marked by the Sun. The denary of Pythagoras and the ternary multiplied by itself represent wisdom applied to the absolute. It is thus of the absolute which we will speak about here.

To find the absolute in the infinite, in the indefinite, and in the finite—such is the Great Work of the sages and what Hermes called the work of the Sun.

To find the unwavering foundations of the true religious faith in philosophical truth and metallic transmutation is Hermes's entire secret; it is the philosopher's stone.

This stone is one and many; it is decomposed through analysis and recomposed through synthesis. Through analysis, it is a powder, the powder of projection of the alchemists; before analysis and after synthesis, it is a stone.

The philosopher's stone, say the masters, should not be exposed to air or the gaze of the profane; one must always keep it hidden and conserve it with care, in the most secret place in one's laboratory, and always keep on one's person the key to the place where it is contained.

He who possesses the Grand Arcanum is a veritable king and more than a king, because he is inaccessible to all fears and vain hopes. For all the maladies of the soul and the body, a single fragment from the precious stone, a single fleck of the divine powder are sufficient to cure them. "He who hath an ear, let him hear!" as the Master said.[491]

Salt, sulfur, and mercury are but accessory elements and passive instruments in the Great Work. All depends, as we have said, on the internal *magnes* of Paracelsus. The work is entirely in the *projection*, and the projection is perfectly accomplished by an effective intelligence and realizable with a single word.

There is only one important operation in the work: it consists of *sublimation*, which is nothing other, according to Geber,[492] than the elevation of the thing which is dry through the means of fire, with adherence to its proper vessel.

He who wishes to attain the understanding of the great word and the possession of the Grand Arcanum must, after having meditated on the principles of our doctrine, carefully read the hermetic philosophers, and he will succeed in becoming initiated as others have before him; but he must take as the key to their allegories the unique doctrine of Hermes, contained in his Emerald Tablet, and follow, in order to classify the knowledge and direct the operation, the order indicated in the Cabalistic alphabet of the Tarot, whose entire and absolute explication we provide in the last chapter of this work.

Among the rare and precious books which contain the mysteries of the Grand Arcanum, one must count the Chemical Pathway, or Manual, by Paracelsus, which contains all the mysteries of demonstrative physics and of the most secret Cabala. This precious and original manuscript is only found in the Vatican's library. Sendivogius made a copy, which the Baron de Tschoudy used to compose the hermetic catechism contained in his work called *The Flaming Star*. This catechism, which we indicate to wise Cabalists as being a working substitute for the incomparable treatise by Paracelsus, contains all the true principles of the Great Work in a manner which is so satisfying and clear that one must totally lack any special intelligence regarding occultism in order to be unable to arrive at the absolute truth by meditating upon it.

---

491   In many places in the Gospels and the book of Revelation, e.g., Matthew 11:15 and
       13:16, Mark 4:9 and 7:16, Revelation 2:7, etc.

492   Jābir ibn Hayyān (c. 751–c. 851), the famous Arabic alchemist.

Raymond Lully, one of the great, sublime masters of the science, has said that to make gold one must first have some gold. Nothing can be made from nothing; one does not create wealth absolutely: one augments and multiplies. Thus aspirants of science well understand that one must not ask of the adept either sleights of hand or miracles. The hermetic science, like all real sciences, is mathematically demonstrable. Its results, even material ones, are as rigorous as those of a properly calculated equation.

The hermetic gold is not just a true doctrine, a light without shadows, a truth without alloy or lies; it is also material gold, real, pure, and the most precious gold that could be found in the mines of the Earth.

But living gold, living sulfur, or the true fire of the philosophers must be searched for in the house of mercury. This fire is fed by air; in order to express its attractive and expansive power, we cannot provide a better comparison than that of lightning, which is primarily a dry and terrestrial exhalation united with humid vapors, but which in exalting itself, coming into contact with the igneous nature, acts on the humidity which is inherent to it, which it attracts to itself and transmutes into its nature, after which it precipitates rapidly to the Earth, where it is attracted by a fixed nature similar to its own.[493]

These words, enigmatic in form, but clear in content, clearly express what the philosophers mean by their mercury which is fertilized by sulfur, which becomes the master and the regenerator of salt: it is the AZOTH, the universal magnesia, the great magical agent, the astral light, the light of life, fertilized by the power of the anima, by intellectual energy, which they compare to sulfur because of its affinities with the divine fire. As to salt, it is the absolute matter. All matter contains salt, and all salt can be converted to pure gold by the combined action of sulfur and of mercury, which sometimes act so rapidly that the transmutation can be done in an instant, in an hour, without tiring the operator and almost without cost; other times, due to more difficult circumstances and atmospheric conditions, the operation requires several days, several months, and sometimes even several years.

---

493   The idea that lightning was the explosion of vapors rising from the earth was standard from ancient times into the nineteenth century; Benjamin Franklin's identification of lightning as an electrical discharge took some decades to find universal acceptance.

As we have already said, there exists in nature two primary and essential laws which produce things by counterbalancing between each other to create the universal equilibrium: they are fixity and movement, analogous, in philosophy, to truth and invention, and, in absolute thought, to necessity and liberty, which are the very essence of God. The Hermetic philosophers give the word fixed to all that has weight, to everything which tends by its nature to rest centrally and be immobile; they call the volatile all which most naturally and voluntarily obeys the law of movement, and they form the stone of analysis, that is to say the volatilization of the fixed, and then of synthesis, that is to say the fixation of the volatile, that which they operate and apply to the fixed, which they call their salt, sulfurized mercury or the light of life directed and rendered all-powerful by a secret operation. They thus take possession of all of nature and their stone is found everywhere that there is salt, which means that no substance is foreign to the Great Work and that we can change to gold even what appears to be the most despicable and vile matter, which is true in the sense that, as we have said, they all contain the principiant salt, represented in our symbols by the cubic stone itself, as we can see in the symbolic and universal frontispiece of the keys of Basilius Valentinus.

To know how to extract the pure salt hidden in all matter is to possess the secret of the stone. This stone is thus a saline stone which the *od* or the universal astral light decomposes or recomposes; it is unique and multiple, because it can be dissolved like ordinary salt and be incorporated in other substances. Obtained through analysis, one could call it the *universal sublimation*; found through synthesis, it is the veritable *panacea* of the ancients, because it cures all maladies, either of the soul or of the body, and was called the medicine par excellence of all of nature. When, through initiation, one disposes of the absolute forces of the universal agent, one always has this stone at one's disposition because the extraction of the stone is then a simple and easy operation very distinct from projection or metallic realizations. This stone, in its sublimated state, should not be left in contact with the air of the atmosphere, which can partially dissolve it and make it lose its virtue. It is without danger, incidentally, to inhale its emanations. The sage prefers to keep it within its natural envelopes, in the knowledge that he can extract it in a single effort of his will and with a single application of the universal agent to its envelopes, which the Cabalists call husks. It is in order to express this law of prudence hieroglyphically that they gave their mercury, personified in Egypt by Hermanubis, the head of a dog, and to their sulfur, represented by the Baphomet of the Temple, or the prince of the Sabbath, that goat head which made the occult associations of the Middle Ages so decried.[494]

---

494   As to the mineral work, the raw matter is exclusively mineral, but it is not a metal. It is a metallized salt. This material is called vegetal because it resembles a fruit, and animal because it yields a sort of milk and a sort of blood. It alone contains the fire that must be used to dissolve it. (Lévi's note.)

CHAPTER XX

THAUMATURGY

We have defined miracles as the natural effects of exceptional causes.[495]

The immediate action of the human will on the body, or at least that action as exercised without visible means, constitutes a miracle in the physical realm.

The influence exercised upon wills or upon intelligences, either suddenly or in a given time, and capable of captivating thought, of changing the most fixed resolutions, of paralyzing the most violent passions, this influence constitutes a miracle in the moral realm.

The common error, with regard to miracles, is to see them as effects without causes, contradictions to nature, sudden fictions of the divine imagination; and we concede that a single miracle of this type would break the universal harmony and plunge us into a universe in chaos.

There are miracles that are impossible for God himself: they are absurd miracles. If God could be absurd even for an instant, neither he nor the world would exist the instant afterward. To expect of divine arbitrariness an effect whose cause we ignore or whose cause does not even exist is what is termed tempting God; it is to leap into the abyss.

God acts through his works: in heaven he operates through the angels, and

---

495   This and the following paragraphs are intended as a direct challenge to the En-
       lightenment claim, first made by British philosopher David Hume, that miracles
       are by definition violations of natural law and therefore cannot take place.

on Earth through men. Thus in the circle of action of angels, angels can do all which is possible for God to do; and in the circle of action of men, men also dispose of the divine omnipotence.

In the heaven of human conceptions, it is humanity who created God, and men think that God made them in his image because they make him in his.

The domain of man is all of corporeal and visible nature on Earth, and though he does not regulate the great celestial bodies and the stars, he can at least calculate their movements and measure the distance and identify his will by their influence; he can modify the atmosphere, act up to a certain point upon the seasons, cure and sicken his fellow men, preserve life and deal out death, and by preservation of life we even mean, as we have said, resurrection in certain cases.

The absolute in reason and in will is the greatest power which is given to man to attain, and it is through the means of this power with which he performs those things that the multitudes admire under the name of miracles.

The most perfect purity of intention is indispensable to the thaumaturge, and then he requires a favorable current and unlimited confidence.

The man who has managed to covet nothing and fear nothing is the master of everything. This is what is expressed by that beautiful allegory in the Gospels where we see the Son of God, thrice victorious over the impure spirit, being served in the desert by the angels.[496]

Nothing on earth can resist a reasonable and free will. When the sage says: I will, it is God himself who will, and all that he commands is accomplished.

It is the science and the confidence of the doctor which makes for the virtue of his remedies, and there exists no medicine more efficient and real than thaumaturgy.

But occult therapy is apart from all common medications. It uses most of all words, insufflations, and communicates by means of the will a varied virtue to the most simple substances: water, oil, wine, camphor, salt. The water of the homeopaths is truly a magnetized and enchanted water, which operates through

---

496   Matthew 4:11.

faith.[497] The energetic substances which they add in infinitesimal quantities are, in a manner of speaking, consecrations and are like the signs of the will of the doctor.

That which is commonly called charlatanism is a great means of real success in medicine if that charlatanism is skillful enough to inspire great confidence and form a circle of faith. In medicine most of all, it is faith which saves.

There is hardly a village which does not have its practitioner of occult medicine, and those people have almost everywhere an incomparably greater success than those doctors approved by some university. The remedies which they prescribe are often ridiculous or bizarre, and for that reason succeed all the more, because they insist upon and realize more faith on the part of the patients and the operators.

An old merchant friend of ours, a man of a strange character with highly exalted religious sentiments, after having retired from commerce, began practicing occult medicine for free through Christian charity in a *département* in France. He only employs oil, insufflations, and prayers. A trial where he was taken to court for the illegal exercise of medicine brought to public attention that, in the space of five years, ten thousand healings were attributed to him, and the number of believers was increasing unceasingly at a rate capable of seriously alarming all the doctors in the country.

We have seen in Mans a poor nun who was considered a little mad by local people, who cured all the sick people in the neighboring countryside with an elixir and a bandage of her own invention. The elixir was for internal illnesses and the bandage for external illnesses, and in this manner nothing escaped this universal panacea. The bandage never stuck to the skin except in those places where its application was necessary; everywhere else it rolled up and fell off on its own; at least this is what the good sister claimed and what her patients confirmed. This thaumaturgist was also taken to court for unlawful competition, since she

---

497   Homeopathic medicine, a common form of alternative medicine in Lévi's time, as it is today, uses extremely small doses of medically active compounds in water or lactose to treat diseases.

was reducing the number of clients of all the doctors in the countryside. She was then strictly cloistered, but soon afterwards they had to give her over to the zeal and the faith of the population. We have seen, on the day of consultations with Sister Jeanne-Françoise, the people of the countryside, having arrived the previous day, waiting for their turn, lying down at the door to the convent; they had slept on the ground and were only waiting for the good sister's elixir and bandage before returning home.

The remedy being the same for all maladies, it would seem that the good sister did not need to know what her patients suffered from. However, she listened to them with great attention, and did not administer her cure without knowledge of the cause. That was the magical secret. The direction of intention given to the remedy gave it its special virtue. The remedy was insignificant on its own. The elixir was flavored eau-de-vie mixed with the juices of bitter herbs: the bandage was covered with something similar to theriac judging by the color and odor: it was perhaps opiated Burgundy pitch.[498] Whatever the case, her cure worked marvels, and you would get into trouble with the people of the countryside if you ever suggested that you doubted the miracles of the good sister.

We knew near Paris an old thaumaturge gardener who also worked miraculous cures and who poured into his vials the juice of Saint John's Wort. This gardener had a brother of strong character who mocked the sorcerer. The poor gardener, unnerved by the sarcasms of this miscreant, then began to doubt himself: the miracles ceased, and the thaumaturge, deprived and despairing, died insane.

Father Thiers, priest of Vibraye, in his curious *Treatise on Superstitions*, reports that a woman, affected by an apparently incurable eye disease, having been suddenly and mysteriously cured, had come to confess to a priest about having taken recourse to magic. She had pestered a cleric whom she believed to be a magician for a long time to give her a sign to carry on her person, the cleric had finally given her a rolled parchment and told her to wash herself three times a day with cold water. The priest had her hand him this parchment, and found these

---

498   A commonly available over-the-counter remedy in Lévi's time, when opium had not yet been prohibited by law.

words written on it: Eruat diabolos oculos tuos et repleat stercoribus loca vacantia.[499] He translated these words for the good woman, who was stupefied; but she was no less cured.

Insufflation is one of the most important practices in occult medicine, because it is the perfect sign of the transmission of life. To inspire in fact means to blow on someone or something, and we already know, through the unique doctrine of Hermes, that the virtue of things created the words and that there is an exact proportion between ideas and words, which are the first forms and the verbal realizations of ideas.

Depending on whether the breath is hot or cold, it attracts or repulses. A hot breath corresponds to positive electricity, and a cold breath to negative electricity. Electric and nervous animals fear cold breath, as we can observe by breathing on a cat whose camaraderie is not welcome. If you gaze fixedly at a lion or a tiger and blow in their face, you would astonish them to the point of forcing them to retreat and back off before you.[500]

Hot and prolonged insufflation reestablishes the circulation of the blood, cures rheumatism and gout pains, reestablishes the equilibrium of the humors,[501] and dissipates lassitude. Coming from a good and pleasant person, it is a universal sedative. Cold insufflation calms pains which arise from congestion and fluidic accumulations. One must therefore alternate the two breaths, while observing the polarity of the human organism, and acting in an opposite manner on the two poles, which one submits, one after another, to a contrary magnetism. Thus, to cure an inflamed eye, one must warmly insufflate the healthy eye, and then practice cold insufflations on the irritated eye at a distance and proportion which is exactly the same as the hot breaths. Magnetic passes[502] themselves act like

---

499   Latin for, "May the devil pluck out your eyes and refill the empty places with shit."

500   Readers are not encouraged to attempt this experiment.

501   In traditional occult medicine, four subtle substances representing the four elements. In equilibrium the humors establish health and in imbalance bring sickness.

502   In Mesmer's system of animal magnetism, "passes"—that is, stroking movements of the hands, made several inches away from the patient's body—play an important role.

breath and are a real breath through transpiration and radiation of the interior air, all phosphorescent with vital light; slow passes are a hot breath which gathers and exalts the spirits; quick passes are a cold breath which disperses forces and neutralizes tendencies towards congestion. Hot breath must be done transversely or from bottom to top; cold breath has more strength if it is directed from top to bottom.

We do not only breathe through the nostrils and the mouth: the universal porosity of our body is a veritable respiratory apparatus, insufficient, no doubt, but very useful to life and health. The extremities of the fingers, where all the nerve endings are, radiate the astral light or draw it in depending on our will. Magnetic passes without physical contact are a simple and light breath; contact adds to that breath a sympathetic and balancing impression. Physical contact is good and even necessary for preventing hallucinations at the beginning of a hypnotism. It is a communion with physical reality, which informs the brain and returns an imagination which has gotten lost; but the contact should not be too prolonged when we only wish to magnetize. If absolute and prolonged contact is useful in certain cases, the actions one will exercise on the subject will be more similar to an incubation or a massage than to magnetism, properly speaking.

We have related examples of incubation taken from the most respected book of the Christians; these examples all have to do with the healing of lethargies reputed to be incurable, since we have agreed to call them resurrections. As to massage, it is still in great use among the Orientals, who practice it in their public baths, and which is found to be very beneficial. It is an entire system of rubbing, pulling, and pressing exercised at length and slowly on all the members and on all the muscles and whose result is a new equilibrium of forces, a feeling of complete relaxation and well-being with a very noticeable renewal of agility and vigor.

All the power of occult medicine is in the consciousness of the will, and all its art consists in producing faith in its patient. "If thou canst believe," said the Master, "all things are possible to him that believeth."[503] One must dominate the subject through physical expression, through tone of voice, through gesture; one

---

503   Mark 9:23.

must inspire confidence with a few paternal affections, loosen him up with a few pleasant and happy phrases. Rabelais, who was more of a magician than he appeared to be, made Pantagruelism into a special panacea.[504] He made the sick laugh, and all the remedies he used thereafter worked better on them; he established between his patients and himself a magnetic sympathy through which he communicated his confidence and his good humor; he flattered them in his prefaces by calling his patients very illustrious and very precious, and dedicating his books to them. We are also convinced that *Gargantua and Pantagruel* cured more black humors, more dispositions to folly, more arbitrary manias, in that era of religious hatred and civil wars, than the entire Faculty of Medicine could have observed and studied.

Occult medicine is essentially sympathetic. There must be a reciprocal affection or at least a sense of good will which is established between the doctor and the patient. Syrups and juleps have hardly any virtue on their own; they are what the common opinion between the agent and the patient make of them: homeopathic medicine completely leaves out both of them without any serious inconvenience. Oil and wine combined either with salt or with camphor could suffice as a bandage for all wounds and all exterior rubbing or sedative applications. Oil and wine are considered the best of medicines in the evangelical tradition. It is the balm of the Samaritan,[505] and in the Book of Revelation the prophet, in describing the great exterminations, begs the avenging powers to spare the oil and wine,[506] that is to say to leave some hope and a remedy for all those wounds. What we call amongst ourselves the extreme unction was among the first Christians, as was the intention of the apostle Saint James, who consigned the precept in his epistle to the faithful of the entire world, the pure and simple practice of the traditional medicine of the Master. "Is any sick among you?" he writes. Let him call for the elders of the Church: and let them pray over him, anointing him with oil in the

---

504 Rabelais's rollicking novel *Gargantua and Pantagruel* is among the funniest books ever penned. Whether or not Rabelais used the book in his medical career—he was a successful physician as well as a Catholic priest—Lévi's comment at the end of this paragraph is doubtless justified.

505 Luke 10:34.

506 Revelation 6:6.

name of the Lord."[507] This divine therapeutic was progressively lost, and people took on the habit of seeing extreme unction as a religious formality which is required before death. Nevertheless, the thaumaturgical virtue of the holy oil was not completely forgotten by the traditional doctrine, and it is mentioned in the passage in the catechism dealing with extreme unction.

What healed most of all among the first Christians was faith and charity. Most sicknesses have their source in moral disorders: one must begin by healing the soul, and the body will be easily healed thereafter.

507   James 5:14.

CHAPTER XXI

THE SCIENCE OF THE PROPHETS

This chapter is dedicated to divination.

Divination, in its widest meaning and according to the grammatical signification of the word, is the exercise of divine power and the realization of the divine science.

It is the priesthood of the mage.

But divination, according to general opinion, has especially to do with the knowledge of hidden things.

To know the most secret thoughts of men, to penetrate the mysteries of the past and the future, to evoke from century to century the rigorous revelation of effects through the exact science of causes: that is what is universally called divination.

Of all the mysteries of nature, the deepest is that of the heart of man, and yet nature does not allow the depths to be inaccessible. Despite the most profound dissimulation, despite the most clever politics, that mystery traces itself and allows a thousand revealing clues to be observed in the form of the body, in the light of glances, in movements, in gait, in the voice.

The perfect initiate does not even need these clues; he sees the truth in the light, he senses an impression which manifests the whole man to him, he traverses hearts with his gaze, and must even feign ignorance, so as to disarm the fears or the hatred of the wicked whom he knows all too well.

The man who has a bad conscience always believes that he is being accused or that he is under suspicion; if he recognizes himself in a line of collective satire, he will take the entire satire as referring to himself and complain loudly that he is being slandered. Always defiant, but as curious as he is fearful, he is for the mage like Satan in the parable or like those scribes who questioned Christ in order to tempt him.[508] Always opinionated and always weak, what he fears above all else is to recognize his wrongdoing. The past troubles him; the future terrifies him; he would like to compromise with himself and believe that he would be a good man under better conditions. His life is a continual battle between good aspirations and evil habits; he sees himself as a philosopher in the manner of Aristippus[509] or Horace,[510] accepting all the corruption of his century as a necessity to which he must submit; he distracts himself with a few philosophical pastimes and deliberately takes on the protective smile of Maecenas,[511] to persuade himself that he is not a simple exploiter of famine in complicity with Verres,[512] or in complaisance like Trimalchio.

Such men are always exploiters, even when they do good works. If they decide to make a donation for the public good, they postpone their good deed in order to gain more credit. This type of person, whom I am forced to describe, is not anybody in particular: it is a whole class of men, with whom the mage most often deals, especially in our century. The mage should mistrust them in the same manner that they mistrust everyone, because he will find in them the most unreliable of friends and the most dangerous of enemies.

The public exercise of divination cannot be, in our era, suitable to the character of a true adept, because he will often be obliged to have recourse to trickery

---

508 For example, Luke 20:19–26.

509 A minor Greek philosopher who argued that the pursuit of pleasure was the point of existence.

510 Quintas Horatius Flaccus, a famous Roman poet of the time of Augustus and author of the abovementioned *Eclogues*, who cultivated a relationship with the emperor and was at times little more than a cheerleader for the imperial regime.

511 The freedman and prime minister of the Roman emperor Augustus, who was a great patron of the arts and literature.

512 The corrupt and rapacious Roman governor of Sicily in 73–71 BCE, who was denounced by Cicero in a set of famous orations.

and sleight of hand in order to keep his clientele and astound his public. Professional seers always have spies who inform them of certain things relative to the personal life or habits of those who consult them. A telegraphy of signals is established between the antechamber and the consulting room; they give a client who they do not know and has come for the first time a number; they give them an appointment for another day and then have them followed; they talk with their doormen, their neighbors and their household servants, and in this manner they manage to acquire the details which will then astonish the naive and provide a charlatan with the esteem which should be reserved to sincere science and to conscientious divination.

Divination of events to come is only possible for those events whose realization are already in some way contained in their cause. The soul, looking through the entire nervous apparatus into the circle of the astral light which influences a man and receives an influence from him, the soul of the seer can embrace in a single intuition all the loves and hatreds that a man had aroused around himself; the seer can read his intentions and his thoughts, predict the obstacles he will encounter along his path, what violent death might await him; but he cannot predict his private, voluntary, and capricious determinations, from the moment which follows after the consultation, unless the craftiness of the seer itself prepares the accomplishment of the prophecy. For example, you say to a woman who is on the rebound and desires a husband, "You will go tonight or tomorrow night to this show, and, by a bizarre set of circumstances, this will result in your future marriage." You can be sure that, dropping all of her other affairs, this lady will go to the indicated show, will see a man who she will believe has noticed her, and then hope for a prompt marriage. If this marriage does not occur, do not worry, she will not blame you, because she will not wish to lose the hope for a new illusion, and she will return, on the contrary, to consult you assiduously.

We have said that the astral light is the great book of divination; those who have the aptitude to read in this book have it naturally or have acquired it. There are therefore two classes of seer, the instinctive and the initiated. It is for this reason that children, the ignorant, shepherds, even idiots, have more of a disposition for natural divination than scholars and intellectuals. David, a simple herdsman, was a prophet as Solomon, the king of the Cabalists and the mages, was after him. The perceptions of instinct are often as reliable as those of the science; the least clairvoyant in the astral light are those who reason the most.

Somnambulism is a state of pure instinct: also somnambulists have need to be directed by a seer of the science; skeptics and reasoners can only mislead them.

Divinatory vision only operates in a state of ecstasy, and to arrive at that state one must render doubt and delusion impossible by enchaining thought or putting it to sleep.

The instruments of divination are thus simply the means of magnetizing yourself and distracting yourself from the exterior light in order to render yourself attentive solely to the interior light. It is for this reason that Apollonius enveloped himself entirely in a coat of wool and in the darkness fixed his gaze on his navel. The magical mirror of du Potet[513] is an analogous means to that of Apollonius. Hydromancy[514] and visions in the thumbnail which is evenly trimmed and blackened[515] are varieties of the magical mirror. Perfumes and evocations numb thought; water or the color black absorb visual rays: and a dazzling glare is then produced, a vertigo, which is followed by a lucidity in the subjects who have a natural aptitude for it or who are suitably disposed to it.

Geomancy and cartomancy are other means of arriving at the same ends: combinations of symbols and numbers, being both fortuitous and necessary at the same time, give a relatively true image of the probabilities of destiny so that the imagination can see the realities occasioned by the symbols. The more that one's interest is excited, the greater the desire to see, the more complete the confidence in one's intuition, the clearer the vision will be. Casting geomantic points haphazardly or drawing cards thoughtlessly is to play at the lottery like children. Random draws are oracular only when they are magnetized by intelligence and directed by faith.

---

513   French occultist Jules Denis du Potet (1796–1881), whose occult manual *La magie dévoilée, ou Principes de science occulte* (1852) gives detailed instructions for making and using a magic mirror.

514   Divination by seeing visions in a bowl or cup of water.

515   A convenient and portable form of magic mirror.

Of all the oracles, the Tarot is the most surprising in its responses, because all the possible combinations of this universal key of the Cabala provide scientific and truthful oracles as their solutions. The Tarot was the unique book of the ancient mages; it is the primordial Bible, as we shall prove in the following chapter, and the ancients consulted it, just as the first Christians would later consult the Lots of the Saints, which is to say verses of the Bible drawn by chance and determined by thinking of a number.[516]

Mlle Lenormand,[517] the most famous of our modern seeresses, knew nothing of the science of the Tarot, or knew no more than Etteilla's explications, which are obscurities thrown at the light. She knew neither high magic nor the Cabala, and her head was stuffed with a misdirected scholarship, but she was intuitive by instinct, and that instinct was rarely wrong. The books she left behind are a sort of legitimistic mumbo jumbo laced with classical citations, but her oracles, inspired by the presence and magetism of her consultants, were often surprising. She was a woman for whom the natural affections of her sex were replaced by a burgeoning imagination and a wandering spirit. She lived and died a virgin, like the ancient Druidesses of the Ile de Sein.[518]

If nature had endowed her with some beauty, she would have easily, in past epochs, played in Gaul the role of a Melusine or a Veleda.[519]

The more you employ ceremonies in the exercise of divination, the more you excite your and your consultant's imaginations. The Conjuration of the Four, the prayer of Solomon, the magic sword used to dismiss phantoms can thus be suc-

---

516 The *sortes apostolorum*, or apostolic lots, was an oracular method much used by early Christians. The diviner, having selected a question, thought of two numbers, then opened the Bible at random and looked up the chapter and verse corresponding to those numbers in the book to which the Bible fell open. For example, if the numbers were nine and six and the Bible fell open to the book of Proverbs, Proverbs 9:6 would be the answer to the question.

517 French diviner Marie-Anne Lenormand (1772–1843), the most successful cartomancer in early nineteenth-century France and the author of several popular books on divination.

518 In Celtic times, nine virgin priestesses lived on this island.

519 Melusine was a legendary witch with serpents for legs; Veleda was a priestess and oracle among the barbarian Bructeri in the first century CE.

cessfully used; you must also evoke the spirit of the day and hour[520] in which you are operating and offer him his particular perfume; then you put yourself in magnetic and intuitive rapport with clients by asking them which animal they find sympathetic to and which they dislike, which flowers they like and which colors they prefer. Flowers, colors, and animals all have an analogical classification with the spirits of the Cabala. Those who like the color blue are idealists and dreamers; those who like red are materialists and prone to anger; those who like yellow are fantastical and capricious; lovers of green often have a mercantile or wily character; the friends of the color black are influenced by Saturn; pink is the color of Venus, etc. Those who like horses work hard and are of noble character, yet they are flexible and docile; the friends of dogs are loving and faithful; friends of cats are independent and libertines. Sincere people are afraid most of all of spiders; proud souls dislike the serpent; upright and delicate people cannot stand rats and mice; pleasure seekers have a horror for the toad, because toads are cold, solitary, hideous, and sad. Flowers have sympathies analogous to those of animals and colors, and since magic is the science of universal analogies, a single preference, a single disposition of a person, allows one to divine all the others. It is the application of Cuvier's analogical anatomy[521] to phenomena of the moral realm.

The physiognomy of the face and the body, the wrinkles on the forehead, the lines on the hands also furnish mages with precious clues. Metoposcopy and chiromancy have become sciences of their own, whose risky and purely conjectural observations, have been compared, discussed, and then united in a body of doctrine by Goclenius, Belot, Rampalle, Indagine, and Taisnier.[522] This last author's book is the most considerable and complete; it reunites and comments on the observations and conjectures of all the others.

---

520   Every hour of the day, as well as every day of the week, is traditionally ruled by one of the seven planets. Tables of the planetary hours can be found in many modern books on magic.

521   The great French anatomist Georges Cuvier (1769–1832) was famous for being able to identify and describe an entire animal, living or extinct, from a single bone due to his exhaustive knowledge of anatomical form.

522   Authors of treatises on metoposcopy and chiromancy from the Renaissance through the nineteenth century.

A modern observer, the Chevalier d'Arpentigny,[523] provided chiromancy with a new degree of certitude with his remarks on the analogies which really exist between a person's character and the form, either complete or in its details, of their hands. This new science was developed and refined since by an artist who is also a man of letters who is full of originality and finesse. The disciple had surpassed the master, and we have already cited the kind and spiritual Desbarolles as a veritable magician of chiromancy, one of the travelers whom the storyteller Alexandre Dumas likes to surround himself with in his cosmopolitan novels.

One must also ask the consultant about his habitual dreams: dreams are reflections of life, either interior or exterior. The ancient philosophers paid a great deal of attention to them, the patriarchs saw assured revelations in them, and the majority of religious revelations occurred in dreams. The monsters of hell are the nightmares of Christianity, and, as the author of *Smarra*[524] has remarked in a spiritual manner, never would the paintbrush or the chisel have produced such horrors if they had not been seen in dreams.

One should be wary of persons whose imagination habitually reflects horrors.

Temperament also manifests itself through dreams, and since temperament exercises a continual influence over life, it is necessary to know it well in order to make conjectures with certitude about the destiny of a person. Dreams of blood, of pleasure, and of light indicate a sanguinary temperament; dreams of water, of mud, of rain, of tears result from a more phlegmatic disposition; nocturnal fires, darkness, terrors, and phantoms belong to the bilious and to melancholics.

Synesius, one of the greatest Christian bishops of the first centuries, disciple of the pure and beautiful Hypatia, who was massacred by fanatics after having been the glorious teacher of that beautiful Alexandrian school of whose heritage Christianity should have partaken; Synesius, a lyrical poet like Pindar and Callimachus, religious as Orpheus, a Christian like Spyridon of Tremetousia, left a treatise on dreams which was commented upon by Cardano. We are little con-

---

523   Casimir d'Arpentigny (1791–1864), whose influential manual *La chirognomie* was published in 1839.

524   French novelist Charles Nodier (1780–1844).

cerned in our day with these magnificent researches into the spirit, because successive fantacisms have virtually forced the world to resign itself to scientific and religious rationalism. Saint Paul burned Trismegistus; Omar burned the disciples of Trismegistus and of Saint Paul. O persecutors! O arsonists! O mockers! when will you have finished your work of darkness and destruction?

Trithemius, one of the greatest mages of the Christian period, the irreproachable abbot of a Benedictine monastery, a scholarly theologian and teacher of Cornelius Agrippa, has left, among his unappreciated and invaluable works, a treatise entitled *De septum secundeis, id est intelligentiis sive spiritibus orbes post Deum moventibus.*[525] It is the key to all the ancient and new prophecies, and a mathematical means, easy and historical, of surpassing Isaiah and Jeremiah in the prediction of all great events to come. The author sketches out the philosophy of history and shares the existence of the entire world between the seven spirits of the Cabala. It is the greatest and widest interpretation that has ever been made regarding the seven angels of Revelation who appear by turns with trumpets then cups to spread the Verb and the realization of the Verb throughout the world. The reign of each angel is 354 years and 4 months. The first is Oriphiel, angel of Saturn, who began his reign on March 13 in the first year of the world (because the world, according to Trithemius, was created on the thirteenth of March): his reign was that of savagery and primitive night. Then came the empire of Anael, the spirit of Venus, which began on June 24 in the 354th year of the world; thus love became the preceptor of men; he created the family, and the family led to association and the primordial city. The first civilizers were poets inspired by love, and then through the exaltation of poetry, religion, fanaticism, and debauchery were produced, which later brought on the flood. And all of this lasted until the eighth month of the 708th year of the world, that is to say until the twenty-fifth of October, and then began the reign of Zachariel, angel of Jupiter, under whom men began to know and fight over ownership of the fields and habitations. It was the epoch of the foundation of cities and the delineation of empires; civilization and war were the consequences. Then the need for commerce was felt, and it was then

---

525   *On the Seven Secondary Causes: That is, On the Intelligences or Spirits That, after God, Move the Celestial Spheres.*

that, in the 1,063th year of the world, on February 24, that Raphael's reign began, the angel of Mercury, the angel of the science and the verb, the angel of intelligence and industry. And thus letters were invented.

The first language was hieroglyphic and universal, and the monument to it which still remains is the book of Enoch, of Cadmus, of Thoth, or of Palamedes, the Cabalistic clavicule later adopted by Solomon, the mystical book of Teraphim, the Urim and Thummim, the primordial Genesis of Zohar and Guillaume Postel, the mystical wheel of Ezekiel, the rota of the Cabalists, the Tarot of the mages and the Gypsies. It was then that the arts were invented and navigation was first attempted; relationships extended, needs were multiplied, and there soon arrived, that is to say on June 26 in the 1,417th year of the world, the reign of Samael, angel of Mars, epoch of the corruption of all men and the universal deluge. After a long breakdown, the world struggled to become reborn under Gabriel, angel of the Moon, who began his reign on March 28 in the 1,771st year of the world: it was then that Noah's family multiplied and repopulated all the areas of the Earth, after the confusion of Babel, up until the reign of Michael, angel of the Sun, which began on February 24 in the 2,126th year of the world, and it is to that era that one must ascribe the origin of the first dominations, the empire of the children of Nimrod, the birth of the sciences and religions on earth, the first conflicts between despotism and liberty.

Trithemius pursues this curious study across the ages and demonstrates over the same eras the return of ruin, then civilization renascent through poetry and love; empires reestablished by the family, aggrandized through commerce, destroyed by war, repaired by universal and progressive civilization, then absorbed by great empires, which are the syntheses of history. The work of Trithemius is, from this point of view, more universal and independent than that of Bossuet, and is an absolute key to the philosophy of history. His rigorous calculations go up to the month of November of the year 1879, the era of the reign of Michael and the foundation of a new universal kingdom. This kingdom has been prepared for by three and a half centuries of anguish and three and a half centuries of hope: epochs which coincide precisely with the sixteenth, seventeenth, eighteenth, and half of the nineteenth centuries of the lunar dusk and hope; with the fourteenth, thirteenth, twelfth, and half of the eleventh centuries with trials, ignorance, anguish, and the plagues of all of nature. We see then, after this calculation, that in 1879, that is to say in twenty-four years, a universal empire which will be founded and which will provide universal peace to the world.[526] This empire will be political and religious; it will provide a solution to all the problems stirred up in our day and will last for 354 years and 4 months; and then the reign of Oriphiel will return, that is to say an epoch of silence and of night. The next universal empire, being under the reign of the Sun, will belong to him who holds the keys to the Orient, which the princes from the four corners of the world fight over at this moment; but intelligence and action are, in the superior realms, the forces which govern the Sun, and the nation which today on Earth now has the initiative of intelligence and of life will also have the keys of the Orient and will found the universal kingdom. Perhaps it will have to suffer a crucifixion and a martyrdom analogous to those of the God-man; but, dead or alive among the nations, its spirit will triumph, and all the peoples of the world will recognize and follow the standard of France, always victorious or miraculously resuscitated. Such is the prophecy of Trithemius, confirmed by all our predictions and backed by our resolutions.

---

526 Lévi's patriotism and idealism here has overwhelmed his common sense. None of the previous eras ruled by Michael in Trithemius's scheme saw a universal empire, much less world peace.

CHAPTER XXII

THE BOOK OF HERMES

We arrive at the end of our work, and it is here that we must provide the universal key and have our last word.

The universal key of the magical arts is the key to all the ancient religious doctrines, the key to the Cabala and to the Bible, it is the Clavicle of Solomon.

This clavicle or little key, which was thought to be lost for centuries, we have found, and with it we have been able to open all the sepulchers of the ancient world, make the dead speak, see again in all their splendor the monuments of the past, understand the enigmas of all sphinxes, and penetrate into all sanctuaries.

Among the ancients, the use of this key was permitted only to the high priests, and they did not even entrust the secret to elite initiates. Nonetheless here is that key:

It was a hieroglyphic and numeral alphabet, expressing in characters and numbers a series of universal and absolute ideas; and then a scale of ten numbers multiplied by four symbols and linked together by twelve figures representing the twelve signs of the zodiac, plus four spirits, those of the four cardinal points.

The symbolic quaternary, figured in the mysteries of Memphis and Thebes[527] by the four forms of the sphinx, the man, the eagle, the lion and the bull, corresponded to the four elements of the ancient world and were represented by

---

527   Two of the great cities of ancient Egypt.

symbols: water, by the cup which is held by man or Aquarius; air, by the circle or halo which encircles the head of the celestial eagle; fire, by the wood which feeds it, by the tree which the heat of the Earth and of the Sun makes fructify, and finally by the scepter of royalty, of which the lion is the emblem; the Earth, by the sword of Mithra, who every year immolates the sacred bull and through its blood makes flow the sap which swells all the fruits of the Earth.

These four signs, with all their analogies, are the explication of the unique word hidden in all sanctuaries, the word which the bacchantes[528] seemed to divine in their drunkenness when in celebrating the feasts of Iacchus they exalted themselves until delirium for IO EVOHE![529] What then did this mysterious word mean? It was the name of the four primordial letters in the mother language: the YOD, symbol of the vine stock, or the scepter of the paternal Noah; the HEH, image of the cup of libations, sign of divine maternity; the VAU, which united the two preceding signs together, and which has as a symbol in India the great and mysterious lingam. Such was, in the divine word, the triple sign of the ternary; and then the maternal letter appeared a second time to express the fecundity of nature and woman, and also to formulate the doctrine of universal and progressive analogies descending from causes to effects and ascending from effects back to the causes. Note that they did not pronounce the sacred word; they spelled it and said it in four words, which are the four sacred words: YOD HEH VAU HEH.

The scholar Gaffarel does not doubt that the Teraphim of the Hebrews, through the means of which they consulted the oracles of urim and thummim, were the figures of the four animals of the Cabala, whose symbols were summarized, as we shall soon explain, by the sphinx or cherubim of the Ark. But he cites, in regards to the usurped teraphim of Micah,[530] a curious passage by Philo Judaeus which is an entire revelation on the ancient and sacerdotal origin of our

---

528   Worshippers of Bacchus in the Dionysian mysteries of ancient Greece.

529   The traditional shout of the Dionysian initiates. Its meaning is unknown to scholars; Lévi's equation of it with the Hebrew tetragrammaton is not as far-fetched as it sounds, as other Semitic divine names show up in ancient Greek usage— compare the biblical figure Japheth with the Greek titan Iapetus, for example.

530   Judges 17:5 and 18:14–31.

Tarot. Here is how Gaffarel expresses himself: "Thus he says (Philo the Jew), speaking of a hidden history in a chapter entitled Judges, that Micah made from fine gold and silver three figurines of young boys and three young calves, as many of a lion, an eagle, a dragon, and a dove: so that if anyone came to ask him to discover some secret regarding their wife, he would ask the dove; regarding their children, he would use the young boy; regarding wealth, through the eagle; regarding strength and power, through the lion; regarding fecundity, through the cherub or calf; regarding the length of days and of years, through the dragon." This revelation of Philo's, even though Gaffarel makes little of it, is for us of the highest importance. Here, in fact, is our key to the quaternary, here are the images of the four symbolic animals which are found in the twenty-first key of the Tarot, which is to say in the third septenary, thus repeating the three and summarizing all the symbolism which the three superimposed septenaries express; then the antagonism of colors, expressed by the dove and the dragon; the circle or ROTA, formed by the dragon or the snake to express the length of days; finally the Cabalistic divination of the entire Tarot as a whole, as it would later be practiced by the Gypsies, whose secrets were guessed at and imperfectly rediscovered by Etteilla.

We see in the Bible that the high priests consulted the Lord on the golden table of the holy Ark, between the cherubim or sphinxes with the body of a bull and the wings of an eagle, and that they consulted with the aid of the teraphim, with the urim, with the thummim and with the ephod.[531] The ephod was, as we know, a magical square of twelve numbers and twelve words engraved on precious stones. The word *teraphim*, in Hebrew, signifies hieroglyphs or figurative signs; the urim and the thummim, were the high and the low, the orient and the occident, the yes and the no, and these signs corresponded to the two columns Jachin and Boaz. Thus when the grand priest wished to make the oracle speak, he drew at random the teraphim or golden strips which had the images of the four holy words on them, and placed them three by three around the rationale or

---

531   This is never said in so many words in the Bible but is a plausible interpretation of
       the fragmentary descriptions of priestly practice in the Old Testament, the writings of Josephus, and the Jewish Talmud.

ephod, between the urim and thummim, that is to say between the two onyx gems which served as clips for the chains of the ephod. The right onyx signified Gedulah, or mercy and magnificence; the left related to Geburah and signified justice and anger, and if, for example, the sign of the lion was found near the stone in which was engraved the name of the tribe of Judah on the left side, the grand priest read the oracle in this manner: "The rod of the Lord is angry at Judah." If the teraphim represented man or the cup and was also found to the left, near the stone of Benjamin, the grand priest read: "The mercy of the Lord is weary of the offenses of Benjamin, who abuses His love. This is why He shall pour upon him his cup of anger, etc." When the sovereign priesthood ended in Israel, when all the oracles of the world were silenced in the presence of the Verb made man, which spoke through the mouth of the most popular and most sweet of sages, when the Ark was lost, the sanctuary profaned, and the temple destroyed, the mysteries of the ephod and the teraphim, which were no longer traced upon gold and precious stones, were then written or rather drawn by a few Cabalist sages on ivory, on parchment, on silvered and gilded leather, and then finally on simple cards, which were always regarded as suspect by the official Church, as though containing a dangerous key to the mysteries. It is from there that those Tarots came from antiquity, as revealed to the scholar Court de Gébelin by the science of hieroglyphs and numbers itself, which later so often exercised Etteilla's doubtful perspicacity and tenacious investigations.

Court de Gébelin, in the eighth volume of his *Monde Primitif*, provided the figures of the twenty-two keys and of the four aces of the Tarot, and demonstrates its perfect analogy with all the symbols from the highest antiquity; he then tries to provide an explanation as to why, and naturally loses his way because he does not take as his point of departure the universal and sacred tetragrammaton, the IO EVOHE of the Bacchanalia, the YOD HEH VAU HEH of the sanctuary, the יהוה of the Cabala.

Etteilla, or Alliette, was solely preoccupied with his system of divination and with the material profit he could extract from it; an ex-barber, having never learned French nor even spelling, pretended to reform and thus claim ownership over the book of Thoth. On the Tarot he had engraved, and which has become very rare, we can read on the twenty-eighth card (the eight of wands) this naive advertisement: "Etteilla, professor of algebra, renovator of cartomancy and editors [*sic*] of modern *errors* of this ancient book of Thoth, resides at 48, rue de l'Oseille, in Paris." Etteilla would certainly have done better in not editing the errors of which he speaks: his work resulted in the ancient book discovered by Court de Gébelin falling into the domain of vulgar magic and fortune-telling. He who wishes to prove too much proves nothing, says an axiom of logic; Etteilla provides another example of this, and yet his efforts brought him to a certain understanding of the Cabala, as we can see in a few rare passages from his generally unreadable books.

The true initiates contemporary with Etteilla, the Rosicrucians, for example, and the Martinists, who were in possession of the true Tarot, as a book by Saint-Martin proves,[532] whose division into chapters is that of the Tarot, and this passage by an enemy of the Rosicrucians: "They pretend to have a volume in which they can learn all that is found in other books which have or could never have existed. This volume is the reason by which they find the prototype for all that exists through the faculty of analysis, to make abstractions, to form a kind of intellectual world, and to create all possible beings. Look upon the philosophical cards, theosophists, microcosmites, etc." *Conspiracy against the Catholic Religion and the Sovereigns*, by the author of *The Veil Raised for the Curious*[533] (Paris: Crapart, 1792). The true initiates, we were saying, who held the secret of the Tarot among their greatest mysteries, made no complaint about Etteilla's errors, and allowed him not to unveil, but to *re-veil* the arcanum of the true clavicle of Solomon. It was not without profound astonishment that we rediscovered, intact and still ignored, that key to all the doctrines and to all the philosophies of the ancient world. I say a key, and it is truly one, having a circle of four decades as a ring, and as its shaft or body the scale of twenty-two characters, then as a turning point the three degrees of the ternary, as was understood and drawn by Guillaume Postel in his *Key to Things Hidden Since the Beginning of the World*, a key which he thus indicates as being its occult name, known only to initiates:

---

532   This is *Tableau naturel des rapports qui existent entre Dieu, l'homme, et l'univers* (*Natural Tableau of the Relationships That Exist between God, Man, and the Universe*), published in 1782, which is divided into twenty-two sections.

533   These are books by Jacques-François Lefranc (1739–92).

a word which can be read as ROTA, and which symbolizes Ezekiel's wheel, or TAROT, and is thus synonymous with the AZOTH of the hermetic philosophers. It is a word which Cabalistically expresses the doctrinal and natural absolute; it is formed from the letters of Christ's monogram, according to the Greeks and the Hebrews. The Latin R or the Greek P is found in the middle, between the alpha and the omega of the Book of Revelation, then the sacred Tau, image of the cross, encloses the word entirely, as we have represented it on page 392 of our Ritual.

Without the Tarot, the magic of the ancients is a book which is closed for us, and it is impossible to penetrate any of the great mysteries of the Cabala. The Tarot alone provides for the interpretation of the magical squares of Agrippa and of Paracelsus, as we can be convinced of by forming these same squares with the keys of the tarot and by reading the hieroglyphs, which are thus found assembled.

Here are the seven magical squares of the planetary spirits according to Paracelsus:

SATURN

JUPITER

MARS

14	10	22	22	18
20	12	7	20	2
8	17	9	9	8
12	3	9	5	26
11	23	8	6	11

SUN

9	22	1	32	25	19
7	11	27	18	8	3
19	14	16	15	23	24
18	20	22	21	17	13
22	29	10	19	26	12
36	5	35	6	12	13

VENUS

22	47	18	41	0	35	8
25	23	47	17	42	11	29
10	6	14	9	18	36	12
3	31	16	25	43	19	37
38	14	32	31	26	44	20
21	39	8	33	22	27	45
46	15	40	19	24	03	27

MERCURY

8	52	39	5	24	61	66	11
49	15	14	52	52	12	10	56
41	43	22	14	45	19	18	48
33	34	35	29	20	38	39	25
40	6	27	59	31	30	31	33
17	47	55	28	25	43	42	24
9	51	53	12	13	51	00	16
64	12	15	64	61	6	7	47

MOON

37	70	29	70	21	62	12	14	44
16	28	70	30	71	12	53	14	46
47	20	11	7	31	72	22	35	15
16	48	68	40	81	32	62	25	56
57	17	49	29	7	66	33	65	25
26	58	40	56	31	42	74	34	66
53	27	59	10	51	2	41	75	35
36	68	19	60	11	65	43	44	76
77	28	20	69	61	12	25	60	5

By adding each of the columns of these squares, you invariably obtain the number which is characteristic of the planet, and, by finding the explication of that number through the hieroglyphs of the Tarot, you look for the meaning of all the figures, either triangular, square, or cruciform, that you shall find formed by the numbers. The consequence of this operation will result in a complete and profound understanding of all the allegories and of all the mysteries hidden by the ancients under the symbol of each planet, or rather of each personification of the influences, either celestial or human, that govern all of life's events.

We have said that the twenty-two keys of the Tarot are the twenty-two letters of the Cabalistic primordial alphabet. Here is a table of variants of this alphabet according to diverse Hebrew Cabalists.

א Being, mind, man, or God; the comprehensible object; the mother unity of numbers, the first substance.

All these ideas are expressed hieroglyphically by the figure of the Magus. His body and his arms form the letter א; he wears around his head a halo in the form of ∞, symbol of life and the universal mind; before him are swords, cups, and pentacles, and he raises a miraculous wand towards the sky. He has a juvenile figure and curly hair, like Apollo or Mercury; he has an assuring smile on his lips and looks out with intelligent eyes.

ב The house of God and man, the sanctuary, the law, Gnosis, the Cabala, the occult church, the binary, woman, mother.

Hieroglyph for the Tarot, High Priestess: a woman crowned with a tiara, having the horns of the Moon or of Isis, her head surrounded by a veil, the solar cross on her chest, and holding upon her knees a book which she hides with her coat.

Your author disagrees with a so-called account of Pope Joan[534] and

---

534 According to a scandalous legend of the Middle Ages, a woman who disguised herself as a man in order to cohabit with her lover, a monk, and made such an effective pretense of sanctity that she ended up becoming pope. She was detected only when she went into labor during a papal procession.

has found and made use of, for better or for worse, regarding his thesis, two curious and ancient figures which he found of the papesse or high priestess of the Tarot. These two figures provide the high priestess with all the attributes of Isis; in one of them, she holds and caresses the hand of her son Horus; in the other, she has long and thin hair; she sits between two binary columns, wears on her breast a four-rayed sun, places one hand on a book, and with the other hand makes the sign of sacerdotal esotericism, which is to say that she stretches out only three fingers and keeps the others folded in the sign of mystery; behind her head is a veil, and on each side of her seat is a sea upon which lotus flowers flourish. I feel deeply sorry for the misguided erudite who only wished to see in this ancient symbol a monumental portrait of his supposed Pope Joan.

ג The verb, the ternary, the plenitude, fecundity, nature, the generation of the three worlds.

Hieroglyph, the Empress: a winged woman, crowned, sitting and holding the world at the end of her scepter; she has as a sign the eagle, image of the soul and of life.

This woman is the Venus-Urania of the Greeks and was represented by Saint John, in his Apocalypse, by a woman dressed in the Sun, crowned by a dozen stars, and having the Moon at her feet. It is the mystical quintessence of the ternary, it is spirituality, it is immortality, it is the queen of heaven.

ד The door or government among the Orientals, initiation, power, the tetragrammaton, the quaternary, the cubic stone or its base.

Hieroglyph, the Emperor: a sovereign whose body represents a right triangle, and the legs a cross, image of the Athanor of the philosophers.

ה Indication, demonstration, teaching, laws, symbolism, philosophy, religion.

Hieroglyph, the Pope or grand hierophant. In more modern Tarots, this sign has been replaced by the image of Jupiter. The grand hierophant, sitting between the two columns of Hermes and Solomon, which makes for the sign of esotericism, leans on a cross with three crossbeams with a triangular form. Before him, two subordinate ministers are kneeling, in such a manner that above him he has the capitals of the two columns and below[535] him the heads of the ministers, he is the center of the quinary and represents the divine pentagram of which he provides the complete meaning. In effect, the columns are necessity or law; the heads are liberty or action. From each column to each head we can draw a line, and two lines from each column to each of the two heads. We thus obtain a square cut in four triangles by a cross, and in the middle of this cross would be the grand hierophant, we might say almost like a garden spider in the center of its web, if this image could be suitable for things of truth, of glory, and of light.

꠸ Chained series, hook, lingam, entanglement, union, embrace, struggle, antagonism, combination, equilibrium.

Hieroglyph, man between Vice and Virtue. Above him shines the Sun of truth, and within this Sun, Love stretches his bow and threatens vice with his arrow. In the order of the ten sephiroth, this symbol corresponds to Tiphareth, that is to say idealism and beauty. The number six represents the antagonism of the two ternaries, that is to say absolute negation and absolute affirmation. It is thus the number of works and of freedom; this is why it also has to do with moral beauty and glory.

꠸ Weapon, glaive, flaming sword of the cherub, sacred septenary, triumph, royalty, priesthood.

Hieroglyph, a cubic chariot of four columns with starry azure drapes. In the chariot, between the four columns, a triumphant victor crowned with a circle upon which arise and radiate three golden pentagrams. The

---

535   The text indicates "above," but this is obviously a misprint. The ministers are depicted below (Levi's note).

THE CHARIOT OF HERMES, SEVENTH KEY OF THE TAROT.

triumphant victor has on his breastplate three superimposed set squares; on the shoulders are the urim and the thummim of the sovereign sacrificator, symbolized by the two crescent moons of Gedulah and Gevurah; he holds in his hand a scepter surmounted by a globe, a square, and a triangle; his attitude is proud and tranquil. Harnessed to the chariot is the double sphinx, or two sphinxes attached at the lower abdomen; one pulls in one direction and one in the other, but one of the two turns its head, and they look in the same direction. The sphinx which turns its head is black; the other is white. On the square which forms the front of the chariot, we see the Indian lingam above, which is found the flying sphere of the Egyptians. This hieroglyph, of which we provide here the exact figure, is the most beautiful and perhaps the most complete of all the hieroglyphs which make up the clavicule of the Tarot.

ה Balance, attraction and repulsion, life, fear, promise and threat. Hieroglyph, Justice with her sword and balance.

ט Good, the loathing of evil, morality, wisdom.

Hieroglyph, a sage leaning on his staff and carrying before him a lamp; he is completely enveloped in his coat. His inscription is The Hermit or The Monk, because of the hood on his oriental coat; but his true name is Prudence, and he thus completes the four cardinal virtues, which had seemed odd to Court de Gébelin and Etteilla.

י Principle, manifestation, praise, virile honor, phallus, virile fecundity, paternal scepter.

Hieroglyph, The Wheel of Fortune, that is to say the cosmogonic wheel of Ezekiel, with an ascending Hermanubis to the right, a descending Typhon to the left, and a sphinx balanced above and holding a sword in its lion claws. An admirable symbol, disfigured by Etteilla, who had replaced Typhon with a man, Hermanubis with a mouse, and the sphinx with a monkey. An allegory worthy of Etteilla's Cabala.

כ The hand in the act of taking and holding.

Hieroglyph, Strength, a woman crowned with the vital ∞ and who peacefully and effortlessly closes the jaws of a furious lion.

ל Example, teaching, public lesson.

Hieroglyph, a man who is hung by one foot and whose hands are tied behind his back in such a manner that his body forms a triangle pointing downwards, and his legs form a cross above the triangle. The gallows have the form of a Hebrew tau; the trees which support it each have six cut branches. We have explained this symbol of sacrifice and the accomplished work elsewhere; we will not repeat it here.

מ The heaven of Jupiter and of Mars, domination and force, rebirth, creation and destruction.

Hieroglyph, Death who scythes crowned heads, in a meadow where we see men growing.

נ The heaven of the Sun, temperatures, seasons, movement, the changes of life, which are always new and always the same.

Hieroglyph, Temperance, an angel with the sign of the Sun on his forehead, and on his breast the square and triangle of the septenary, pours from one cup to another the two essences which compose the elixir of life.

ס The heaven of Mercury, occult science, magic, commerce, eloquence, mystery, moral strength.

Hieroglyph, The Devil, the goat of Mendes or the Baphomet of the temple with all its pantheistic attributes. This hieroglyph is the only one which Etteilla perfectly understood and properly interpreted.

ע The heaven of the Moon, alterations, subversions, changes, weakness.

Hieroglyph, a tower struck by lightning, probably the tower of Babel. Two persons, no doubt Nimrod and his false prophet or his minister, are thrown down below the ruins from above. One of the persons, in falling, perfectly represents the letter ע, Ayin.

ם The heaven of the soul, effusions of thought, the moral influence of the idea over the forms, immortality.

Hieroglyph, the brilliant star and eternal youth. We have provided the description of this figure elsewhere.

צ The elements, the visible world, the reflected light, the material forms, symbolism.

Hieroglyph, the Moon, dew, a crawfish in water rising towards the Earth, a dog and a wolf howling at the Moon and standing at the foot of two towers, a path which becomes lost in the horizon and which is sprayed with droplets of blood.

ק Mixtures, the head, the summit, the prince of the sky.

Hieroglyph, a radiant Sun and two naked children who hold hands in a fortified enclosure. In other Tarots, it is a spinner uncoiling the destinies; in others, a naked child astride a white horse, holding a scarlet standard.

ר The vegetative, the generative virtue of the earth, eternal life.

Hieroglyph, Judgment. A spirit sounds a trumpet and the dead come out of their tombs; these dead who become again living are a man, a woman, and a child: the ternary of human life.

ש The sensory, the flesh, eternal life.

Hieroglyph, The Fool: a man dressed as a jester, walking haphazardly, loaded with a bag which he carries behind him, and which are no doubt full of his absurdities and his vices; his disorderly clothes display openly what should be hidden, and a tiger who is following him bites him without his thinking of avoiding it or defending himself.

ת The microcosm, the summary of everything in everything.

Hieroglyph, Kether, or the Cabalistic crown between four mysterious animals; in the middle of the crown, we see Truth holding a magic wand in each hand.

Such are the twenty-two keys of the Tarot, which explain the numbers. Thus the mage, or the key of unity, explains the four aces with their quadruple and progressive signification in the three worlds and the first principle. Thus the ace of coins or of the circle, is the soul of the world; the ace of swords is the active intelligence; the ace of cups is the loving intelligence; the ace of wands is the creative intelligence; they are also the principles of movement, of progress, and of fecundity and power. Each number, multiplied by a key, gives another number, which, explained in its turn by the keys, completes the philosophical and religious revelation contained in each sign. Yet each of the fifty-six cards can be multiplied by the twenty-two keys, one after the other; the result is a series of combinations providing all of the most surprising results of revelation and of light. It is a veritable philosophical machine, which prevents the spirit from becoming lost while allowing for its initiative and freedom; it is mathematics applied to the absolute, it is the alliance of the positive with the ideal, it is an assemblage of thoughts which are as rigorously correct as numbers, finally it is perhaps that which the human genius has ever conceived which is the most simple and the most grand.

The manner in which to read the hieroglyphs of the Tarot is to dispose them either in a square or in a triangle, by placing the even numbers in antagonism with and by reconciling them with the odd numbers. Four signs always express the absolute within any order and are explained by the fifth. Thus the solution to all magical questions is that of the pentagram, and all the antinomies are explained by the harmonious unity.

Thus disposed, the Tarot is a true oracle and responds to all possible questions with more clarity and infallibility than the android of Albertus Magnus,[536] to such an extent that a prisoner without any books could, in a few years, if he had only a Tarot deck and knew how to use it, acquire universal science, and would speak of everything with a doctrine without equal and with an inexhaustible eloquence. This wheel is the true key to the notory art[537] and the Great Art of Raymond Lully;[538] it is the true secret of the transmutation of darkness into light, it is the first and the most important of all the arcana of the Great Work.

By the means of this universal key to symbolism, all the allegories of India, of Egypt, and of Judea become clear; the Revelation of Saint John is a Cabalistic book whose meaning is rigorously indicated by the figures and by the numbers of the urim, of the thummim, of the teraphim, and of the ephod, all summarized and completed by the Tarot; the ancient sanctuaries have no more mysteries, and we understand for the first time the signification of the occult objects of the He-

---

536   According to legend, as already noted, this great medieval scholar had a brass sculpture of a head that spoke, giving answers to all questions.

537   A branch of medieval magic almost forgotten today, the *ars notoria,* or notory (not "notary") art was a set of practices for learning at an accelerated rate by contemplating certain abstract diagrams while repeating appropriate incantations.

538   The *ars magna,* or Great Art, of Ramon Llull was a system of conceptual algebra by which a handful of basic ideas are combined and recombined to produce all human knowledge. The prisoner in Lévi's parable gains universal knowledge by using the tarot in this way, not by divination.

brews.[539] Who does not see in the golden tablet, crowned and supported by the cherubim, which covered the Ark of the Covenant and served as a propitiatory, the same symbols as those in the twenty-first key of the Tarot? The Ark was a hieroglyphic summary of all the Cabalistic doctrine, it contained the Yod or the flowering wand of Aaron, the He or the cup, the omer containing the manna, the two tablets of the law, a symbol which is analogous to the sword of justice, and the manna contained in the omer, four things which marvelously translate the letters of the divine Tetragrammaton.

Gaffarel skillfully proved that the cherubim or cherubs of the Ark were in the form of calves; but what he did not know was that instead of two there were four, two at each end, as it is expressly stated in the text, a section which is misunderstood by most commentators.

Thus in the verses 18 and 19 of chapter 25 of Exodus, one must translate the Hebrew text in this manner:

You shall make two calves or sphinxes made of gold and worked by hammer at each side of the oracle.

And you shall place one facing one side, and the other facing the other side.

The cherubs or sphinxes were in effect coupled in pairs at each side of the Ark, and their heads turned towards the four corners of the Mercy Seat, which they covered with their wings which were curved into a vault, thus shading the crown and the golden tablet, which they supported on their shoulders while looking at each other in the eyes and looking at the Mercy Seat. (See the figure.)

The ark thus had three sections, or three levels, representing Atziluth, Yetzirah, and Briah, the three worlds of the Cabala: the base of the coffer, to which were attached the four rings for the two carrying poles analogous to the columns of the temple, Jachin and Boaz; the body of the coffer, from which the sphinxes came out in relief; and the cover, shaded by the wings of the sphinxes. The base represented the realm of salt, to speak in the language of the adepts of Hermes; the coffer was the realm of mercury or of azoth and the cover was the realm of sulfur, or of fire. The other cultic objects were no less allegorical, but we would need an entire book to describe and explain them.

---

539   See chapter 25 of the book of Exodus for a detailed description of these objects.

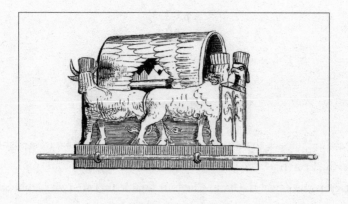

Saint-Martin, in his *Natural Tableau of the Relationships which Exist between God, Man, and the Universe*, had followed, as we have said, the division of the Tarot, and provides for the twenty-two keys a rather lengthy mystical commentary. Postel had the same discretion, and while only naming the Tarot in the figure of his key to the arcanum, he designates it in the rest of the book under the name of Genesis of Enoch. The character of Enoch, author of the first sacred book, is effectively identical with that of Thoth for the Egyptians, of Cadmus for the Phoenicians, and of Palamedes for the Greeks.[540]

We have found, in a rather extraordinary manner, a medal from the sixteenth century, which is a key to the Tarot. We do not really know if we should mention that this medal and the place where we had found it was shown to us in a dream by the divine Paracelsus: whatever the case, the medal is in our possession. It represents, on one side, the mage, in German dress of the sixteenth century, holding his belt in one hand and in the other the pentagram; before him, on his table, between an open book and a closed purse, ten coins or talismans are placed in two lines of three each and in one square of four; the feet of the table form two ה, and the feet of the mage form two upturned ר which look like this ⌐ ∟. The reverse side of the medal contains the letters of the alphabet placed in a magical square in this way:

---

540   All these figures, according to legend, created the alphabets of their respective
       languages.

A B C D E

F G H I K

L M N O P

Q R S T V

X V Z N

We should remark that this alphabet has only twenty-two letters, the V and the N having been repeated twice, and that it is arranged in four quinaries and a quaternary as the key at the base. The four final letters are two combinations of the binary and the ternary, and read Cabalistically they form the word AZOTH, by rendering the configurations of the letters into their values in primordial Hebrew and by taking the N for a א, the Z for what it is in Latin, the V for the Hebrew vau ו, which is pronounced like O between two vowels or letters which function as vowels, and the X for the primordial Tau, which had that same shape. The entire Tarot is thus explained on this marvelous medal, worthy of Paracelsus, and which we hold at the disposition of the curious. The letters, placed four times by five, have as a summary the word א Z ות analogous to יהוה, to INRI, and containing all the mysteries of the Cabala.

The book of the Tarot having such high scientific importance, it is worth hoping that it shall no longer be altered. We have gone through the collection of ancient Tarots in the Imperial Library, and it is there that we gathered all the hieroglyphs for which we provide the description. There remains an important work to be done: that is to engrave and publish a Tarot which is rigorously complete and carefully executed. Perhaps we shall do so soon.

We find vestiges of the Tarot among all the peoples of the world. The Italian Tarot is, as we have said, the best conserved and the most faithful, but we could perfect it more with precious information borrowed from Spanish decks: the two of cups, for example, in Naibis is completely Egyptian, and we see therein two antique vases whose handles are formed by ibises,[541] with a cow superimposed; we find in this same set of cards a unicorn in the middle of the four of

---

541   The ibis in Egyptian symbolism is sacred to the god Thoth, while the cow is sacred to the goddesses Isis and Hathor.

coins; the three of cups presents the figure of Isis coming out of a vase, and out of the two other vases two ibises come out, one carrying a crown for the goddess, the other a lotus flower which he seems to offer her. The four aces contain the image of the hieratic and sacred serpent, and, in certain decks, in the middle of the four of coins, instead of a symbolic unicorn, we find the double triangle of Solomon.

German Tarot decks are more altered, and we find little more than the numbers of the keys overloaded with bizarre or absurd figures. We have in our possession a Chinese Tarot, and there is to be found in the Imperial Library several samples from a similar deck. Paul Boiteau, in his remarkable book on playing cards,[542] provided several very well-made specimens of such a deck. The Chinese Tarot conserves several other primordial emblems, we can clearly distinguish the coins and the swords, but it is more difficult to find the cups and wands in them.

It was in the time of the Gnostic and Manichaean heresies that the Tarot must have become lost to the Church, and it is in that same era that the meaning of the Book of Revelation was also lost. It was no longer understood that the seven seals of this Cabalistic book are the seven pentacles whose figure we provide, and that they are explained by the analogy of the numbers of the characters and the figures of the Tarot. Thus the universal tradition of the unique religion was momentarily interrupted, the shadows of doubt were spread all over the earth, it resembled ignorance rather than true Catholicism, and the universal revelation had disappeared for a time. The explication of the book of Saint John through the characters of the Cabala will be a new revelation, which has already been foreseen by several distinguished mages. Here is how one among them, Agosti Xaho,[543] expresses himself:

The poem of Revelation supposes of the young evangelist a complete system of traditions developed by him alone.

It is written in the form of visions, and compresses into the dazzling

---

542   *Les cartes à jouer, et la cartomancie*, published in Paris in 1854.

543   Basque romantic author (1811–58).

frame of poetry all of the erudition, all of the philosophy of the civilizing African.

An inspired bard, the author skims through a series of primary facts; he describes in general terms the history of society from one cataclysm to another and even beyond.

The truths which he reveals are prophecies come from on high and afar, of which he sounds the echo.

He is the voice which cries out, the voice which sings the harmonies of the desert and prepares the paths towards the light.

His words explode with influence and command our faith, because he had just brought to the barbarians the oracles of Lao and revealed for the admiration of future civilizations the firstborn of the suns.

The theory of the four ages[544] is found in Revelation as it is found in the books of Zoroaster and the Bible.

The gradual reestablishment of the primordial federations and the reign of God among the peoples, free of the tyrants' yoke and the blindfold of error, is clearly prophesied for the end of the fourth age and the renovation of the cataclysm described, first in the distant future, with the consummation of time.

The description of the cataclysm and its duration; the new world, having been cleared of the waves and appearing under the sky with all its charms; the great serpent, tied by an angel to the bottom of the well of the abyss for a time; the dawn at long last of the time to come as prophesied by the Verb, which appears to the apostle right at the start of his poem:

"His head and his hair were white, his eyes sparkled, his feet seemed of fine bronze when still in the furnace, his voice equaled the noise of great waters.

"He held seven stars in his right hand, and from his mouth arose a

---

544   Found in Hindu scriptures, the theory of four ages holds that all of time follows a repeating sequence of four periods, each of which is worse than the one before it; the fourth age ends in catastrophe, and then the first, golden, age recurs.

APOCALYPTIC KEY:

THE SEVEN SEALS OF SAINT JOHN.

well sharpened double-edged glaive. His visage was as bright as the sun in full force.

"Here is Ormuzd, Osiris, Surya,[545] the lamb, the Christ, the Ancient of Days, the man of time and the river as sung by Daniel.

"He is the first and the last, he who was and who must be, the alpha and the omega, the beginning and the end.

"He holds in his hand the key to the mysteries; he opens the great abyss

---

545   Ormuzd, or Ahura Mazda, is the Zoroastrian god of light; Osiris is the Egyptian god of resurrection; Surya is the Hindu god of the sun.

of the central fire where death rests under a tent of darkness, where the great serpent sleeps while waiting for the awakening of the centuries."

The author draws together Saint John's allegory with that of Daniel's, where the four forms of the sphinx are applied to the great periods of history, and where the man-sun, the Verb of light, consoles and instructs the seer.

The prophet Daniel saw a sea agitated in the contrary direction by the four winds of heaven.

And the beasts all very different from one another arose from the depths of the Ocean.

The empire of everything on earth was accorded to them until an age, two ages and half of the fourth age.

And there arose four.

The first beast, symbol of the solar race of the seers, came from Africa; it resembled a lion and had eagle's wings: it was given a human heart.

The second beast, emblem of the conquerors of the north who regenerates through iron during the second age, resembled a bear.

It had in its jaws three rows of sharp teeth, symbol of the three great conquering families, and it was told: Arise and satiate yourself with carnage.

After the apparition of the fourth beast, the thrones were raised, and the ancient of days, the Christ of the seers, the lamb of the first age, appears seated.

His clothing was of a blinding whiteness, his head radiated; his throne, from which lively flames spouted out, was carried by burning wheels; a very lively flame arose from his visage, and a myriad angels or stars shone about him.

The judgment rung out; the allegorical books were opened.

The new Christ arrived in a multitude of lightning and stopped before the ancient of days; he gained a share of power, honor, and the reign over all the peoples, all the tribes, all the languages.

Daniel then approached one of those who were present and asked him for the truth of things.

And he is answered that the four animals are the four powers which reign successively over the earth.

Mr. Xaho then explains several images whose analogies are striking, and which are found in almost all the sacred books. His words are highly noteworthy.

In all primordial verbs, the parallels between physical relationships and moral relations are established along the same radical lines.

Each word carries with it its material and perceptible definition, and this living language is so perfect and true that it is simple and natural for creative man.

The seer expresses with the same word, slightly modified, the sun, day, light, truth, and when applying the same epithet to the white sun and the lamb, he says lamb or Christ instead of sun, and sun instead of truth, light, civilization, there is no allegory, but true relationships, grasped and expressed with inspiration.

But when the children of the night say in their barbarous and incoherent dialect, sun, day, light, truth, lamb, the wise relationship so clearly expressed by the primordial Verb is erased and disappears, and through simple translation, the lamb and the sun become allegorical beings, become symbols.

Note that, in effect, the word allegory itself signifies in its Celtic definition change of discourse, translation.

The observation which we have just made rigorously applies to all the cosmogonical language of the barbarians.

The seers made use of the same inspired radicals to express food and instruction. Is not the science of truth the food of the soul!

Thus, the papyrus scroll or the biblos devoured by the prophet Ezekiel;[546] the little book which an angel has the author of the Book of Rev-

---

546   Ezekiel 3:1–3.

elation eat;[547] the feasts in the magical palace of Asgard to which Gangleri is invited by Har the Sublime;[548] the miraculous multiplication of the seven loaves, as recounted by the evangelists of the Nazarene;[549] the living bread which Sun-Jesus has his disciples eat, while saying to them, "This is my body;"[550] and the masses of other similar lines are the repetition of the same allegory: the lives of souls, which are nourished by the truth; the truth, which multiplies itself, without ever diminishing and, to the contrary, augments as we eat it.

That exalted by a noble sentiment of nationalism, blinded by the idea of an immense revolution, there arises a revealer of hidden things, and he looks to popularize the discoveries of the ancient science among crude men, ignorant, stripped of the most simple and elementary notions.

That he says, for example: The Earth turns, the Earth is as round as an egg.

What can the barbarian who listens do, if not believe! Is it not evident that any proposition of this type becomes for him a doctrine from on high, an article of faith?

And does not the veil of a wise allegory suffice to make a myth?

In the schools of seers the terrestrial globe was represented by an egg of paper or of painted wood, and when they asked little children: What is this egg? And they responded: It is the Earth.

As big children, the barbarians having heard this, repeated after the children of the seers: The world is an egg.

But they understood by that the physical world, the material world, and the seers had meant the geographical world, the ideal world, the world image, created by the spirit and the Verb.

Thus the priests of Egypt represented the spirit, intelligence, Kneph,

---

547   Revelation 10:10.

548   A reference to *Gylfaginning*, one of the books of the Norse Edda.

549   Matthew 14:17 and 15:32, Mark 6:35, Luke 9:12, and John 6:5.

550   Matthew 26:26.

with an egg laying on lips, to better express that the egg was only a comparison, an image, a manner of speaking.

Shumontou, the philosopher of the Ezourvedam, explains to the fanatic Biache in the same manner what one must understand by the golden egg of Brahma.[551]

One must not completely lose hope for an epoch in which we are again occupied with serious and reasonable research: it is also with great relief and profound sympathy that we have just quoted from the pages of M. Xaho. This here is no longer the negative and despairing critique of Dupuis and of Volney. It is a tendency towards a single faith, towards a single cult which must link all the future to all of the past; it is the rehabilitation of all the great men falsely accused of superstition and idolatry; lastly it is the justification of God himself, that sun of intelligences who is never veiled to upright souls and pure hearts.

"He is great, the seer, the initiate, the elect of nature and of supreme reason," cries out still the author we have just quoted in conclusion.

"To him alone that faculty of imitation which is the principle of his advance towards perfection and whose inspirations, quick as lightning, direct his creations and discoveries.

"To him alone a Verb of perfect convenience, of propriety, of flexibility, of wealth, the harmony of thought created by physical reaction; of thought whose insights, still independent of language, always reflect the nature exactly reproduced by its impressions, well judged, and well expressed through their connections.

"To him alone the light, the science, the truth, because imagination, bounded in its secondary, passive role, never dominates reason, the

---

551   The Ezourvedam was a faux-Hindu scripture manufactured by French Jesuits sometime before 1760, when a manuscript copy was presented to Voltaire. It consisted of an assortment of passages from genuine Hindu writings pulled out of context and used to justify Christian ideas. It was proved to be a fraud in 1822 but remained in circulation in French romantic circles for some time thereafter.

natural logic which results from the comparison of ideas, which are born, and extend out in the same proportion as his needs, and whose circle of knowledge thus widens by degrees without a confusion of false judgments and errors.

"To him alone an infinitely progressive light, because the rapid multiplication of the population, after the terrestrial renovations, combined in just a few centuries a new society with all the possible connections of its destiny, either moral or political.

"And we could add, absolute light.

"The man of our times is immutable by nature; he changes no more than the nature by which he is organized.

"The social conditions in which he finds himself placed, alone determine the degree of his perfectionment, which has as its limits virtue, the holiness of man and his happiness within the law."

Will people still ask us after such insights what use are the occult sciences? Will they treat with disdain these living mathematics called mysticism and illuminism, these dimensions of ideas and of forms, this permanent revelation within universal reason, this liberation of the spirit, this unshakable foundation given to faith, this omnipotence revealed to the will? Children in search of magic tricks, are you disappointed because we give you miracles! A man said to us one day: "Make the devil appear, and I will believe you." We answered, "You ask for very little; we would prefer, instead of making the devil to appear, but to disappear from the entire world; we wish to chase him from your dreams! The devil is ignorance, it is darkness, it is incoherent thought, it is ugliness! Awake, dreamer of the Middle Ages! Do you not see that it is day? Do you not see the light of God which fills all of nature? Where then would the fallen prince of the hells dare show himself now?"

It remains for us to provide our conclusions and to determine the goal and the extent of this work in the religious domain, the philosophical domain and in the domain of positive and material realizations.

In the religious domain, first of all, we have demonstrated that cultic practices are by no means of indifferent value, that the magic of religions is in their rites, that their moral force is in the ternary hierarchy, and that the hierarchy has unity as its foundation, principle, and synthesis.

We have demonstrated that the unity and the universal orthodoxy of the doctrine was successively dressed up in several allegorical veils, and we have followed the truth saved by Moses from the profanations of Egypt, conserved in the Cabala of the prophets, emancipated by the Christian school from servitude to the Pharisees, attracting to it all the poetic and generous aspirations of the Greek and Roman civilizations, and then protesting against a new Phariseeism even more corrupt than the first, with the great saints of the Middle Ages and the bold thinkers of the Renaissance. We have shown, I say, that eternal universal truth, always one, always living, which alone conciliates reason with faith, science with submission; the truth of being demonstrated by being, the truth of harmony demonstrated by harmony, the truth of reason manifested by reason.

By revealing to the world for the first time the mysteries of magic, we did not wish to resuscitate those practices buried under the ruins of ancient civilizations, but we say to the humanity of today that it is also called to make itself immortal and omnipotent by its works.

Liberty is not given, it is taken, said a modern writer;[552] the same is true for science, and it is for this reason that the divulging of the absolute truth is never useful for the vulgar. But in an era where the sanctuary has been devastated and has fallen into ruins, because we had thrown the key across the fields to no one's profit, I believed it my duty to pick up that key, and I offer it to he who will know how to take it: because that person will in his turn be a doctor of nations and a liberator of the world.

We need and we will always need fables and toys for children; but it must not be the case that those who hold up the toys are also children and listeners to fables.

---

552   French priest Jean-Baptiste Henri Lacordaire (1802–61), by many accounts the best
       preacher of the nineteenth century.

May the most absolute science, may the most highest reason again become the allotment of the leaders of the people; may the sacerdotal and royal art again take up the double scepter of the ancient initiations, and the world will arise once again from chaos.

Let us stop burning the holy images, let us stop demolishing the temples: man needs temples and images; but let us chase off the merchants from the house of prayers; let us stop allowing the blind to lead the blind; let us reconstitute the hierarchy of intelligence and holiness, and let us only recognize those who know as the doctors for those who believe.

Our book is Catholic; and if the revelations it contains are of a nature which alarms the conscience of simpletons, our consolation is to think that they will not read it. We write for men without prejudices, and we do not want to flatter irreligiousness any more than fanaticism.

But if there is something in this world which is essentially free and inviolable, it is belief. We must, through science and through persuasion, turn imaginations lead astray away from the absurd; but to threaten or constrain them would be to provide their errors with all the dignity and truth of a martyr.

Faith is but superstition and folly if it does not have reason as its base, and we can only suppose what we do not know through analogy with what we do know. To define what we do not know is presumptuous ignorance; to positively affirm what we do not know is to lie.

Faith is also an aspiration and a desire. So be it, I desire it to be so, such is the last word of all professions of faith. Faith, hope, and charity are three sisters who are so inseparable that we can take one for the other.

Thus in religion, the universal and hierarchical orthodoxy, the restoration of the temples in all their splendor, the reestablishment of all the ceremonies in their primordial glory, the hierarchic teaching of symbols, mysteries, miracles, legends for children, light for mature men who will take care not to scandalize the little ones in their simplicity and their beliefs. There is the religion of our utopia, and it is also the desire and the need of humanity.

Let us come to philosophy.

Ours is that of realism and positivism.

Being is due to the being which no one doubts. All exists for us through science. To know is to be. Science and its object are identified in the intellectual life of he who knows. To doubt is to be ignorant. Yet that which we do not know exists does not yet exist for us. To live intellectually is to learn.

Existence develops and is amplified by science. The first conquest of science is the first results of the exact sciences, it is the opinion of reason. The laws of nature are algebraic. The only reasonable faith is the student's provisional acceptance of theorems: he does not ask about their correctness in and of themselves but whether their applications and their results have been sufficiently demonstrated to him. Thus the true philosopher believes in what is and only accepts a posteriori that all is reasonable.

But no more charlatanism in philosophy, no more empiricism, no more systems; just the study of existence and its comparative realities! A metaphysics of nature! Then away with mysticism! No more dreams in philosophy: philosophy is not a poem; it is the pure mathematics of the realities, either physical or moral. Let us leave to religion the freedom of infinite aspirations, but let religion leave science its rigorous conclusions of absolute experimentalism.

Man is the son of his works: he is what he wants to be, he is the image of God who makes himself; he is the realization of his ideal. If his ideal lacks a foundation, the entire edifice of his immortality collapses. Philosophy is not the ideal, but it must serve as a foundation for the ideal. The known for us is the measure of the unknown; the visible allows us to appreciate the invisible, sensations are to thoughts what thoughts are to aspirations. Science is a celestial trigonometry: one of the sides of the absolute triangle is nature submitted to our investigations; the other side is our soul, which embraces and reflects nature; the third side is the absolute within which our soul grows! Atheism is no longer possible, because we no longer have the arrogance to define God. God is for us the most perfect and the best of intelligent beings, and the ascending hierarchy of being demonstrates well enough that he exists. Let us not ask for more; but, to understand him better and better, shall we not perfect ourselves by climbing towards him?

No more ideology; existence is what it is and is only perfected by following the real laws of being. Let us observe, not prejudge; let us exert out faculties, not falsify them; let us expand the domain of life in life; let us see truth in the truth!

All is possible for he who only wants what is true. Remain within nature, study, know, then dare; dare to want, dare to act, and remain silent!

No more hatred directed at anybody. Each will reap what he sows. The result of work is fate, and that is the supreme reason for judging and punishing the wicked. He who goes down a dead-end road will backtrack or will be broken. Warn him kindly, if he can still hear you; then leave him to it: human freedom must run its course.

We are not set to judge each other. Life is a battlefield. Let us not stop fighting because of those who fall, but let us avoid stepping on them. Then comes victory, and the wounded of both parties, having become brothers through suffering and before humanity, shall be reunited in the ambulances of the victors.

Such are the consequences of the philosophical doctrine of Hermes; such was the philosophy of the Rosicrucians, inheritors of all the ancient wisdom; such is the secret doctrine of those associations which were treated as dangerous to the public order and which have always been accused of conspiring against thrones and altars!

The true adept, far from troubling the public order, is its firmest support, he respects liberty too much to desire anarchy; child of the light, he loves harmony, and he knows that the shadows produce confusion. He accepts all that is and denies only what is not. He wants the true religion, practical, universal, believing, palpable, realized throughout his entire life; he wants it to have a wise and powerful priesthood, surrounded by all the virtues and all the glamour of faith. He wants universal orthodoxy, absolute Catholicism, hierarchical, apostolic, sacramental, incontestable, and uncontested. He wants an experimental philosophy, real, mathematical, modest in its conclusions, indefatigable in its researches, scientific in its progress. Who then could be against us if God and reason are with us? What does it matter if they prejudge us and they slander us? Our entire justification is our thoughts and our works. We do not come, like Oedipus, to kill the sphinx of symbolism; we undertake, to the contrary, to resuscitate it. The sphinx only devours blind interpreters, and he who killed it did not know how to divine it well: one must tame it, enchain it, and force it to follow. The sphinx is the living palladium of humanity, it is the conquest of the king of Thebes; it would have been Oedipus's salvation if Oedipus had guessed its enigma entirely!

In the positive and material domain, what must one conclude of this work? Is magic a force which science can abandon to the most audacious and the most wicked? Is it the trickery and lies of the most clever used to fascinate the ignorant and the weak? Is the philosopher's mercury the exploitation of the credulous through misdirection? Those who have understood us know already how to respond to these questions. Magic can no longer in our day be the art of fascination and illusions: one now only fools those who wished to be fooled. But the narrow and reckless incredulity of the previous century is refuted by nature itself. We live surrounded by prophecies and miracles; in the past, doubt denied them recklessly; the science of today explains them. No, monsieur Comte de Mirville, it is not given to a fallen spirit to trouble the empire of God! No, unknown things are not explained by impossibilities; no, it is not at all given to invisible beings the ability to fool, to torment, to seduce, to even kill the living creatures of God, men, already so ignorant and so weak, and who have so much difficulty defending themselves from their own illusions. Those who told you as much in your childhood have fooled you, monsieur Count, and if you were childish enough to listen to them, be man enough now to no longer believe them.

Man is himself the creator of his heaven and his hell, and there are no other demons than those of madness. The spirits that truth punishes are corrected through punishment and no longer imagine troubling this world. If Satan exists, he can only be the most unhappy, the most ignorant, the most humiliated, and the most impotent of beings.

The existence of a universal agent of life, of a living fire, of an astral light has been demonstrated to us through facts. Magnetism allows us to understand today the miracles of ancient magic: the occurrences of second sight, aspirations, sudden healings, penetrations of thought are now things which are recognized and familiar, even to our children. But we have lost the ancient traditions, we thought they were new discoveries; we searched for the latest word regarding the observed phenomena, heads have been troubled by manifestations without apparent cause, we were subjected to fascinations without understanding them. We have come to say to the table turners: These illusions are not new; you can operate even greater ones if you study the secret laws of nature. And what will be the result of the renewed knowledge of these powers? A new pathway opened to the activity and the intelligence of man, the combat of life organized anew with the most perfect weapons, and the possibility rendered unto elite intelligences to again become masters of all the destinies by providing the world to come with true priests and great kings!

END OF THE RITUAL

THE *NUCTEMERON* OF APOLLONIUS OF TYANA

Published in Greek, based on an ancient manuscript, by Gilbert Gaulminus in *De vita et morte Moysis*, book III, page 206; reproduced by Laurent Moshemius in his sacred observations and historical criticisms, Amsterdam, 1721; translated and explained for the first time, by Eliphas Lévi.[553]

Nuctemeron means day and night or the night illuminated by the day.[554] It is a title which is analogous to that of *Light Arising from Darkness*, a relatively well-known hermetic work;[555] we could also translate it in this way:

The Light of Occultism

This monument to the high magic of the Assyrians[556] is interesting enough for us to have taken the trouble to have its importance noticed. We not only evoked Apollonius, we have perhaps managed to resuscitate him.[557]

---

553 Lévi has the right author but the wrong book. The *Nuctemeron* is found in Gilbert Gaulminus's *Michael Psellus de operatione daemonum dialogus* (Paris: Hieronymus Drovart, 1615), 126–28.

554 From the Greek νυκτος, "night," and έμερος, "day."

555 The *Aurora consurgens*, an alchemical text falsely attributed to Thomas Aquinas; the title means "light surging forth."

556 In Lévi's time, the different cultures of ancient Mesopotamia were still hopelessly confused by scholars, and it was quite common for writers to say "Assyrian" when they meant to refer to ancient Near Eastern cultures in general.

557 Fans of modern opera may be interested to know that Hans van Eck's opera *Nuctemeron: The Twelve Hours of Apollonius of Tyana* (2008) quotes Lévi's version of the *Nuctemeron* of Apollonius in English translation.

The *Nuctemeron*

FIRST HOUR.

I. Ἐν ᾗ δαίμονες ἀνοῦντες (*lege* ὑμνοῦντες *vel* αἰνοῦντες) τὸν θεὸν, οὔτε ἀδικοῦσιν, οὔτε κολάζουσιν. (In which demons, praising God, neither injure nor punish.)[558]

In the unity, the demons sing the praises of God, they shed their wickedness and their anger.

SECOND HOUR.

II. Ἐν ᾗ αἰνοῦσιν οἱ ἰχθύεςτὸν θεὸν, καὶ τὸ τοῦ πυρὸς βάθος. Ἐν ᾗ ὀφείλει στοιχειοῦσθαι ἀποτελέσματα εἰς δράκοντας καὶ πῦρ. (In which the fishes praise God, and the depth of fire. In which one ought to deploy talismans against dragons and fire.)

Through the binary, the fish of the Zodiac sing the praises of God, the serpents of fire intertwine themselves around the caduceus, and the lightning becomes harmonious.

THIRD HOUR.

III. Ἐν ᾗ αἰνοῦσιν ὄφεις καὶ κύνες καὶ πῦρ. (In which snakes and dogs and fire praise [God].)

The serpents of Hermes's caduceus intertwine themselves three times, Cerberus opens his triple mouth, and the fire sings the praises of God with three tongues of lightning.

---

558 The passages in parentheses are literal translations of the Greek texts, for which I am indebted to Robert Mathiesen. They may be compared with Lévi's paraphrase.

FOURTH HOUR.

IV.   Ἐν ᾗ διέρχονται δαίμονες ἐν τοῖς μνήμασιν, καὶ ὁ ἐρχόμενος ὁ ἐκεῖσε βλαβήσεται, καὶ φόβον καὶ φρίκην ἐκ τῆς δαιμόνων λήψεται φαντασίας. Ἐν ᾗ ὀφείλει ἐνεργεῖν ἐπὶ μαγικοῦ καὶ παντὸς γοητικοῦ πράγματος. (In which demons go about inside the tombs, and a [demon] that comes from there will injure one, and he will take fear and shuddering from the fantasy of demons. In [this hour] one ought to work on every deed of magic and sorcery.)

In the fourth hour the soul returns to visit the tombs, it is the moment when the magic lamps at the four corners of the circles are lit, it is the hour of enchantments and illusions.

FIFTH HOUR.

V.   Ἐν ᾗ αἰνοῦσιν τὰ ἄνω ὕδατα τὸν θεὸν τοῦ οὐρανοῦ.[559] (In which the waters on high praise the God of heaven.)

The voices of the great waters sing out to the God of the celestial spheres.

SIXTH HOUR.

VI.   Ὅτε δέον ἡσυχάζειν καὶ ἀναπαύεσθαι, διότι ἔχει φόβον. (When it is right to be silent and take one's rest, lest one take fright.)

The spirit remains immobile, it sees the infernal monsters marching against it, and it is without fear.

SEVENTH HOUR.

VII.   Ἐν ᾗ ἀναπαύσει πάντα τὰ ζῷα. Καὶ ἐάν τις καθαρὸς ἄνθρωπος ἁρπάσῃ καὶ βάλλῃ αὐτὸ ὁ ἱερεύς, καὶ μίξει ἐλαίῳ καὶ ἁγιάσῃ αὐτὸ καὶ ἀλείψῃ ἀπ'αὐτοῦ ἀσθενῆ, παρευθὺ τῆς νόσου ἀπαλλαγήσεται. (In which all animals take their rest. And if any pure person

---

559   The waters above heaven (the marble table of the world according to the Hebrews). This note is in Lévi's source.

seizes up, and the priest throws it down, and mixes it with oil, and hallows it, and anoints his weaknesses from him, he will be delivered at once from his illness.)

A fire which gives life to all animated beings is directed by the will of pure men. The initiate extends his hand and the sufferings subside.

EIGHTH HOUR.

VIII.　Ἐν ᾗ ἀποτέλεσμα στοιχείων καὶ παντοίον φυτῶν. (In which a talisman of elements and of plants of all sorts [ought to be made].)

The stars speak, the soul of the suns correspond with the breath of flowers, the chains of harmony link all the beings of nature together.

NINTH HOUR.

IX.　Ἐν ᾗ τελεῖται οὐδὲν. (In which nothing is brought to completion.)

The number which must not be revealed.

TENTH HOUR.

X.　Ἐν ᾗ ἀνοίγωνται αἱ πύλαι τοῦ οὐρανοῦ, καὶ ἄνθρωπος ἐν κατανύξει ἐρχόμενος εὐήκοος γενήσεται. (In which the gates of heaven are opened and a person who has gone into deep sleep will be ready to hear.)

This is the key of the astronomical cycle and the circular movement of the lives of men.

ELEVENTH HOUR.

XI.　Ἐν ᾗ πέτονται ταῖς πτέρυξιν σὺν ἤχῳ οἱ ἄγγελοι καὶ χερουβὶμ καὶ σεραφὶμ, καὶ ἔστιν χαρὰ ἐν οὐρανῷ καὶ γῇ, ἀνατέλλει δὲ καὶ ὁ ἥλιος ἐξ Ἀδὰμ (*lege* Ἐδὲμ). (In which the angels take wing vociferously, and the cherubim and seraphim; and there is joy in heaven and on earth, and the Sun rises up out of Eden.)

The wings of the spirits flap with a mysterious rushing sound, they fly from one sphere to another and carry from world to world the messages of God.

TWELFTH HOUR.

XII. Ἐν ᾗ ἀναπαύονται τὰ πύρινα τάγματα. (In which the fiery ranks [of creatures] take their rest.)

Here the works of the eternal light are accomplished through fire.

EXPLICATION.

These twelve symbolic hours, analogous to the signs of the magical Zodiac and to the allegorical trials of Hercules, represent the series of works towards initiation.

Thus one must start by:

First, taming wicked passions and strength, using the expression of the wise Hierophant, to make the demons themselves praise God.

Second, studying the balanced forces of nature so as to know how harmony results from the analogy of opposites. To recognize the great magical agent and the double polarization of the universal light.

Third, becoming initiated into the symbolism of the ternary, the principle of all theogonies and of all religious symbols.

Fourth, knowing how to dominate all the phantoms of the imagination and triumph over all illusions.

Fifth, understanding how the universal harmony is produced in the center of the four elementary forces.

Sixth, becoming inaccessible to fear.

Seventh, acting in the direction of the magnetic light.

Eighth, learning to predict effects by the calculation of the weighting of causes.

Ninth, understanding the hierarchy of teachings, respecting the mysteries of the doctrine, and remaining silent before the profane.

Tenth, studying astronomy fully.

Eleventh, becoming initiated through analogy with the laws of life and
　　　of universal intelligence.

Twelfth, operating great works of nature with the guidance of the
　　　light.

Here now are the names and the attributions of the spirits which preside over
the twelve hours of the *Nuctemeron*.

By these spirits the ancient hierophants meant neither gods nor angels nor
demons, but moral forces or personified virtues.

SPIRITS OF THE FIRST HOUR.

PAPUS, doctor.

SINBUCK, judge.

RASPHUIA, necromancer.

ZABUN, spirit of scandal.

HEIGLOT, spirit of the snows.

MIZKUN, spirit of amulets.

HAVEN, spirit of dignity.

EXPLICATION.

One must become one's own *doctor* and *judge* in order to vanquish the evil spells
of the *necromancer*. Banish and scorn the spirit of *scandal*, triumph over opinions
which freeze all enthusiasm and confound all things with the same cold pallor as
does the *spirit of the snows*. Know the virtue of the signs and thus enchain the *spirit
of the amulets* to arrive at the *dignity* of the mage.

SPIRITS OF THE SECOND HOUR.

SISERA, spirit of desire.

TORVATUS, spirit of discord.

NITIBUS, spirit of the stars.

HIZARBIN, spirit of the seas.

SACHLUPH, spirit of plants.

BAGLIS, spirit of moderation and equilibrium.

LABEZERIN, spirit of success.

EXPLICATION.

One must learn to want and thus transform *the spirit of desire* into power, the obstacle to the will is *the spirit of discord* which one enchains with the science of harmony. Harmony is *the spirit of the stars and the seas*, one must study the virtue *of plants*, understand the laws of *equilibrium in moderation* to arrive *at success*.

SPIRITS OF THE THIRD HOUR.

HAHABI, spirit of fear.

PHLOGABITUS, spirit of ornaments.

EIRNEUS, spirit destroyer of idols.

MASCARUN, spirit of death.

ZAROBI, spirit of chasms.

BUTATAR, spirit of calculations.

CAHOR, spirit of deception.

EXPLICATION.

When, by the growing force of your will, you will have vanquished the *spirit of fear*, you will know that the doctrines are sacred *ornaments* of the truth which is unknown to the vulgar, but with your intelligence you will upturn all of *the idols* and you will enchain *the spirit of death*, you will sound all the *chasms*, and you will submit infinity itself to the measurement of your calculations, and thus you will forever avoid the snares of the *spirit of deception*.

SPIRITS OF THE FOURTH HOUR.

PHALGUS, spirit of judgment.

THAGRINUS, spirit of confusion.

EISTIBUS, spirit of divination.

PHARZUPH, spirit of fornication.

SISLAU, spirit of poisons.

SCHIEKRON, spirit of animal love.

ACLAHAVR, spirit of games.

EXPLICATION.

The power of the mage is in his *judgment*, which allows him to avoid the *confusion* resulting from the antinomy and the antagonism of the principles; he practices the *divination* of the sages but he scorns the illusions of enchanters, who are slaves to *fornication*, artists of *poisons*, and the servants of *animal love*, he triumphs thus over fatalism, which is the *spirit of games*.

SPIRITS OF THE FIFTH HOUR.

ZEIRNA, spirit of infirmities.

TABLIBIK, spirit of fascination.

TACRITAU, spirit of goetia.

SUPHLATUS, spirit of dust.

SAIR, spirit of the stibium[560] of the mages.

BARCUS, spirit of the quintessence.

CAMAYSAR, spirit of the marriage of opposites.

EXPLICATION.

Triumphant over the human *infirmities*, the mage is no longer the toy of *fascination*, he tramples beneath his feet the vain and dangerous practices of *goetia*, all of his power is in a *dust* that the wind carries off; but he possesses the *stibium* of the sages, he arms himself with all the creative forces of the *quintessence* and produces at will the harmony which results from the analogy and the *marriage of opposites*.

---

560   Tin ore.

SPIRITS OF THE SIXTH HOUR.

TABRIS, spirit of free will.

SUSABO, spirit of journeys.

EIRNILUS, spirit of fruits.

NITIKA, spirit of precious stones.

HAATAN, spirit who hides the treasures.

HATIPHAS, spirit of finery.

ZAREN, spirit of vengeance.

EXPLICATION.

The mage is free, he is the king of the occult and of the earth and he travels across it as though it were his domain. In his *journeys*, he learns to recognize the juices of *plants* and of *fruits*, the virtues of the *precious stones*, he forces the *spirit who hides the treasures* of nature to surrender all its secrets, he thus penetrates the mysteries of form, he understands the *finery* of the earth and of speech, and if he is little known, if the people are inhospitable towards him, if he passes by doing good but gathers insults, he is always followed by the *spirit of vengeance*.

SPIRITS OF THE SEVENTH HOUR.

SIALUL, spirit of prosperity.

SABRUS, spirit who supports.

LIBRABIS, spirit of the hidden gold.

MIZGITARI, spirit of eagles.

CAUSUB, spirit who enchants serpents.

SALILUS, spirit who opens doors.

JAZER, spirit who makes himself loved.

EXPLICATION.

The septenary expresses the triumph of the mage, he gives *prosperity* to men and to nations and he *supports* them through his sublime teachings; he soars like the *eagle*, he directs the currents of the astral fire represented by the *serpents*, all the doors of the sanctuary are open to him and all souls who aspire to the truth give him their trust; he is beautiful with moral grandeur and he carries everywhere with him the spirit with whose power one is *loved*.

SPIRITS OF THE EIGHTH HOUR.

NANTUR, spirit of writing.

TOGLAS, spirit of treasures.

ZALBURIS, spirit of therapy.

ALPHUN, spirit of doves.

TUKIPHAT, spirit of the Shamir.

ZIZUPH, spirit of mysteries.

CUNIALI, spirit of association.

EXPLICATION.

Such are the spirits who obey the true mage, *the doves* represent religious ideas; the Shamir is an allegorical diamond, which in the magical traditions represents the stone of the sages, or that force based on truth and which nothing can resist. The Arabs still say that the Shamir, given in primordial times to Adam, and lost by him after his fall, was rediscovered by Enoch and possessed by Zoroaster, that Solomon received it next from an angel when he had asked God for wisdom. Solomon, by the means of this magical diamond, cut all by himself and without a hammer all the stones of the temple, simply by touching them with the Shamir.

SPIRITS OF THE NINTH HOUR.

RISNUCH, spirit of agriculture.

SUCLAGUS, spirit of fire.

KIRTABUS, spirit of languages.

SABLIL, spirit who discovers thieves.

SCHACHLIL, spirit of the horses of the Sun.

COLOPATIRON, spirit who opens the prisons.

ZEFFAR, spirit of the irrevocable choice.

EXPLICATION.

This number, says Apollonius, must be passed by in silence, because it encloses the great secrets of the initiate, the power *which renders the earth fertile*, the mysteries of *the occult fire*, the universal key to *languages*, the second sight before which *wrongdoers* do not know how to remain hidden. The great laws of equilibrium and of luminous movement represented by the four symbolic animals in the Cabala and in the mythology of the Greeks by the four *horses of the Sun*. The key to the emancipation of the bodies and the souls which opens *all the prisons* and that force of eternal choice which completes the creation of man and fixes him in immortality.

SPIRITS OF THE TENTH HOUR.

SEZARBIL, devil or enemy spirit.

AZEUPH, killer of children.

ARMILUS, spirit of cupidity.

KATARIS, spirit of dogs or the profane.

RAZANIL, spirit of the onyx stone.

BUCHAPHI, spirit of the stryges.

MASTHO, spirit of vain appearances.

EXPLICATION.

The numbers end with nine, and the distinctive sign of ten is the zero, without any value of its own, added to the unity. The spirits of the tenth hour thus represent all which, being nothing on their own, receive great power from opinion and can in consequence set back the omnipotence of the sage. We walk here upon burning ground, and you will allow me to not explain it to the profane nor *the devil* who is their master, nor *the killer of children* who is their love, nor to *cupidity* who is their god, nor to *the dogs* to whom we compare them, nor to *the stone of onyx* which escapes them, nor to *the stryges* who are their courtesans, nor *the false appearances* which they take for reality.

SPIRITS OF THE ELEVENTH HOUR.

AEGLUN, spirit of lightning.

ZUPHLAS, spirit of forests.

PHALDOR, spirit of oracles.

ROSABIS, spirit of metals.

ADJUGHAS, spirit of rocks.

ZOPHAZ, spirit of pentacles.

HALACHO, spirit of sympathies.

EXPLICATION.

Lightning obeys man, it becomes the vehicle of his will, the instrument of his force, the light of his torches, the oaks of the sacred *forests* which render *oracles*, *the metals* are transformed and change into gold, or become talismans, *the rocks* are detached from their base and, carried away by the lyre of the grand hierophant, touched by the mysterious schamir, they change into temples and palaces, the doctrines are formulated, the symbols represented by the pentacles become effective, the spirits are enchained by powerful *sympathies* and obey the laws of family and friendship.

SPIRITS OF THE TWELFTH HOUR.

TARAB, spirit of corruption.

MISRAN, spirit of persecution.

LABUS, spirit of the inquisition.

KALAB, spirit of sacred vases.

HAHAB, spirit of the royal tables.

MARNES, spirit of the discernment of spirits.

SELLEN, spirit of the favors of the great.

EXPLICATION.

Here is the fate which mages must expect and the way in which their sacrifice will be consummated because after the conquest of life, one must know how to sacrifice oneself to be reborn immortal. They will suffer *corruption*; their gold, their pleasure, and vengeance will be demanded of them, and, if they do not satisfy the cupidity of the vulgar, they will be exposed to *persecution*, to the *inquisition*; but one does not profane the *sacred vases*, they are made for the *royal tables*, that is to say for the banquets of intelligence. Through the *discernment of spirits*, they will know how to keep the *favors of the great* and will remain invincible in their force and in their liberty.

THE *NUCTEMERON*

According to the Hebrews[561]

The *Nuctemeron* of Apollonius, borrowed from Greek theurgy, completed and explained by the Assyrian hierarchy of angels, corresponds perfectly with the philosophy of numbers as we find it presented in the most curious pages of the ancient Talmud.

Thus the Pythagorean traditions rise higher than Pythagoras, thus Genesis is a magnificent allegory, which in the form of a story hides the secrets, not only

---

561 Extract from the part of the ancient Talmud called the Mishnah by the Jews. (Lévi's note.)

of the past accomplishment of creation, but of permanent and universal creation, of the eternal generation of beings.

Here is what we read in the Talmud:

"God stretched the sky out like a tabernacle, he dressed the world like a richly served table, and he created man as though he were inviting a guest."

Listen to what King Shlomo[562] says:

"The divine Chokmah, wisdom, the wife of God, built herself a house, she carved seven columns.

"She immolated her victims.

"She mixed her wine, she dressed the table, and she sent for her servants."

This wisdom who establishes her house according to regular and numerical architecture is the exact science which presides over the works of God.

It is her compass and her set square. The seven columns are the seven distinctive and primordial days.

The victims are the natural forces which fertilize themselves which results in a sort of death.

The mixed wine is the universal fluid, the table is the world with its seas filled with fish.

The servants of Chokmah are the souls of Adam and Chavah (Eve).

The earth from which Adam was formed was taken from the entire mass of the world.

His head is Israel, his body is the empire of Babylon and his members are the other nations of the Earth.

(Here are revealed the hopes of the initiates of Moses for the constitution of a universal Oriental kingdom.)

Yet there are twelve hours in the day in which man's creation was accomplished.

---

562   That is, Solomon. The passage that follows is a close paraphrase of Proverbs 9:1–2.

FIRST HOUR.

God reunites the scattered fragments of the Earth, and he kneads them together, from it he forms a single mass which he wishes to animate.

EXPLICATION.

Man is the synthesis of the created world, in him the creative unity begins, he is made in the image and the resemblance of God.

SECOND HOUR.

God roughs out the form of the body, he separates it in two so that the organs are dual, because all force and all life results from two, and it is thus that the Elohim had made all things.

EXPLICATION.

Everything lives through movement, everything maintains itself through equilibrium, and harmony results from the analogy of opposites; this law is the form of forms, it is the first manifestation of the activity and the fecundity of God.

THIRD HOUR.

The members of man, obeying the law of life, reproduce from themselves and are completed by the generative organ, which is composed of one and of two, symbol of the ternary number.

EXPLICATION.

The ternary comes of itself from the binary; the movement which produces two, produces three; three is the key to all numbers, because it is the first numeral synthesis, its geometry is the triangle, the first complete and enclosed figure, generator of an infinity of triangles, either dissimilar or the same.

FOURTH HOUR.

God blows on the face of man and gives him a soul.

EXPLICATION.

The quaternary which in geometry is the cross and the square is the perfect number and it is in the perfection of form that the intelligent soul manifests itself, according to this revelation of the Mishnah, the child will only be animated in the womb of the mother after the form completes all its members.

FIFTH HOUR.

Man stands on his feet, he detaches himself from the earth, he walks, he goes where he wishes.

EXPLICATION.

The number five is that of the soul symbolized by the quintessence which results from the equilibrium of the four elements, in the Tarot this number is symbolized by the grand-priest or the spiritual autocrat, symbol of the human will, that grand-priest who alone decides our eternal destinies.

SIXTH HOUR.

The animals pass before Adam and he gives each of them a name of his choosing.

EXPLICATION.

Through work, man subdues the earth and tames the animals; by manifesting his liberty, he produces his Verb, or Word, and creation obeys him; here primordial creation is completed. God created man on the sixth day, but on the sixth hour of that day, man finishes the work of God and creates himself anew in a way, since he makes himself the king of nature, which he subjects to his word.

SEVENTH HOUR.

God gives Adam a companion taken from the substance of man itself.

EXPLICATION.
God, after having created man in his image, rested on the seventh day, because he gave himself a fertile wife who would work ceaselessly for him; nature is the wife of God, and God rests on her. Man, having become a creator in his turn through the Verb, provides himself with a companion similar to himself and upon whose love he can now rest; woman is the work of man, it is he, who in loving her, renders her beautiful, it is he who makes her a mother; woman is the veritable daughter of human nature and mother of man, granddaughter and little mother[563] of God.

EIGHTH HOUR.

Adam and Eve get into the nuptial bed, they are two when they lie down and when they arise, they are four.

EXPLICATION.
The quaternary joined to the quaternary represents form balancing form, creation coming from creation, the eternal balance of life, seven being the number of God's rest, the unity which comes after represents man who works and cooperates with nature for the work of creation.

NINTH HOUR.

God imposes his law upon man.

---

563 A play on words; In French, *petite-fille*, "little daughter," means "granddaughter" while *petite mère*, "little mother," does not mean grandmother but mother-in-law! The latter reference is of course to the Virgin Mary, considered mother of God by Catholics.

EXPLICATION.

Nine is the number of initiation because, being composed of three times three, it represents the divine idea and the absolute philosophy of numbers, that is why Apollonius says that the mystery of the number nine must not be revealed.

TENTH HOUR.

In the tenth hour Adam falls into sin.

EXPLICATION.

According to the Cabalists, ten is the number of matter whose special sign is the zero, in the tree of the sephiroth, ten represents Malkhut or the exterior and material substance; Adam's sin is thus materialism and the fruit which he picks from the tree represents the flesh isolated from the spirit, the zero separated from its unity, the splitting of the number ten, which gives on one side the dispossessed unity and on the other the void or death.

ELEVENTH HOUR.

On the eleventh hour the guilty one is condemned to work and must expiate his sin by submitting to suffering.

EXPLICATION.

In the Tarot eleven represents strength, yet strength is acquired through ordeals; God gives man suffering as the means for his salvation, one must thus struggle and suffer to conquer intelligence and life.

TWELFTH HOUR.

Man and woman submit to their suffering, the expiation begins, and the liberator is promised.

EXPLICATION.

Such is the complement to the birth of morality, man is complete, because he is fated for the sacrifice which regenerates him. Adam's exile is similar to Oedipus's exile; like Oedipus, Adam is the father of two enemies; Oedipus has as a daughter the pious and virginal Antigone,[564] and the race of Adam gives rise to Mary.

These mysterious and divine revelations of the religious unity in the ancient mysteries is found, as we have said, in the Talmud, but without having recourse to this voluminous compilation, we can also find them in Paolo Riccio's commentary on the Talmudists which has as its title Epitome de talmudica Doctrina, p. 280 of tome I from the collection of the Cabalists by Pistorius.[565]

OF COUNTRY MAGIC
AND THE SORCERY OF SHEPHERDS

In his solitude, in the middle of his work with vegetation, the instinctive and magnetic forces of man are augmented and are exalted, the powerful emanations of sap, the odor of hay, the aromas of certain flowers fill the air with euphoria and vertigo; and then impressionable people easily fall into a sort of ecstasy which makes them dream while awake. It is then that the nocturnal washerwomen[566] appear, the werewolves, the imps who fling riders from their mounts and climb up on horses, whipping them with their long tails. These visions of men while still awake are real and frightful, and one should not laugh at our old Breton farmers when they recount what they have seen.

These passing intoxications, when they are multiplied and prolonged, communicate an impressionability and particular sensibility to the nervous system, people become waking somnambulists, the senses acquire a keenness which is sometimes miraculous and even incredible; they hear revealing sounds at tre-

---

564 The symbolism of these Greek stories has been suggested already in the introduction to "The Doctrine."

565 Johann Pistorius, *Artis cabbalisticae* (Basel, 1587).

566 Mysterious figures from French legend, curiously similar to the banshees of Irish tradition.

mendous distances, they see the thoughts of men on their faces, they are suddenly struck by presentiments of misfortune which threaten them.

Nervous children, idiots, old women, and in general all instinctive or unwilling celibates are the most susceptible to this type of magnetism; and it is thus that those pathological phenomena which we regard as the mysterious powers of the medium are produced and develop complications. Around these unruly souls, magnetic whirlpools are formed and wonders often occur, wonders analogous to those of electricity, the attraction and repulsion of inert objects, atmospheric currents, highly pronounced sympathetic or antipathetic influences. The human magnet acts at great distances and upon all bodies, with the exception of wood charcoal, which absorbs and neutralizes the terrestrial astral light in all its transformations.

If these natural accidents merge with a perverse will, this sick person can become a great danger to his neighbors, especially if his organism has exclusively absorbent properties. It is in this manner that enchantments and spells are explained; thence that strange ailment which the Romans called the evil eye and which is still feared in Naples under the name of Jettatura becomes admissible and can be submitted to medical diagnostics.

In our *Key to the Great Mysteries*[567] we have said why shepherds are more easily subject than others to these magnetic deregulations; drivers of herds, whom they magnetize with their good or evil will, are subject to influence from the animal souls which are united under their direction and which become like appendages of their will; their moral infirmities produce physical maladies in their sheep, and they are subject in turn to the petulance of their billy goats and the caprices of their nannies; if a shepherd has an absorbent nature, the flock becomes absorbent and sometimes fatally attracts to itself all the vigor and health of a neighboring flock. It is thus that mortalities occur in the stables without anyone knowing why, and all precautions or remedies that are taken have no effect.

This contagious sickness within flocks is sometimes determined by the

---

567 *La clef des grands mystères* (1861), one of Lévi's later books; this appendix was added with the second, revised edition of *Dogme et rituel de la haute magie.*

enmity of a rival shepherd who sneaked in during the night and buried a pact[568] under the threshold of the stable. This will make the incredulous smile, but this no longer has to do with credulity. That which superstition blindly believed in the past, science now observes and explains.

For it is certain and demonstrated by numerous experiments, first, that the magnetic influence of man directed by his will attaches itself to any object chosen and influenced by that will.

Second, that human magnetism acts at a distance and its power is centered upon magnetized objects.

Third, that the will to magnetize acquires even more power as it is multiplied by the expressive acts of that will.

Fourth, that if these acts are of a nature which strongly impresses the imagination, if to accomplish them one had to surmount great exterior obstacles and vanquish great interior resistances, the will becomes fixed, relentless, and invincible like the will of madmen.

Fifth, that men alone, due to their free will, can resist human will, but that animals do not resist for long.

Let us now examine how rural sorcerers create their evil spells, veritable pacts with the spirit of perversity which serve as the fatal consecration of their evil will.

They form a composition of substances which cannot be procured without criminal acts or combined without sacrilege, they pronounce over these horrible mixtures, sometimes soaked with their own blood, formulas of execration, and they bury these signs of infernal hatred, which are irrevocably magnetized under the field or the door to the stable of their enemy.

The effect is infallible; from that moment the flock begins to perish and the entire stable will soon be depopulated, unless the master of the stable opposes an energetic and victorious resistance towards the magnetism of his enemy.

---

568   That is, a pact with the devil, consigning the neighbor's flock to Satan. This is a fascinating survival of the ancient Greek and Roman habit of writing and burying *defixiones* (curse tablets) to invoke the powers of the underworld against an enemy.

This resistance is easy when we make it using circles and currents, that is to say through the association of wills and efforts. Contagion hardly ever affects farmers who know how to make themselves liked by their neighbors. Their goods are thereby protected by everyone's interest and the associated good wills soon triumph over an isolated malevolence.

When an evil spell is thus cast off, it turns against its author, the malevolent magnetizer suffers intolerable torments, which soon force him to destroy his evil work and go back himself and disinter his pact.

People in the Middle Ages also had recourse to conjurations and prayers, they blessed the stables and the animals, they said mass as a means of repelling, by the association of Christian wills in the faith and in prayer, the impiety of the enchanter.

They aired the stables, they practiced fumigations, and they mixed magnetized salt into the animals' feed with special exorcisms.

At the end of our *Key to the Great Mysteries* we reproduced several of these exorcisms, whose original text we had reestablished with particular attention.

These formulas, copied and recopied by ignorant hands, thereafter senselessly printed by exploiters of popular credulity, did not come into our hands without strange alterations.

Here are a few of them as they are still found in the latest grimoires:

Before all else, pronounce upon the salt: *Panem coelestem accipiat sit nomen Domine invocabis.*[569] Then take recourse in the castle of Beauty and do the casting and the frictions while pronouncing the following:

"*Eum ter ergo docentes omnes gentes baptizantes eos. In nomine atris,* etc."[570]

Protection against scabies. "When Our Lord rose up to heaven, he left his holy virtue on earth. Pasle, Colet, and Hervé; all that which God said

---

569   "Let him receive celestial bread; let it be the name of God you will invoke." All these bits of Latin are more or less garbled; see Lévi's corrections below.

570   "Therefore he taught three times all people, baptizing them. In the name of the (F)ather," etc.

was said well. Beast of red, white, or black, of whatever color you are, if there are any scabies or ringworms on you, even if they were placed and made nine feet underground, it is just as true that they shall leave and die, just as Saint John was in the skin and was born of a camel; just as Saint Joseph Nicodemus of Arimathea brought down the body of my sweet Savior Redeemer Jesus Christ, from the tree of the cross, on the day of Good Friday."

"You shall use for the casting and the frictions the following words, and have recourse to that which we said in the castle of Beauty:

"Salt, I cast you with the hand that God gave me. *Volo et vono Baptista Sancta Aca latum est.*"[571]

Protection to stop wolves from entering the grounds where the sheep are. "Place yourself in the corner of the rising sun, and pronounce five times that which follows. If you only wish to pronounce it once, you will do so five days in a row.

"Come, beast of wool, this is the Lamb of humility, I protect you, *Ave, Maria.* This is the Lamb of the Redemptor who fasted for forty days without rebelling, without having taken any meal from the enemy, who was in truth tempted. Go straight, gray beast, to the gray grasper; search out your prey, wolves and she-wolves and wolf cubs; you shall not visit this meat which is here. In the name of the Father, the Son, and the Holy-Spirit, and the blessed saint Stag. Also *vade retro, o Satana!*"[572]

Another protection. "Beast of wool, I take you in the name of God and the very holy sacred Virgin Mary. I pray to God that the domain that I shall make takes on and profits from my will. I conjure you so that you will break and shatter any kinds of enchantments which may be passed under the body of my living flock of beasts of wool, who are here present before God and before myself; who are under my care and my guard. In the

---

571   "I will and I go, Saint Aca the Baptist at my side."

572   "Go back, O Satan!"

name of the Father, the Son, and the Holy Spirit and of M. Saint John the Baptist and M. Saint Abraham."

See above regarding what we have said for operating in the castle of Beauty, and you shall use the casting and friction of the words which follow:

"Pasqueflower, Jesus is resuscitated."

Protection against scabies, ringworm and sheep pox. "It was on a Monday morning that the Savior of the world passed, the Holy Virgin after him, M. Saint John his shepherd boy, his friend, who searches for his divine flock, which is besotted with that malign sheep pox, with which he is fed up, because of the three shepherds who came to adore my Savior Redemptor Jesus Christ in Bethlehem, and who adored the voice of the child." Say the Our Father five times and the Ave Maria five times.

"My flock, who are subject to me, shall be healthy and beautiful. I pray to Mme Saint Genevieve that she may serve me as my friend with regard to this malign sheep pox here. Sheep pox banished by God, renounced by Jesus Christ, I command you, on behalf of the great God, that you leave from here, and that you go and dissolve and be confounded before God and before me, as does the dew before the sun. By the so glorious Virgin Mary and Holy Spirit, sheep pox, leave from here, because God commands you, as true as Joseph Nicodemus of Arimathea had descended the precious body of my Savior and Redemptor Jesus Christ, the day of Good Friday, from the tree of the cross: by the Father, by the Son, and by the Holy Spirit, worthy flock of beasts of wool, approach here, to God and to me. Here is the divine offering of salt which I present to you today; since without the salt nothing was done and with the salt everything was done, as I believe, by the Father, etc.

"O salt! I conjure you, on behalf of the great living God, that you may serve as I say, that you may protect and guard my flock from ringworm, scabies, dyspnea, from the lesser dyspnea, from poisoned pellets and from contaminated water. I command you, as Jesus Christ my savior commanded his disciples in the boat, when they said to him: Lord, wake up, because the sea frightens us. The Lord awoke immediately and commanded the sea to stop; then the sea became calm, commanded by the Father, etc."

It is evident that one should read:

For the prayer on the salt: *panem coelestem accipiam et nomen Domini invocabo.*[573]

And below that:

Euntes ergo docete omnes gentes baptizantes eos, etc.[574]

The names of Pasle, Colet, and Hervé are those of shepherds associated with magnetic works. Instead of *mortira* (line 14) read *sortira*; and in the following line read hamlet rather than camel which is an absurd and grotesque nonsense here.

In one of the following formulas, instead of pasque flower (*passe flori*), one should read flowery Easter (*pâques fleuri*).

That which follows was written primitively in verse and we can see, by restoring it, how much it had been disfigured:

> It was on a Monday morning that
> Jesus passed by the road,
> With the holy Virgin beside him
> And M. Saint John his friend,
> M. Saint John his shepherd boy,
> who searches for his divine flock.
> Besotted with malign sheep pox,
> Malign sheep pox which will be cured
> And from my flock will leave

---

573   "I will receive celestial bread and I will invoke the name of God."

574   "As you go, therefore, you will teach all people, baptizing them," etc.

By the three kings and the shepherds;
From the adorers of Jesus Christ
Who went to Bethlehem
In passing by Jerusalem
And turn by turn prostrated themselves
Adoring the cross of the child.

This example will suffice for understanding to what point these little vulgar books on sorcery and the so-called magic they still dare to peddle in the countryside are altered and have become ridiculous.

We can also see that in principle these formulas derive from an ardent and naive faith. It was in the name of the little child born in a stable, the shepherds who came to visit him, Saint John the Baptist, man of the desert, always accompanied by a lamb without blemishes, that the old Christian herdsman conjured against the evil spells of their enemies. These prayers, or rather these acts of faith, were pronounced upon salt, so salutary on its own and so indispensable to the good health of the herd. Our false scholars may now laugh at these rustic enchanters; but they knew well what they were doing and their instinct, directed by experience, guided them more surely than the poor science of the time could have.

Now that faith has weakened in the countryside as elsewhere, these naive prayers have almost no power or prestige. At the best we can search them out as curious monuments to the beliefs of our ancestors. We find them in handwritten grimoires and in Leo III's *Enchiridion*, a famous little book from the Middle Ages, of which various editions with more or less errors have multiplied in our day. We have extracted and provided here the conjurations which were considered the most effective.

Here begin the mysterious prayers of Pope Leo.

Prayers against all sort of charms, enchantments, curses, characters, visions, illusions, possessions, obsessions, evil obstructions to marriage, and anything that can occur due to the evil spells of sorcerers, or through the incursion of devils; also very good against all types of misfortune caused to horses, mares, bulls, cows, sheep, ewes, and other animal species. Prayer *Qui Verbum caro factum est*, etc.

May the Verb which had been made into flesh, and which had been attached to the cross, and which sits at the right hand side of the Father fulfill the prayers of those who believe in him, he who by his holy name, all knees kneel; and by the merits of the blessed Virgin Mary his mother, and also by the prayers of all the saints of God. Deign to protect this creature N from all that could harm it, and from demonic attacks, you who live and reign in the perfect unity; because here is †[575] the cross of our Lord Jesus Christ, in whom is found our salvation, our life and our resurrection, and the confusion of all those who wish to harm us and from malign spirits; flee then, adversaries, because I conjure you, demons of hell, and you malign spirits, whatever type you may be; whether you had been called or invoked, whether you come of your own will, or you were sent; either by enchantment or by the art of evil men or women; who encouraged you to dwell or molest. Until that time when you have left your diabolic trickery, you shall depart forthwith † in the name of the true † living God † holy † Father †, Son †, and Holy Spirit. Especially by he † who was sacrificed and † who was killed as a lamb †, who was crucified as a man, in the blood with which we had vanquished, when Saint Michael battled with us, and preceded victory, and made you retreat by the amount you had approached, and so that you cannot, under any pretext there is, molest or trouble this creature, neither in its body, nor outside its body, through visions, nor by fright, nor by day, nor by night, nor in sleeping, nor in waking, nor while eating, nor while praying, nor while doing other things, either natural or spiritual: otherwise I spread over you † all the maledictions, excommunications † degrees and punishments and torments, as though you were thrown into a pool of fire and of sulfur by the hands of your enemies, by the command of the Holy Trinity, the archangel Saint Michael executes it. Because if

575 In Catholic prayers, as here, the cross symbol instructs the person repeating the prayer to make the sign of the cross.

you have previously taken any bond of adoration, any perfume, any subtle and evil affliction that might be, either with herbs or with words, or in stones, or in the elements, whether natural, whether they are simple or mixtures, or temporal, or spiritual, or sacramental, or in the names of the great God and his angels, whether they are in the characters of the hours, of minutes, of days, of the year, of months, observed superstitiously by an expressed or tacit pact, even strengthened by vows. I break † all these things, I annul them and destroy them by the power of the Father who created this world †, by the wisdom of the redeeming Son, by the grace of the Holy Spirit †, by he who accomplished the entire law †, who is †, who was †, who is to come †, all-powerful, holy †, immortal †, Savior †, which is composed of four letters †, Jehovah †, Alpha and Omega †, the beginning and the end. May all the diabolical virtue in this creature be extinguished, and be driven away by the virtue of the very holy cross, by the invocation of the angels, the archangels, the patriarchs, the prophets, the apostles, the martyrs, the confessors, the virgins, and also the blessed Virgin and all those who reign in heaven, with the dead Lamb since the beginning of the world and those who live well in the holy Church of God. Retreat then; in the manner of the smoke of liver, of burned fish, according to Raphael's advice, who chased off the spirit which had tormented Sara, in the same manner that these benedictions drive you away, so that you do not dare approach this creature. Marked with the sign of the holy cross, with the area of one hundred thousand feet, because my mandate is not mine, but that of he who was sent by the Father in order to destroy your works, as he had destroyed them on the tree of the cross, he gave us such a power, to the glory and utility of the faithful, to command you, as we command you and order you; that you dare not approach by Our Savior Jesus Christ †; here is the cross of the Lord, flee, adversaries; the lion of the tribe of Judah has vanquished. Root of David, halleluiah, amen, amen, fiat, fiat.

HERE ARE THE SEVEN PRAYERS
THAT ONE MUST SAY DURING THE WEEK.

For Sunday. *Libera me, Domine*, etc.

Our Father, etc.[576]

Deliver me, I beg you, Lord, your servant N., from all past ills, present ills, and ones to come, as much of the soul as of the body, and by the intercession of the blessed Virgin Mary, mother of God, and of your blessed apostles Saint Peter, Saint Paul, and Saint Andrew, with all your saints, favorably provide peace to your servant N., and holiness in all the days of my life, so that, being aided by the help of your mercy, I shall always be free from the slavery of sin and from all the fears of any troubles. By the same Jesus Christ your Son, Our Lord, who, being God, lives and reigns with you in the unity of the Holy Spirit, in all the centuries of centuries. Amen. May the peace of the Lord be always with me. Amen. May your celestial peace, Lord, which you had left to your disciples, always firmly dwell in my heart, and may it always be between me and my enemies, visible or invisible. Amen. May the peace of Our Lord Jesus Christ, his face, his body and his blood, come to my aid, I N., sinner that I am, and serve me as a favorable protection and defense, and as a consolation to my soul and my body. Amen. Lamb of God, who deigned to be born of the Virgin Mary, and to carry the sins of the world on the tree of the cross, have pity on my body and on my soul; Lamb of God through whom all the faithful are saved, give me in this century and the centuries to come eternal peace. Amen.

For Monday. *O Adonai, per quem*, etc.

O Adonai! O Savior through whom all things were liberated, deliver me from all evil. O Adonai! O Savior through whom all things were saved, save me in all my needs and anxieties, affairs and perils, and from all the traps of my visible and invisible enemies, deliver me ✝ in the

---

576   That is to say, repeat the Our Father, or Lord's Prayer, here.

name of the Father who created the world †, in the name of the Son who redeemed everyone †, in the name of the Holy Spirit who fulfilled all the laws. I align myself with you entirely. Amen †. May the blessing of God the all-powerful Father, who created all things with a single word, be always with me. Amen †. May the blessing of Our Savior Jesus Christ, Son of the living God, be always with me. Amen †. May the blessing of the Holy Spirit with his seven gifts be always with me †. Amen. May the blessing of the blessed Virgin Mary with her Son be always with me. Amen. May the blessing and the consecration of the bread and the wine which Our Savior Jesus Christ had made when he had given it to his disciples, in saying to them:

For Tuesday. *Accipite et comedite*, etc.

Take and eat all this, because it is my body which shall be given to you, in memory of me. Amen. May the blessing of the angels and the archangels, of the virtues, of the Principalities of the thrones, of the dominations, of the cherubim and the seraphim be always with me. Amen. May the blessing of the patriarchs, of the prophets, of the apostles, of the martyrs, of the confessors, of the virgins, and of all the saints of God be always with me. Amen. May the blessings of all the heavens of God be always with me. Amen †. May the adorable majesty protect me; may his eternal kindness raise me; may the power of the Father conserve me; may the wisdom of the Son vivify me; may the virtue of the Holy Spirit always be between me and my visible and invisible enemies. Amen. Power of the Father, fortify me; wisdom of the Son, deliver me; consolation of the Holy Spirit, console me. The Father is peace; the Son is life, the Holy Spirit is the remedy of consolation and of salvation. Amen. May the divinity of God bless me; may his humanity fortify me. Amen. May his piety warm me; may his love conserve me: O Jesus Christ, Son of the living God, have pity on me.

For Wednesday. *O Emmanuel, ab hoste*, etc.

O Emmanuel! defend me from the malign spirit and all my visible and invisible enemies, and from all evil; the Christ king came in peace; God became man, and he suffered with mercy for us; may Jesus Christ, peaceful king, always be between me and my enemies. Amen †. Christ conquers †; Christ reigns †; Christ commands †. May Christ always defend me from all evil. Amen. May Christ deign to command that I be victorious over all my adversaries. Amen. Here is the cross of Our Lord † Jesus Christ; flee, adversaries. The lion of the tribe of Judah has vanquished; root of David, halleluiah, halleluiah, halleluiah. Savior of the world, save me, and rescue me, you who by your cross and by your precious blood had redeemed me; aid me, I beg you, O God, O Agios, O Theos †, Agios Ischyros †, Agios Athanatos †, eleison himas;[577] holy God, powerful God, merciful and immortal God, have pity on me N., your servant. Lord, come to my aid; do not abandon me; never look upon me with contempt, God my salvation; but always come to my aid, Lord God my Savior.

For Thursday. *Illumina oculos meos*, etc.

Illuminate my eyes, Lord, so that I may never fall asleep in death, and that my enemy does not say that he was stronger than me. May the Savior come to my aid, and I will not fear what man could do against me; my very kind Jesus Christ, protect me, rescue me, and save me: that in the name of Jesus all knees kneel in the heavens, on earth and in the hells, and that all tongues confess that Our Lord Jesus Christ is in the glory of God our Father. Amen. I know very truly, O Jesus, that on any day and hour that may be that I invoke you, I shall be saved. O so clement Lord Jesus Christ, Son of the living God, who, by the virtue of your very precious name, had operated so many miracles, and who gave the so abundant remedy to us who have so great a need, because, by the virtue of your name, the demons fled, the blind saw, the deaf heard, the lame walked, the dumb spoke, the lepers were cured, the sick found health, and the dead were resuscitated; because, when we pronounce

---

577 These words in Greek are translated exactly in the following sentence.

the name of your so sweet son, Jesus, we hear a sweet melody in our ears, honey is tasted on our lips, the demon flees, all knees kneel, the celestial spirits rejoice, evil intentions are uprooted, all infirmities are cured; we are granted several indulgences; the struggles between the world, the flesh, and the devil are exhausted, and many other good things follow, because whoever invokes the name of God shall be saved, that name that was named by an angel before he was conceived in the womb.

For Friday. *O nomen dulce*, etc.

O sweet name, name which fortifies the heart of man, name of life, of salvation, and of joy; precious name, joyous, glorious, and gracious; name which fortifies the sinners, name which saves us and which guides and governs the entire machine of the universe. May it please you then, O so pious Jesus! that by the same so precious virtue of your name you deign to make the demons before me flee; illuminate me, I who am blind; make it so I hear, I who am deaf; guide my steps, I who am lame; make it so I speak, I who am dumb; cure my leprosy, give me health, I who am infirm; wake me from death, surround me entirely inside and out, such that being equipped with your so sacred name, I can always live within you, in praising you and in honoring you, you who are worthy of praises, because you are the glorious Lord and the eternal Lord and the eternal Son of God, within whom, to whom and by whom all things rejoice and are governed, to you the praise, the honor and the glory over all the centuries. Amen. May Jesus always be in my heart, may Jesus always be in my mouth; may Jesus always be in my inward parts. Amen. May God my Lord Jesus Christ be within me to bring me back to health; may he be around me to guide me; may he be next to me to conserve me, in front of me to protect me, on me to bless me; may he be between me to vivify me, close to me to govern me, above me to fortify me; may he always be with me to take away all the sorrow of an eternal death, he who, with the Father and the Holy Spirit, lives and reigns during all the centuries of centuries. Amen.

For Saturday. *Jesus Mariae filius*, etc.

May Jesus, son of Mary, Lord and Savior of the world, be clement and favorable to me, may he give us a healthy and submissive spirit, honor be to God, and may he accord us deliverance from our evils in the place where we are: and no one laid their hands upon him, because his hour had not yet come, he who is, who was, and will always be Alpha and Omega, God and man, the beginning and the end; may this invocation be my eternal protection, name of Jesus of Nazareth, king of the Jews, mark of triumph, son of the Virgin Mary, have pity on me, in accordance with your clemency, on the road to eternal salvation. Amen. But Jesus, knowing all that must occur to him, came forwards and said to them: "Whom do you search for?" They answered him, "Jesus of Nazareth." Jesus said to them, "It is I." Now Judas, who betrayed him, was also present with them. And when Jesus had told them: "It is I," they were overset and fell to the ground. He asked them again: "Whom do you search for?" They said to him, "Jesus of Nazareth." Jesus answered them, "I have already told you that it is I; if it is thus for me that you search, let these others go." May Jesus, who made himself a victim for me, through his cross effacing my crime, render me agreeable in his eyes, so that at last my purified soul, being separated from my body, reigns with him in the heavens. Amen. Jesus is the way †, Jesus is life †, Jesus is the truth †, Jesus suffered †, Jesus was crucified †, Jesus Christ, Son of the living God, have pity on me. But Jesus, passing † amongst them, was standing, and no one laid violent hands upon Jesus, because his hour had not yet come.

For Sunday, Oremus. *Dulcissime Domine*, etc.

Sweetest Lord Jesus Christ, living Son of God, who answered thus to the Jews who wanted to take you: It is I; thus if it is I who you search for, let these others go; then the Jews were upturned and fell to the ground. In this way, my so kind Savior Jesus Christ, deign to protect me now and always from all my enemies who look to harm me, and make them upturn and fall, so that they may do me no harm in any manner that there is, but that I withdraw in safety from their hands onto the road of peace and of rest, in the praise and the glory of your name, which is blessed in the centuries of centuries. Amen.

These prayers, as we can see, are nothing but very pious and very Christian in their simplicity and can still be the expression of confidence and upright will of a submissive child of the Church.

Prayers said together and which are in accord with the ardent faith of the majority, truly constitute a magnetic current and what we mean by magnetism works *in circles*.

Evil spells are only dangerous for isolated individuals; it is thus important, especially for people from the countryside, to live in families, to have peace in their household, and to make numerous friends.

One must also, for the health of the herds, properly air and expose the stables to the sun; batten the ground well which one can cover with a sort of pavement of wood charcoal, purify unhealthy water with a charcoal filter,[578] give the beasts salt that is not exorcised, but magnetized according to the intentions of the master, avoid as much as possible neighboring herds belonging to an enemy or a rival, rub sick ewes with a mix of pulverized wood charcoal and sulfur, then often change their litter and give them good grass.

One must also carefully avoid the company of persons afflicted with black or chronic sicknesses, never speak to village seers and enchanters, because in consulting these sorts of people, one in a way places oneself under their power, finally, one must have confidence in God alone and let nature do its work.

Priests often pass for sorcerers in the countryside, and they are believed to be relatively capable of exercising an evil influence, which is unfortunately true in regards to evil priests; but a good priest, far from bringing bad luck for anyone, is a benediction for families and the regions.

There also exist dangerous madmen who believe in the influence of the spirit of darkness, and who are not afraid of evoking him so as to make him a servant

---

578   Modern as this sounds, charcoal filters were in common use in Europe long before Lévi's time.

to their evil desires; one must apply to these types that which we have said about diabolical evocations, and most of all to guard oneself well against believing them or imitating them.

To command the elementary forces, one must have pure morals and a strong sense of justice. The man who makes a worthy and noble use of his intelligence and his liberty is truly the king of nature, but beings of human shape who allow themselves to be dominated by bestial instincts are not even worthy of commanding animals. The Desert Fathers were served by lions and by bears.

Daniel, in the lion's den, was not touched by any of those starving animals, and, in fact, say the masters of the great art of the Cabala, ferocious beasts naturally respect men and only attack them when they take them for other animals who are hostile or inferior to them. Animals, in effect, communicate through their physical soul with the universal astral light and are endowed with a particular intuition for seeing the plastic mediator of men under the form which had been given to it through the regular exercise of free will.

The veritable truth alone appears to them, in the splendor of the human form, and they are forced to obey its regard and its voice; other animals attract them as prey or scare them and irritate them as dangers. It is for this reason, according to the prophet Isaiah, that when justice will reign on earth, and when men will raise their families in true innocence, a little child will lead the tigers and the lions, and will play with impunity in their midst.

Prosperity and joy should be the privilege of the just; for them misfortune itself changes into a blessing, and the pain they experience is like the goad of the divine shepherd who forces them to always walk and progress along the ways of perfection. The Sun greets them in the morning, and the Moon smiles at them at night. For them, sleep is without anxiety, and dreams without terror, their presence blesses the Earth and brings happiness to the living. Happy are those who resemble them! happy are those who take them for friends!

Physical evil is often a consequence of moral evil, disorder necessarily follows unreason. And unreason in action is injustice. The laborious life of the inhabitants of the countryside too often render them hard and greedy. From there a host of errors in judgment and there follows an imbalance of actions which forces nature to protest and to react. That is the secret of those evil destinies which sometimes seem to attach themselves to a family or a house. The ancients would then say: one must appease the offended gods, and they tell us still: the good acquired through evil profits no one, one must give back, one must repair the evil committed, one must satisfy justice, or justice will take revenge in a fatal manner.

A power, invincible if we wish it, was given to us to vanquish fatality: it is our moral liberty. With the aid of this power, we can correct destiny and remake the future. That is why religion does not want us to consult the seers to know what will happen to us; it wants only that we learn from our pastors what we should do. What do obstacles matter to us? A brave man should not count his enemies before the battle. To provide for evil is to render it in a way necessary. We will arrive at the result that we had wanted: there is the universal prophecy.

To observe nature, to follow the laws in our work, to obey reason in all things, to sacrifice, if need be, one's own interest for justice. That is the true magic which brings happiness, and those who act thus fear neither the malice of enchanters not the sorcery of shepherds.

RESPONSES TO SOME QUESTIONS AND CRITICISMS

FIRST QUESTION

Question: Do you hope that serious Catholics will accept your Cabalistic
   beliefs, your philosophical interpretations of doctrine, and even
   your definition of Catholicism, that is to say universality in matters
   of religion?
Response: If by serious Catholics you mean those who deny civilization and
   its progress, I certainly hope not.

Q: So you are a Protestant?
R: Yes, if one is a Protestant when he believes in civilization and progress.

Q: **Why then do you call yourself a Roman Catholic?**

R: Because I do not believe that we should even exclude Romans from the universal communion.

Q: **What do you hope to achieve if, while calling yourself Catholic, you do not hope to convert true Catholics?**

R: I would like to bring back to the hierarchical unity, to the integrity of the doctrine and the effectiveness of the cult, the dissident Christian communions, and this is possible for the communions emancipated by the reform, since they accept civilization and progress.

SECOND QUESTION

Q: **Do you perform miracles and can you teach the means of performing them?**

R: If by miracles you mean works counter to nature or effects unjustified by their causes, no, I neither perform nor teach how to perform such miracles. God himself would not know how to do such things.

THIRD QUESTION

Q: **How do you answer those who accuse you of credulity, of superstition, or of charlatanism?**

R: I answer that they have not read my books or that, having read them, they did not understand them. It was thus that a Sir Tavernier, in a so-called critique of the *Key to the Great Mysteries*, was not afraid to write that I evoked Archaea, Azoth and Hyle, well known devils, he adds. Yet who does not know that by Archaea the ancients meant the universal soul, by Azoth, the mediating substance, and by Hyle, the passive matter?

FOURTH QUESTION

Q: How do you answer to those, like Sir Gougenot des Mousseaux, who call your writings abominable books?

R: I take care not to answer their offenses with more offenses, and feel sorry for them because they are subject to beliefs which translate into reckless judgments and insults.

—*Eliphas Lévi*

THE RELIGIOUS, PHILOSOPHICAL, AND MORAL TENDENCIES OF OUR BOOKS ON MAGIC

Since the first edition of this book was published,[579] several major events have occurred in the world, and others which are perhaps even greater will soon come to pass.

As usual, these events were forecast by various prophecies: the tables had spoken, voices had arisen from the walls, and disembodied hands had written mysterious words as at Belshazzar's feast.

Fanaticism, in the last convulsions of its agony, signaled this final persecution of Christians as predicted by all the prophets. The martyrs of Damas[580] asked the dead of Perugia[581] for the name of the one who saves and who blesses; then the sky clouded over and the earth remained silent.

More than ever, science and religion, despotism and liberty seem to be fighting a relentless war and swearing irreconcilable hatred for each other. Do not believe in bloody appearances, however: they are on the cusp of uniting and embracing each other forever.

---

579 This essay was originally published as a preliminary discourse to the second edition of *Dogme et rituel de la haute magie*. It deals primarily with issues and incidents relevant to Lévi's own time, though, and so has been placed here as an appendix instead.

580 A town in Syria where eleven Franciscan monks were killed by Muslim rebels in 1860.

581 The site of an 1859 uprising against the papacy, which was suppressed by a massacre of citizens by the pope's troops.

The discovery of the great secrets of religion and of the primitive science of the Mages, in revealing to the world the unity of the universal dogma, annihilates fanaticism by proving the prophecies to be correct. The human word, the creator of the marvels of man, unites forever with the word of God, and ends the universal antimony within us, making us understand that harmony is the result of the analogy of opposites.

The greatest Catholic genius of modern times, Count Joseph de Maistre,[582] had foreseen this great event. "Newton," he said, "brings us back to Pythagoras, and the analogy that exists between science and faith must sooner or later come closer together. The world is without religion, but such a monstrosity cannot exist for long; the eighteenth century continues on, but it will end."

Sharing the faith and hope of this great man, we dared to search through the ruins of the old sanctuaries of occultism; we asked of the secret doctrines of the Chaldeans, the Egyptians, and the Hebrews, to provide the secrets of the transfiguration of the dogmas, and the eternal truth answered us: the truth, which is one and universal, like existence; the truth, which belongs to science as much as to faith; the truth, mother of reason and of justice; the living truth in the forces of nature, the mysterious Elohim which remake the sky and the earth when chaos takes over creation and its marvels for a time, and when the spirit of God soars alone over the abyss of the oceans.

The truth is above all opinions and all parties.

The truth is like the Sun; blind is he who does not see it. This was the meaning, we do not doubt it, of a famous speech of Bonaparte's, spoken by him at a time when the conqueror of Italy, summarizing the French revolution incarnate in him alone, began to understand how the Republic could be a truth.

Truth is life, and life is revealed through movement. Also through movement, through willed and effective movement, through action, to use a single word, life develops and takes on new forms. Yet, the developments of life by itself, and its giving birth to new forms; we call creation. The intelligent power which works through universal movement, we call the Verb, in a transcendental and absolute manner. It is the initiative of God, which can never remain without effect, and

---

582   French philosopher and conservative politician (1754–1821).

never stops without achieving its goal. For God, speaking is doing; and such should be the power of speech even among men: true speech is the seed of action. An emission of intelligence and will cannot be sterile unless there was abuse or profanation of its original dignity. And it is for this reason that the Savior of men must hold us severely to account for all disorienting thoughts without a legitimate goal, and even more importantly, for idle speech.

Jesus, according to the Gospel, was powerful in his deeds and in his words; deeds before words: it is in this manner that one's right to speak is established and proven. Jesus began to do and to speak, says an evangelist elsewhere, and often, in the primitive language of the holy Scripture, an action is called a verb. In every language in fact, we call a VERB that which expresses at the same time being and action, and there is no verb that cannot be replaced by the verb to do by diversifying the structure of the sentence. In the principle was the Verb, said Saint John the evangelist. In what principle? In the first principle; in the absolute principle which comes before all things. Thus, in this principle was the Verb, that is to say, action. This is incontestable in philosophy, since the first principle is necessarily the first driving force. The Verb is not an abstraction: it is the most positive principle in the world, because it is continually made evident by deeds. The philosophy of the Verb is essentially the philosophy of action and of done deeds, and it is in this manner that we can distinguish a verb from a word. Words can sometimes be sterile, like a harvest of empty corn husks, but such is never the case with the Verb. The Verb, is the full and fertile word; men do not amuse themselves by listening to and applauding it; they always fulfill it! Often without understanding it, almost never without having resisted it. The doctrines we repeat are not the ones which succeed. Christianity was still a mystery when the Caesars sensed that they were dethroned by the Christian Verb. A system which the world admires and the crowds applaud, can only be a brilliant assembly of sterile words; a system to which humanity is subjected to, in a manner of saying, despite itself, is a Verb.

Power is demonstrated by results, and as was written, it is said, by a profound politician from modern times: Responsibility is only important when one does not succeed.[583] These words, which some intelligent minds had found to be im-

---

583 Attributed to Louis Philippe I, the last king of the French.

moral, are equally true if applied to all the particular notions which distinguish the word from the Verb, the will from action, or, more precisely, the imperfect act from the perfect act. The man who damns himself, according to Catholic theology, is he who is unable to save himself. To sin is to lack happiness. The man who does not succeed is always wrong: whether in literature, in ethics, or in politics. The bad person of all types is the beautiful and the good poorly achieved. And if we have to go higher up to the domain of the eternal dogma, two spirits met in the old days, each of whom wished divinity for themselves alone: one succeeded, and it is he who is God; the other failed and became the devil!

To succeed is to be able to; to fail forever is to try eternally: these two words summarize the opposing destinies of the spirit of good and the spirit of evil.

When a will modifies the world, it is the Verb which speaks, and all voices are silenced before it, as is said in the book of Maccabees, in regards to Alexander: but Alexander died with his Verb of power, because there was no future in him; unless the grandeur of Rome was the realization of his dreams! Yet in our times something even stranger is occurring: a man who died in exile in the middle of the Atlantic Ocean has silenced Europe a second time before his Verb, and he holds the entire world suspended before the power of his name alone![584]

This is because Napoleon's mission was great and saintly; it is because the Verb of truth was in him. Napoleon alone could, after the French Revolution, raise the altars of Catholicism, and it was Napoleon's moral heir alone who had the right to bring Pius IX back to Rome.[585] We will explain why.

In the Catholic doctrine of Incarnation there is a dogma known to the theological schools under the title of Communication of Idioms. This dogma affirms that in the union of divinity and humanity accomplished by Jesus Christ the joining of the two natures was so close that the result was one identity and a very

---

584 A sly if politically dangerous comment. Napoleon III, the nephew of Napoleon Bonaparte, was the emperor of France at the time Lévi wrote, though he had practically nothing in common with his illustrious uncle but the name.

585 From the unification of Italy in 1861 to the beginning of the Franco-Prussian War in 1870, French troops were garrisoned in Rome and the countryside around it by order of Napoleon III, to keep the Italian government from invading the pope's secular dominions.

simple unity of personhood, which means that Mary, mother of man, could and should be called the Mother of God. (The entire world debated in favor of this prerogative at the time of the Council of Ephesus.) Which means as well that we can attribute to God the sufferings of man and to man the glories of God. In one word, the Communication of idioms is the solidarity of the divine and human natures in Jesus Christ; a solidarity in the name of which we can say that God is man, and that man is God.

Zoroastrianism, in revealing to the world the universal law of equilibrium and harmony resulting from the analogy of opposites, takes all the sciences at their base and was the prelude by the reform of mathematics to a universal revolution in all the branches of human knowledge: to the principal generator of numbers it attaches the principal generator of ideas, and in consequence the principal generator of worlds, thus bringing to the light of science the unpredictable result of the overly physical intuitions of Pythagoras; he confronts the theurgical esotericism of the school of Alexandria with a clear, precise, and absolute formula which all the regenerated sciences reveal and justify: the first reason and the last final universal movement, whether through ideas or through the forms, can, for him, be definitively summarized in a few algebraic signs in the form of an equation.

Mathematics, thus understood, brings us to religion, because it becomes, in all its forms, the demonstration of the infinite generator of the firmament and proof of the absolute, from which emanates all the calculations of all the sciences. This supreme and inevitable consequence of the works of the human spirit, this conquest of divinity by intelligence and by study, must complete the redemption of the human soul and provide the definitive emancipation of the Verb of humanity. And thus, what we still call today the natural law will have all the authority and all the infallibility of a *revealed law*; and thus also, we will understand that the positive and divine law is at the same time a natural law, since God is the creator of nature and would be unable to contradict himself in his creations and his laws.

From this reconciliation of the human Verb shall be born true morality, which does not yet exist in a complete and definitive manner. And so a new path will also open up for the universal Church. Indeed, up until the present, the infallibility of the Church was just dogma, and for this reason, no doubt, the Divinity did not wish to have to deal with men who were asked to understand what previously they were simply required to believe. But to constitute morality, the situation is different, because morality is as human as it is divine; and man must have the choice of consent to a pact which obliges him the most. Do you know what the epoch which we are heading towards lacks the most? It is morality. Everyone senses it, everyone says so, yet the schools of ethics are open everywhere. What do these schools need? A teaching which would inspire confidence; in a word, a reasonable authority instead of reason without authority on the one hand, and authority without reason on the other.

Let us note that the question of morality was the pretext for the great defection which has now left the Church widowed and desolate. It is in the name of *humanity*, that material expression of *charity*, that we raised the instincts of the people against the dogmas, which were falsely accused of being inhuman.

Catholic morality is not inhuman, but it is often *superhuman*; it is also not meant for men of the old world and is part of a dogma which sees as possible the destruction of old man and the creation of a new man. High magic receives this dogma with enthusiasm and promises this spiritual renaissance to humanity during the future epoch of the rehabilitation of the human Verb. And so, he said, man, having become Creator in the place of God, will be the architect of his moral development and the author of his glorious immortality. *To create oneself*, that is the sublime vocation of man reestablished in all his rights by the baptism of the spirit; and such a connection will manifest itself between immortality and morality that one will be the complement and the consequence of the other.

The light of truth is also the light of life. But truth, for it to be fertile in immortality, wishes to be received by souls which are both free and submissive, that is to say voluntarily obedient. In the splendor of this clarity, order is established in the forms as in the ideas, while the deceiving twilight of the imagination gives birth, and can only give birth, to monsters. Thus hell is peopled with nightmares and phantoms; thus the temple of soothsayers is filled with dreadful and deformed divinities; thus the shadowy invocations of theurgy give the chimeras of the Sabbath a fantastical existence. The symbolic and popular images of the temptation of Saint Anthony represent a pure and simple faith, at the dawn of Christianity, fighting against all the specters of the old world: but the human Verb, manifest and victorious, was depicted in the admirable Saint Michael, whom Raphael painted vanquishing, with a simple threat, an inferior being who also had a human face, but of a brutish aspect.

The religious mystics wish us to do good uniquely by obeying God. In the order of the true morality, one must still do good according to the will of God, no doubt, but also for good itself. Goodness is within God the just by his essence, which does not constrain, but which determines his liberty. God *cannot* damn the majority of men through capricious despotism. There must exist an exact proportion between the actions of man and the creation determined by His will from which definitively arises a power of good or an auxiliary of evil, and it is this which is demonstrated by the exact science of high magic.

Here is what we wrote in a book published in 1845: "The time of blind faith has now passed, and we arrive at an epoch of intelligent faith and reasonable obedience, a time where we no longer only believe in God, but where we will observe him in his works, which are the exterior forms of his being.

"But here is the great problem of our times:

"To trace, complete, and close the circle of human knowledge, then, through the convergence of radii, to find the center, which is God.

"To find a proportional scale between the effects, desires, and the causes and to go up from there to arrive at the first cause and the first will.

"To constitute a science of analogies between ideas and their first source.

"To render all religious truth as certain and as clearly demonstrable as the solution to a geometry problem."

Here, now, is what one man says who was lucky enough to discover before us the demonstration of the absolute according to the ancient sages, but also unlucky enough to see in this discovery only an instrument of fortune and a pretext for cupidity.

"It suffices to say here, in anticipation of the Messianic doctrine, that on one hand, the application of absolute reason upon our psychological faculty of cognition produces in us the superior faculty of the creation of principles and the deduction of consequences, which is the great goal of philosophy; and, on the other hand, that the application of absolute reason upon our psychological faculty of feeling produces in us the superior faculty of moral and religious sentiment, which is the great goal of religion. We can thus begin to see how Messianism will achieve the final union of philosophy and religion by freeing both from their physical and terrestrial constraints and by bringing them, beyond their temporal conditions, to absolute reason, which is their common source. We can also already recognize how, through the influence of these temporal conditions or through these physical constraints, on one hand, Error in the philosophical domain, and on the other, Sin is the religious domain, become possible; especially when these physical conditions are part and parcel of the hereditary moral depravity of the human species, which is an aspect of its terrestrial nature. And we can thus understand how absolute reason, which is above these physical conditions, these terrestrial contaminants, and which, in Messianism, must destroy the very source of error and sin, forms, under the allegorical expression of the Virgin who must crush the Serpent's head, the accomplishment of this holy prediction. It is thus this august Virgin that Messianism introduces today into the sanctuary of humanity."

Believe, and you shall understand, said the Savior of the world; study, and you shall believe, the apostles of high magic now can say.

To believe is to know through the word. Yet that divine Word, which was ahead of and replaced the Christian science for a time, we only understood later, according to the Master's promise. That, then, is the agreement between science and faith demonstrated by faith itself.

But, to establish the necessity of that agreement through science, one must recognize and establish a grand principle: it is that the absolute is not found at either of the two extremities of the antinomy, and that men who take sides, who always pull towards the opposite extremes, are at the same time fearful of arriving at those extremes, and consider those who clearly admit to their tendencies as dangerous madmen, and within their own system they instinctively fear the ghost of the absolute as if it were the void or death. This is why the pious archbishop of Paris formally disapproves of the conceited inquests of the *Univers*,[586] and why the entire revolutionary party was outraged by the cruelties of Proudhon.[587]

---

586   A liberal Catholic newspaper of Lévi's time.

587   French anarchist Pierre-Joseph Proudhon (1809–65).

The power of this negative proof consists of this simple observation: that a central link must unite two apparently opposite tendencies, which cannot take a step without having the other being pulled along backwards; and which will then require an equal reaction. And that is what has been happening for two centuries: chained to one another without their knowledge and from behind, these two powers are condemned to a Sisyphean labor and mutually obstruct each other. Turn them around and direct them to the central point, which is the absolute, then they will meet each other head on, and, supporting each other, they will produce a stability which is equal to the power of their contrary efforts, multiplied by the one times the other.

To thus turn around the human powers, which seems at first to be a Herculean effort, it suffices to disabuse minds and show them the goal which they thought an obstacle.

Religion is reasonable. That is what one must tell philosophy, and through the simultaneity and the correspondence of the generative laws of dogma and of science we can prove it completely. *Reason is holy.* That is what one must tell the Church, and we will prove it to her by applying to the triumph of its doctrine of charity all the conquests of emancipation and all the glories of progress.

Jesus Christ being the example of humanity born anew, the divinity rendered human had as his mission to render humanity divine: The Verb made flesh allowed the flesh to become the Verb, and that is what the doctors of the Church did not understand to start with; their mysticism had them absorb humanity in the divinity. They denied the human right in the name of the divine right; they believed that faith must annihilate reason, without remembering the profound words of one of the greatest Christian hierophants: "Any intellect which divides the Christ is an intellect of the Antichrist."[588]

The revolt of the human spirit against the Church, a revolt which was punished by a terrible negative success, was thus, from this point of view, a protest in favor of the doctrine of the whole, and the revolution, which has lasted for three centuries and a half, was only due to an immense misunderstanding!

---

588   Saint Cyril of Alexandria (376–444) used this slogan during his struggle against the Nestorians.

In fact, the Catholic Church has never denied, nor can it deny, human divinity, the Verb made flesh, the human Verb! The Church never consented to those absorbing and irritating doctrines which destroy human liberty in a senseless quietism.[589] Bossuet had the courage to hector Madame Guyon,[590] whom he admired nonetheless and whom we admired after him for her conscientious folly; but Bossuet lived, unfortunately, only after the Council of Trent. The divine experience had to inevitably go through stages of sickness.

Yes, we call the French Revolution a divine experience, because God, at that time, allowed the human genius to measure itself against Him; a strange conflict which had to end up in a tight ligature; the downfall of the prodigal son whose sole future was a decisive return and a solemn celebration in the house of the family father.[591]

The divine Verb and the human Verb, conceived separately, but with a sense of solidarity that rendered them inseparable, had from the start founded the papacy and the empire: the struggle of the papacy to reign alone had been through the absolute affirmation of the divine Verb; with that affirmation, to reestablish the balance of the dogma of Incarnation, there had to be a corresponding absolute affirmation of the human Verb in the empire. Such was the origin of the Reform, which resulted in the Rights of Man.

The Rights of Man! Napoleon manifested them by the glory with which he surrounded his sword. Incarnate and summed up in Napoleon, the revolution stopped being disorderly, and produced with its resounding success the irrefutable proof of his Verb. It is then that one lives, a thing unheard of in the ceremonious pomp of religions! For man to extend, in turn, his hand to God, as though to raise him from his fall. A pope, whose piety and orthodoxy was never questioned, had just sanctioned, with the authority of all the Christian centuries, the *holy usurpation* of the new Caesar, and the revolution incarnate was conse-

---

589   Quietism is the belief, common in some schools of mysticism, that salvation is obtained by abandoning all thought and action in a submergence of the self in God.

590   French religious author and teacher Jeanne-Marie Bouvier de la Motte-Guyon (1648–1717), a leading quietist.

591   The reference is to Napoleon, who reestablished the Catholic Church in France and was crowned emperor in Rome.

crated, that is to say Napoleon received the anointment of the Christ from the very hand of the most venerable successor of the fathers of authority!

It is due to the same type of occurrences, just as universal, just as incontestable and as brilliantly clear as the light of the Sun, it is due to the same type of occurrences, that Messianism was founded in the past.

The affirmation of the divine Verb by the human Verb, insisted upon by the latter right up to suicide, through abnegation and holy frenzy, that is the history of the Church since Constantine up until the Reformation.

The immortality of the human Verb proven through terrible convulsions, by a frenzied revolt, by gigantic battles and by suffering similar to that of Prometheus, until the arrival of a man strong enough to reconnect humanity to God: that is the history of the entire revolution!

Faith and reason! Two terms which we believe are opposites and which are identical.

Authority and liberty, two opposites which are at bottom the same thing, since one cannot exist without the other.

Religion and science, two contradictions which mutually destroy each other as contradictions, and reciprocally affirm each other if we consider them as two fraternal affirmations.

That is the problem already posed and resolved by history. That is the enigma of the Sphinx explained by the Oedipus of modern times, the Napoleonic genius.

It is assuredly a spectacle worthy of all the sympathies of the human genius, and we would add, worthy of the admiration of even the coldest minds, that such a movement, this simultaneous progress, these equal tendencies, those predicted falls, and those equally infallible rebounds, of divine wisdom, on one hand, poured into humanity, and human wisdom, on the other hand, steered by divinity! They are rivers arising from the same source, they separate only to embrace the world more readily, and when they reunite, they will carry off everything with them. All the higher souls predicted this synthesis, this triumph, this driving force, this definitive salvation of the world: but who then, before these great events which revive and raise to such heights the power of human magic and the intervention of God in the works of reason, who, then, had dared predict them?

We have said that the objective of the revelation was the affirmation of the divine Verb, and that the affirmation of the human Verb was the transcendental and providential result of the European revolution started in the sixteenth century.

The divine founder of Christianity was the Messiah of the revelation, because the divine Verb was incarnate in him, and we consider the emperor as the Messiah of the revolution, because the human Verb is summarized and manifested in him in all its power.

The divine Messiah had been sent to save humanity, which was wasting away, worn out by the tyranny of the senses and the orgies of the flesh.

The human Messiah came in a way to save God who offended the obscene cult of reason, and to save the Church, which was threatened by revolts of the human spirit and by saturnalias of false philosophy.

After the reform and the revolution in Napoleon's wake had shaken the base of all of Europe's powers, after the negation of the divine right had transformed almost all the masters of the world into usurpers and handed over the political universe to atheism or the fetishism of the parties, one sole people, guardians of the doctrines of unity and authority, had become the people of God in politics. And that people grew in strength in an impressive manner, inspired by an idea that could be transformed into a Verb, that is to say into a word of action: that people were the vigorous Slavic race, and the idea was that of Peter the Great.

INDEX

Abel, 42, 45, 54, 146, 348, 349
Abracadabra, 228–30, 232
Abraham, 180
Abraham, Rabbi, 291, 293
Abraxas, 87, 251, 292
Absolute, 364, 465
Achilles, 17, 36
Acts, 298
Adam, 40, 54, 55, 89, 124, 137, 280
Adramelech, 103, 305
Aeons, 54
Aesch Mezareph, 180
Aeschylus, 17
Agrippa, Cornelius, 11, 25, 31, 52, 81, 86*n*144, 99, 112, 120, 179, 181, 220, 225–26, 261, 294, 328, 384, 392
Air, 63–64, 67
Albertus Magnus, 339, 401
Alchemy, 5, 63, 65, 120–21, 169, 170, 210, 221, 289–90, 293, 294
Aleph, 12, 31, 37, 41*n*83, 178, 342
Alexander VI, Pope, 341
Alexander the Great, 173, 353, 461
Alexandria:
    library of, 167
    school of, 4, 7, 58, 85, 290, 383, 462
Alliette, Jean-Baptiste, *see* Etteilla
Altar, 267, 270
Althea, 95
Ammonius Saccas, 7, 19
Amphiaraus, 17
Amphitheatrum Sapientiae Aeternae (Khunrath), 292
Anacreon, 91, 254
Anael, 259, 384
Analogies, 97–98, 183–86, 201, 276, 388, 462

Ancient of Days, 103
Androids, 339–40, 401
Angela of Foligno, Saint, 361–62
Anger, 336–37
Animal magnetism. *See* Magnetism
Animals, 86, 87, 147, 254
Anteros, 44
Anthony, Saint, 69, 140, 235, 361, 463
Antichrist, 61–62, 466
Antigone, 17
Apollonius of Tyana, 4, 15, 31, 71, 79–80, 99, 112, 128–30, 298, 303, 309, 322, 380
    mantle of, 96, 98
Apuleius, 18, 19, 31, 33, 132, 137, 308, 310, 355, 359
Aqua Tofana, 160, 163
Archimedes, 23, 54, 111, 116, 253
Aristippus, 378
Ark, 44, 123, 388–90, 402–3
Ashburner, John Archibald, 357
Ashes, 238
Aspergillus, 237
Assiah, 55
Assyria, 345, 353, 354*n*
Astral body, 91, 133–34, 136, 256
Astral intoxication, 147
Astral light, xx–xxii, 70, 71, 76–82, 89–91, 97, 110, 111, 113, 114, 116, 118, 134–35, 140, 180, 220, 234, 256, 290–92, 366, 417
    enchantments and, 146–48
    necromancy and, 124–26, 130, 131
    pregnancy and, 72, 91, 152
    stars and, 152, 154

ABOUT THE TRANSLATORS

JOHN MICHAEL GREER is a widely respected author, translator, and blogger in the occult field. He is most recently the editor of the new, substantially revised seventh edition of Israel Regardie's occult landmark *The Golden Dawn* (Llewellyn 2016).

MARK MIKITUK, currently a resident of France, has extensive experience as a translator and has also taught English to Francophone students. This is his first book project.